Religion and Political Thoug

Religion and Political Thought

Edited and annotated by

MICHAEL HOELZL and GRAHAM WARD

continuum
LONDON • NEW YORK

The Continuum International Publishing Group
The Tower Building, 11 York Road, London SE1 7NX
80 Maiden Lane, Suite 704, New York, NY 10038

www.continuumbooks.com

British Library Cataloguing-in-Publication Data
A catalogue record for this book is available from the British Library

ISBN 0–8264–8005–5 (hardback)
ISBN 0–8264–8006–3 (paperback)

Typeset by Servis Filmsetting Ltd, Manchester
Printed on acid-free paper in Great Britain by MPG Books Ltd, Bodmin, Cornwall

Contents

PART THREE: RELIGION IN DEMOCRATIC CULTURE

PART FOUR: POLITICS AFTER RELIGION

PART FIVE: THE CONTEMPORARY DEBATES

CONTENTS

Contributors

Marcella Althaus-Reid is Reader in Christian Ethics, Practical Theology and Systematic Theology at the University of Edinburgh, School of Divinity, UK.

Michael Hoelzl is Lecturer in Philosophy of Religion at the University of Manchester, UK.

Jürgen Manemann is Chair-Professor of the Department of *Christliche Weltanschauung, Religions und Kulturtheorie* at the University of Erfurt, Germany.

John Milbank is Professor in Religion, Politics and Ethics at the University of Nottingham, UK.

Charles Taylor is Professor em. at McGill University, Department of Philosophy, Canada.

Graham Ward is Professor in Ethics and Contextual Theology at the University of Manchester, UK.

Slavoj Žižek is Professor at the University of Lubljana, Department of Philosophy, Slovenia.

Acknowledgements

We gratefully want to thank Marcella Althaus Reid, Charles Taylor, Slavoj Žižek, John Milbank and Jürgen Manemann for their willingness to contribute to this book. We would also like to thank Continuum for their patience and cooperation. Last, but not least, we want to acknowledge our debt to Tim Stanley.

Acknowledgments

In memory of Geoffrey Price

General Introduction

There is no neutral position in a game of chess. The opening move is a bid for power on a level playing field. The hierarchy of figures (kings, queens, bishops, knights and pawns) is deployed in the desire to dominate. The very confrontational alignment of two kingdoms establishes a drama that will inevitably unfold. Even if, finally, there is only the exhaustion of stalemate. No wonder the game has been used in the past to train a military aristocracy in the art of war. But a war governed by rules. The world of chess is not a war of 'every man against every man' (Hobbes), because a well-defined social order and conventions govern social interaction. Clausewitz, writing at the beginning of the nineteenth century, could therefore still say 'war is a continuation of politics by other means'. In conventional warfare, as in chess, two distinct parties encounter each other. In the march, one against the other, there are stratagems, tricks, feints and decisions. As Miranda accuses Ferdinand in Shakespeare's play *The Tempest*: 'Sweet lord, you play me false'. In chess, as in a medieval society, figures belong to specific classes with specific functions. Each side constitutes not only a differentiated social body but also a cosmological body. This is figured in the chess board itself as a common and mapped-out ground. This is the order of things; what came to be understood as 'natural law'. The battles that commence then are not simply between temporal powers. They take place within a religious context in which even the spiritual estate is a political player in temporal concerns. The function of religion was to guarantee the stability of this world-view and provided both a common knowledge of the right social order on earth, and the order of things in the next life.[1] This religious dimension is not limited to the moves made by 'bishops', for the order of the whole social world (from the pawn to the king) is governed by a religious world-view. Perhaps then it is not surprising that when the Reformation split Christendom and this cosmological order was torn apart it expressed itself in what we call the Wars of Religion. The 'chessboard' fissured, the common ground was rent apart and gave way to the random construction of trenches and no-man's-land. No rules

---

1. We would draw attention here to Ingmar Bergman's *The Seventh Seal* in which, in the opening scenes, the knight on return from the crusades is summoned by Death, whom he invites to play chess on a wild and rocky beach. The allegory of the chess game, which continues throughout the film, dramatizes an interplay between the temporal order and the spiritual order in which Death too has to play according to the rules.

could then limit the use of violence, because each individual considered themselves to be king of their personal domain. The equality among players informed Hobbes' understanding of the natural condition of humankind.

The game of chess illustrates the long and abiding association between religion and politics, which this volume aims to explore and provide resources for further research. The profundity of this association is evident when we examine the twofold roots of political thought in the West.[2] For, on the one hand, there is the biblical tradition, and we will observe the continuation of this tradition right up to the nineteenth century. Both the Hebrew and the Christian Bibles provided sources for the *legitimation of power*; the exercise of political power was based upon biblical authority. While, on the other, there is the classical Greek tradition that has given us basic classificatory *concepts* in political science as well as a definition of the *political* itself. In the opening book of Aristotle's *Politics*, we find: '. . . it is evident that the state is a creation of nature and that man is by nature a political animal. And he who by nature, and not by mere accident, is without a state, is either above humanity or below it . . .'[3]. Therefore, the political condition of things is written into the constitution of what it means to be human. The social task is to create the best form of polity. Although modern understandings of democracy bear little direct relation to the classical Greek *polis*, nevertheless the category of democracy as defined in the context of Aristotle's typology of government remained a benchmark until the nineteenth century. But when we consider Hannah Arendt's return to the Aristotelian understanding of the nature of politics in *The Human Condition* (or Alasdair MacIntyre's in *After Virtue*), then we recognize the enduring significance of the classical Greek tradition. To return to an old similitude, the history of political thought is founded upon two cities – Jerusalem and Athens – such that its association with religion (the Judaeo-Christian and the Greek notion of the Good) cannot be ignored.

Religion and politics in the Scripture

If politics, as its name implies, is related to the city (*polis*) then, when examining the relationship between religion and politics in the Hebrew Bible we would have to return to the early chapters of Genesis. For Cain, the son of Adam and Eve and the slayer of his brother Abel, founded the *first* city 'which he named Enoch after his son' (Gen. 4.18). We know nothing of the political organization of this city, but the Hebrew Bible has been the source of inspiration for thinking through the right order of living in a community and the understanding of a community among other communities. This is a further meaning of the word 'politics'. For the *polis* is not only the city, but also the *community* of that city and its ethos.

---

2. There is of course another source for Western political thought. The heritage of Roman law has undeniably shaped our present understanding of politics in a legal sense. In this context we do not explicitly refer to this strand in political theory because we are primarily focusing on the history of ideas rather then the evolution of modern law.

3. Aristotle (1966), *The Politics and the Constitution of Athens*, ed. Stephen Everson (Cambridge: Cambridge University Press), I.2.

From the story of Cain to the covenants made by God with first Noah, then Abraham, then Jacob and, finally, Moses; from the exile into Egypt and the crossing of the Red Sea, to the return to the Promised Land, the division of the kingdoms, the fall of the northern kingdom and the deportation into Babylon; from the return under the Persian monarchs of Ezra, the rebuilding of the Temple, the conquest of Alexander and the Maccabean revolts, to the destruction of the second Temple under Tiberius and the Jewish diaspora – the religious and the political are indissociable. In the Hebrew Bible, as O'Donovan makes clear in his own exposition of the roots of political theology, we 'rediscover politics not as a self-enclosed field of human endeavour but as the theatre of the divine self-disclosure; to rediscover God as the one who exercises rule.'[4] Furthermore, the Hebrew Bible is not simply a compilation of narratives in which religion is a political force, it also contains influential reflections on the nature of government. As distinct from the Greek tradition, this nature of government, and the just organization of society it advocated, was directly related to the belief in the one God, YHWH.

With a view to the selected classical passages we have chosen, four aspects of the relationship between religion and politics in the Hebrew Bible become pertinent. These are kingship, equality, justice and covenant.[5] The first category, *kingship*, concerns the question of the best form of government; while the next two categories (equality and justice) constitute norms for social life; and the covenant between God and His chosen people, the final category, is the foundational principle of both kingship and the norms for social life. Covenant and kingship had a profound and continuing influence on political theory, as the examples in this book demonstrate. We will return to this. For the moment we will briefly treat equality and justice as they are given expression in the Hebrew Bible and the New Testament.

The basis for *equality* in the Hebrew Bible is the place of each human being before God. Genesis 1.27: 'so God created man in his own image; in the image of God he created him; male and female he created them'. Whatever disputes have been fought over the story of Eve coming from the rib of Adam, in this verse there is no hierarchy between male and female; unlike in the classical Greek accounts.[6] For the moment, one further aspect of this equality should be noted. We are all equally images of God, but, according to the Hebrew Bible, we are all equally the children of Adam and Eve. We will observe how the proto-democratic thinking of Luther and the fully democratic thinking of Paine are both indebted to these two biblical notions of equality: the first being theological and the second genetic.

4. O. O'Donovan (1999), *The Desire of the Nations: Rediscovering the Roots of Political Theology* (Cambridge: Cambridge University Press), p. 2.
5. It is undeniable that in the Hebrew Bible rules for social policy are explicitly named and related to theology, which we have not included here, e.g. the *ius talionis* or the institution of the 'year of the jubilee'. These, and other, theologico-juridical regulations are outlined in detail in Lev. 24.20 and Lev. 25.8–55. The influence of some of these regulations are still present today. For example *lex talionis* is still practised in certain countries of the world and the year of the jubilee (the fiftieth year in which all debts were forgiven and slaves freed) remains inspirational for those combating Third World debts.
6. See Aristotle, *The Politics and the Constitution of Athens*, I.2.

The New Testament talks about the foundations of equality in a different manner. St Paul, writing to the community in Galatia, transforms and extends the universalism of human beings made in the image of God. 'For through faith you are all sons of God in union with Christ Jesus. Baptised into union with him, you have all put on Christ as a garment. There is no such thing as Jew and Greek, slave and freeman, male and female; for are you are all one person in Christ Jesus' (Galatians 3.28). Jesus Christ, as the second Adam, transcends all differences of ethnicity, class and gender.[7] Luther will base his notion of equality upon this Christian interpretation; whereas Paine will found his notion of equality upon a literal understanding of the Hebrew Bible's depiction of all humankind as being the children of Adam.

The understanding of *social justice* has its background in the writings of the Hebrew prophets like Amos. The call is on behalf of the poor, the widowed and the orphaned; and is pitched against 'you who grind the destitute and plunder the humble' (Amos 8.4). In the Book of Nehemiah there is a telling story that demonstrates the nature of justice in the Hebrew Bible. Nehemiah has been chosen by the Persian king to lead many of the deported Jews back to Jerusalem to rebuild its walls and the Temple. But the Jews who have returned later complain to Nehemiah that they are being exploited and oppressed by the Jews who remained in the land throughout the Babylonian exile. Nehemiah summons these people to him and demands that they 'Restore to them [the Jews who have returned], this very day, their fields, their vineyards, their olive orchards, and their houses, and the interest on the money, grain, wine, and oil that you have extracted from them' (Nehemiah 5.11). The failure to do so will bring the curse of Nehemiah upon them: 'May God shake out everyone from house and from property who does not perform this promise' (Nehemiah 5.13). If there is any significant difference about the New Testament understanding of social justice, then it is in the emphasis upon love as *caritas*. 'You have learned that they were told, "Love your neighbour, hate your enemy". But what I tell you is this: Love your enemies and pray for your persecutors, only so can you be children of your Heavenly father, who makes his sun rise on good and bad alike, and sends the rain on the honest and the dishonest' (Matthew 5.45). Here, as with the New Testament understanding of equality, there is an extension beyond the ethnic borders of a specific people. Justice is to be done to all, even the unjust, the alien and the enemy.

To summarize: compared to a modern understanding of the principles of right sociality, equality and justice, the biblical traditions cannot be divorced from God. If we take the Ten Commandments as illustrative here, the last seven relate specifically to norms for human behaviour. But they cannot be understood without reference to the first three commandments which concern right relations with God Himself. God is the source and measure for equality and justice; their realization cannot be achieved by human endeavour alone. A distinction between the sacred and the secular would not make sense. Furthermore, we do not find

---

7. See A. Badiou (2003), *St Paul: The Foundation of Universalism*, trans. Ray Brassier, (Stanford, CA: Stanford University Press). For Badiou, Paul is a paradigmatic figure for the first universal and absolute religion. He introduces, as Badiou calls it, the first 'universal singularity'.

in either the Hebrew Bible or the New Testament any notion of freedom in the modern understanding of this term. Freedom, in the biblical tradition, is only achieved through a deepening obedience to God. Freedom as being a self-governing rational agent, making informed choices without necessarily referring to the will of God, is entirely alien to such orthodoxy. We will see a continuation of this biblical tradition, which is simultaneously a criticism of modernity, in the conservative and counter-revolutionary writings of Joseph de Maistre and, more recently, with John Milbank.[8]

The most contentious biblical category is *kingship*. The reason for the contention in the Hebrew Bible lies in the two forms of government outlined in the Pentateuch and the Books of Samuel, Kings and Chronicles. The early form of Israel's political organization appears to be a confederacy of what is symbolically referred to as the Twelve Tribes. These were governed first by an oligarchy of elders and then a single judge. The transition from Samuel as judge over Israel to Saul as the first anointed king is not without fierce resistance. Appeal is made to God to intervene when Israel demands of Samuel that he appoints them a king like the other nations around them. For God is the true and only king over his people, Samuel argues. The concession made to Israel is hedged about with descriptions of future sufferings and oppressions.

> He [the king] will take your sons and make them serve in his chariots and with his cavalry, and will make them run before his chariot. Some he will appoint officers over units of a thousand and units of fifty. Others will plough his fields and reap his harvest; others again will make weapons of war and equipment for mounted troops. He will take your daughters for perfumers, cooks, and confectioners, and will seize the best of your cornfields, vineyards, and olive-yards, and give them to his lackeys. He will take a tenth of your grain and your vintage to give to his eunuchs and lackeys. Your slaves, both men and women, and the best of your cattle and your asses he will seize and put to his own use. He will take a tenth of your flocks and you and yourselves will become his slaves. When that day comes, you will cry out against the king whom you have chosen; but it will be too late, the Lord will not answer you. (1 Samuel 8.11–18).

On the other hand, even the Pentateuch refers to good kings – most particularly, Melchisedek, who in the New Testament is a foreshadow of the Messiah. This figure was both ruler and priest, bridging both Court and Temple. Saul, the first king anointed by Samuel, is abandoned by God, but, in his place, there arises David who again becomes an archetype for the coming Messiah. Solomon, David's son, becomes the embodiment of divine wisdom. With these two monarchs is instituted the notion of sacral kingship that conflates the temporal with the spiritual. The 'kingship' of Jesus Christ in the New Testament is explicitly related, in the genealogies of Matthew (1.1–17) and Luke (3.23–38) to both the Davidic and Solomonic monarchies. All later notions of the Divine Right of Kings will be based upon these royal archetypes.

8. See pp. 161–72 and pp. 225–36 in this volume.

With Jesus Christ the Hebrew Bible's ambivalent attitude to kingship finds its most dramatic development. In the Gospel's narrative reports of the trial, Jesus is brought face to face with imperial authority in the figure of Pontius Pilate.

> Pilate . . . summoned Jesus. 'Are you the king of the Jews?' he asked. Jesus said, 'Is that your own idea, or have others suggested it to you?' 'What! Am I a Jew?' said Pilate. 'Your own nation and their chief priests have brought you before me. What have you done?' Jesus replied, 'My kingdom does not belong to this world. If it did, my followers would be fighting to save me from arrest by the Jews. My kingly authority comes from elsewhere.' 'You are a king, then?' said Pilate. Jesus answered, ' "King" is your word.' (John 18.33–7)

The controversy of Jesus' kingship is emphasized throughout both the trial and the crucifixion narratives. For Pilate has Jesus flogged by the Romans and presented with a crown of thorns and royal cloaks and hailed ironically as 'King of the Jews' (John 19.2–3). A few lines later, when Jesus was crucified,

> . . . Pilate wrote an inscription to be fastened to the cross; it read, 'Jesus of Nazareth, King of the Jews'. This inscription was read by many Jews. . . . Then the Jewish chief priests said to Pilate, 'You should not write "King of the Jews"; write, "He claimed to be king of the Jews." ' Pilate replied, 'What I have written, I have written.' (John 19.19–22)

From this New Testament tradition will arise the distinction, and the debates, between the 'Kingdom of God' (and its authority) and the authority of terrestrial kingship. The tension between spiritual and temporal authority provokes a conflict of loyalties that the New Testament writings do not resolve. This is illustrated by the story of when the lawyers and chief priests came to Jesus and asked:

> 'Are we or are we not permitted to pay taxes to the Roman Emperor?' . . . [Jesus said] 'Show me a silver piece. Whose head does it bear, and whose inscription?' 'Caesar's', they replied. 'Very well then', he said, 'pay Caesar what is due to Caesar, and pay God what is due to God.' (Luke 19.22–5).

St Paul reiterates a similar principle of submission to temporal authority in his Letter to the Romans when he advises the Christians to discharge their obligations and pay both tax and toll (Rom. 13.7). But St Paul goes much further when he tells them:

> Every person must submit to the supreme authorities. There is no authority but by act of God, and the existing authorities are instituted by Him; consequently anyone who rebels against authority is resisting a divine institution, and those who so resist have themselves to thank for the punishment they will receive . . . they are God's agents working for your good . . . they are God's agents of punishment. . . . The authorities are in God's service and to these duties they devote their energies. (Rom. 13.1–6)

This notion of unconditional obedience to temporal authority is at the heart of debates from Augustine to Dietrich Bonhoeffer and Oscar Romero concerning whether it is right or wrong to resist and even overthrow tyrannical forms of government.

The implications of both the Hebrew Bible and the New Testament with respect to kingship and authority for later developments in Christian political thought are profound. In almost every text we have chosen, from Augustine to Luther, and even to Rousseau's *Social Contract*, the controversy of spiritual and temporal powers is evident.[9]

The last of the categories of particular significance here is covenant. Biblical commentators, working within the historical-critical school, inform us that 'covenant' comes from treaties made between suzerainties or rulers and their clients or people. These were written down and constituted a legally binding relationship. The so-called covenants with Noah, Abraham and Jacob were verbal promises exchanged between God and these figures who stood for their people. Only with Moses do we find written covenants made between God and the people of Israel. There are two such covenants. The first is in Exodus 34, where we can read that on Mount Horeb

> The Lord said to Moses, 'Write these words down, because the covenant I make with you and with Israel is in these words.' Moses stayed there with the Lord forty days and forty nights, neither eating nor drinking, and wrote down the words of the covenant, the ten commandments . . .' (Exodus 34.7–8).

The second covenant was an extended one given to Moses at Moab in order to compliment the first (Deuteronomy 28.29). What both these covenants regulate is a social order that is to be maintained through a right relation to God. As with the suzerainty treatises, two parties are involved here and make binding commitments one to the other. God promises to remain faithful in guiding and supporting His people and the people bind themselves to fulfilling God's commandments. The vertical axis of the God/people covenant facilitates a horizontal axis in which the people bind themselves legally and morally to one another. The Jewish law provides rules for the regulation of reciprocal duties, the exercise of which can be found in various places in the Hebrew Bible (for example, the Book of Ruth, chapter 4). Religion always shapes and produces social norms and a moral order.

Later, with the prophets Jeremiah and Ezekiel there is an eschatological vision of a new covenant. It would seem that covenantal relations need to be renewed and made more perfect. The new covenants of Jeremiah and Ezekiel arise because of new political situations. In Jeremiah God tells his people:

> 'I will make a new covenant with Israel and Judah. It will not be like the covenant I made with their forefathers . . . I will set my law within them and write it on their hearts; I will become their God and they shall become my people. No longer need they teach one another to know the Lord; all of them, high and low alike, shall know me', says the Lord, 'for I will forgive their wrongdoing and remember their sin no more'. (Jeremiah 31.31–4).

---

9. An interesting discussion of the symbolic impact of the dichotomy of the temporal and the spiritual on political theory can be found in E. Voegelin (1986), *Political Religions* (New York: Edward Mellen Press).

This inner covenant of the heart politically infers (and would require) major social reform. In Ezekiel, the new covenant is made in order to unify a people and build a single nation. Moreover, it will install one God and one mediating king who is also viewed as the shepherd of the people (Ezekiel 37.21–8). This messianic political constellation (one God, one ruler, one people) becomes the ideal Christian polity throughout the medieval period. It is still echoed in the sixteenth-century political scientist Jean Bodin's concept of sovereignty and the notion of *cuius regio eius religio* expressed at the peace treaty at Augsburg in 1630. Even contemporary understandings of being a 'nation under God' makes subtle appeal to this ideal.

In the New Testament, the covenant between God and a particular nation becomes universal through Jesus Christ. Christian theologians would debate for many centuries the way in which Christ was both mediator of this covenant and God Himself. Central to this notion of covenant is the liturgy of the Eucharist and the community it constitutes. St Paul, writing to the Church in Corinth, rehearses the founding institutional narrative:

> The Lord Jesus, on the night of his arrest, took bread and, after giving thanks to God, broke it and said: 'This is my body, which is for you; do this as a memorial of me.' In the same way, he took the cup after supper, and said: 'This cup is the *new covenant* sealed by my blood. Whenever you drink it, do this as a memorial of me.'
> (1 Corinthians 11.23–5, editors' italics)

This new covenant promulgates a new law: '"I give you a new commandment: love one another; as I have loved you, so you are to love one another. If there is this love among you, then all will know that you are my disciples."' (John 13.34–5) The reference to 'all' here was interpreted as a new universalism, inclusive of every people and nation. The early Christians defined the community this constituted as an *ecclesia* – adopting what was a Greek political term for an assembly. The social order of this community was founded upon love. How one understands an act of love is highly contestable, as the history of intra-Christian relationships demonstrates. With Augustine we will find that this love is employed in defining certain forms of social behaviour, moral norms and the quality of a community. That is why Augustine opposes the kingdom of God (governed by *amor dei* – love of God) to the terrestrial kingdom (governed by *amor sui* – love of self). It is important to observe with this new covenant that politics must not be understood either in a technical and bureaucratic sense, or in terms of juridical prescriptions. This new community is an ethical and spiritual one; it is not a society as such.

To summarize: the Hebrew and Christian Bibles have impacted upon political theory in numerous ways. We have drawn attention to four of the most important influences of the biblical tradition: kingship, equality, justice and covenant. Throughout the texts that follow attention should be paid to the different ways in which the Jewish and Christian Scriptures were used as: sources for legitimating the exercise of power; sources of visions for the perfect polity; and sources offering norms for social conduct.

The classical heritage

Compared with the influence of the Scripture on Western political theory, the influence of the classical tradition is much more circumscribed. For the texts we have included the importance of certain figures is indisputable. Augustine is evidently influenced by Plato and Cicero; Aquinas and Dante refer explicitly to Aristotle; and Machiavelli's account of religion and politics is designed as a commentary on the history of the Romans by the Latin historian Livy. But, by the time we come to the work of Rousseau (for whom Seneca is particularly important, among many other classical authors) we are already discerning a loss of common knowledge of the classical tradition. Even in his time Rousseau appears to be old-fashioned by building his argument with reference to these ancient resources. This is most evident when he borrows the term 'civil religion' from the Roman antiquarian, polymath and philosopher Varro (116–27 BCE). In the context of the passages we have chosen for this volume and its aim to provide a student resource, it is sufficient to outline the impact of Plato and Aristotle on the development of political thought.

Plato developed the notion of the city as a community of souls. In his *Republic* he elaborated a vision of the perfect society governed by the form of the Good. The Good is a transcendent source from which politics, aesthetics, ethics and theology issue. Plato compares the Good, which is beyond Being, to the operation of the Divine. The ordering of the *polis* is to be governed by the soul in its contemplation of the Good. Ruled over by the philosopher king, Plato envisages a perfect society and form of government in which the ongoing education of the soul and its knowledge of the Good takes place. The importance of Plato's political writings can be seen in the patristic literature, and they underscore the central idea that by nature human beings are good and just. It is because of ignorance that corruption and social evil manifest themselves. By being educated as to their true nature, human beings can naturally create good and just social orders. For this reason education becomes fundamental in Plato's scheme for the training of those capable of governing well. Augustine transforms these thoughts in line with his doctrine of humans being originally sinful, but the Platonic influence is nevertheless clear. After Augustine, the utopia of Plato's perfect 'city' significantly influenced the ideal of Christian polity. The word 'utopia' (*ou-topos*) literally means 'no place'. So the speculative outline of the perfect city has no concrete manifestation. From early modernity, with Thomas More's *Utopia* and Francis Bacon's *Atlanta*, these utopian visions of a perfected society became a literary genre bordering on science fiction.

In the sixteenth century, the Italian Renaissance artist Raphael painted a fresco for the Vatican chambers in which he depicted the most celebrated classical thinkers, entitled *School of Athens*. One's perspective is directed in the painting to the foregrounded figures of Plato and Aristotle (portrayed as Michelangelo and Leonardo da Vinci). Each is making a distinctive gesture which is characteristic of his philosophical position. While Plato, with a raised right arm, points one finger towards heaven, Aristotle extends his left arm and spreads his fingers as if he would encompass all things beneath him. In contrast to Plato's speculative or even con-templative thinking, Aristotle is more concerned with concrete details and their causal relationship. It is for this reason that Aristotle's political thinking provides a set of categories and distinctions which have had a profound impact on those who rethought the art of governing after him. To borrow and amend a phrase by the philosopher Alfred Whitehead, one could say that all political science is a footnote to Aristotle.

We have already drawn attention to the importance of Aristotle's political anthropology, that is, his definition of a human being as a political animal. This definition was taken up by Aquinas almost seventeen hundred years later, as we will discover in the text included in this volume. Aquinas emphasized that the *political* animal is a *social* animal. What is significant for the development of political theory is that neither Aristotle nor Aquinas saw the relations between human beings in terms of 'contract'. For Aristotle, the identity of the social and political is founded upon ethics, on the one hand, and economics, on the other. The ethical is crucial because the telos or governing purpose of political action is to augment the common good. Unlike in Plato, the good is not a transcendent idea, beyond being, but an idea being worked out in the concreteness of action and living and the good for Aristotle is not related to a deity. This notion that political life is ori-entated towards maximizing the common good re-emerges with Aquinas, as we have said, but it also continues to be the fundamental doctrine for politics in Renaissance republics. This is illustrated by an inscription at the entrance to the Palace of the Prince in Dubrovnic, a town which was at that time influenced by Venice and Renaissance republicanism: *obliti privatoru[m] publica curate*. This translates as: Forget the private, care for the public. The public was understood to be the common good of the city and its citizens. In Renaissance England (and through to the mid-seventeenth century) this notion was enshrined in the concern for the 'common weal' or Commonwealth. The economic, for Aristotle, was crucial because doing politics was the business of those who could afford to spend time on public issues and fund public events. This economic dimension of political life has become dominant with the rise of political economy in the work of Ricardo, Smith and Marx (who is included among the classic texts chosen) and more recently with the advent of globalism and the resistance to it, evident in the essay by Althaus-Reid.

The common good, for Aristotle, is the basis for discerning between just and unjust forms of government. In the *Politics*, he outlines six types of government. Each is organized in sets of pairs. Monarchy is paired with tyranny; aristocracy with oligarchy; and polity with democracy. Monarchy is the rule of one; aristoc-racy is the rule of the few; and polity is the rule of the many – *in the interests of the social whole*. These forms of government constitute a typology of just political regimes. Their obverse are tyranny as the rule of one; oligarchy as the rule of few; and democracy as the rule of many – *in the interests of those who govern*. Aristotle is aware that this is a formal classification and in reality types of government can change. For example, monarchy can become tyranny and this, subsequently, may turn into a democracy. Moreover, real forms of government are always a contingent mixture of different types of rule. For example, a democracy like the one in Athens was a mixture of aristocratic power and the rule of the many (that is, of those who were counted as citizens, i.e. neither slaves, nor women, nor people in commercial business). We can see from this form of democracy that it differs significantly from any modern understanding. The recognition that government never exists in its pure type, but is always composed of many different styles of exercising power, is foregrounded in the work of Rousseau.

The history of the relationship between religion and Western political thought draws substantially from both the biblical and the classical traditions, as we will see. Evidently, there are other religious traditions that are embedded in their own political cultures and which have developed their own characteristic style of religion and politics. Only since the nineteenth century has the Western world become interested in examining these other traditions in any depth.[10] Islam has had a long history of involvement with the West, but other than its philosophical schools (see Introduction to Aquinas) it has had no impact upon the development of political theory in the West until the twentieth century.

Key topics in the history of Western religion and politics

Four major themes can be identified from the material we have selected that are representative of the relationship between religion and political thought in the West: a) the use of the body as both metaphor and analogy for the social; b) the divine legitimation of sovereignty; c) a functional approach in which religion is a tool for politics; and d) the religious character of political atheism.

a)   The body: from St Paul to Hobbes

The most celebrated and influential passages that refer to the body as a political metaphor can be found in St Paul's letters (to the Romans, the Corinthians and the Church at Ephesus). The body being defined here in the first century CE is the body of Christ as the Christian Church. This was not simply the material body constituting a local *ekklesia*. For while each community was made up of various 'members', the community itself was also a 'member' of the universal body of Christ. The use of 'body' does not distinguish between the spiritual and the

---

10. Hegel was one of the first to systematically analyse the traditions of other faiths. But it was Max Weber (1978) who in his unfinished *Economy and Society. An Outline of Interpretative Sociology*, 2 vols, eds Guenther Roth and Claus Wittich (Berkeley, CA: University of California Press) and his works on the sociology of world religions, most ambitiously attempted to compare and identify common elements in the relationship between religion and politics. He endeavoured to take into account Buddhism, Hinduism, ancient Chinese and Egyptian religions as well as different sects of Christianity. For an examination of Islamic political thought see M. Watt (1988), *Islamic Political Thought* (Edinburgh: Edinburgh University Press) and recently P. Crone (2005), *God's Rule – Government and Islam: Six Centuries of Medieval Islamic Political Thought* (New York: Columbia University Press). For Hinduism and political theory see Vishwanath Prasad Varma (1974), *Studies in Hindu Political Thought and its Metaphysical Foundations* (Delhi: Motilal Banarsidass) and, more recently, J. Zaros (2000), *The Emergence of Hindu Nationalism in India* (Delhi: Oxford University Press).

material, at this point in history. For they interpenetrate each other in the Eucharist, where the historical body of Jesus Christ is extended into the sacramental notion of Christ's abiding presence. The material community is poised between the spiritual body of the resurrected Christ, on the one hand, and the sacramental body of Christ (in the Eucharist), on the other. So, when St Paul employs the 'body' as an image for the community, he is not simply arguing for a necessary and natural hierarchy. For, as he writes in his famous First Letter to the Corinthians:

> For Christ is like a single body with its many limbs and organs, which, many as they are, together make up one body. . . . A body is not a single organ, but many. Suppose the foot should say, 'Because I am not a hand, I do not belong to the body', it does belong to the body none the less. . . . But, in fact, God appointed each limb and organ to its own place in the body, as He chooses. If the whole were a single organ, there would not be a body at all; in fact, however, they are many different organs, but one body. Now you are Christ's body, and each of you a limb or organ of it. (1 Corinthians 12.12–27)

Furthermore, in what is still contested to be St Paul's Letter to the Ephesians, we find:

> They [the people of God] are measured by His [God's] strength and the might He exerted in Christ when He raised him from the dead, when He *enthroned* his son at His right hand in the heavenly realms, far above all government and authority, all power and dominion, and any title of sovereignty. . . . He put everything in subjection beneath his feet, and appointed him [Christ] as supreme head to the Church, which *is* his body . . . (Ephesians 1.19–23, editors' italics)

These passages have been at the centre of a prolonged politics in the Christian world. Indeed, they have shaped the history of political life in the West, triggering schisms and initiating reformations. For the perspective of this volume, attention needs to be drawn to several controversial aspects in this teaching by St Paul. First, there is the matter of the ontological status of the Church. Is it *like* the single body of Christ or is it *actually* the body of Christ? To say something is *like* something is to offer a description of one thing in terms of another. To say something *is* something is to be prescriptive and make the claim that something is *the same* as something else. So what kind of claim is St Paul making here both for Christ and for the nature of the Church? Is the body being used as an illustration, or a description, of the social order? Second, if the Church *is* the body of Christ, and Christ is its head, then who *represents* the head of this body? Third, how does the community of the Church maintain its association with Christ? For St Paul, the renewal of the presence of Christ in the community takes place in the memorial celebration of the Eucharist, which is the actualization *of* the body of Christ. But the 'memorial' element here has raised numerous questions concerning the relationship between the actual crucifixion of Jesus Christ and the Last Supper, which inaugurated the new covenant in Christ (see above). Fourth, closely related to all these aspects, there is the question of who has the authority to define the nature of one's place within this community. St Paul only mentions how *God* chooses who will be a foot, an eye, a hand, etc., but who or what in any given society makes the actual decision about the choice of one's role? In other words, given there is no hierarchy other than the head and the rest of the body, then who, among the various organs constituting this body, submits to the authority of whom? We might think that today class, gender, race and money play a decisive role in allocating social functions. But we should not forget that the charismatic qualities of a person are, by definition, a gift and not an achievement. And these play a profound role in obtaining hierarchical status, as Weber has convincingly argued.[11] One can see from this list of ambiguities how the body as a political metaphor was contested and rendered complex. One might also see how changes to the understanding of the body may affect this body-politics and its complexity.

In 1628 the Oxford scholar and close friend of Thomas Hobbes, William Harvey,[12] published his groundbreaking study *De motu cordis*. As Richard Sennett comments: 'Harvey launched a scientific revolution in the understanding of the body: its structure, its healthy state, and its relation to the soul. A new master image of the body took form.'[13] This revolution of the understanding of the body affected not only medicine and physiology, but also political science and theology. We can measure the changes incurred by returning to Aristotle and Aquinas, for whom the soul was the moving force within the body, causing motion, appetite, desire and will.[14] With Harvey, for the first time, the body is a self-regulating organism. There is no need to refer to any transcendent principle – like the soul in its relationship to the divine – to account for its maintenance and development. What Harvey did for the biological understanding of the body, Hobbes did for political science, Descartes did for philosophy and Rembrandt did with his painting, *The Anatomy Lessons of Dr Tulp*, for fine art. The body was now conceived purely in terms of its materiality. In his *Leviathan*, published in 1651, Hobbes writes:

> Nature (the activity by which God hath made and governs the world) is by the art of man, as in many other things, so in this also imitated, that it can make an *artificial animal*. . . . Art goes yet further, imitating that rational and most excellent work of Nature, man. For by art is created that great LEVIATHAN called a COMMON WEALTH, or STATE (in Latin, CIVITAS), which is but an *artificial man*, though of greater stature and strength than the natural, for whose protection and defence it was intended.

What is new here can be appreciated with respect to three points. First, Hobbes is not referring in his account of the body to the classical passages by St Paul, but employs the mythological depiction of Leviathan, the sea monster described in the Book of Job. He continues using the Bible as a form of legitimation, but the idea of the state for him (employing this narrative) changes. It now becomes a reality in which *non est potestas super terram quae comparetur ei* (there is no power on earth that can be compared to it) (Job 41.33). This encapsulates the notion of

---

11. See M. Weber (1978), *Economy and Society*, ed. Guenther Roth and Klaus Wittich (Los Angeles, CA: University of California Press), vol. I, pp. 212–301 and vol. 2, pp. 1111–57.
12. See A. P. Martinich (1999), *Hobbes. A Biography* (Cambridge: Cambridge University Press).
13. R. Sennett (1996), *Flesh and Stone: The Body and the City in Western Civilization* (London: W.W. Norton and Company), p. 255.
14. See J. Le Goff (1989), *Head or Heart?: The Political Use of Body Metaphors in the Middle Ages* in Michael Feher (ed.), *Fragments for a History of the Body*, vol. 3 (New York: Zone Books), pp. 11–26.

absolute monarchy. Second, a distinction is now made between nature and art; art perfects ('and goes yet further') nature. So the natural body is inferior to the 'artificial man'. Besides this move towards a more materialistic politics, aligned with the advance of the physical sciences, the knowledge of government also changed. Prior to modernity, the concern with the soul was identical to the management of the body, physical and social.[15] Now the management of the body, physically and spiritually, was a matter of social policy, that is of implementing specific regimes from above. Third, Hobbes is transferring notions of the body of Christ to the body of the state or the body of the king.

The ambiguity in St Paul's employment of 'body', between 'Christ is *like* a single body' and the 'Church, which *is* his body', is now resolved. For Hobbes, and those after him, the physiological and literal body is employed as a *metaphorical* map for analysing the social body. This use of the body as a metaphor for an agglomeration of single entities coming together as a unit continues up to the present day. The tradition is preserved in various modern languages that inflect the Latin *corporis* (body) and form contemporary terms like *corps medical* and *corps diplomatique* (in French), *Volkskörper* and *Körperschaft* (in German), and 'corporate identity' and 'corporation' (in English).

b) The divine legitimation of sovereignty

The second key topic concerns divine kingship. We discovered earlier the complexities concerning kingship in the Hebrew Bible as well as the question of the kingship of Jesus Christ. These questions take on a new relevance with the medieval debates over the subordination of temporal to spiritual power (and vice versa). After the Reformation and the Wars of Religion that followed, the nature of kingship was further challenged by, on the one hand, the raise of the nation state and, on the other, the development of government by parliament. Theories of absolute monarchy mark one extreme position, opposing theories of collective and representative government. What is at stake here is whether sovereign power is indivisible (as Jean Bodin has argued in his *Six Books on the Commonwealth*, 1576), or divisible and therefore shared and delegated (as James Harrington argued in his *Commonwealth of Oceania*, 1656). This is the old Aristotelian question of the best form of government: by one or by many. Theories of absolute monarchy took their legitimation from divine law; hence the Divine Right of Kings. We can see something of this emerging conflict with King James VI of Scotland being appointed King James I of England. Debates in Parliament in the early part of his reign focused on the kind of union there should be between Scotland and England and the state of the royal income. James petitioned Parliament for an annual income that would make him largely independent of Parliament.[16] A struggle ensued in which James gave his famous 'Speech Before Parliament, March 21st, 1609'.

---

15. *Curia animarum* (care of souls) entailed *regimen animarum* (rules for the care of souls). More recently, this distinction has been re-examined in the late work of Michel Foucault.
16. G. Davies (1937), *The Early Stuarts 1603–1660* (Oxford: Oxford University Press), p. 12.

Interestingly, James makes appeal here to the metaphor of chess and the supreme position of the King:

> Kings are justly called Gods, for that they exercise a manner or resemblance of divine power upon earth. For if you will consider the attributes to God, you shall see how they agree in the person of a king God hath power to create, or destroy, make or unmake at his pleasure, to give life or send death, to judge all, and to be judged nor accountable to none. To raise low things, and to make high things low at his pleasure, and to God are both soul and body due. And the like power have Kings: they make and unmake their subjects: they have power of raising, and casting down: of life and of death: judges over all their subjects, and in all causes, and yet accountable to none but God only. They have power to exalt low things, and abase high things, and make of their subjects like men at the chess. A pawn to take a bishop or a knight, and to cry up or down any of their subjects, as they do their money. And to the king is due both the affection of the soul, and the service of the body of his subjects . . .

James maintained his royal rank before Parliament (unlike his son, Charles I), but he did not win the battle for his royal prerogative. Furthermore, Parliament refused to grant the King's veto on certain subjects being discussed.

With the Divine Right of Kings, religion and political thought are again inseparable. The King derived his power from God to whom he was bound by a covenant. The King was both maker of the law and above the law, only accountable to God. But the King was crowned, and at his coronation he took an oath which also bound him to his people. The nature of the reciprocal duties of the King and his subjects became, increasingly, matter of contestation. From this struggle arose the distinctions between covenantal promise and contract, on the one hand, and the distinction between right and law, on the other. Covenant is related to right as contract is related to law. As Carl Schmitt at the beginning of the twentieth century observed in *Legality and Legitimacy*,[17] these agonistic parallels between law and right, contract and covenant, elected parliament and sacral kingship and secular and spiritual authority haunted the development of modern politics.

c) Religion as a tool for politics

The doctrine of the Divine Right of Kings lingered on into the nineteenth and early twentieth centuries (in Prussia, the Habsburg Empire and Russia, for example), but predominantly the political theory of society was informed by the idea of a social contract. According to this mode of political thinking, society is consolidated on the basis of the mutual transferral of rights by its members. Equality, freedom and solidarity became the new catchwords that prepared the ground for a modern understanding of democratic polity. The role of religion was diminished to the extent that it withdrew from the public sphere and became a matter of personal conscience and moral education. Nevertheless, it maintained an important function in the building and sustaining of a democratic society. As the contemporary

---

17. C. Schmitt (2004), *Legality and Legitimacy*, trans. Jeffery Seitzer (Durham: Duke University Press).

theorist of constitutional law and member of the Supreme Court in Germany Ernst-Wolfgang Boekenfoerde has aptly stated: 'The livelihood of the liberal, secularized state depends on preconditions which itself cannot guarantee. That is the great risk the state took for the sake of freedom.'[18] What are the preconditions at stake here? From a secular and liberal perspective it is the *task of religion*, and also the *legitimation* for its continuing existence, to foster certain values needed for the development of responsible citizenship. We can illustrate this supporting principle with reference to the world's first democracy. In his reflections on democracy in America, Alexis de Tocqueville observed: 'In the United States religion exercises but little influence upon the laws and upon the details of public opinion; but it directs the customs of the community, and, by regulating domestic life, it regulates the state'. Religion is portrayed here as both indispensable and strictly apolitical; it has become a *political tool*. This instrumental use of religion has a long history. We can find it explicitly in the work of the Renaissance diplomat, Niccolò Machiavelli, and most famously in Constantine's appeal to Christianity as the religion of the Empire. For both of these figures religion provides a cohesive force for a people. In the early twentieth century a sociological analysis of the function of religion as a generator for solidarity was undertaken by the French thinker Emil Durkheim. According to Durkheim, religion is the social cement.

Broadly speaking, two traditions of political thinking emerged in the eighteenth and nineteenth centuries. Both employed religion in a different manner. First, there were the liberal theorists (like Rousseau, Paine, Tocqueville and John Stuart Mill). These figures supported the Boekenfoerde axiom in which religion was understood positively. The apolitical nature of religion did not necessarily rest upon the developing secularization of the European mind – as Tocqueville demonstrated. Nevertheless secularism's notion of neutrality (that the government transcends any religion sectarianism or ideology) did foster principles such as *laicité*. The privatization of religion as advocated in the tradition of liberalism harmonized with the internalization of religion by Protestantism, since Protestantism was always sceptical about the Church as a public institution and a political agent. On the other hand, the Catholic Church always insisted on its public and political role in society. It is not surprising, then, that the second political tradition that emerged at this time was associated with the Catholic faith. Conservatives (like de Maistre, Maurras and Schmitt) were all Catholics radically opposed to Protestantism, not simply on dogmatic grounds but because of the Protestant liberal agenda. Only after the Second World War, for example, did the Catholic Church recognize the legitimacy of democratic polity, for democracy was the political form of government that liberalism enshrined. The conservative tradition has a long history that includes figures such as Machiavelli and Hobbes. Two distinguishing characteristics are evident in this tradition: a) a negative anthropology – according to which human beings were sinful and would war against each other unless subservient to a supreme authority; they were unable to save themselves; b) the guarantee for the

---

18. See E.-W. Boekenfoerde (1992), *Recht, Staat, Freiheit: Studien zur Rechtsphilosophie, Staatstheorie und Verfassungsgeschichte* (Frankfurt: Suhrkamp).

maintenance of a republic lay in the *fear* which could be aroused by that supreme authority. So contrary to the positive role religion played in governing in the liberal tradition, in the conservative tradition religion played a negative and delimiting role. For if the people feared God, this fear could be used to coerce obedience to a supreme political authority. The young Friedrich Engels intuitively recognized this theo-political principle of fear when he said: 'The origins of the State and religion are the same: it is the fear of the people of themselves.'

What the two traditions, liberal and conservative, have in common is that both led to the development of what Foucault called biopolitics.[19] With the notion of biopolitics Foucault drew attention to how governing power concerned itself with the regulation of biological life: establishing national concerns for health, for example. We saw above that Tocqueville viewed the family as the arena in which values were produced and nurtured. The family became seen as the fundamental unit in the constitution of the state. Foucault's analysis of biopower and biopolitics facilitated an understanding of the relation between how the state governs and how the basic unit of the state, the family, is affected (by the regulation of sexuality, reproduction and diet, for example). It is significant that Foucault elaborates his analysis of biopower by studying pastoral practices as they developed in the Church (such as the obligation to confess and by doing this making oneself transparent).

d) The religious character of political atheism

In the wake of the Enlightenment, the new intellectual context fostering political science can be measured by a statement made by Dostoievsky: 'Without God everything is permitted.' Although the critique of religion is evident throughout the Enlightenment, represented by Kant,[20] Rousseau and Paine, none of these figures denied the existence of God. God remained the condition for the possibility of ethical and political conduct. In contrast to this, with Marx we enter a cultural condition in which the belief in God *prohibits* any possible change in society for the good. Atheism was not intrinsic to socialism (as the British Christian Socialists exemplify), but with Marx and Engels, and later with Stalin, in the realization of socialism as a political programme, religion had to be abandoned. With respect to this transformation, the text in this volume by Lenin presents a transition from the toleration to the rejection of the political role of religion. Marx begins by announcing that the critique of religion is the prerequisite of all critique. He states explicitly that, in Germany, the critique of religion is over and now a new agenda has been set. 'Thus, the criticism of Heaven turns into the criticism of Earth, the criticism of religion into the criticism of law, and the criticism of theology into the criticism of

19. See the Afterword by Michel Foucaul in H. Dreyfus, and P. Rainbow (1982), *Michel Foucault: Beyond Structuralism and Hermeneutics* (Harvester: New York), pp. 208–26, and J. Carrette (1999) *Religion and Culture by Michel Foucault* (Manchester: Manchester University Press), pp. 154–87.
20. See, for example, Kant's famous essay 'What is Enlightenment?' in which he rejects any external authority and particularly the Church in the formation of moral conduct, but not the idea of the existence of God as such.

politics.' Nevertheless, Marx's 'atheism' and his account of political economy is couched in a religious terms. The Enlightenment Rights of Man, developed into a humanism for Marx in which social freedom lay in the overthrowing of thrones, dominions and oppressions; the raising up of the poor as described in Engels' famous account of *The Social Conditions of the Working-Class People in England*. Thus Marx, when he writes that *'man is the highest essence for man* – hence, [there is] the *categoric imperative to overthrow all relations* in which man is a debased, enslaved, [and] abandoned' (editors' italics), calls for a new realization of a messianic formula already found in the Magnificat. 'He has brought down monarchs from their throne, but the humble have been lifted high' (Luke 1.52). Lenin embraces the secularization thesis understood in terms of the process of rationalization as the driving force of modernity (not unlike Max Weber's thesis of the disenchantment of the world). He is convinced religion will naturally disappear over time so its present toleration is simply pragmatic. But the continuing critique of religion is challenged by a return to religion as an intellectual arsenal for critique itself. This becomes evident in the attack of Simone Weil on Lenin's religious reductionism and her rediscovery of the spiritual roots of socialism in her own resistance to totalitarianism. Ironically, Schmitt recognizes (alongside Eric Voeglin), that totalitarianism was itself a surrogate religion. Refiguring a book title by Hannah Arendt, we sadly have to admit that the twentieth century proved that where totalitarianism gave birth to the banality of evil, the banality of religion gave birth to totalitarianism.

In the tradition of political thinkers like Weil and Schmitt, the awareness of religion as a source for criticizing corrupt forms of dominion is evident today in the theological interventions of Althaus-Reid, Manemann and Milbank. In fact, Žižek is most prominently a contemporary representation of a philosopher who demonstrates the continuing religious character of political atheism in his own work. Hence we can speak of different aspects of the religious nature of political atheism in a manner that connects with where we are today.

Of course, in the rich array of material presented in this volume, other themes are evident. We have drawn attention to just four: the use of the body as both metaphor and analogy for the social; the divine legitimation of sovereignty; a functional approach in which religion is a tool for politics; and the religious character of political atheism. These themes demonstrate the ongoing game between religion and politics. At stake in this game is the continuing quest for sovereign power. To change the nature of this game may well require different players. This is what Shakespeare conceived in the final scene of his final play, *The Tempest*. Here, two kingdoms face each other, the Kings of Naples (Alonso) stands alongside the Duke of Milan (Prospero) and observe the future of both their kingdoms in terms of a marriage between Alonso's son, Ferdinand, and Prospero's daughter, Miranda. These two are playing chess in Prospero's cell.

Miranda: Sweet lord, you play me false.
Ferdinand: No, my dearest love, I would not for the world.
Miranda: Yes, for a score of kingdoms you should wrangle, and I call it fair play . . .

At this point they are interrupted by the old order (Alonso and Prospero) and Miranda responds with her famous expression:

> O, wonder how many goodly creatures are they here! How beauteous mankind is!
> O brave new world, that has such people in it!

Her father responds more ambivalently: 'Tis new to thee'. The game of chess is suspended, the allegory it suggests shifts into the political world that all four main characters will now encounter in returning to Italy. The game will continue there, albeit in a different way.

From reading to research

We want to conclude this introduction to the study of *Religion and Political Thought* by remarking on the pedagogical intention behind this book and the structure of its composition. Our intention is twofold: to make key primary texts of political philosophy accessible; and to provide a sourcebook which enables the reader to understand the history of current issues in religion and politics and their complexity. There is today a major re-evaluation of the relation between religion and politics. However vague the concept of religion and the notion of politics are, the study of the past sheds light on the present and we want to contribute to the clarification of the understanding of religion and politics in terms of a history of ideas.[21] This volume is of an introductory character and it will have served its purpose if it is an incentive for the reader to move from reading to research. Over the last years the availability of primary sources on the Internet has grown enormously and this has changed traditional research culture. Therefore we have suggested some Internet databases in addition to selected secondary readings at the end of the introduction to each classical thinker. In making the decision of whom we would like to include in this selection, representative of the history of religion and politics, we observed two governing principles. First, the texts chosen for each of the five sections bring into dialogue celebrated and well-known figures with less-known people from both sides, that is political theory and Christian theology. Second, the order of the key texts is, in the main, chronological but at the same time intends to set out an arena of questions, alternatives, standpoints and problems in each epoch at stake. Therefore this volume can be read in terms of an unfolding story of the relation of religion and politics from Augustine to Lenin, but also as a synthesis and analysis of key topics in this dense and unfinished relationship. Finally, Parts One to Four of the book introduce classical themes and Part Five draws attention to the current debate about religion and politics.

---

21. For a vast source of empirical data on 'religion and politics' see R. Wuthnow, ed. (1998), *The Encyclopedia of Politics and Religion*, 2 vols (Washington, DC: Congressional Quarterly Books).

PART ONE

The Division of Christ's Political Body

Prologue to Part One

It is evident from the General Introduction that the relation between religion and political thinking did not begin in the early fifth century CE, nor did it fall into abeyance when Augustine died until the time of Aquinas. Selections have been made; and made in accordance with certain criteria with respect to where we are in the West today. The first of those criteria is related to the profound influence one religion in particular has had on so many of our conceptions and categories – legal, philosophical, economic, anthropological, sociological and political – and that is Christianity. It is little wonder that even now as Europe debates the nature of its own identity and contemplates the possibility of Turkey's entry into the EU, the question of its Christian heritage (and whether this should be acknowledged, even protected in some way) has been foregrounded.[1] That is not to undervalue the contributions of the other two main monotheistic faiths – Judaism and Islam. No one acquainted with the four books of the Maccabees, written while Israel was feeling the effects of Hellenistic infiltration, or Josephus' *History of the Jews*, written in Rome by a Jewish historian witnessing the triumph of the Roman Empire over his homeland, the expansion of the Jewish diaspora and the end of the traditional Jewish cult in Jerusalem, could say Judaism was not involved in a debate that was both profoundly religious and political. Islam too had a political character from its development in the seventh century CE.

Nevertheless, as many of the seminal texts in the history of political thought in the West demonstrate, until recently, it was the vision and values of the Christian religion that impressed themselves upon political thinkers. The reason is clear, and it is for this reason that we begin with Augustine – the continuing relationship between the Christian religion and state power. Eusebius of Caesarea tells the story in his ecclesiastic history of the Emperor Constantine facing a major battle at the Bridge of Milvian. Concerned how things would go,

---

1. See Project Syndicate (2004), *Spiritual and cultural dimensions of Europe*, published on the Web at europa.eu.int/comm/research.

he called on [Jesus Christ] with earnest prayer and supplications that he would reveal to him who he was, and stretch forth his right hand to help him in his present difficulties. And while he was thus praying with fervent entreaty, a most marvellous sign appeared to him from heaven, the account of which it might have been hard to believe had it been related by any other person. But since the victorious emperor himself long afterwards declared it to the writer of this history, when he was honoured with his acquaintance and society, and confirmed his statement by an oath, who could hesitate to accredit the relation, especially since the testimony of after-time has established its truth? He said that about noon, when the day was already beginning to decline, he saw with his own eyes the trophy of a cross of light in the heavens, above the sun, and bearing the inscription, CONQUER BY THIS. At this sight he himself was struck with amazement, and his whole army also, which followed him on this expedition, and witnessed the miracle.[2]

Whatever the truth behind this story, with Constantine's conversion Church and state entered into a new set of relations. The impact of these relations might be gauged by the first Ecumenical Council of Nicaea (325 CE). In the face of Arian heresy it was this council that defined the major doctrine of Christ as of the same substance (*homousios*) as the Father. But the council was summoned by the Emperor Constantine. Augustine was not the first to reflect in a theo-political manner on relations between Church and Empire. Setting aside the letters of St Paul, in Oliver O'Donovan and Joan Lockwood's sourcebook for Christian political thought,[3] there are eight entries from theological figures prior to Augustine. Some of these figures were writing prior to the developments later known as Constantinianism, but Augustine himself has to be set within the Latin (Western) context of Ambrose of Milan and the Greek (Eastern) context of Eusebius of Caesarea and John Chrysostom. In fact, the difference between the Western and Eastern approaches to Church–state relations is already quite apparent, and will set up debates that continue down to Martin Luther. Generally, Ambrose and Augustine held to a position in which the Church maintained a critical distance from state power that reflected their sense of Nicaean orthodoxy and the recent political history of the Christian Roman Empire, in which emperors (in order to maximize peace) compromised on doctrine. Eusebius and Chrysostom, on the other hand, viewed imperial power as a divine provision for the maintenance of the Church's faith.

Our selection in this section of Augustine, Aquinas, Dante and Luther reflects the ongoing debates between these two positions, under changing cultural and historical conditions. The debates over episcopal and imperial jurisdiction became transformed in the centuries following Augustine which saw the rise and centralization of papal power, concurrent with what is known as 'Romano-Germanic' discussions in the West concerning kingship and the revival of Roman law.

2. Eusebius of Caesarea (1999), *Life of Constantine*, trans. A. Cameron and S. G. Hall (Oxford: Clarendon Press), p. 86.
3. O. O'Donovan and J. Lockwood (2004), *Bonds of Imperfection: Christian Politics Past and Present* (Grand Rapids, MI: Eerdmans).

To chart these transformations in some detail, we would refer you to the O'Donovan sourcebook. In particular, attention should be paid to the theo-political thinking of Popes Gelasius I (492–6 CE) and Gregory I (ca.540–604 CE), and Isidore of Seville (ca.560–636 CE). Gelasius became important for distin-guishing between secular imperial power and papal spiritual authority, advocating what seems to be a balance between the two. His thinking coincided with a growing schism between the Eastern and Western Churches brought about, in part, by an appeal to the primacy of the Roman See. Gregory I and Isidore of Seville developed the notion of political power as implicated in God's providential rule. The wield-ing of authority in the institution and execution of civil law was a divine office for the subjugation and limitation of human sinfulness. Even tyrants had to be toler-ated as God's punishment for wickedness. There are echoes of Augustine here, but also traces of what will eventually emerge as a notion of sacral royalty, where kings have powers both temporal and spiritual. Politically, such ideas, when developed, will become important for fledging nation–state ideology.

But the sharpness of the controversy between papal and imperial sovereignty did not arise until several more centuries had wrought changes across Europe. The Byzantine Empire declined and Europe became fragmented until the advent of Charlemagne. On Christmas Day 800 CE Charlemagne, King of the Franks, was invested by Pope Leo III as the Roman Emperor, since Charlemagne had reunited much of the Western part of the old Empire. Charlemagne's Frankish kingdom was itself divided on his death between his grandsons, but in 962 CE when the north-ern parts of the Papal States in Italy were invaded, Pope John XII requested aid from the Franks. In 962 CE he crowned Otto I as the Holy Roman Emperor. It is a matter of debate whether he was the first of such, but the investiture by the Pope became, in the eyes of some, a bestowal by the Pope of temporal authority that belonged, *de jure*, to him alone. Much earlier, in the eighth century, a document had been forged entitled the *Constitutum Constantini*, or the Donation of Constantine, in which it was alleged that as Constantine was moving his own court to the East and Constantinople, he gave into the hands of Pope Sylvester I prime jurisdiction over all the Churches and territories in the West, claiming it was 'not right that the earthly emperor should have authority there, where the rule of priests and the head of the Christian religion have been established by the Emperor of heaven'.[4] The document found its way to Rome in the eleventh century, and it was then that the debates over sovereignty of the Empire could begin.

We have chosen Aquinas and Dante to represent aspects of the struggle that began when reforming Popes, most notably Gregory VII, determined to tackle the feudal system in which the appointment of senior clerics to spiritual and temporal office was made by kings. Then the battle cry went up, *plenitude potestatis!*, and the Pope claimed the 'fullness of power' over all things spiritual and temporal. Kings and emperors took up the counter-offensive: the divinity of kings. In a remarkable and very influential document by 'Norman Anonymous', composed around the begin-ning of the twelfth century, we have the first articulation (outside the Scriptures – to

---

4. 'Donation of Constantine', in O. O'Donovan, and J. Lockwood, *Bonds of Imperfection*, pp. 255–62.

which the document makes extensive appeal) of *sacral kingship*. Based on a doctrine of Christ as the bearer of two offices – the divine and kingly, the priestly and human – kings were portrayed as consecrated at their coronation and fashioned as *icon Christi* in his divine relationship to the Father. Priests are consecrated as *images of Christ* in his office as redeemer of mankind. The king's office then is superior, and it matters not a whit whether he is consecrated by the bishop or the Pope, for these are only the administrators of God's grace. The king's role is to reign over all God's people. He is as Christ to them in his government and defence of the true faith. As such, the king is a 'double person: one by nature, the other by grace'.[5] As the political historian Kantorowicz points out, the 'Norman Anonymous' is one of the main sources for the Elizabethan and Stuart attention to the king's two bodies.[6] In fact, we will find the notion of sacral kingship remains politically fundamental even in nineteenth-century Prussia. Significantly, the 'Norman Anonymous' refers back to the thinking of Gelasius I. But whereas Gelasius I had left the power balance between secular and sacral authority open to interpretation, what we have now is both a hierarchy and a fusion. Hierarchy, because the king is supreme ruler within his or her domains; fusion, because while the king does not usurp to the sacerdotal office of the priest, he or she nevertheless holds a sacral office that is nearer to the divinity of Christ than the priests.

We conclude this section with Luther and the struggles between temporal and spiritual power as they were conceived by that reformer. Again, there were a number of important political thinkers prior to Luther, among whom are Marsilius of Padua (ca.1275–1342), John Wyclif (ca.1330–84) and Nicholas of Cusa (1401–64). But space allowed for only so many possibilities and the striking difference between Luther's position and that of Aquinas and Dante not only points to a considerable cultural and political sea change, but also presages an even greater one. For where early medieval thinkers, influenced by Augustine's notion of two cities that were profoundly intermingled, sought to find either a balance between temporal and spiritual power or a hierarchical order, Luther divides them entirely. With that division, secular power attains an autonomy to act that it did not have earlier – an autonomy that was culturally attuned with the new *realpolitik* advocated by Machiavelli. So that although the division between the public sphere and private concerns with one's own spiritual development did not enter the political arena until after the Wars of Religion (at the end of the seventeenth and beginning of the eighteenth century in Britain), Luther's theopolitical imagination has already provided the space for that possibility. Luther even goes some way to showing us the polity of such a secular state – a collection of free-standing individuals, living according to the dictates of their own consciences and bound by protective laws that are safeguarded by a secular authority. We are on the threshold of a new era of religious and political thinking entirely.

5. 'Norman Anonymous', in O. O'Donovan, and J. Lockwood, *Bonds of Imperfection*, pp. 296–301.
6. E. Kantorowicz (1958), *The King's Two Bodies: A Study in Mediaeval Political Theology* (Princeton, NJ: Princeton University Press).

Chapter 1

Augustine (354–430)

. . . two cities have been formed by two loves: the earthly by the love of self, even to the contempt of God; the heavenly by the love of God, even to the contempt of self.

Introduction

On 18 August 410 CE the unthinkable happened. Rome, that great though now fading symbol of a glorious empire defined in Luke's Gospel as 'the world', fell to Alaric, the barbarian Goth from the North. The sacred city, which had fallen to no one and withstood even two besieges by Alaric, was sacked for three days. Pelagius, a British monk, gave contemporary testimony to the shock: 'Rome, the mistress of the world, shivered, crushed with fear, at the sound of blaring trumpets and the howling of the Goths'. Augustine's *City of God* (from which the excerpt below is taken) was written in the aftermath of this unthinkable event. He was far across the other side of the Mediterranean in a Roman city on the African coast called Hippo Regius, but the waves of panic and dread raged across the waters as many of the Roman nobility fled, taking refuge in African cities such as Carthage. These aristocratic refugees reinforced a simmering nostalgia for the old days of imperial and pagan splendour. There was talk that the sacking of Rome was a consequence of turning away from the traditional gods who protected the city. *City of God*, which Augustine himself called his *magnum opus*, was written to exorcise such nostalgia through a rigorous and detailed presentation of the new, Christian order and systematically refute the idea that the imperial turn towards Christianity was the root of Rome's ruin.

City of God is the mature fruit of Augustine's theology. Born in 354 CE in a small African town called Thagaste, Augustine, Bishop of Hippo, was 59 when he began writing it – three years after the Goth invasion. He had been trained as a teacher of rhetoric and left Africa to make his fortune in the imperial civil service whose headquarters were in Milan. It was whilst in Milan that he came under the influence of its powerful bishop, Ambrose, eventually being baptized by him on 24 April 387 CE at the age of 33. Later, two years into his office as Bishop of Hippo, Augustine wrote down the narrative of his spiritual journey from Thagaste to conversion, entitling it *Confessions*. It was far from being the first book he wrote; there had been important works like *De vere religione* (389 CE) and commentaries on the Psalms (392 CE) and the Book of Genesis (393 CE). But *Confessions* is undoubtedly his most ambitious book to date. Other important works followed, particularly *De trinitate* (399 CE – though it did not appear until 414 CE) and a sustained polemic against a Gnostic set called the Manichees.

City of God is the most carefully structured of Augustine's lengthier writings and also his longest. It took 12 years to complete, is composed of 22 books and is divided into five parts. The first five books treat the pagan pursuit of happiness on earth and the myths of the old religion that had been given memorable expression by the prolific Roman writer Marcus Terentius Varro (116–27 BCE). The second five books treat the pagan pursuit of eternal happiness, examining in particular Graeco-Roman philosophers (like Porphyry) or philosophical schools (like Stoicism). If, in these books, Augustine's voice is sternly critical, it is with the remaining 12 books that he becomes constructive – as he outlines the emergence of the two cities, the Jewish God, the incarnation of that God in Jesus Christ, the Church and its final destiny. These 12 books are divided into three groups of four. We have taken two excerpts. The first comes from the first division (Books XIII–XVI), the second comes for the second division (Books XVII–XX), and both concern Augustine's famous two cities – *civitas terrena* and *civitas aeterna*. It was composed in 418 CE amidst Augustine's struggles with the 'heresy' of Pelagius.

The context in which the writing took place is significant for two reasons. The first concerns form. *City of God* is not a systematic political philosophy such as we find in Aristotle[1] or as we will meet later (in Dante, for example). Augustine's political thinking issues from, and is never independent of, a theological account of history and society. The political thinking is important and highly influential, but it is one aspect of Augustine's vision of human beings caught in a temporality suspended within the grace of God. Second, the context is also significant culturally. Augustine's life was a public one and the emerging Roman Church was caught up in a dense set of political relations with their own tensions and pragmatic activities: with the imperial court, the Roman aristocracy's pagan conservatism, with the Church in Africa (as distinct from Rome), with the Greek Church, with Gnostics like Mani and heretical sectarians like the Donatists and Pelagians. The cultural ethos was changing. With Augustine's writing we are immersed in a culture on the cusp of a major shift from what we now call Late Antiquity to early medieval Christendom. Politics were inescapable and the sacred was the necessary imprimatur for any form of power. The Goths negotiated a financial deal with Rome and left. The real war was a cultural one. And at stake was the authority to shape (by coercion if necessary) a new world order. One must never forget that, like St Paul, Augustine was schooled in polemics. The *City of God* is honed like one of the pebbles David used in his fight against Goliath. It is a literary and intellectual missile.

The representation of the two cities makes manifest both the tensions and the pragmatics of Roman Christian living at this time. Given later medieval political thought that draws the distinction between the temporal and the spiritual orders, the rule of the Emperor and the rule of the Pope, it is important to understand that

1. Aristotle (2000), *Politics* (Toronto: Dover Publications).

the cities have no *material* existence for Augustine. They only have *formal* existence, and that formal existence is based upon a reading of the Scriptures. The two cities will only have material existence on the Day of Judgement when God separates out the wheat from the tares, the sheep from the wolves. Until that time the two cities are intermingled and work out their different destinies in the *saeculum*: this realm of temporal duration. They do not constitute, then, two different kinds of political society, but two kinds of moral society. Augustine has little to say about the best form of government (unlike Aristotle and Cicero) or political relations between ruler and ruled. Furthermore, he does not equate the City of God with the Church. He acknowledges there may be many in the Church who will discover they were actually citizens of the earthly city that will perish.

Nevertheless, the cities are distinguished in terms of power relations between citizens; they are caught up in a subtle and psychological warfare. The origins of these relations lie for Augustine in certain moral orientations of the soul. Augustine follows Aristotle in viewing all human beings as desiring happiness; and happiness is a state of being at peace. Thus there needs to be a right ordering of these 'peturbations', but Augustine's argument is that there is only one right ordering: when the soul is orientated towards the supreme Good, 'the Creator good' and not 'the created good'. The two cities issue, then, from two different desires or loves. The actions of their citizens are in accord with these different loves, and Augustine distinguishes them in terms of *amor sui* (love of self) and *amor dei* (love of God). The love of self is driven by a rapacious individualism, a lust for power (*libido dominandi*) and a desire both to possess and use the temporal goods of this world. The love of God is governed by a liberality expressed in terms of adoration towards the supreme Good, a denial of self, a care for one's neighbour and an enjoyment of the temporal goods of this world.

On the basis of this theological and psychological approach to politics, Augustine can argue that the best citizens in the *saeculum* are going to be Christian citizens. For they will foster right relations and a just social order governed by being formed in the image of the supreme Good. This idea radically challenges classical political theory that would agree on the importance of self-denial, but view the highest good as the common good of the city (particularly its survival). Augustine recognizes the challenge – that is why he spends time in Book XIV talking about the moral virtues of Stoicism that Cicero saw as fundamental for the development of civic virtue. He argues on two counts. First, Christians do not wish to expurgate the affections – 'the affections have their place when love is rightly placed'. The temporal order is such that there will always be change and this will create fear, desire, grief and joy. But the citizens of the City of God are part of a pilgrim city (*civitas peregrina*), ruled over by God's good providence. Second, he argues the Stoic virtues are not virtues at all. They cannot be because they are not orientated towards the supreme Good. The restraint they exhort is governed by the love of self, particularly self-control. Civic virtues are founded upon 'ungodly pride' and a desire for personal glory.

It is important to emphasize again that the two cities are not two distinct political societies. They issue from the depths of human motivation; and the abiding message throughout Augustine's *Confessions* is that the endless mystery of God finds its echo in the endless mystery of human motivation. Only God knows the orientation of a human heart. And so, although Augustine champions Christians as good citizens and the Christian ruler is therefore the best ruler of all (see Book V), Augustine allows for the overthrow of even a Christian ruler. Unlike the sycophantic apologists for Christian imperialism (such as Eusebius), Augustine was wary of the conflation of Church and state. Because of human sin and the subsequent fragility of human goodness, political authority has a therapeutic role to play, even a coercive role (endorsed by Augustine for the persecution of Donatists and Pelegians), but only a pragmatic one. And if this raises tensions in Augustine's theological politics – tensions that surface more clearly in his defence of a just war and Christian warriors – that should not alarm us too much. The tensions mirror the conflicts in Augustine's own soul, the cities like Hippo Regius and Carthage that he lived in, and that late Roman culture standing on the edge of the Dark Ages.

Further reading

Selected English translations

Confessiones is translated by H. Chadwick (1991), *Confessions* (Oxford: Oxford University Press).
De Civitate Dei is translated by R. W. Dyson (1998), *The City of God Against the Pagans* (Cambridge: Cambridge University Press).
The Works of Saint Augustine: A Translation for the 21st century (New York: New City Press, 1999–2004).

General introductions

Brown, P. (1967), *Augustine of Hippo* (London: Faber and Faber/Berkeley, CA: University of California Press).
Chadwick, H. (1986), *Augustine* (Oxford: Oxford University Press).
O'Daly G. (1999), *Augustine's City of God: A Reader's Guide* (New York: Oxford University Press).

Reception of key ideas

Donnelly, D. F. (ed.) (1995), *The City of God: A Collection of Critical Essays* (New York: Peter Lang).
Elshtain, J. (1995), *Augustine and the Limits of Politics* (Notre Dame, IN: University of Notre Dame).
Markus, R. (1970), *Saeculum: History and Society in the Theology of Saint Augustine* (Cambridge: Cambridge University Press).

Excerpt from *City of God*

Book 14

Chapter 1 – that the disobedience of the first man would have plunged all men into the endless misery of the second death, had not the grace of God rescued many

We have already stated in the preceding books that God, desiring not only that the human race might be able by their similarity of nature to associate with one another, but also that they might be bound together in harmony and peace by the ties of relationship, was pleased to derive all men from one individual, and created man with such a nature that the members of the race should not have died, had not the two first (of whom the one was created out of nothing, and the other out of him[2]) merited this by their disobedience; for by them so great a sin was committed, that by it the human nature was altered for the worse, and was transmitted also to their posterity, liable to sin and subject to death. And the kingdom of death so reigned over men, that the deserved penalty of sin would have hurled all headlong even into the second death, of which there is no end, had not the undeserved grace of God saved some therefrom. And thus it has come to pass, that though there are very many and great nations all over the earth, whose rites and customs, speech, arms, and dress are distinguished by marked differences, yet *there are no more than two kinds of human society, which we may justly call two cities, according to the language of our Scriptures* [editors' italics]. The one consists of those who wish to live after the *flesh*, the other of those who wish to live after the *spirit*; and when they severally achieve what they wish, they live in peace, each after their kind. [. . .]

Chapter 28 – of the nature of the two cities, the earthly and the heavenly

Accordingly, two cities have been formed by two loves: the earthly by the love of self, even to the contempt of God; the heavenly by the love of God, even to the contempt of self. The former, in a word, glories in itself, the latter in the Lord. For the one seeks glory from men; but the greatest glory of the other is God, the witness of conscience. The one lifts up its head in its own glory; the other says to its God, 'Thou art my glory, and the lifter up of mine head.' In the one, the princes and the nations it subdues are ruled by the love of ruling; in the other, the princes and the subjects serve one another in love, the latter obeying, while the former take thought for all. The one delights in its own strength, represented in the persons of its rulers; the other says to its God, 'I will love Thee, O Lord, my strength.' And therefore the wise men of the one city, living according to man, have sought for profit to their own bodies or souls, or both, and those who have known God 'glorified Him not as God, neither were thankful, but became vain in their imaginations, and their foolish heart was darkened; professing

2. Genesis chapters 2–4.

themselves to be wise,' – that is, glorying in their own wisdom, and being possessed by pride, – 'they became fools, and changed the glory of the incorruptible God into an image made like to corruptible man, and to birds, and four-footed beasts, and creeping things.' For they were either leaders or followers of the people in adoring images, 'and worshipped and served the creature more than the Creator, who is blessed for ever.' But in the other city there is no human wisdom, but only godliness, which offers due worship to the true God, and looks for its reward in the society of the saints, of holy angels as well as holy men, 'that God may be all in all.'

Book 15

Chapter 1 – of the two lines of the human race which from first to last divide it

Of the bliss of Paradise, of Paradise itself, and of the life of our first parents there, and of their sin and punishment, many have thought much, spoken much, written much. We ourselves, too, have spoken of these things in the foregoing books, and have written either what we read in the Holy Scriptures, or what we could reasonably deduce from them. And were we to enter into a more detailed investigation of these matters, an endless number of endless questions would arise, which would involve us in a larger work than the present occasion admits. We cannot be expected to find room for replying to every question that may be started by unoccupied and captious men, who are ever more ready to ask questions than capable of understanding the answer. Yet I trust we have already done justice to these great and difficult questions regarding the beginning of the world, or of the soul, or of the human race itself. This race we have distributed into two parts, the one consisting of those who live according to man, the other of those who live according to God. And these we also mystically call the two cities, or the two communities of men, of which the one is predestined to reign eternally with God, and the other to suffer eternal punishment with the devil. This, however, is their end, and of it we are to speak afterwards. At present, as we have said enough about their origin, whether among the angels, whose numbers we know not, or in the two first human beings, it seems suitable to attempt an account of their career, from the time when our two first parents began to propagate the race until all human generation shall cease. For this whole time or world-age, in which the dying give place and those who are born succeed, is the career of these two cities concerning which we treat.

Of these two first parents of the human race, then, Cain was the first-born, and he belonged to the city of men; after him was born Abel, who belonged to the city of God. For as in the individual the truth of the apostle's statement is discerned, 'that is not first which is spiritual, but that which is natural, and afterward that which is spiritual,' whence it comes to pass that each man, being derived from a condemned stock, is first of all born of Adam evil and carnal, and becomes good and spiritual only afterwards, when he is grafted into Christ by regeneration: so was it in the human race as a whole. When these two cities began to run their course by a series of deaths and births, the citizen of this world was the first-born, and after him the stranger in this world, the citizen of the city of God, predestinated by grace, elected by grace, by grace a stranger below, and by grace a citizen above. By grace – for so far as regards himself he is sprung from the same mass, all of which is condemned in its origin: but God, like a potter (for this comparison is introduced by the apostle judiciously, and not without thought), of the same lump made one vessel to honor, another to dishonor. But first the vessel to dishonor was made, and after it another to honor. For in each individual, as I have already said, there is first of all that which is reprobate, that from which we must begin, but in which we need not necessarily remain; afterwards is that which is well-approved, to which we may by advancing attain, and in which, when we have reached it, we may abide. Not, indeed, that every wicked man shall be good, but that no one will be good who was not first of all wicked but the sooner any one becomes a good man, the more speedily does he receive this title, and abolish the old name in the new. Accordingly, it is recorded of Cain that he built a city, but Abel, being a sojourner, built none. For the city of the saints is above, although here below it begets citizens, in whom it sojourns till the time of its reign arrives, when it shall gather together all in the day of the resurrection; and then shall the promised kingdom be given to them, in which they shall reign with their Prince, the King of the ages, time without end.

Chapter 4 – of the conflict and peace of the earthly city

But the earthly city, which shall not be everlasting (for it will no longer be a city when it has been committed to the extreme penalty), has its good in this world, and rejoices in it with such joy as such things can afford. But as this is not a good which can discharge its devotees of all distresses, this city is often divided against itself by litigations, wars, quarrels, and such victories as are either life-destroying or short-lived. For each part of it that arms against another part of it seeks to triumph over the nations through itself in bondage to vice. If, when it has conquered, it is inflated with pride, its victory is life-destroying; but if it turns its thoughts upon the common casualties of our mortal condition, and is rather anxious concerning the disasters that may befall it than elated with the successes already achieved, this victory, though of a higher kind, is still only short-lived; for it cannot abidingly rule over those whom it has victoriously subjugated. But the things which this city desires cannot justly be said to be evil, for it is itself, in its own kind, better than all other human good. For it desires earthly peace for the sake of enjoying earthly goods, and it makes war in order to attain to this peace; since, if it has conquered, and there remains no one to resist it, it enjoys a peace which it had not while there were opposing parties who contested for the enjoyment of those things which were too small to satisfy both. This peace is purchased by toilsome wars; it is obtained by what they style a glorious victory. Now, when victory remains with the party which had the juster cause, who hesitates to congratulate the victor, and style it a desirable peace? These things, then, are good things, and without doubt the gifts of God. But if they neglect the better things of the heavenly city, which are secured by eternal victory and peace never-ending, and so inordinately covet these present good things

31

that they believe them to be the only desirable things, or love them better than those things which are believed to be better – if this be so, then it is necessary that misery follow and ever increase.

Chapter 5 – of the fratricidal act of the founder of the earthly city, and the corresponding crime of the founder of Rome

Thus the founder of the earthly city was a fratricide. Overcome with envy, he slew his own brother, a citizen of the eternal city, and a sojourner on earth. So that we cannot be surprised that this first specimen, or, as the Greeks say, archetype of crime, should, long afterwards, find a corresponding crime at the foundation of that city which was destined to reign over so many nations, and be the head of this earthly city of which we speak. For of that city also, as one of their poets has mentioned, 'the first walls were stained with a brother's blood,' or, as Roman history records, Remus was slain by his brother Romulus. And thus there is no difference between the foundation of this city and of the earthly city, unless it be that Romulus and Remus were both citizens of the earthly city. Both desired to have the glory of founding the Roman republic, but both could not have as much glory as if one only claimed it; for he who wished to have the glory of ruling would certainly rule less if his power were shared by a living consort. In order, therefore, that the whole glory might be enjoyed by one, his consort was removed; and by this crime the empire was made larger indeed, but inferior, while otherwise it would have been less, but better. Now these brothers, Cain and Abel, were not both animated by the same earthly desires, nor did the murderer envy the other because he feared that, by both ruling, his own dominion would be curtailed – for Abel was not solicitous to rule in that city which his brother built – he was moved by that diabolical, envious hatred with which the evil regard the good, for no other reason than because they are good while themselves are evil. For the possession of goodness is by no means diminished by being shared with a partner either permanent or temporarily assumed; on the contrary, the possession of goodness is increased in proportion to the concord and charity of each of those who share it. In short, he who is unwilling to share this possession cannot have it; and he who is most willing to admit others to a share of it will have the greatest abundance to himself. The quarrel, then, between Romulus and Remus shows how the earthly city is divided against itself; that which fell out between Cain and Abel illustrated the hatred that subsists between the two cities, that of God and that of men. The wicked war with the wicked; the good also war with the wicked. But with the good, good men, or at least perfectly good men, cannot war; though, while only going on towards perfection, they war to this extent, that every good man resists others in those points in which he resists himself. And in each individual 'the flesh lusteth against the spirit, and the spirit against the flesh.' This spiritual lusting, therefore, can be at war with the carnal lust of another man; or carnal lust may be at war with the spiritual desires of another, in some such way as good and wicked men are at war; or, still more certainly, the carnal lusts of two men, good but not yet perfect, contend together, just as the wicked contend with the wicked, until the health of those who are under the treatment of grace attains final victory.

Chapter 6 – of the weaknesses which even the citizens of the city of God suffer during this earthly pilgrimage in punishment of sin, and of which they are healed by God's care

This sickliness – that is to say, that disobedience of which we spoke in the fourteenth book – is the punishment of the first disobedience. It is therefore not nature, but vice; and therefore it is said to the good who are growing in grace, and living in this pilgrimage by faith, 'Bear ye one another's burdens, and so fulfill the law of Christ.' In like manner it is said elsewhere, 'Warn them that are unruly, comfort the feeble-minded, support the weak, be patient toward all men. See that none render evil for evil unto any man.' And in another place, 'If a man be overtaken in a fault, ye which are spiritual restore such an one in the spirit of meekness; considering thyself, lest thou also be tempted.' And elsewhere, 'Let not the sun go down upon your wrath.' And in the Gospel, 'If thy brother shall trespass against thee, go and tell him his fault between thee and him alone.' So too of sins which may create scandal the apostle says, 'Them that sin rebuke before all, that others also may fear.' For this purpose, and that we may keep that peace without which no man can see the Lord, many precepts are given which carefully inculcate mutual forgiveness; among which we may number that terrible word in which the servant is ordered to pay his formerly remitted debt of ten thousand talents, because he did not remit to his fellow-servant his debt of two hundred pence. To which parable the Lord Jesus added the words, 'So likewise shall my heavenly Father do also unto you, if ye from your hearts forgive not every one his brother.' It is thus the citizens of the city of God are healed while still they sojourn in this earth and sigh for the peace of their heavenly country. The Holy Spirit, too, works within, that the medicine externally applied may have some good result.

Otherwise, even though God Himself make use of the creatures that are subject to Him, and in some human form address our human senses, whether we receive those impressions in sleep or in some external appearance, still, if He does not by His own inward grace sway and act upon the mind, no preaching of the truth is of any avail. But this God does, distinguishing between the vessels of wrath and the vessels of mercy, by His own very secret but very just providence. When He Himself aids the soul in His own hidden and wonderful ways, and the sin which dwells in our members, and is, as the apostle teaches, rather the punishment of sin, does not reign in our mortal body to obey the lusts of it, and when we no longer yield our members as instruments of unrighteousness, then the soul is converted from its own evil and selfish desires, and, God possessing it, it possesses itself in peace even in this life, and afterwards, with perfected health and endowed with immortality, will reign without sin in peace everlasting.

Book 19

Chapter 17 – what produces peace, and what discord, between the heavenly and earthly cities

But the families which do not live by faith seek their peace in the earthly advantages of this life; while the families which live by faith look for those eternal blessings which are promised, and use as pilgrims such advantages of time and of earth as do not fascinate and divert them from God, but rather aid them to endure with greater ease, and to keep down the number of those burdens of the corruptible body which weigh upon the soul. Thus the things necessary for this mortal life are used by both kinds of men and families alike, but each has its own peculiar and widely different aim in using them. The earthly city, which does not live by faith, seeks an earthly peace, and the end it proposes, in the well-ordered concord of civic obedience and rule, is the combination of men's wills to attain the things which are helpful to this life. The heavenly city, or rather the part of it which sojourns on earth and lives by faith, makes use of this peace only because it must, until this mortal condition which necessitates it shall pass away. Consequently, so long as it lives like a captive and a stranger in the earthly city, though it has already received the promise of redemption, and the gift of the Spirit as the earnest of it, it makes no scruple to obey the laws of the earthly city, whereby the things necessary for the maintenance of this mortal life are administered; and thus, as this life is common to both cities, so there is a harmony between them in regard to what belongs to it. But, as the earthly city has had some philosophers whose doctrine is condemned by the divine teaching, and who, being deceived either by their own conjectures or by demons, supposed that many gods must be invited to take an interest in human affairs, and assigned to each a separate function and a separate department, – to one the body, to another the soul; and in the body itself, to one the head, to another the neck, and each of the other members to one of the gods; and in like manner, in the soul, to one god the natural capacity was assigned, to another education, to another anger, to another lust; and so the various affairs of life were assigned, – cattle to one, corn to another, wine to another, oil to another, the woods to another, money to another, navigation to another, wars and victories to another, marriages to another, births and fecundity to another, and other things to other gods: and as the celestial city, on the other hand, knew that one God only was to be worshipped, and that to Him alone was due that service which the Greeks call *latreia*, and which can be given only to a god, it has come to pass that the two cities could not have common laws of religion, and that the heavenly city has been compelled in this matter to dissent, and to become obnoxious to those who think differently, and to stand the brunt of their anger and hatred and persecutions, except in so far as the minds of their enemies have been alarmed by the multitude of the Christians and quelled by the manifest protection of God accorded to them. This heavenly city, then, while it sojourns on earth, calls citizens out of all nations, and gathers together a society of pilgrims of all languages, not scrupling about diversities in the manners, laws, and institutions whereby earthly peace is secured and maintained, but recognizing that, however various these are, they all tend to one and the same end of earthly peace. It therefore is so far from rescinding and abolishing these diversities, that it even preserves and adopts them, so long only as no hindrance to the worship of the one supreme and true God is thus introduced. Even the heavenly city, therefore, while in its state of pilgrimage, avails itself of the peace of earth, and, so far as it can without injuring faith and godliness, desires and maintains a common agreement among men regarding the acquisition of the necessaries of life, and makes this earthly peace bear upon the peace of heaven; for this alone can be truly called and esteemed the peace of the reasonable creatures, consisting as it does in the perfectly ordered and harmonious enjoyment of God and of one another in God. When we shall have reached that peace, this mortal life shall give place to one that is eternal, and our body shall be no more this animal body which by its corruption weighs down the soul, but a spiritual body feeling no want, and in all its members subjected to the will. In its pilgrim state the heavenly city possesses this peace by faith; and by this faith it lives righteously when it refers to the attainment of that peace every good action towards God and man; for the life of the city is a social life.

Chapter 20 – that the saints are in this life blessed in hope

Since, then, the supreme good of the city of God is perfect and eternal peace, not such as mortals pass into and out of by birth and death, but the peace of freedom from all evil, in which the immortals ever abide; who can deny that that future life is most blessed, or that, in comparison with it, this life which now we live is most wretched, be it filled with all blessings of body and soul and external things? And yet, if any man uses this life with a reference to that other which he ardently loves and confidently hopes for, he may well be called even now blessed, though not in reality so much as in hope. But the actual possession of the happiness of this life, without the hope of what is beyond, is but a false happiness and profound misery. For the true blessings of the soul are not now enjoyed; for that is no true wisdom which does not direct all its prudent observations, manly actions, virtuous self-restraint, and just arrangements, to that end in which God shall be all and all in a secure eternity and perfect peace.

Chapter 26 – of the peace which is enjoyed by the people that are alienated from God, and the use made of it by the people of god in the time of its pilgrimage

Wherefore, as the life of the flesh is the soul, so the blessed life of man is God, of whom the sacred writings of the Hebrews say, 'Blessed is the people whose God is the Lord.' Miserable, therefore, is the people which is alienated from God. Yet even this people has a peace of its own which is not to be lightly esteemed, though, indeed, it shall not in the end enjoy it, because it makes no good use of it before the end. But it is our interest that it enjoy this peace meanwhile in this life; for as long as the two cities are commingled, we also enjoy the peace of Babylon. For from Babylon the people of God is so freed that it meanwhile sojourns in its company.

And therefore the apostle also admonished the Church to pray for kings and those in authority, assigning as the reason, 'that we may live a quiet and tranquil life in all godliness and love.' And the prophet Jeremiah, when predicting the captivity that was to befall the ancient people of God, and giving them the divine command to go obediently to Babylonia, and thus serve their God, counselled them also to pray for Babylonia, saying, 'In the peace thereof shall ye have peace,' – the temporal peace which the good and the wicked together enjoy.

Chapter 27 – that the peace of those who serve God cannot in this mortal life be apprehended in its perfection

But the peace which is peculiar to ourselves we enjoy now with God by faith, and shall hereafter enjoy eternally with Him by sight. But the peace which we enjoy in this life, whether common to all or peculiar to ourselves, is rather the solace of our misery than the positive enjoyment of felicity. Our very righteousness, too, though true in so far as it has respect to the true good, is yet in this life of such a kind that it consists rather in the remission of sins than in the perfecting of virtues. Witness the prayer of the whole city of God in its pilgrim state, for it cries to God by the mouth of all its members, 'Forgive us our debts as we forgive our debtors.'

Chapter 2

Thomas Aquinas (1225/7–74)

*Among the forms of unjust rule, therefore, democracy is the most tolerable and
tyranny the worst.*

Introduction

Three important and culturally defining events mark out the time between
Augustine and Aquinas. The first, historically, is the pontificate of Leo the Great
(440–61). The second is the Investiture Controversy (1075–1122). And the third
event is the rediscovery of Aristotle through two medieval Islamic commentators:
Avicenna (980–1037) and Averroes (1126–96).

Leo became Pope in 440 CE, ten years after the death of Augustine. Rome again
faced invasion from the northern barbarians, under the infamous Attila the Hun.
The last shreds of the Roman Empire were tattered and torn and it was Leo who
negotiated with Attila for the safety of Rome itself. At the same time as effectively
becoming the major political figure in what was left of the Empire, Leo centralized
the Catholic Church around the Roman pontificate. The Bishop of Rome now
became Primate of the Universal Church in the West and in the East.

It was this primacy and its relations to the rule of the Emperor that paved the way,
over 600 years later, for the second cultural event, the Investiture Controversy. The
question upon which the controversy hinged concerned whether the Emperor's
temporal authority was subservient or equal to the Pope's authority over both the
secular and spiritual domain. The papal position held that all power was derived
from the Pope, who could make and divest both kings and emperors. The imperial
position held that all power came from God and the consent of those being governed, even the Pope's temporal power (in his own Papal States) was derived from
the secular ruler. These two positions met in a head-on collision when Pope
Gregory VII (1020–85) believed the Emperor (Henry IV) was not carrying out the
reforms of the Church he proposed, particularly with respect to clerical appoint-
ments. Henry IV maintained the right to invest his own candidates as bishops,
deposing those invested by the Pope. The power struggle reached such a pitch that
Gregory VII excommunicated Henry IV and all his ecclesiastical supporters.
Canvassing then began for the election of a new Emperor, who would be crowned,
as all the emperors were, by the Pope. At the castle of Canossa, in the Italian Alps,
Henry IV met Gregory VII as a penitent. Gregory VII stripped him of his royal robes

and made him walk barefoot through snow and ice before admitting Henry IV into his presence. If Gregory had won this first round, his victory was to remain short-lived. For the German princes elected a new Emperor (Rudolf of Swabia) and Henry IV announced a new Pope (Clement III). Henry IV was once again excommunicated, but now he drove his armies down through Italy, took Rome and had his own Pope, Clement III, crown him as Emperor yet again. The Duke of Normandy came to liberate Gregory VII, causing both Henry IV and Clement III to flee.

The importance of this struggle, which continued until the pontificate of Callistos II (1119–24), cannot be overestimated in any discussion of the relationships between religion and politics, the Church and the state, spiritual and temporal powers. The reflections upon the nature of authority in Aquinas, Dante and Luther are (each in their way) affected by the conceptual consequences of this struggle, as we will see.

The third event is a cultural one. Contact with the Islamic world (through the Crusades) introduced a number of texts by Aristotle that were not part of the Latin translations known at that time in the West. In particular, Aristotle's *Ethics* and *Politics* began to circulate among scholars in the latter part of the twelfth and early part of the thirteenth century. Aquinas's teacher, Albertus Magnus, was one of these scholars. This rediscovery of Aristotelian thought rejuvenated intellectual life in Europe, creating conflicts, accusations of heresy and creative syntheses.

Aquinas was immersed in the feverish disputations, both political and intellectual. His uncle, now dead, was the Emperor Frederick I (Barbarossa) and his father, the Count of Aquino, was an important ally in the Pope Urban IV's struggles with the Hohenstaufer, the ruling family of Germany. In 1264, the Emperor Manfred, who had some claim to the kingship of Rome, marched towards the Papal States with a huge army. The Pope moved north to the hilltop fortress of Orvieto in Umbria only to be encircled by the troops of a powerful Italian family, which we will meet again with Dante, the Ghibellines. Thomas Aquinas had been teaching at the Dominican priory in Orvieto since September 1261, where he composed his first major work, *Summa Contra Gentiles*. He was known to Urban IV, who had requested a work from Thomas on the Greek Fathers in 1263. In Orvieto the Pope waited for French forces, supported by the second most powerful Italian family, the Guelfs, to liberate him. But they didn't come and the Pope fled further north to Perugia where he died. The French army reoccupied Rome in the early summer of 1265, now with its new Pope (Clement IV), and it was later that summer that Thomas came from Orvieto to Rome to establish a centre for theological studies or *studium* for the Dominican order. Meanwhile, on 26 February 1266, the two armies, the French and the Hohenstaufer, gathered for a final showdown in which Thomas's family once again fought.

This is the context within which *De regno* was composed (either at Oriveto, with Urban IV, or Rome). It is significant that *regnum* was the Latin term for 'secular authority', as distinct from *sacerdotium*, which is 'spiritual authority'. The treatise, then, concerns the limits and legitimacy of secular rule (a concern central to the excerpts taken from Dante and Luther). The origin, intention and purpose of the treatise are encompassed with mystery. For why would Aquinas wish to address an unsolicited work on secular authority to the King of Cyprus, who he names as Henry, but who was in fact Hugh II? Furthermore, why did he leave the work unfinished? (Books I and II up to chapter 4 are Aquinas's, the remainder was completed by Aquinas's disciple and confessor, Tolomeo of Lucca, presumably after his master's death in 1274.) Was he asked to write it, and, if so, by whom? The Pope? There is also a mystery about its contents, insofar as elsewhere (*Summa Theologica* IaIIae 105:1) he recommends that the best form of government is a mixed one, in which the king's authority works with a group of aristocrats (oligarchy). These were not hereditary noblemen, for Thomas's model for this kind of government comes from the Book of Deuteronomy where Moses appointed 72 elders to assist him in his rule (Deut. 1.15). He enjoins, then, 'a democratic government' collaborating with the rule of the monarch. In *De regno* some have thought he advocates an absolute monarchy that contradicts his position in the *Summa Theologica*. The *Summa Theologica* was begun in Rome, but the question concerning good government belongs to what is known as the second half of the first part of the *Summa* (the *Prima Secundae*), which is thought to have been written in 1270 or 1271 (when Thomas was in Paris).

In the excerpt we have chosen it would certainly appear that Thomas allows the king absolute rule (and therefore the text can be compared to those of James VI/I and Hobbes on the nature of sovereignty). But later in the text,[1] when the question of the tyrant emerges in Book I, chapter vii, Thomas suggests that 'once the king has been appointed, the government of the kingdom should be so arranged as to remove from the king, the opportunity of becoming a tyrant; and, at the same time, his power should be restricted so that he will not easily be able to fall into tyranny'. Rather unhelpfully, Thomas promises he will go into the details of such restrictions later in the text – but the treatise ends before any discussion of these details takes place. But what is interesting is that, compared to James VI/I on absolute monarchy, Thomas does leave open the possibility of removing the tyrannous ruler through 'public authority'. So there may not be a contradiction at all between Thomas's views on secular authority, and question 105:1 of the *Prima Secundae* may well be a development of what Thomas means by 'public authority' and the restrictions on the powers of any king.

The excerpt from *De regno*, as the footnotes indicate, shows the considerable influence of Aristotle. Throughout his work, Thomas frequently refers to Aristotle as 'the Philosopher' and he wrote a number of commentaries on major works by Aristotle: *De anima* (1268), *Nicomachean Ethics* (1270), *Politics* (1269–72). The commentaries are part of Thomas's late work, when he was in Paris – where there was much controversy over the importance of Aristotle for theology. Aristotle's philosophy, with its affirmation of reasoning, facilitated new approaches to both creation and society for a number of medieval thinkers at this time. We can measure his impact by comparing Thomas to Augustine. As we saw, Augustine sketches a limited and largely negative role for secular authority and rule; he does not develop a political theology as such. Thomas, on the other hand, views secular government

---

1. R. W. Dyson, ed. (2002), *Aquinas: Political Writings* (Cambridge: Cambridge University Press).

as a positive contribution to what he calls, after Aristotle, the 'common good'. Secular rule has an end in itself, 'the unity of peace'. But, as we observed above, Thomas reads Aristotle through the Christian tradition and its Scriptures. The *telos* or end of the common good is the ordering of right relations between the created order and God as Maker and Ruler of all. The created order is what Thomas calls 'nature' and governance is an art that should *imitate* nature as much as possible. We can note here how the body as an analogy is used to move between the natural and the socio-political. We will see this same analogy appearing, in different guises, in Dante, Luther, James VI/I and Hobbes. It is derived from St Paul's picture of the Church as the body of Christ made up of several different members. Here, Thomas employs it to emphasize how the government of any part (city, state, province) has to be in accord with the principle governing the whole (God). God is the source of the Good. In fact, the tradition understood the Good to be one of the 'names' of God – along with the True, the Just and the Beautiful. The common good is then only truly good when it is related to the principle of Goodness (which is also the principle of Justice, Truth and Beauty). This is analogical thinking: 'good' is used with respect to the socio-political but its meaning and perfection lies in God as the Good. A similar analogy associates the king with God as the supreme King and associates law as a 'rule and measure' of reason, natural law and divine law. The analogical association is made possible because it is the natural condition of all things to desire and seek that which is universally Good. God has ordained His creation in this way. The end of all things is heavenly blessedness, as Thomas outlines later (in Book I, chapter x). Because of this *telos*, in Book I, chapter xiv he argues that the administration of God's kingdom 'is entrusted not only to earthly kings, but to priests, so that spiritual and earthly things may be kept distinct; and in particular to the Supreme Priest, the successor of Peter, the Vicar of Christ, the Roman Pontiff, to whom all the kings of the Christian people should be subject . . . For those who are responsible for intermediate ends should be subject to one who is responsible for the ultimate end, and be directed by his command'. It would seem, then, that Thomas advocates the Guelf rather than the imperial position on the plenitude of papal power.

Further reading

Selected English translations

Dyson, R. W. (ed.) (2002), *Aquinas: Political Writings* (Cambridge: Cambridge University Press).

General introductions

Gilson, E. (1954), *The Christian Philosophy of St. Thomas Aquinas*, trans. L. Shook (New York: Random House).
Kretzmann, N. and Stump, E. (eds) (1993), *The Cambridge Companion to Aquinas* (New York: Cambridge University Press).

Torrell, J.-P. (1996), *Saint Thomas Aquinas, Vol. 1: The Person and His Work*, trans. R. Royal (Washington, DC: Catholic University of America Press).

Torrell, J.-P. (2003), *Saint Thomas Aquinas, Vol. 2: Spiritual Master*, trans R. Royal (Washington, DC: Catholic University of America Press).

Weisheipl, J. A. (1984), *Friar Thomas D'Aquino: His Life, Thought, and Work* (Washington, DC: Catholic University of America Press).

Reception of key ideas

Finnis, J. (1998), *Aquinas: Moral, Political, and Legal Theory* (Oxford: Oxford University Press).

Excerpt from *De regimine (De regno)*

Preface: The author sets forth his intention in writing to the king of Cyprus.

As I considered with myself what I should undertake that would be worthy of royal majesty and in keeping with my calling and office, it occurred to me that what I might offer a king above all would be a book written on the subject of kingship, in which I should, to the best of my powers, diligently draw out both the origin of a kingdom and what pertains to the king's office, according to the authority of Divine Scripture, the teachings of the philosophers, and the examples given by those who praise princes, relying for the beginning, progression and completion of the work upon the aid of Him Who is King of kings and Lord of lords, by Whom kings reign: the Lord, 'a great God, and a great King above all gods' (Psalm 95:3).

Book 1

Chapter 1: That it is necessary for men who live together to be subject to diligent rule by someone.

To fulfil this intention, we must begin by explaining how the title 'king' is to be understood. Now in all cases where things are directed towards some end but it is possible to proceed in more than one way, it is necessary for there to be some guiding principle, so that the due end may be properly achieved. For example, a ship is driven in different directions according to the force of different winds, and it will not reach its final destination except by the industry of the steersman who guides it into port. Now man has a certain end towards which the whole of his life and activity is directed; for as a creature who acts by intelligence, it is clearly his nature to work towards some end.[2] But men can proceed towards that end in different ways, as the very diversity of humankind shows. Man therefore needs something to guide him towards his end.

Now each man is imbued by nature with the light of reason, and he is directed

---

2. Aristotle, *Ethics* 1:7 (1098a5).

towards his end by its action within him. If it were proper for man to live in solitude, as many animals do, he would need no other guide towards his end; for each man would then be a king unto himself, under God, the supreme King, and would direct his own actions by the light of reason divinely given to him. *But man is by nature a social and political animal, who lives in a community* [*in multitudine vivens*]:[3] more so, indeed, than all other animals; and natural necessity shows why this is so. For other animals are furnished by nature with food, with a covering of hair and with the means of defence, such as teeth, horns or at any rate speed in flight. But man is supplied with none of these things by nature. Rather, in place of all of them reason was given to him, by which he might be able to provide all things for himself by the work of his own hands.[4] One man, however, is not able to equip himself with all these things, for one man cannot live a self-sufficient life. It is therefore natural for man to live in fellowship with many others.

Moreover, other animals are endowed with a natural awareness of everything which is useful or harmful to them. For example, the sheep naturally judges the wolf to be an enemy. Some animals even have a natural awareness which enables them to recognize certain medicinal plants and other things as being necessary to their lives. Man, however, has a natural understanding of the things necessary to his life only in a general way, and it is by the use of reason that he passes from universal principles to an understanding of the particular things which are necessary to human life. But it is not possible for one man to apprehend all such things by reason. It is therefore necessary for a man to live in community, so that each man may devote his reason to some particular branch of learning: one to medicine, another to something else, another to something else again. And this is shown especially by the fact that only man has the capacity to use speech, by means of which one man can reveal the whole content of his mind to another.[5] Other animals express their feelings to each other in a general way, as when a dog shows his anger by barking and the other animals show their feelings in various ways; but one man is more able to communicate with another than any other animal is, even those which are seen to be gregarious, such as cranes, ants and bees.[6] Solomon, therefore, is thinking of this at Ecclesiastes 4:9 where he says: 'Two are better than one, because they have the reward of mutual companionship.'

If, therefore, it is natural for man to live in fellowship with many others, it is necessary for there to be some means whereby such a community of men may be ruled. For if many men were to live together with each providing only what is convenient for himself, the community would break up into its various parts unless one of them had responsibility for the good of the community as a whole, just as the body of a man and of any other animal would fall apart if there were not some general ruling force to sustain the body and secure the common good of all its parts. Solomon is thinking of this at Proverbs 11:14 where he says: 'Where there is no governor, the people shall be scattered.' This accords with reason; for individ-

3. Aristotle, *Politics* 1:2 (1253a2).
4. Aristotle, *De partibus animalium* 4:10 (687a19).
5. Aristotle, *Politics* 1:2 (1253a1).
6. Aristotle, *Historia animalium* 1:1 (488a10).

ual interests and the common good are not the same. *Individuals differ as to their private interests, but are united with respect to the common good*, and such differences have various causes. It is fitting, therefore, that, beyond that which moves the individual to pursue a good peculiar to himself, there should be something which promotes the common good of the many. It is for this reason that whatever things are organized into a unity, something is found that rules all the rest.[7] For by a certain order of Divine providence all bodies in the material universe are ruled by the primary, that is, the celestial body, and all bodies by rational creatures. Also, in one man the soul rules the body, and, within the soul, the irascible and concupiscible appetites are ruled by reason. Again, among the members of the body there is one ruling part, either the heart or the head, which moves all the others.[8] It is fitting, therefore, that in every multitude there should be some ruling principle.[9]

Chapter 2: The various forms of lordship or government.

But where matters are directed towards some end, there may be one way of proceeding which is right and another which is not right; and so we find that the government of a community can be directed both rightly and not rightly.[10] Now something is directed rightly when it is led to its proper end, and not rightly when it is led to an end not proper to it. But the end proper to a community of free men is different from that of slaves. For a free man is one who is the master of his own actions, whereas a slave, insofar as he is a slave, is the property of another.[11]

If, therefore, a community of free men is ordered by the common good, such rule will be right and just insomuch as it is suitable to free men. If, however, the government is not directed towards the common good but towards the private good of the ruler, the rule of this king will be unjust and perverted;[12] and such rulers are warned by the Lord at Ezekiel 34:2, where He says: 'Woe be to the shepherds that do feed themselves' – because they seek only gain for themselves. 'Should not the shepherds feed flocks?' Shepherds must seek the good of their flock, and all rulers the good of the community subject to them.

If, therefore, government is exercised unjustly by one man alone, who, in ruling, seeks gain for himself and not the good of the community subject to him, such a ruler is called a tyrant, a name derived from [the Greek word, τύραννις, which means] 'force', because he oppresses with power and does not rule with justice. Hence, among the ancients all men of power were called 'tyrants'.[13] If, however, unjust government is exercised not by one but by several, when this is done by a few it is called 'oligarchy', that is, 'rule by the few'; and this comes about when, by

7. Aristotle, *Politics* 1:5 (1254a28).
8. Aristotle, *Metaphysics* 5:1 (1013a5).
9. See John of Salisbury, *Policraticus* 5:2.
10. Aristotle, *Politics* 3:6 (1279a17).
11. Aristotle, *Metaphysics* 1:2 (982b25).
12. Aristotle, *Politics* 3:7 (1279a22); *Ethics* 8:10 (1159b31).
13. Augustine, *De civitate Dei* 5:89.

reason of their wealth, the few oppress the people, and it differs from tyranny only with respect to number. Again, if wrongful government is exercised by the many, this is named 'democracy', that is, 'rule by the people'; and this comes about when the common people oppress the rich by force of numbers. In this way the whole people will be like a single tyrant.

Similarly, it is proper to distinguish the various kinds of just government. For if the administration is in the hands of a certain section of the community [*aliquam multitudinem*], as when the military class [*multitudo bellatoruni*] governs a city or province, this is commonly called polity.[14] If, again, administration is in the hands of a few but virtuous men, rule of this kind is called aristocracy: that is, 'the best rule', or 'rule of the best men' [*optimorum*], who for this reason are called aristo-crats [*optimates*]. And if just government belongs to one man alone, he is properly called a king. Hence the Lord, at Ezekiel 37:24, says: 'And David my servant shall be king over them, and they all shall have one shepherd'. It is clearly shown by this verse that it is the nature of kingship that there should be one who rules, and that he should be a shepherd who seeks the common good and not his own gain.[15]

Now since it is fitting for man to live in a community because he would not be able to provide all the necessaries of life for himself were he to remain alone, it must be that a society of many men will be perfect to the extent that it is self-sufficient in the necessaries of life. The self-sufficient life is certainly present to some extent in the family of one household, with respect, that is, to the natural activities of nourishment and the procreation of children and other things of this kind; and one locality may be sufficient in all those things belonging to a particu-lar trade; and a city, which is a perfect (i.e. a complete) community, is sufficient in all the necessaries of life.[16] But this is all the more true of a single province, because of the need for common defence and mutual assistance against enemies. Hence, he who rules a perfect community, that is, a city or province, is properly called a king; but he who rules a household is not a king, but the father of a family. He does, however, bear a certain resemblance to a king and for this reason kings are some-times called the 'fathers' of their people.

From what we have said, therefore, it is clear that *a king is one who rules over the community or province, and for the common good.* Hence Solomon, at Ecclesiastes 5:8, says: 'The king commands all the lands subject to him.'

Chapter 3: That it is more beneficial for a community of men living together to be ruled by one than by many.

Having said these things, we must next ask whether it is more suitable for a province or city to be ruled by many or by one. This can be answered by considering the end of government itself. For it must be the task of anyone who exercises rule to secure the well-being of whatever it is that he rules. For example, it is the task of the steers-

14. Aristotle, *Politics* 3:7 (1279b1).
15. Aristotle, *Politics* 3:7 (1279a25).
16. Aristotle, *Politics* 1:2 (1252b9).

man to preserve the ship from the perils of the sea and to guide it into a safe harbour. But the good and well-being of a community united in fellowship lies in the preservation of its unity. This is called peace,[17] and when it is removed and the community is divided against itself social life loses its advantage and instead becomes a burden. It is for this end, therefore, that the ruler of a community ought especially to strive: to procure the *unity of peace* [editors' italics]. Nor may he rightly wonder whether he ought to bring about peace in the community subject to him, any more than the physician should wonder whether he ought to heal the sick entrusted to him: for no one ought to deliberate about an end for which he must strive, but only about the means to that end.[18] Thus the Apostle, commending the unity of the faithful people, says at Ephesians 4:3: 'Be ye solicitous for the unity of the Spirit in the bond of peace.' The more effectively government preserves the unity of peace, the more beneficial it is; for we all find something 'more beneficial' when it leads more effectively to its end. Clearly, however, something which is itself one can bring about unity more effectively than something which is many can, just as the most effective cause of heat is that which is itself hot. Government by one is therefore more advantageous than government by several.

Moreover, it is clear that a plurality of rulers will in no way preserve a community if they are wholly at odds with one another. Some kind of unity is required as between a plurality of individuals if they are to govern anything whatsoever, just as a group of men in a boat cannot pull together as one unit unless they are in some measure united. But a plurality is said to be united to the degree that it approaches to one. It is therefore better for one to rule than many, who only approach to one.

Again, those things are best which are most natural, for in every case nature operates for the best; and in nature government is always by one. Among the multitude of the body's members there is one part which moves all the others, namely, the heart; and among the parts of the soul there is one force, namely the reason, which chiefly rules; also there is one king of the bees,[19] and in the whole universe one God is the Maker and Ruler of all. And this accords with reason, for every multitude is derived from unity. Thus, if those things which come about through art do so by imitation of those which exist in nature, and if a work of art is better to the degree that it achieves a likeness to what is in nature, it is necessarily true in the case of human affairs that that community is best which is ruled by one.

This appears also to be borne out by experience. For provinces or cities which are not ruled by one man toil under dissensions and are tossed about without peace, so that the complaint which the Lord made through the prophet (Jeremiah 12:10) may be seen to be fulfilled: 'Many pastors have destroyed my vineyard.' By contrast, provinces and cities governed by a single king rejoice in peace, flourish in justice and are gladdened by an abundance of things. Hence the Lord promises His people through the prophets that, as a great gift, He will put them under one head and that there will be one prince in the midst of them.

17. Augustine, *De civitate Dei* 19:13.
18. Aristotle, *Ethics* 3:3 (1112b13).
19. Aristotle, *Historia animalium* 5:21 (553b6).

Chapter 4: That just as the rule of one is the best when it is just, so its opposite is the worst: and this is proved by many reasons and arguments.

But just as the rule of a king is the best, so the rule of a tyrant is the worst. Now democracy is the opposite of polity, since, as is apparent from what has been said, rule is in each case exercised by the many; and oligarchy is the opposite of aristocracy, since in each case it is exercised by the few; and tyranny of kingship, since in each case it is exercised by one. But it has been shown already that kingship is the best form of government. If, therefore, that which is the opposite of the best is the worst, tyranny is necessarily the worst.

Again, a power which is united is more efficient at bringing about its purposes than one which is dispersed or divided. For many men united at the same time can pull what no one of them would be able to pull if the group were divided into its individual parts. Therefore, just as it is more beneficial for a power which produces good to be more united, because in this way it is able to produce more good, so is it more harmful for a power which produces evil to be united than divided. The power of an unjust ruler produces evil for the community inasmuch as it replaces the good of the community with a good peculiar to himself. Therefore, just as, in the case of good government, rule is more beneficial to the extent that the ruling power is more nearly one, so that kingship is better than aristocracy and aristocracy than polity; so the converse will be true in the case of unjust rule: that is, it will be more harmful to the extent that the ruling power is more nearly one. Tyranny is therefore more harmful than oligarchy and oligarchy than democracy.

Again, what renders government unjust is the fact that the private good of the ruler is sought at the expense of the good of the community. The further it departs from the common good, therefore, the more unjust will the government be. But there is a greater departure from the common good in an oligarchy, where the good of the few is sought, than in a democracy, where the good of the many is sought; and there is a still greater departure from the common good in a tyranny, where the good of only one is sought. A large number comes closer to the whole than a small one, and a small one closer than only one. Tyranny, therefore, is the most unjust form of government.

The same thing becomes clear from a consideration of the order of Divine providence, which disposes all things for the best. For goodness arises in things from one perfect cause, as from the working together of everything that can assist in the production of good; whereas evil arises singly, from individual defects. For there is no beauty in a body unless all its members are properly disposed, and ugliness arises when even one member is improperly so. And so ugliness arises for many reasons and from a variety of causes, whereas beauty does so in one way and from one perfect cause; and this is true in all cases of good and evil, as if it were by the providence of God that good should be the stronger because coming from a single cause, while evil should be the weaker because coming from many. It is fitting, therefore, that just government should be exercised by one man alone, so that it may for this reason be stronger. But if the government should fall away into injustice, it is more fitting that it should belong to many so that it may be weaker, and so that they may hinder one another. Among the forms of unjust rule, therefore, democracy is the most tolerable and tyranny the worst.

The same conclusion is especially apparent if one considers the evils which arise from tyranny. For when the tyrant, despising the common good, seeks his own private good, the consequence is that he oppresses his subjects in a variety of ways, according to the different passions to which he is subject as he tries to secure whatever goods he desires. For one who is in the grip of the passion of greed will seize the property of his subjects; hence Solomon says at Proverbs 29:4: 'The just king makes rich the earth, but the greedy man destroys it.' If he is subject to the passion of wrath, he will shed blood for no reason; hence it is said at Ezekiel 22:27: 'Her princes in the midst thereof are like wolves ravening their prey, to shed blood.' The wise man admonishes us that such rule is to be shunned, saying (Ecclesiasticus 9:13), 'Keep thee far from the man that hath power to kill': that is, because he kills not for the sake of justice, but through power and from the lust of his own will. There will, therefore, be no security, but all things uncertain, when the law is forsaken; nor will it be possible for any trust to be placed in that which depends upon the will, not to say the lust, of another. Nor does such rule oppress its subjects in bodily matters only, but it impedes them with respect to their spiritual goods also; for those who desire to rule their subjects rather than benefit them put every obstacle in the way of their progress, being suspicious of any excellence in their subjects that might threaten their own wicked rule. Tyrants 'suspect good men rather than bad, and are always afraid of another's virtue'. Tyrants therefore endeavour to prevent their subjects from becoming virtuous and increasing in nobility of spirit, lest they refuse to bear their unjust dominion. They prevent the bond of friendship from becoming established among their subjects, and hinder them from enjoying the rewards of mutual peace, so that, for as long as they do not trust one another, they will not be able to unite against a tyrant's rule. For this reason, tyrants sow discord among their subjects, nourish strife, and prohibit those things which create fellowship among men, such as wedding feasts and banquets and other such things by which familiarity and trust are usually produced among men. They also endeavour to prevent anyone from becoming powerful or rich, because, suspecting their subjects according to their own evil conscience, they fear that, just as they themselves use power and riches to do harm, so the power and wealth of their subjects will be used to do harm to them in return. Hence Job (15:21) says this of the tyrant: 'The sound of dread is ever in his ears, and even when there is peace' – that is, even when no ill is intended towards him – 'he is ever suspicious of treacheries'. For this reason, then, when rulers who ought to cultivate the virtues in their subjects look upon their subjects' virtues with wretched envy and do everything in their power to impede them, few virtuous men will be found under a tyrant. For according to what the Philosopher says, brave men are found among those who honour the bravest;[20] and, as Cicero says, 'Things which are despised by everyone always fail and have little strength.'

20. Aristotle, *Ethics* 1:3 (1095b28); 3:8 (1116a20).

It is, indeed, natural that men who are nourished in a climate of fear should degenerate into a servile condition of soul and become fearful of every manly and strenuous act. This is shown by the experience of those provinces which have remained long under a tyrant. Hence the Apostle says at Colossians 3:21: 'Fathers, provoke not your children to anger, lest they be discouraged.' And Solomon is thinking of these harmful effects of tyranny when he says (Proverbs 28:12): 'When the wicked reign, men are ruined': because, that is, subjects fall away from the perfection of virtue through the wickedness of tyrants. And he goes on to say (29:2): 'When the wicked beareth rule, the people mourn'; and again (28:28): 'When the wicked rise, men hide themselves' in order to escape the cruelty of tyrants. And no wonder; for a man who rules without reason according to the lusts of his own soul is no different from a beast. Hence Solomon says (Proverbs 28:15): 'As a roaring lion and a hungry bear, so is a wicked ruler over the poor people.' And so it is that men remove themselves from a tyrant as from cruel beasts, and to be subject to a tyrant seems the same as to be mauled by a ferocious animal.

Chapter 3
Alighieri Dante (1265–1321)

It is therefore clear that the authority of temporal Monarchy comes down, with no intermediate will, from the fountain of universal authority.

Introduction

In his *Life of Dante*, composed around 1351, the medieval writer Giovanni Boccaccio records: 'There is nothing in this world that is more unstable than public grace. No hope is more insane, no advice more foolish than that which encourages one to find consolation in it'. It is a moral sentiment drawn from a meditation upon the political turmoil with which Dante found himself embroiled and that led not only to his exile from Florence and the confiscation of his property, but to his being condemned to death on 10 March 1302. The events that led to this situation, the movements of power far beyond that of a middle-class citizen and poet, constitute the context within which we must read Dante's *De Monarchia* – even though this work was written sometime between 1314 and 1317. The political philosophy outlined here was the fruit of a complex involvement with, and a long meditation upon, conflicting currents in the history of human relations. It became his last testimony to Florence, to Italy, to France, to the papacy and to the Emperor.

The events began and ended in the hot summer of 1300, the year declared as a Jubilee by Pope Boniface VIII, the year, significantly, in which Dante's *Commedia* is set. But the origins of the events of that summer lay in earlier configurations of circumstance. There are four significant aspects of the complex situation that emerged, each of which reveals that Dante had only a small walk-on part in a drama that engulfed him. First, returning us to Aquinas's context, in 1250 the Emperor Frederick II died and the vacancy found no undisputed successor before Dante's death in 1321. Second, Boniface VIII became Pope in 1294. We saw, with Aquinas, that there were two positions towards the sovereignty of the Pope over matters temporal and spiritual, the Ghibelline and the Guelf. The papal cause was supported by the Guelfs. But, third, the Guelfs (a Tuscan family to whom Dante was related) had become divided into two factions: the Whites, who tended to belong to the merchant class, the *nouveaux riches* and the Blacks, who were the older aristocratic line. Finally, there were the ambitions of the French to gain imperial power through the papacy. In fact, in 1305, the newly appointed French Pope, Clement V, established his papal court at Avignon. So in that fateful summer of 1300, Dante was a minnow, elected to one of the six executive offices of Prior for the city of Florence, allied with the White faction of the Guelfs, and swimming in a pool of piranhas.

It started with a dance in May in the Piazza Santa Trinità, with both sides of the Guelf clan in attendance. A brawl turned into two months of civil war, after which the city banished the leaders of both parties. Dante, as one of the Priors, ratified this punishment. It ended in a coup in the winter of 1301 when the Blacks, aided by the French who had come to assist them at the request of the Pope, took control of the city. Dante, ironically, was in Rome at the papal court leading a delegation seeking to dissuade the Pope from calling upon French help. Back in Florence, his house was plundered and he himself was charged with fraud, corruption, extortion and opposition to the policies of the Pope and the military help of Charles de Valois (brother of the French king). Unable to return '[Dante] wandered from here to there, in uncertainty, in various Tuscan localities', Boccaccio tells us. Abandoning all hope of reconciliation, Boccaccio narrates that he decided to leave Italy and, crossing the high mountains into the province of Gaul, went to Paris for two years (1307–9). Biographers cannot verify the stay in Paris, but it was during this time that he made the acquaintance of Henry, Count of Luxemburg, who was elected Holy Roman Emperor in 1308, and crowned by Pope Clement V, not in Rome but Aix. Dante's support for Henry VII is well attested in his *Letters V–VII* written between 1310 and 1311. Though scholars now doubt whether *De monarchia* itself was written to support the Emperor Henry VII, what is not in doubt is the use made of the argument following Dante's death by followers of Ludwig of Bavaria, who was elected Emperor and subsequently excommunicated by Pope John XXII in 1324. In fact, the book was considered both dangerous and damning by the Church, who ordered its public burning in 1329. The bones of Dante would likewise have been publicly burned had not the Lord of Ravenna (where Dante was buried) intervened.

Whatever Dante's aspirations for the quiet life of a poet and philosopher, he was enmeshed in the feverish politics of popes, emperors, powerful families and republican city states. The same conflict between temporal and spiritual power was being played out, only this time, unlike with Aquinas, we have a writer who had suffered much at the hands of the papacy. In fact, when Dante came to write his *Commedia* (from 1308 until his death in 1321), Boniface VIII is confined to hell as a simoniac and usurper. In the third part of that epic poem *Il Paradiso*, no less a person than St Peter condemns him. It is important for understanding the position Dante adopts towards papal authority in *De monarchia* that, in 1302, Boniface VIII had published his famous Bull 'Unam sanctam'. The Bull proclaimed:

> We are told by the word of the Gospel that in this His fold there are two swords – a spiritual, namely, and a temporal. For when the apostles said, 'Behold here are two swords' – the Lord did not reply that this was too much, but enough. Surely he who denies that the temporal sword is in the power of Peter wrongly interprets the word of the Lord when He says, 'Put up thy sword in its scabbard'. *Both swords, the spiritual and the material, therefore, are in the power of the Church* [editors' italics]; the one, indeed, to be wielded for the Church, the other by the Church; the one by the hand of

the priest, the other by the hand of kings and knights, but at the will and sufferance of the priest. One sword, moreover, ought to be under the other, and the temporal authority to be subjected to the spiritual. For when the Apostle says 'There is no power but of God, and the powers that are of God are ordained', they would not be ordained unless sword were under sword and the lesser one, as it were, were led by the other to great deeds. . . . Therefore if the earthly power err, it shall be judged by the spiritual power; but if the lesser spiritual power err, by the greater. But if the greatest, it can be judged by God alone, not by man, the Apostle bearing witness. A spiritual man judges all things, but he himself is judged by no one. This authority, moreover, even though it is given to man and exercised through man, is not human but rather divine, being given by divine lips to Peter and founded on a rock for him and his successors through Christ Himself whom He has confessed; the Lord Himself saying to Peter: 'Whatsoever thou shalt bind', etc. Whoever, therefore, resists this power thus ordained by God, resists the ordination of God, unless he makes believe, like the Manichean, that there are two beginnings. This we consider false and heretical, since by the testimony of Moses, not 'in the beginnings', but 'in the beginning' God created the heavens and the earth. *Indeed we declare, say, pronounce, and define that it is altogether necessary to salvation for every human creature to be subject to the Roman Pontiff* [editors' italics].

Beneath the placid, elegantly organized and logical surface of *Monarchia* not only the bruising of Dante's life in exile is evident; but what is also evident is a rhetorical war. For here Dante conducts a forensic argument for a strong, just and peacemaking Emperor. The argument is constructed over three books. This structure parallels the three stages in a favoured philosophical demonstration, known as the syllogism: major premise, minor premise and conclusion. Each of the books is structured similarly, beginning, in Aristotelian fashion, with a first principle. The first book, owing much, like Aquinas, to Aristotle's *Ethics* and *Politics*, has as its first principle: 'that the activity proper to mankind considered as a whole is constantly to actualise the full intellectual potential of humanity, primarily through thought and secondarily through action'. To do this what is needed is peace; and so the argument concludes that such peace is best obtainable by having one temporal ruler. The exemplar for such a rule and such a ruler is the Roman Empire under Augustus. The second book takes up this Roman example (in a way comparable to Machiavelli's use much later of the writings of Livy). Dante sets about developing a theology of history, beginning from the question of the significance of the Roman Empire for Christianity. In arguing for the necessity of this prior Empire (however pagan) for the subsequent development of the Church, he again works from a first principle: 'that what God wills in human society must be considered true and pure right'. He then sets about demonstrating that this Empire was part of God's providential grace. The arguments of Books I and II constitute the major and minor premises that set up the concluding argument of Book III.

The excerpt we have chosen is taken from Book III. The thrust of this argument is that the temporal power of the Emperor or monarch does not rely upon the spiritual power of the Pope, but has its distinct and autonomous part to play in God's dealings with the world. Again the demonstration that follows is a rational development from a first principle: 'what is contrary to nature's intention is against God's will'. This is clearly in line with both Aristotle and Aquinas (though Aquinas, of course, reaches a different conclusion). He then proceeds to refute three classes of argument against his overall thesis: arguments drawn from Scripture (chapters 4–9); arguments drawn from the history of the Church (chapters 10–11) and arguments drawn from reason (chapters 12–13). The arguments from reason are given the highest place in the ascending order of the demonstration. It is then that Dante makes his own rational proof that imperial authority is derived solely from God (and not mediated by the Pope), drawing also upon nature (the body analogy in chapter xvi) and Scripture.

Dante's argument is both sophisticated and dazzling. It makes an interesting comparison with both Aquinas and Luther. There are numerous points of inter-section with Aquinas, but we can observe (with respect to Luther's argument against papal authority) Dante's deft refutation of the Donation of Constantine. Dante presupposes the authenticity of this document. By the time we come to Luther the document has been shown to be a forgery. One further point remains: the profound ambiguity of the final sentence of the text. For having argued throughout for the *distinction* between the two offices (temporal and spiritual) and their *integrity* as both deriving their authority from God, Dante concludes: 'Let Caesar therefore show that reverence towards Peter which a firstborn son should show his father, so that, illumined by the light of paternal grace, he may the more effectively light up the world, over which he has been placed by Him alone who is ruler over all things spiritual and temporal'. How do we interpret this final remark? Is Dante contradicting himself or has the text been interpolated? As Aristotle wrote at the conclusion of his *Nicomachean Ethics*: 'Let the debate now begin'.

Further reading

English translation

Shaw, P. (tr.) (1996), *De monarchia* (Cambridge: Cambridge University Press).
Sisson, C. (1980), *The Divine Comedy* (Harmondsworth: Penguin).

General introductions

Bemrose, S. (2000), *A New Life of Dante* (Exeter: University of Exeter Press).
Jacoff, R. (1993), *The Cambridge Companion to Dante.* (Cambridge: Cambridge University Press).
Vossler, K. (1958), *Mediaeval Culture: an Introduction to Dante and His Times* (New York: Ungar).

Reception of key ideas

Fortin, E. (2002), *Dissent and Philosophy in the Middle Ages: Dante and his Precursors, Applications of Political Theory* (Lanham: Lexington Books).

Passerin d'Entráeves, A. (1952), *Dante as a Political Thinker* (Oxford: Clarendon Press).

Excerpt from De Monarchia

Book III, 1

The present question, then, concerning which we have to inquire, is between two great luminaries, the Roman Pontiff and the Roman Prince: and the question is, does the authority of the Roman Monarch, who, as we have proved in the second book, is the monarch of the world, depend immediately on God, or on some minister or vicar of God; by whom I understand the successor of Peter, who truly has the keys of the kingdom of heaven ? [. . .]

Book III, 3

Now three classes of men chiefly strive against the truth which we are trying to prove. First, the Chief Pontiff, Vicar of our Lord Jesus Christ and the successor of Peter, to whom we owe, not indeed all that we owe to Christ, but all that we owe to Peter, contradicts this truth, urged it may be by zeal for the keys; and also other pastors of the Christian sheepfolds, and others whom I believe to be only led by zeal for our mother, the Church. These all, perchance from zeal and not from pride, withstand the truth which I am about to prove.

But there are certain others in whom obstinate greed has extinguished the light of reason, who are of their father the devil, and yet pretend to be sons of the Church. They not only stir up quarrels in this question, but they hate the name of the most sacred office of Prince, and would shamelessly deny the principles which we have laid down for this and the previous questions. There is also a third class called Decretalists, utterly without knowledge or skill in philosophy or theology, who, relying entirely on their Decretals (which doubtless, I think, should be venerated), and hoping, I believe, that these Decretals will prevail, disparage the power of the Empire. And no wonder, for I have heard one of them, speaking of these Decretals, assert shamelessly that the traditions of the Church are the foundation of the faith. May this wickedness be taken away from the thoughts of men by those who, antecedently to the traditions of the Church, have believed in Christ the Son of God, whether to come, or present, or as having already suffered; and who from their faith have hoped, and from their hope have kindled into love, and who, burning with love, will, the world doubts not, be made co-heirs with Him.

And that such arguers may be excluded once for all from the present debate, it must be noted that part of Scripture was *before* the Church, that part of it came *with* the Church, and part *after* the Church.

Before the Church were the Old and the New Testament – the covenant which the Psalmist says was 'commanded for ever,' of which the Church speaks to her

Bridegroom, saying: 'Draw me after thee.' *With* the Church came those venerable chief Councils, with which no faithful Christian doubts but that Christ was present. For we have His own words to His disciples when He was about to ascend into heaven: 'Lord, I am with you always, even unto the end of the world,' to which Matthew testifies: There are also the writings of the doctors, Augustine and others, of whom, if any doubt that they were aided by the Holy Spirit, either he has never beheld their fruit, or if he has beheld, he has never tasted thereof.

After the Church are the traditions which they call Decretals, which, although they are to be venerated for their apostolical authority, yet we must not doubt that they are to be held inferior to fundamental Scripture, seeing that Christ rebuked the Pharisees for this very thing; for when they had asked: 'Why do thy disciples transgress the tradition of the elders?' (for they neglected the washing of hands), He answered them, as Matthew testifies: 'Why do ye also transgress the commandment of God by your tradition?' Thus he intimates plainly that tradition was to have a lower place.

But if the traditions of the Church are *after* the Church, it follows that the Church had not its authority from traditions, but rather traditions from the Church; and, therefore, the men of whom we speak, seeing that they have nought but traditions, must be excluded from the debate. For those who seek after this truth must proceed in their inquiry from those things from which flows the authority of the Church.

Further, we must exclude others who boast themselves to be white sheep in the flock of the Lord, when they have the plumage of crows. These are the children of wickedness, who, that they may be able to follow their evil ways, put shame on their mother, drive out their brethren, and when they have done all will allow none to judge them. Why should we seek to reason with these, when they are led astray by their evil desires, and so cannot see even our first principle?

Therefore there remains the controversy only with the other sort of men who are influenced by a certain kind of zeal for their mother the Church, and yet know not the truth which is sought for. With these men, therefore – strong in the reverence which a dutiful son owes to his father, which a dutiful son owes to his mother, dutiful to Christ, dutiful to the Church, dutiful to the Chief Shepherd, dutiful to all who profess the religion of Christ – I begin in this book the contest for the maintenance of the truth. [. . .]

Book III, 4

Those men to whom all our subsequent reasoning is addressed, when they assert that the authority of the Empire depends on the authority of the Church, as the inferior workman depends on the architect, are moved to take this view by many arguments, some of which they draw from Holy Scripture, and some also from the acts of the Supreme Pontiff and *of* the Emperor himself. Moreover, they strive to have some proof of reason. For in the first place they say that God, according to the book of Genesis, made two great lights, the greater light to rule the day, and the lesser light to rule the night; this they understand to be an allegory, for that the lights are the two powers, the spiritual and the temporal. And then they maintain that as the moon, which is the lesser light, only has light so far as she receives it from the sun, so the temporal power only has authority as it receives authority from the spiritual power.

For the disposing of these, and of other like arguments, we must remember the Philosopher's words in his book on Sophistry, 'the overthrow of an argument is the pointing out of the mistake.' Error may arise in two ways, either in the matter, or in the form of an argument; either, that is, by assuming to be true what is false, or by transgressing the laws of the syllogism . . . I use 'false' in a large sense, as including the inconceivable, that which in matters admitting only of probability has the nature of falseness.

If the error is in the form of an argument, he who wishes to destroy the error must do so by showing that the laws of the syllogism have been transgressed. If the error is in the matter, it is because something has been assumed which is either false in itself, or false in relation to that particular instance. If the assumption is false in itself, the argument must be destroyed by destroying the assumption; if it is false only in that particular instance, we must draw a distinction between the falseness in that particular instance and its general truth.

Having noted these things, to make it more clear how we destroy this and the further fallacies of our adversaries, we must remark that there are two ways in which error may arise concerning the mystical sense, either by seeking it where it is not, or by accepting it in a sense other than its real sense.

On account of the first of these ways, Augustine says, in his work *City of God*, that we must not think that all things, of which we are told, have a special meaning; for it is on account of that which means something, that that also which means nothing is woven into a story. It is only with the plough-share that we turn up the earth; but the other parts of the plough are also necessary. On account of the second way in which error touching the interpretation of mysteries may arise, Augustine, in his book *Concerning Christian doctrine*, speaking of those who wish to find in Scripture something other than he who wrote the Scripture meant, says, that such 'are misled in the same way as a man who leaves the straight path, and then arrives at the end of the path by a long circuit.' And he adds: 'It ought to be shown that this is a mistake, lest through the habit of going out of the way, the man be driven to going into cross or wrong ways.' And then he intimates why such precautions must be taken in interpreting Scripture. 'Faith will falter, if the authority of Scripture be not sure.' But I say that if these things happen from ignorance, we must pardon those who do them, when we have carefully reproved them, as we pardon those who imagine a lion in the clouds, and are afraid. But if they are done purposely, who has deigned to unfold to us His will.

Having thus first noted these things, I will proceed, as I said above, to destroy the argument of those who say that the two great lights are typical of the two great powers on earth: for on this type rests the whole strength of their argument. It can be shown in two ways that this interpretation cannot be upheld. First, seeing that these two kinds of power are, in a sense, accidents of men, God would thus appear to have used a perverted order, by producing the accidents, before the essence to which they belong existed; and it is ridiculous to say this of God. For the two great lights were created on the fourth day, while man was not created till the sixth day, as is evident in the text of Scripture. Secondly, seeing that these two kinds of rule are to guide men to certain ends, as we shall see, it follows that if man had remained in the state of innocence in which God created him, he would not have needed such means of guidance. These kinds of rule, then, are remedies against the weakness of sin. Since, then, man was not a sinner on the fourth day, for he did not then even exist, it would have been idle to make remedies for his sin, and this would be contrary to the goodness of God. For he would be a sorry physician who would make a plaster for an abscess which was to be, before the man was born. It cannot, therefore, be said that God made these two kinds of rule on the fourth day, and therefore the meaning of Moses cannot have been what these men pretend.

We may also be more tolerant, and overthrow this falsehood by drawing a distinction. This way of distinction is a gentler way of treating an adversary, for so his arguments are not made to appear consciously false, as is the case when we utterly overthrow him. I say then that, although the moon has not light of its own abundantly, unless it receives it from the sun, yet it does not therefore follow that the moon is from the sun. Therefore be it known that the being, and the power, and the working of the moon are all different things. For its being, the moon in no way depends on the sun, nor for its power, nor for its working, considered in itself. Its motion comes from its proper mover, its influence is from its own rays. For it has a certain light of its own, which is manifest at the time of an eclipse; though for its better and more powerful working it receives from the sun an abundant light, which enables it to work more powerfully. Therefore I say that the temporal power does not receive its being from the spiritual power, nor its power which is its authority, nor its working considered in itself. Yet it is good that the temporal power should receive from the spiritual the means of working more effectively by the light of the grace which the benediction of the Supreme Pontiff bestows on it both in heaven and on earth. [. . .]

Book III, 6

Again, from the first book of Kings they take the election and the deposition of Saul; and they say that Saul, an enthroned king, was deposed by Samuel, who, by God's command, acted in the stead of God, as appears from the text of Scripture. From this they argue that, as that Vicar of God had authority to give temporal power, and to take it away and bestow it on another, so now the Vicar of God, the bishop of the universal Church, has authority to give the sceptre of temporal power, and to take it away, and even to give it to another. And if this were so, it would follow without doubt that the authority of the Empire is dependent on the Church, as they say.

But we may answer and destroy this argument, by which they say that Samuel was the Vicar of God for it was not as Vicar of God that he acted, but as a special delegate for this purpose, or as a messenger bearing the express command of his Lord. For it is clear that what God commanded him, that only he did, and that only he said. Therefore we must recognize that it is one thing to be another's vicar, and that it is another to be his messenger or minister, just as it is one thing to be a doctor, and

56

another to be an interpreter. For a vicar is one to whom is committed jurisdiction with law or with arbitrary power, and therefore within the bounds of the jurisdiction which is committed to him, he may act by law or by his arbitrary power without the knowledge of his lord. It is not so with a mere messenger, in so far as he is a messenger; but as the mallet acts only by the strength of the smith, so the messenger acts only by the authority of him that sent him. Although, then, God did this by His messenger Samuel, it does not follow that the Vicar of God may do the same. For there are many things which God has done and still does, and yet will do through angels, which the Vicar of God, the successor of Peter, might not do. [. . .]

Book III, 10

Certain persons say further that the Emperor Constantine, having been cleansed from leprosy by the intercession of Sylvester, then the Supreme Pontiff, gave unto the Church the seat of Empire which was Rome, together with many other dignities belonging to the Empire. Hence they argue that no man can take unto himself these dignities unless he receive them from the Church, whose they are said to be. From this it would rightly follow, that one authority depends on the other, as they maintain.

The arguments which seemed to have their roots in the Divine words, have been stated and disproved. It remains to state and disprove those which are grounded on Roman history and in the reason of mankind. The first of these is the one which we have mentioned, in which the syllogism runs as follows: no one has a right to those things which belong to the Church, unless he has them from the Church; and this we grant. The government of Rome belongs to the Church; therefore no one has a right to it unless it be given him by the Church. The minor premiss is proved by the facts concerning Constantine, which we have touched on. This minor premiss then will I destroy; and as for their proof, I say that it proves nothing. For the dignity of the Empire was what Constantine could not alienate, nor the Church receive. And when they insist, I prove my words as follows: no man on the strength of the office which is committed to him, may do aught that is contrary to that office; for so one and the same man, viewed as one man, would be contrary to himself, which is impossible. But to divide the Empire is contrary to the office committed to the Emperor; for his office is to hold mankind in all things subject to one will: as may be easily seen from the first book of this treatise. Therefore it is not permitted to the Emperor to divide the Empire. If, therefore, as they say, any dignities had been alienated by Constantine, and had passed to the Church, the 'coat without seam' – which even they, who pierced Christ, the true God, with a spear, dared not rend – would have been rent. Further, just as the Church has its foundation, so has the Empire its foundation. The foundation of the Church is Christ, as Paul says in his first Epistle to the Corinthians: 'For other foundation can no man lay than that which is laid, which is Jesus Christ.' He is the rock on which the Church is built; but the foundation of the Empire is human right. Now I say that, as the Church may not go contrary to its foundation – but must always rest on its foundation, as the words of the Canticles say: 'Who is she that cometh up from the desert, abounding in delights, leaning on her beloved?' – in the same way I say that the Empire may not do aught that transgresses human right. But were the Empire to destroy itself, it would so transgress human right. Therefore the Empire may not destroy itself. Since then to divide the Empire would be to destroy it, because the Empire consists in one single universal Monarchy, it is manifest that he who exercises the authority of the Empire may not destroy it, and from what we have said before, it is manifest that to destroy the Empire is contrary to human right.

Moreover, all jurisdiction is prior in time to the judge who has it; for it is the judge who is ordained for the jurisdiction, not the jurisdiction for the judge. But the Empire is a jurisdiction, comprehending within itself all temporal jurisdiction: therefore it is prior to the judge who has it, who is the Emperor. For it is the Emperor who is ordained for the Empire, and not contrariwise. Therefore it is clear that the Emperor, in so far as he is Emperor, cannot alter the Empire; for it is to the Empire that he owes his being. I say then that he who is said to have conferred on the Church the authority in question either was Emperor, or he was not. If he was not, it is plain that he had no power to give away any part of the Empire. Nor could he, if he was Emperor, in so far as he was Emperor, for such a gift would be a diminishing of his jurisdiction.

Further, if one Emperor were able to cut off a certain portion of the jurisdiction of the Empire, so could another; and since temporal jurisdiction is finite, and since all that is finite is taken away by finite diminutions, it would follow that it is possible for the first of all jurisdictions to be annihilated, which is absurd. Further, since he that gives is in the position of an agent, and he to whom a thing is given in that of a patient, as the Philosopher holds in the fourth book to Nicomachus, therefore, that a gift may be given, we require not only the fit qualification of the giver, but also of the receiver; for the acts of the agent are completed in a patient who is qualified. But the Church was altogether unqualified to receive temporal things; for there is an express command, forbidding her so to do, which Matthew gives thus: 'Provide neither gold, nor silver, nor brass in your purses.' For though we find in Luke a relaxation of the command in regard to certain matters, yet I have not anywhere been able to find that the Church after that prohibition had licence given her to possess gold and silver. If therefore the Church was unable to receive temporal power, even granting that Constantine was able to give it, yet the gift was impossible; for the receiver was disqualified. It is therefore plain that neither could the Church receive in the way of possession, nor could Constantine give in the way of alienation; though it is true that the Emperor, as protector of the Church, could allot to the Church a patrimony and other things, if he did not impair his supreme lordship, the unity of which does not allow division. And the Vicar of God could receive such things, not to possess them, but as a steward to dispense the fruits of them to the poor of Christ, on behalf of the Church, as we know the Apostles did. [. . .]

Book III, 12

But from *reason* they thus argue: they take the principle laid down in the tenth book of 'Philosophia Prima,' saying that all things which belong to one genus are to be brought under one head, which is the standard and measure of all that come under that genus. But all men belong to one genus: therefore they are to be brought under one head, as the standard and measure of them all. But the Supreme Pontiff and the Emperor are men; therefore if the preceding reasoning be true, they must be brought under one head. And since the Pope cannot come under any other man, the result is that the Emperor, together with all other men, must be brought under the Pope, as the measure and rule of all; and then, what those who argue thus desire follows. To overset this argument, I answer that they are right when they say that all the individuals of one genus ought to be brought under one head, as their measure; and that they are again right when they say that all men belong to one genus, and that they are also right when they argue from these truths that all men should be brought under one head, taken from the genus man, as their measure and type. But when they obtain the further conclusion concerning the Pope and the Emperor, they fall into a fallacy touching accidental attributes. That this thing may be understood, it must be clearly known that to be a man is one thing, and to be a pope or an emperor is another; just as to be a man is different from being a father or a ruler. A man is that which exists by its essential form, which gives it its genus and species, and by which it comes under the category of substance. But a father is that which exists by an accidental form, that is, one which stands in a certain relation which gives it a certain genus and species, and through which it comes under the category of relation. If this were not so, all things would come under the category of substance, seeing that no accidental form can exist by itself, without the support of an existing substance; and this is not so. Seeing, therefore, that the Pope and the Emperor are what they are by virtue of certain relations: for they owe their existence to the Papacy and the Empire, which are both relations, one coming within the sphere of fatherhood, and the other within that of rule; it manifestly follows that both the Pope and the Emperor, in so far as they are Pope and Emperor, must come under the category of relation; and therefore that they must be brought under some head of that genus. I say then that there is one standard under which they are to be brought, as men; and another under which they come, as Pope and Emperor. For in so far as they are men, they have to be brought under the best man, whoever he be, who is the measure and the ideal of all mankind; under him, that is, who is most one in his kind, as may be gathered from the last book to Nicomachus. When, however, two things are relative, it is evident that they must either be reciprocally brought under each other, if they are alternately superior, or if by the nature of their relation they belong to connected species; or else they must be brought under some third thing, as their common unity. But the first of these suppositions is impossible: for then both would be predicable of both, which cannot be. We cannot say that the Emperor is the Pope, or the Pope the Emperor. Nor again can it be said that they are connected in species, for the idea of the Pope is quite other than the idea of the Emperor, in so far as they are Pope and Emperor. Therefore they must be reduced to some single thing above them.

Now it must be understood that the relative is to the relative as the relation to the relation. If, therefore, the Papacy and the Empire, seeing that they are relations of paramount superiority, have to be carried back to some higher point of superiority from which they, with the features which make them different, branch off, the Pope and Emperor, being relative to one another, must be brought back to some one unity in which the higher point of superiority, without this characteristic difference, is found. And this will be either God, to whom all things unite in looking up, or something below God, which is higher in the scale of superiority, while differing from the simple and absolute superiority of God. Thus it is evident that the Pope and the Emperor, in so far as they are men, have to be brought under some one head; while, in so far as they are Pope and Emperor, they have to be brought under another head, and so far is clear, as regards the argument from reason.

Book III, 13

We have now stated and put on one side those erroneous reasonings on which they, who assert that the authority of the Roman Emperor depends on the Pope of Rome, do most chiefly rely. We have now to go back and show forth the truth in this third question, which we proposed in the beginning to examine. The truth will appear plainly enough if I start in my inquiry from the principle which I laid down, and then show that the authority of the Empire springs immediately from the head of all being, who is God. [. . .]

We prove that the authority of the Church is not the cause of the authority of the Empire in the following manner. Nothing can be the cause of power in another thing when that other thing has all its power, while the first either does not exist, or else has no power of action. But the Empire had its power while the Church was either not existing at all, or else had no power of acting. Therefore the Church is not the cause of the power of the Empire, and therefore not of its authority either, for power and authority mean the same thing. [. . .]

Book III, 14

Again, if the Church had power to bestow authority on the Roman Prince, she would have it either from God, or from herself, or from some Emperor, or from the universal consent of mankind, or at least of the majority of mankind. There is no other crevice by which this power could flow down to the Church. But she has it not from any of these sources; therefore she has it not at all.

It is manifest that she has it from none of these sources; for if she had received it from God, she would have received it either by the divine or by the natural law: because what is received from nature is received from God; though the converse of this is not true. But this power is not received by the natural law; for nature lays down no law, save for the effects of nature, for God cannot fail in power, where He brings anything into being without the aid of secondary agents. Since therefore the Church is not an effect of nature, but of God who said: 'Upon this rock I will build my Church,' and elsewhere: 'I have finished the work which Thou gavest me to do,' it is manifest that nature did not give the Church this law. Nor was this power bestowed by the divine law; for such care taken away from the priests of the Old

Testament by the express command of God to Moses, and from the priests of the New Testament by the express command of Christ to His disciples. But it could not be that this care was taken away from them, if the authority of the temporal power flowed from the priesthood; for at least in giving the authority there would be an anxious watchfulness of forethought. and afterwards continued precaution, lest he to whom authority had been given should leave the straight way.

Then it is quite plain that the Church did not receive this power from herself; for nothing can give what it has not. Therefore all that does anything, must be such in its doing, as that which it intends to do, as is stated in the book 'of Simple Being.' But it is plain that if the Church gave to herself this power, she had it not before she gave it. Thus she would have given what she had not, which is impossible.

But it is sufficiently manifest from what we have previously made evident that the Church has received not this power from any Emperor. And further, that she had it not from the consent of all, or even of the greater part of mankind, who can doubt? Seeing that not only all the inhabitants of Asia and Africa, but even the greater number of Europeans, hold the thought in abhorrence. It is mere weariness to adduce proofs in matters which are so plain. [. . .]

Book III, 15

And from this it may be collected that the power of bestowing authority on this kingdom is contrary to the nature of the Church; for contrariety which is in thought or word follows from contrariety which is in the thing thought and the thing said; just as truth and falsehood in speech come from the being or the not-being of the thing, as we learn from the doctrine of the *Categories*. [. . .]

Book III, 16

Although it has been proved in the preceding chapter that the authority of the Empire has not its cause in the authority of the Supreme Pontiff; for we have shown that this argument led to absurd results; yet it has not been entirely shown that the authority of the Empire depends directly upon God, except as a result from our argument. For it is a consequence that, if the authority comes not from the vicar of God, it must come from God Himself. And therefore, for the complete determination of the question proposed, we have to prove directly that the emperor or monarch of the world stands in an immediate relation to the King of the universe, who is God.

For the better comprehending of this, it must be recognized that man alone, of all created things, holds a position midway between things corruptible and things incorruptible; and therefore philosophers rightly liken him to a dividing line between two hemispheres. For man consists of two essential parts, namely, the soul and the body. If he be considered in relation to his body only, he is corruptible; but if he be considered in relation to his soul only, he is incorruptible. And therefore the Philosopher spoke well concerning the incorruptible soul when he said in the second book 'Of the Soul': 'It is this alone which may be separated, as being eternal,

61

from the corruptible.' If, therefore, man holds this position midway between the corruptible and the incorruptible, since every middle nature partakes of both extremes, man must share something of each nature. And since every nature is ordained to gain some final end, it follows that for man there is a double end. For as he alone *of* all beings participates both in the corruptible and the incorruptible, so he alone of all beings is ordained to gain two ends, whereby one is his end in so far as he is corruptible, and the other in so far as he is incorruptible.

Two ends, therefore, have been laid down by the ineffable providence of God for man to aim at: the blessedness of this life, which consists in the exercise *of* his natural powers, and which is prefigured in the earthly Paradise; and next, the blessedness of the life eternal, which consists in the fruition of the sight of God's countenance, and to which man by his own natural powers cannot rise, if he be not aided by the divine light; and this blessedness is understood by the heavenly Paradise. But to these different kinds of blessedness, as to different conclusions, we must come by different means. For at the first we may arrive by the lessons of philosophy, if only we will follow them, by acting in accordance with the moral and intellectual virtues. But at the second we can only arrive by spiritual lessons, transcending human reason, so that we follow them in accordance with the theological virtues, faith, hope, and charity. The truth of the first of these conclusions and of these means is made manifest by human reason, which by the philosophers has been all laid open to us. The other conclusions and means are made manifest by the Holy Spirit, who by the mouth of the Prophets and holy writers, and by Jesus Christ, the co-eternal Son of God, and His disciples, has revealed to us supernatural truth of which we have great need. Nevertheless human passion would cast them all behind its back, unless, that men, going astray like the beasts that perish, were restrained in their course by bit and bridle, like horses and mules. Therefore man had need of two guides for his life, as he had a twofold end in life; whereof one is the Supreme Pontiff, to lead mankind to eternal life, according to the things revealed to us; and the other is the Emperor, to guide mankind to happiness in this world, in accordance with the teaching of philosophy. And since none, or but a few only, and even they with sore difficulty, could arrive at this harbour of happiness, unless the waves and blandishments of human desires were set at rest, and the human race were free to live in peace and quiet, this therefore is the mark at which he who is to care for the world, and whom we call the Roman Prince, must most chiefly aim at: I mean, that in this little plot of earth belonging to mortal men, life may pass in freedom and with peace. And since the order of this world follows the order of the heavens, as they run their course, it is necessary, to the end that the learning which brings liberty and peace may be duly applied by this guardian of the world in fitting season and place, that this power should be dispensed by Him who is ever present to behold the whole order of the heavens. And this is He who alone has preordained this, that by it in His providence He might bind all things together, each in their own order.

But if this is so, God alone elects, God alone confirms: for there is none higher than God. And hence there is the further conclusion, that neither those who now are, nor any others who may, in whatsoever way, have been called 'Electors,' ought to have that name; rather they are to be held as declarers and announcers of the providence of God. And, therefore, it is that they to whom is granted the privilege of announcing God's will sometimes fall into disagreement; because that, all of them or some of them have been blinded by their evil desires, and have not discerned the face of God's appointment. It is therefore clear that the authority of temporal Monarchy comes down, with no intermediate will, from the fountain of universal authority; and this fountain, one in its unity, flows through many channels out of the abundance of the goodness of God.

And now, methinks, I have reached the goal which was before me. I have unravelled the truth of the questions which I asked: whether the office of Monarchy was necessary to the welfare of the world; whether it was by right that the Roman people assumed to themselves the office of Monarchy; and, further, that last question, whether the authority of the Monarch springs immediately from God, or from some other. Yet the truth of this latter question must not be received so narrowly as to deny that in certain matters the Roman Prince is subject to the Roman Pontiff. For that happiness, which is subject to mortality, in a sense is ordered with a view to that happiness which shall not taste of death. Let, therefore, Caesar be reverent to Peter, as the first-born son should be reverent to his father, that he may be illuminated with the light of his father's grace, and so may be stronger to lighten the world over which he has been placed by Him alone, who is the ruler of all things spiritual as well as temporal.

Chapter 4

Martin Luther (1483–1546)

Christians can be governed by nothing except the Word of God alone.

Introduction

Martin Luther stands on the threshold between the medieval ages and modernity. On the one hand, he is deeply rooted in medieval thinking because his political thought still revolves around the medieval division of spiritual and temporal authority. For example, in his early works Luther mainly addresses the problem of the *precedence* of spiritual over temporal, not unlike Dante. On the other hand, Luther anticipates modernity in terms of equality, proto-democratic forms of political action, individualism and freedom of conscience. His writings had an enormous impact on the course of Western history and it is almost impossible to understand the Reformation and its aftermath without his theological ideas and pastoral–political engagement. The Reformation not only triggered the Catholic (counter-)revolution and the Council of Trent (1545–63) which divided Christendom between Catholics and Protestants, but also caused a period of religious wars for more than 100 years, which eventually brought about the requirement by governments for the strict division between secular politics and privatized religion. With Luther and the Reformation a religious, political and cultural process of change started to evolve which we now call modernity.

The two texts we have chosen date back to 1520 and 1523 and provide two different and contrary solutions to the problem of the dichotomy[1] of temporal and spiritual power, or in Augustine's terminology, of the Kingdom of God and the Kingdom of the World. We can call this binary opposition the 'great dichotomy' of medieval religion and politics. This creates a division between two separate spheres, where one cannot be reduced to the other. This is important for understanding the medieval world in which the spiritual and temporal domains are completely divided but at the same time inextricably linked. Each sphere represents a political system in its own right. The factual interdependence also explains why the Reformation was not just a religious revolution restricted to theological matters, but also had serious

---

1. An interesting parallel can be drawn between the dichotomy of the spiritual/temporal and the dichotomy of public/private. See N. Bobbio (2002), *Democracy and Dictatorship* (Cambridge: Polity Press).

political and cultural consequences. As we will see later on, the interdependence of spiritual and temporal power was particularly important for jurisprudence.

In all his writings Luther speaks as a political theologian; in particular, a politically engaged pastoral theologian. In the texts below, Luther critically discusses and seeks to overcome the hierarchical connection between temporal and spiritual power. It is crucial for understanding these texts to keep in mind that he is not speaking as a politician in the secular sense of the word but as a *theologian primarily expressing pastoral concerns*. In the first text, 'Address to the Christian Nobility of the German Nation' (1520) he offers a conclusion to the problem of spiritual–temporal authority, which differs significantly from that drawn in the second text, 'On the Limits of Secular Authority' (1523). In fact, the solution to the problem of the great dichotomy between spiritual and temporal power in the first text is dramatically qualified by the solution he offers in the second. In his 'Address to the Christian Nobility' Luther emphatically rejects the subordination of secular authority to spiritual authority and subsequently the primacy of papal jurisdiction over secular jurisdiction. In the opening paragraph of the 'Address' the Pope and all his followers (called the Romanists) are heavily attacked. Employing a highly rhetorical language, which is typical of Luther, he calls the Pope the Antichrist and the intentions and deeds of the Romanists the work of the devil. There is no doubt for Luther that there is manifest evil in the Church of his time. Luther is convinced that only a radical reform of the Church can re-establish her true vocation to represent the inchoate dominion of God. Right at the beginning Luther recalls the true vocation of the Church and makes its malfunctions explicit. He talks about the 'three walls' of the Romanists, which they have drawn around themselves to be protected and secure from any reform. These three walls are: the claim of the supremacy of spiritual authority; the monopoly of the interpretation of the Scripture; and the reservation of the right to convene a council. The last two walls are clearly aimed to make a reform of the Church illegitimate and illegal by any other people than those subject to the Pope. It is illegitimate, because every reform of the Church must be in accordance with the Scripture and every attempt to interpret the meaning of the Scripture in a way different from the official doctrine lacks any theological authority. This is why Luther's principle of *sola scriptura*, alongside making the Scriptures available for everyone through his translation of the Bible into German, were highly contested at that time. Furthermore, the attempt of reforming the Church by means of a council is also an illegal act if the council is not convened by the Pope. The discussion of whether the authority of the Pope is above the council, or whether the Pope is subject to decisions made by a council, has a long history in the Church and the question of the highest form of authority in the Church is still debated today. Compared to these two walls 'erected' by the Romanists, the first wall, that of the subordination of secular power, is a more general but also more fundamental one. It simply defines the order of the two components of political government.

Luther's solution to the problem of temporal and spiritual power outlined in 'Address to the Christian Nobility' is a radical one. In the first step of his threefold argument, the binary opposition of spiritual and temporal is unmasked as a 'lie and hypocritical device' by the Romanists. According to Luther the division between spiritual and temporal lacks any foundation in the Scripture. Moreover, if we take St Paul's metaphor of the body of Christ seriously, then it is evident that Christendom is indivisible. No body can have two heads. Luther must have realized that theologically there are difficulties with this argument. Because theologically speaking, neither the Pope nor the Emperor can be the head of the body of Christ. Christ alone is the head and those baptized in his name are members with different functions of his 'body', visible and invisible. But Luther's main argument does not rest on St Paul's use of the body metaphor. 'All Christians', the argument starts, 'are truly of the spiritual estate, and there is no difference among them, save of office alone'. The main point of this is: 'we are all consecrated as priests by baptism'. This is a remarkable statement for two reasons. First, Luther articulates a politically significant equality among Christians anchored in the sacrament of baptism. The sacrament of baptism dissolves all essential differences among the members of the body of Christ. Secondly, as a result, there is no division of the temporal and spiritual 'estate' in the ontological sense of the word any more. The difference between temporal and spiritual is merely one of different vocations. In short, Luther rejects the ontological claim of two separate estates while still holding to a functional differentiation. Thus, any man is able to become a priest and exercise a spiritual office whenever his vocation is ratified and given a mandate from the congregation. Conversely, members of the clergy have no special prerogative whatsoever and are therefore subject to secular jurisdiction like every other person. In the Roman Catholic Church, clergy were outside the civil law and only subject to ecclesiastical courts.

Luther's 'Address' was truly dynamite for the social order and very much appreciated by those German princes struggling for power with the Pope and Church. These German princes were the successors of the Holy Roman Empire.

The second text we have chosen is a response to the negative consequences and the misuse of secular authority which emerged in the following years on the basis of Luther's argument. Luther, who once argued for an augmentation of secular power, now has to counterbalance an all too powerful use of this power by defining its limits. In 1523, only three years after the publication of the 'Address', the Reformation had begun to involve major political figures from all over Germany and the Austrian–Spanish Empire under Charles V. Luther complains in this text about the development of the Reformation and the self-empowerment of secular rulers who 'have had the temerity to put themselves in God's place, to make themselves masters of consciences and belief and to undertake to give lessons to the Holy Spirit from what is in their addled brains'. This secular interference into matters of belief and conscience was clearly an illegitimate act in which secular authority overreached itself. But how can secular power be restricted to its proper domain? Is it possible, as Luther had earlier advocated, to draw a clear line between temporal and spiritual power without reintroducing the old (ontological) doctrine of the two estates?

Luther now introduces the temporal/spiritual distinction but in a different manner. Human beings, Luther writes, echoing Augustine, are divided between the Kingdom of God and the Kingdom of the World. 'We must divide Adam's children, all mankind, into two parts: the first belong to the Kingdom of God, the second to the Kingdom of the World. All those who truly believe in Christ belong to God's Kingdom . . . Now: these people need neither secular sword nor law. And if all the world were true Christians . . . there would be neither need nor use for princes, kings, lords, the sword or law.' The distinction between the Kingdom of God and the Kingdom of the World is different from the old dichotomy of the two estates (spiritual and temporal), that is domains of government. The Kingdom of God is an ideal and perfect society of true Christians which cannot be completely realized in this world. It is the 'counterfactual ideal' of a *societas perfecta*. The gap between an ideal society and the imperfect real society legitimizes the use of the temporal sword. The anthropological assumption here is that every Christian is divided. On the one hand, as baptized in Christ, he/she belongs to the Kingdom of God. On the other, he/she is also a sinner, belonging to the Kingdom of the World and therefore subject to secular authority. Luther expresses the twofold condition of human nature in the formula: *simul iustus et peccator*, which means that a Christian is justified by God alone and is not in need of any other form of authority while, at the same time, he/she is under the law of sin and is subject to worldly jurisdiction. It is the task of every single individual to obey God's word and to follow his/her own conscience; even if this involves struggling against secular authority. 'Each must decide at his own peril what he is to believe, and must see to it that he believes rightly.' Religion here is conceived as a strictly private and intimate affair. This privacy of religion, the authority of the conscience and religious conviction, defines the limits of secular authority. Luther concludes:

> Secular government has laws that extend no further than the body, goods and outward, earthly matters. . . . No one can or should lay down commandments for the soul, except those who can point it on the way to heaven. But no human being can do that; only God.

In Luther, who was himself an Augustinian monk, the Augustinian division of the *civitas dei* and the *civitas terrena* became a material distinction rather than just a formal one. 'Church' and 'state' are becoming independent entities. After Luther, religious belief in what became known as the Protestant tradition was increasingly conceived as an individual matter. This is the presupposition for political deism which we will encounter in Part Three where we talk about the Enlightenment and the emergence of democratic forms of government. This transition from a Christian Holy Roman Empire to the formation of democratic nation states instigated a period of vicious and bloody confessional warfare – as we will see in the next section.

Further reading

Selected English translations

Höpfl, H. (1991), *Luther and Calvin on Secular Authority* (Cambridge: Cambridge University Press).

General introductions

Bainton, R. (1990), *Here I Stand: A Life of Martin Luther* (Nashville, TN: Abingdon Press).

Lohse, B. (1986), *Martin Luther: An Introduction to his Life and Work*. Philadelphia, PA: Fortress Press).

Oberman, H. (1981), *Masters of the Reformation: The Emergence of a New Intellectual Climate in Europe* (Cambridge: Cambridge University Press).

Reception of key ideas

Davies, R. (1978), *The Problem of Authority in the Continental Reformers: A Study in Luther, Zwingli, and Calvin* (Westport, CN: Greenwood Press).

Ozment, S. E. (1969), *Homo Spiritualis. A Comparative Study of the Anthropology of Johannes Tauler, Jean Gerson and Martin Luther (1509–16) in the Context of their Theological Thought, Studies in Medieval and Reformation Thought*, vol. 6 (Leiden: E.J. Brill).

Excerpt from 'Address to the Christian Nobility of the German Nationality'*

To his most Serene and Mighty Imperial Majesty and to the Christian Nobility of the German Nation. Dr. Martinus Luther.

The grace and might of God be with you, Most Serene Majesty, most gracious, well-beloved gentlemen!

It is not out of mere arrogance and perversity that I, an individual poor man, have taken upon me to address your lordships. The distress and misery that oppress all the Christian estates, more especially in Germany, have led not only myself, but every one else, to cry aloud and to ask for help, and have now forced me too to cry out and to ask if God would give His Spirit to any one to reach a hand to His wretched people. Councils have often put forward some remedy, but it has adroitly been frustrated, and the evils have become worse, through the cunning of certain men. Their malice and wickedness I will now, by the help of God, expose, so that, being known, they may henceforth cease to be so obstructive and injurious. God has given us a young and noble sovereign,[2] and by this has roused great hopes in many hearts; now it is right that we too should do what we can, and make good use of time and grace.

The first thing that we must do is to consider the matter with great earnestness, and, whatever we attempt, not to trust in our own strength and wisdom alone, even if the power of all the world were ours; for God will not endure that a good work should be begun trusting to our own strength and wisdom. He destroys it; it is all useless, as we read in Psalm 33, 'There is no king saved by the multitude of a host; a mighty man is not delivered by much strength.' And I fear it is for that reason that those beloved princes the Emperors Frederick, the First and the Second, and many other German emperors were, in former times, so piteously spurned and

---

* Italics have been added by the editors for emphasis.
2. Charles V was at that time not quite twenty years of age.

oppressed by the Popes, though they were feared by all the world. Perchance they trusted rather in their own strength than in God; therefore they could not but fall; and how would the sanguinary tyrant Julius II have risen so high in our own days but that, I fear, France, Germany, and Venice trusted to themselves? The children of Benjamin slew forty-two thousand Israelites, for this reason: that these trusted to their own strength (Judges 20, etc.).

That such a thing may not happen to us and to our noble Emperor Charles, we must remember that in this matter we wrestle not against flesh and blood, but against the rulers of the darkness of this world (Eph. 6, 12), who may fill the world with war and bloodshed, but cannot themselves be overcome thereby. We must renounce all confidence in our natural strength, and take the matter in hand with humble trust in God; we must seek God's help with earnest prayer, and have nothing before our eyes but the misery and wretchedness of Christendom, irrespective of what punishment the wicked may deserve. If we do not act thus, we may begin the game with great pomp; but when we are well in it, the spirits of evil will make such confusion that the whole world will be immersed in blood, and yet nothing be done. Therefore let us act in the fear of God and prudently. The greater the might of the foe, the greater is the misfortune, if we do not act in the fear of God and with humility. If Popes and Romanists have hitherto, with the devil's help, thrown kings into confusion, they may still do so, if we attempt things with our own strength and skill, without God's help.

The Three Walls of the Romanists

The Romanists have, with great adroitness, drawn three walls round themselves, with which they have hitherto protected themselves, so that no one could reform them, whereby all Christendom has fallen terribly.

Firstly, if pressed by the temporal power, they have affirmed and maintained that the temporal power has no jurisdiction over them, but, on the contrary, that the spiritual power is above the temporal.

Secondly, if it were proposed to admonish them with the Scriptures, they objected that no one may interpret the Scriptures but the Pope.

Thirdly, if they are threatened with a council, they pretend that no one may call a council but the Pope.

Thus they have secretly stolen our three rods, so that they may be unpunished, and entrenched themselves behind these three walls, to act with all the wickedness and malice which we now witness. And whenever they have been compelled to call a council, they have made it of no avail by binding the princes beforehand with an oath to leave them as they were, and to give moreover to the Pope full power over the procedure of the council, so that it is all one whether we have many councils or no councils, in addition to which they deceive us with false pretences and tricks. So grievously do they tremble for their skin before a true, free council; and thus they have overawed kings and princes, that these believe they would be offending God, if they were not to obey them in all such knavish, deceitful artifices.

Now may God help us, and give us one of those trumpets that overthrew the walls of Jericho, so that we may blow down these walls of straw and paper, and that we may set free our Christian rods for the chastisement of sin, and expose the craft and deceit of the devil, so that we may amend ourselves by punishment and again obtain God's favour.

The First Wall: That the Temporal Power has no Jurisdiction over the Spiritual

Let us, in the first place, attack the first wall. It has been devised that the Pope, bishops, priests, and monks are called the spiritual estate, princes, lords, artificers, and peasants are the temporal estate. This is an *artful lie and hypocritical device*, but let no one be made afraid by it, and that for this reason: that all Christians are truly of the spiritual estate, and there is no difference among them, save of office alone. As St Paul says (1 Cor. 12), we are all one body, though each member does its own work, to serve the others. This is because we have one baptism, one Gospel, one faith, and are all Christians alike; for baptism, Gospel, and faith, these alone make spiritual and Christian people.

As for the unction by a pope or a bishop, tonsure, ordination, consecration, and clothes differing from those of laymen – all this may make a hypocrite or an anointed puppet, but never a Christian or a spiritual man. Thus we are all consecrated as priests by baptism, as St Peter says: 'Ye are a royal priesthood, a holy nation' (1 Peter 2, 9); and in the book of Revelations: 'and hast made us unto our God (by Thy blood) kings and priests' (Rev. 5, 10). For, if we had not a higher consecration in us than pope or bishop can give, no priest could ever be made by the consecration of pope or bishop, nor could he say the mass, or preach, or absolve. Therefore the bishop's consecration is just as if in the name of the whole congregation he took one person out of the community, each member of which has equal power, and commanded him to exercise this power for the rest; in the same way as if ten brothers, co-heirs as king's sons, were to choose one from among them to rule over their inheritance, they would all of them still remain kings and have equal power, although one is ordered to govern.

And to put the matter even more plainly, if a little company of pious Christian laymen were taken prisoners and carried away to a desert, and had not among them a priest consecrated by a bishop, and were there to agree to elect one of them, born in wedlock or not, and were to order him to baptize, to celebrate the mass, to absolve, and to preach, this man would as truly be a priest, as if all the bishops and all the Popes had consecrated him. That is why in cases of necessity every man can baptize and absolve, which would not be possible if we were not all priests. This great grace and virtue of baptism and of the Christian estate they have quite destroyed and made us forget by their ecclesiastical law. In this way the Christians used to choose their bishops and priests out of the community; these being afterwards confirmed by other bishops, without the pomp that now prevails. So was it that St Augustine, Ambrose, Cyprian, were bishops.

Since, then, the temporal power is baptized as we are, and has the same faith and Gospel, we must allow it to be priest and bishop, and account its office an office that is proper and useful to the Christian community. For whatever issues from baptism may boast that it has been consecrated priest, bishop, and pope, although it does not beseem every one to exercise these offices. For, since we are all priests alike, no man may put himself forward or take upon himself, without our consent and election, to do that which we have all alike power to do. For, if a thing is common to all, no man may take it to himself without the wish and command of the community. And if it should happen that a man were appointed to one of these offices and deposed for abuses, he would be just what he was before. Therefore a priest should be nothing in Christendom but a *functionary*; as long as he holds his office, he has precedence of others; if he is deprived of it, he is a peasant or a citizen like the rest. Therefore a priest is verily no longer a priest after deposition. But now they have invented *characteres indelebiles*,[3] and pretend that a priest after deprivation still differs from a simple layman. They even imagine that a priest can never be anything but a priest – that is, that he can never become a layman. All this is nothing but mere talk and ordinance of human invention.

It follows, then, that between laymen and priests, princes and bishops, or, as they call it, between spiritual and temporal persons, the only real difference is one of *office and function*, and not of estate; for they are all of the same spiritual estate, true priests, bishops, and popes, though their functions are not the same – just as among priests and monks every man has not the same functions. And this, as I said above, St Paul says (Rom. 12; 1 Cor. 12), and St Peter (1 Peter 2): 'We, being many, are one body in Christ, and severally members one of another.' Christ's body is not double or twofold, one temporal, the other spiritual. He is one Head, and He has one body.

We see, then, that just as those that we call spiritual, or priests, bishops, or popes, do not differ from other Christians in any other or higher degree but in that they are to be concerned with the word of God and the sacraments – that being their work and office – in the same way the temporal authorities hold the sword and the rod in their hands to punish the wicked and to protect the good. A cobbler, a smith, a peasant, *every man has the office and function of his calling*, and yet all alike are consecrated priests and bishops, and every man should by his office or function be useful and beneficial to the rest, so that various kinds of work may all be united for the furtherance of body and soul, just as the members of the body all serve one another.

Now see what a Christian doctrine is this: that the temporal authority is not above the clergy, and may not punish it. This is as if one were to say the hand may not help, though the eye is in grievous suffering. Is it not unnatural, not to say unchristian, that one member may not help another, or guard it against harm? Nay, the nobler the member, the more the rest are bound to help it. Therefore I say, forasmuch as the temporal power has been ordained by God for the punishment of the bad and the protection of the good, therefore we must let it do its duty throughout the whole Christian body, without respect of persons, whether it strikes popes, bishops, priests, monks, nuns, or whoever it may be. If it were sufficient reason for fettering the temporal power that it is inferior among the offices of Christianity to the offices of priest or confessor, or to the spiritual estate – if this were so, then we ought to restrain

---

3. In accordance with a doctrine of the Roman Catholic Church, the act of ordination impresses upon the priest an indelible character, so that he immutably retains the sacred dignity of priesthood.

tailors, cobblers, masons, carpenters, cooks, cellarmen, peasants, and all secular workmen, from providing the Pope or bishops, priests and monks, with shoes, clothes, houses or victuals, or from paying them tithes. But if these laymen are allowed to do their work without restraint, what do the Romanist scribes mean by their laws? They mean that they withdraw themselves from the operation of temporal Christian power, simply in order that they may be free to do evil, and thus fulfil what St Peter said: 'There shall be false teachers among you, . . . and in covetousness shall they with feigned words make merchandise of you' (2 Peter 2, 1, etc.).

Therefore the temporal Christian power must exercise its office without let or hindrance, without considering whom it may strike, whether pope, or bishop, or priest: whoever is guilty, let him suffer for it.

Whatever the ecclesiastical law has said in opposition to this is merely the invention of Romanist arrogance. For this is what St Paul says to all Christians: 'Let every soul' (I presume including the popes) 'be subject unto the higher powers; for they bear not the sword in vain: they serve the Lord therewith, for vengeance on evildoers and for praise to them that do well' (Rom. 13, 1–4). Also St Peter: 'Submit yourselves to every ordinance of man for the Lord's sake . . . for so is the will of God' (1 Peter 2, 13, 15). He has also foretold that men would come who should despise government (2 Peter 2), as has come to pass through ecclesiastical law.

Now, I imagine, the first paper wall is overthrown, inasmuch as the *temporal power has become a member of the Christian body*; although its work relates to the body, yet does it belong to the spiritual estate. Therefore, it must do its duty without let or hindrance upon all members of the whole body, to punish or urge, as guilt may deserve, or need may require, without respect of pope, bishops, or priests, let them threaten or excommunicate as they will. That is why a guilty priest is deprived of his priesthood before being given over to the secular arm; whereas this would not be right, if the secular sword had not authority over him already by Divine ordinance.

It is, indeed, past bearing that the spiritual law should esteem so highly the liberty, life, and property of the clergy, as if laymen were not as good spiritual Christians, or not equally members of the Church. Why should your body, life, goods, and honour be free, and not mine, seeing that we are equal as Christians, and have received alike baptism, faith, spirit, and all things? If a priest is killed, the country is laid under an interdict:[4] why not also if a peasant is killed? Whence comes this great difference among equal Christians? Simply from human laws and inventions.

It can have been no good spirit, either, that devised these evasions and made sin to go unpunished. For if, as Christ and the Apostles bid us, it is our duty to oppose the evil one and all his works and words, and to drive him away as well as may be, how then should we remain quiet and be silent when the Pope and his followers are guilty of devilish works and words? Are we for the sake of men to allow the commandments and the truth of God to be defeated, which at our baptism we

---

4. By the interdict, or general excommunication, whole countries, districts, or towns, or their respective rulers, were deprived of all the spiritual benefits of the Church, such as divine service, the administering of the sacraments, etc.

vowed to support with body and soul? Truly we should have to answer for all souls that would thus be abandoned and led astray.

Therefore it must have been the arch-devil himself who said, as we read in the ecclesiastical law, if the Pope were so perniciously wicked, as to be dragging souls in crowds to the devil, yet he could not be deposed. This is the accursed and devilish foundation on which they build at Rome, and think that the whole world is to be allowed to go to the devil rather than they should be opposed in their knavery. If a man were to escape punishment simply because he is above the rest, then no Christian might punish another, since Christ has commanded each of us to esteem himself the lowest and the humblest (Matt. 18, 4; Luke 9, 48).

Where there is sin, there remains no avoiding the punishment, as St Gregory says, 'We are all equal, but guilt makes one subject to another'. Now let us see how they deal with Christendom. They arrogate to themselves immunities without any warrant from the Scriptures, out of their own wickedness, whereas God and the Apostles made them subject to the secular sword; so that we must fear that it is the work of Antichrist, or a sign of his near approach.

Excerpt from 'On the Limits of Secular Authority: how far does the Obedience owed to it extend?'*

To the illustrious and noble Prince and Lord, John, Duke of Saxony, Landgrave of Thüringen and Margrave of Meissen, my gracious Lord, Grace and peace in Christ. The force of circumstances, and the fact that many have asked me, but above all your Grace's [express] wishes, my most excellent and noble Prince and gracious Lord, oblige me to write once again about secular authority and its Sword: how can a Christian use be made of it and how far do Christians owe it obedience! [. . .]

Some time ago, I wrote a pamphlet to the German nobility. In it I set out their tasks and duties as Christians. How much notice they took of it is plain for all to see. And so I must turn my efforts in another direction and write instead about what they ought not to do, and desist from doing. I am confident that they will pay as little attention this time as they did to my last piece. Long may they remain princes, and never become Christians. For God Almighty has driven our princes mad: they really think they can command their subjects whatever they like and do with them as they please. And their subjects are just as deluded, and believe wrongly that they must obey them in all things. It has now come to this, that rulers have begun to order people to hand over books and to believe and think as their rulers tell them. They have had the temerity to put themselves in God's place, to make themselves *masters of consciences* and belief and to undertake to give lessons to the Holy Spirit from what is in their addled brains. And after all that, they will not allow anyone to dare to tell them [the truth], and still insist on being called 'My gracious Lords'. They write and issue edicts, [pretending that these] are the Emperor's commands, and that they [themselves] are merely acting as the Emperor's obedient Christian princes, as if they meant it seriously and as if people were incapable of seeing

---

* Italics have been added by the editors for emphasis.

through that sort of subterfuge. If the Emperor were to take away one of their castles or towns, or to command something else that did not seem right to them, we would soon see them finding reasons why they were entitled to resist and disobey him. But as long as it is a question of harassing the poor man and subjecting God's will to their own arbitrary whims, it must be called 'obedience to the Emperor's commands'. In days gone by, people like that were called scoundrels, but now we are to call them 'Christian and obedient princes'. And yet they will allow no one to obtain a hearing or to reply to charges against them, however humbly you plead with them, even though they would think it intolerable to be treated in that way themselves, by the Emperor or anyone else. These are the princes that rule the German territories of the Empire, and it is little wonder that things there are in such a state. Now, because the raging of these fools tends to the destruction of Christian faith, the denial of God's Word and blasphemy against God's majesty, I can no longer stand idly by and merely watch my ungracious lords and angry princes. I must resist them, even if it is only with words. And since I was not afraid of their idol the Pope when he threatened me with the loss of heaven and my soul, I must show the world that I am not afraid of the Pope's lackeys either, who threaten me [only] with the loss of my life and worldly possessions. May God let them rage to the end of time and help us to survive their threats. Amen. [. . .]

Here we must divide Adam's children, all mankind, into two parts: the first belong to the kingdom of God, the second to the kingdom of the world. All those who truly believe in Christ belong to God's kingdom, for Christ is king and lord in God's kingdom, as the second Psalm (5, 6) and the whole of Scripture proclaims. [. . .]

Now: these people need neither secular [*weltlich*] Sword nor law. And if all the world [*Welt*] were true Christians, that is, if everyone truly believed, there would be neither need nor use for princes, kings, lords, the Sword or law. What would there be for them to do? Seeing that true Christians have the Holy Spirit in their hearts, which teaches and moves them to love everyone, wrong no one, and suffer wrongs gladly, even unto death. Where all wrongs are endured willingly and what is right is done freely, there is no place for quarrelling, disputes, courts, punishments, laws or the Sword. And therefore laws and the secular Sword cannot possibly find any work to do among Christians, especially since they of themselves do much more than any laws or teachings might demand. As Paul says in 1 Tim. 1, 9: 'Laws are not given to the just, but to the unjust.' Why should this be? It is because the just man of his own accord does all and more than any law demands. But the unjust do nothing that is right, and therefore they need the law to teach, compel and urge them to act rightly. [. . .]

Part Two: How far secular authority extends

We now come to the main part of this sermon. We have learnt that there must be secular authority on this earth and how a Christian and salutary use may be made of it. Now we must establish how long its reach is, and how far it may stretch out its arm without overreaching itself and trenching upon God's kingdom and government. [. . .]

The first point to be noted is that the two parts into which the children of Adam are divided (as we have said above), the one the kingdom of God under Christ, the other the kingdom of the world under secular authority, have each their own kind of law. Everyday experience sufficiently shows us that every kingdom must have its own laws and that no kingdom or government can survive without law. Secular government has laws that extend no further than the body, goods and outward, earthly matters. But where the soul is concerned, God neither can nor will allow anyone but himself to rule. And so, where secular authority takes it upon itself to legislate for the soul, it trespasses on what belongs to God's government, and merely seduces and ruins souls. [. . .]

If someone imposes a man-made law on souls, compelling belief in what he wants to be believed, then there will probably be no word of God to justify it. If there is nothing in God's Word about it, then it is uncertain whether this is what God wants. If he himself has not commanded something, there is no way of establishing that it is pleasing to him. Or rather, we can be sure that it is not pleasing to him, for he will have our faith grounded solely in his divine Word; [. . .]

It is therefore utter folly for them to order us to believe the Church, the Fathers and the Councils, even though there is no Word of God for what they tell us to believe. It is the apostles of the devil that issue that sort of command, not the Church. The Church commands nothing except what it is certain is God's Word. As St Peter says (1 Peter 4, 11): 'Whoever speaks, let him speak according to God's word.' But they will never be able to show that the decrees of Councils are the Word of God. And what is even more ridiculous is when it is argued that, after all, this is what kings and princes and people generally believe. But, my friends, we are not baptized in the name of kings and princes and people in general, but in the name of Christ and of God himself. And our title is not 'kings' or 'princes' or 'people in general', but Christians. *No one can or should lay down commandments for the soul, except those who can point it on the way to heaven. But no human being can do that; only God.* And therefore in those things which concern the salvation of souls, nothing is to be taught or accepted except God's Word. [. . .]

Each must decide at his own peril what he is to believe, and must see to it that he believes rightly. Other people cannot go to heaven or hell on my behalf, or open or close the gates to either for me. And just as little can they believe or not believe on my behalf, or force my faith or unbelief. *How he believes is a matter for each individual's conscience, and this does not diminish the authority of secular governments.* They ought therefore to content themselves with attending to their own business, and allow people to believe what they can, and what they want, and they must use no coercion in this matter against anyone. Faith is free, and no one can be compelled to believe. More precisely, so far from being something secular authority ought to create and enforce, faith is something that God works in the spirit. Hence that common saying which also occurs in Augustine: no one can or ought to be forced to believe anything against his will. [. . .]

So, if a prince or a secular lord commands you to adhere to the papacy, to believe this or that, or to surrender books, then your answer should be: it is not fitting for Lucifer to sit next to God. My good Lord, I owe you obedience with my life and goods. Command me what lies within the limits of your authority, and I will obey. But if you command me to believe, or to surrender my books, I will not obey. For then you will have become a tyrant and overreached yourself, commanding where you have neither right nor power. If he then takes away your goods and punishes you for your disobedience, then blessed are you, and you should thank God for counting you worthy to suffer for the sake of his Word. Let the fool rage; he shall surely find his judge. But I say to you: if you do not resist him and let him take away your faith or your books, then you will truly have denied God. [. . .]

But what if you were to say: how are Christians to be ruled outwardly, seeing that there ought to be no secular Sword amongst them? Surely there must be superiors amongst Christians too! My answer is that there neither can, nor ought to be any superiors amongst Christians. Rather, each is equally subject to all the rest, as St Paul says in Romans 12, 10: 'Each is to regard the next person as his superior.' And Peter (1 Peter 5, 5): 'Be ye all subject one to another.' And this is what Christ wants (Luke 14, 10): 'If you are invited to a wedding, take the lowest place of all.' Among Christians there is no superior except Christ alone. And how can there be superiority or inferiority when *all are equal*, and all have the same right, power, goods and honor? No one desires to be another's superior, for everyone wants to be the inferior of the rest. How could one establish superiors amongst such people, even if one wanted to? Nature will not tolerate superiors when no one wants to be, or can be, a superior. But where there are no people of the latter sort, there are no true Christians either. What of priests and bishops? Their government is not one of superiority or power, but rather a service and an office. For they are not higher or better than other Christians. And therefore they ought not to impose any laws or commands on others without their consent and permission. Their government, on the contrary, is nothing but furtherance of the Word of God, guiding Christians and overcoming heresy by means of it. As has been said, *Christians can be governed by nothing except the Word of God alone.* For Christians must be governed in faith, not by outward works. But faith cannot come by human words, only by God's Word. As St Paul says in Romans 10, 17: 'Faith comes by hearing, but hearing comes through the Word of God.' Those who do not have faith are not Christians and do not belong to Christ's kingdom, but to the kingdom of the world, to be coerced and ruled by the Sword and by external government. Christians on the other hand do everything that is good, without any compulsion, and have all they need in God's Word. But of this I have written much and often elsewhere.

PART TWO
The Legitimation of Sovereign Power

Prologue to Part Two

It is always difficult to define exactly when a certain era in history ends and a new one begins. In this section we cover a period of nearly 200 years stretching from the Late Renaissance and the Reformation to the second half of the seventeenth century. During this period of time the golden era of the Christian world came to an end. The decline of the *orbis christianus*, the Holy Roman Empire, started as a reform *within* Christendom by Martin Luther. But it took only a few years for the Reformation to divide Europe into the Catholic south and the Protestant north. The drawing of these new boundaries led to a cultural fracture effecting Europe in general as well as countries individually. Except for the Peasants' War (1524–6) in Germany, which was provoked by the Reformation, the initial phase of the religious schism seemed to be solved by diplomacy. In 1530 Philip Melanchthon, the first systematic theologian of Protestantism and Luther's foremost collaborator, composed the *confessio augustana*, the creed of the reformed Church, to be approved at the Reichstag of Augsburg by the Habsburg Emperor Charles V. But the devout Catholic Charles V rejected the new faith, which led to the formation of the Schmalkaldic league by the Protestant princes and subsequently to the Schmalkaldic War (1546–7). In this war, the Emperor allied with the Pope and even other Protestant princes. The extent to which the confessional split was motivated by other political and territorial reasons now became manifest. After this war, which the Schmalkaldic league lost, the last opportunity for a peaceful solution occurred in 1555. The so-called 'Peace of Augsburg' was a treaty between Charles V and the besieged Protestant princes, declaring that the faith of a prince determines the faith of his subjects (*cuius regio, eius religio*). However, this treaty clearly provided an enormous economic advantage for the Catholic party. Moreover, it did not include Calvinism and this would turn out to be fatal. The limited freedom of religion only applied to Lutheran princes of the *confessio augustana*.

Calvinism started to spread from Geneva to France and England establishing different confessional sects. Only seven years after the Peace of Augsburg was ratified, the first major set of religious wars began. A time of fierce and brutal wars of religion started and they would last almost 100 years until the Peace of Westphalia in 1648. Almost every European country was involved in these years of civil and international warfare. The wars of religion led to the war of Philip II of Spain and the Netherlands and England, the Massacre of St Bartholomew in France in 1572 (where thousands of civilian Huguenots were slaughtered), the Civil War in England and, finally, the Thirty Years' War (1618–48). It was a period in Europe's history of which Friedrich Schiller retrospectively said:

> From the beginning of the war about religion in Germany, to the Peace of Münster [i.e. Peace of Westphalia], scarcely anything great or remarkable occurred in the political world of Europe in which the Reformation had not an important share. All the events of this period, if they did not originate in, soon became mixed up with, the question of religion, and no state was either too great or too little to feel directly or indirectly more or less of its influence.[1]

The historical context from which the excerpts (from Niccolò Machiavelli, King James VI/I and Thomas Hobbes) composing this section are taken is governed by war. Fundamentally the war of religion among Christians shaped the period from the end of the Renaissance to the baroque era. The Franco-Habsburg War (1521–9) over Italian territory, which is reflected in the political writings of Machiavelli (and in which he was actually involved), and the war against the Ottoman expansion are both significant. The first military encounter with Islam in this context took place in 1526 when Sultan Suleiman the Magnificent endeavoured to take Vienna, one of the capitals of the Habsburg Empire, and had to retreat after three years of battle which devastated almost all of Hungary. The conflict on the borders of the Habsburg Empire culminated again in the Battle of Vienna in 1683 and continued until the second half of the eighteenth century.

War was waging all over Europe and Hobbes's famous words that the life of man is 'solitary, poor, nasty, brutish, and short' illustrate the atmosphere of a whole epoch. Borrowing a phrase from Karl Marx, not religion but this war of religions was the 'sigh of the oppressed creature'. In times of war and crises strong leadership is needed. Thus it is not surprising that the notion of authority, concepts of sovereignty, absolutist monarchy, divine kingship, etc. are central to the political thinking of Machiavelli, James VI/I and Hobbes. For Machiavelli the fortune of the state depends on the quality of the prince and his leadership quality in particular. In his analysis of *realpolitik*, Machiavelli treats religion as a tool for the maintenance of political power. During his lifetime he experienced how the Holy See acted as a political agent like every other secular ruler. The warlike Pope Julius II conquered Italian republics in the name of the papacy and the Church of Christ. According to Machiavelli, religion can be used to generate loyal bounds between the ruler and his subjects and must be used if the situation requires it. The idea of the use of religion as a tool for political means is explic-

---

1. This is the opening paragraph of Friedrich Schiller's *History of the Thirty Years War*. See F. Schiller (2001), *History of the Thirty Years' War in Germany* (Honolulu: University Press of the Pacific).

itly expressed for the first time by Machiavelli. Although it has a long history before and after him.

Machiavelli shares the concept of strong authority with James VI/I and Hobbes, but he still belongs to the era of Renaissance republicanism and the concept of absolutist monarchy as it is advocated by James VI/I or the concept of the state in the sense Hobbes uses it is different. Moreover, there are undeniable differences between the Florentine Renaissance and Stuart England in terms of arts, literature, architecture and the social imagination in general. But despite these fundamental differences in the socio-historical contexts in which Machiavelli, on the one hand, and James VI/I and Hobbes, on the other, lived, connections can be drawn. Both James VI/I and Hobbes were familiar with Machiavelli's work and often referred to it. By the second half of the seventeenth century, Machiavelli was already seen as a classical source for political theory. Machiavelli represents a tradition of moral-political literature for the advice to princes. Together with the ancient classical works (including Greek sources like Thucydides' *History of the Peloponnesian War*, Plato's *Republic*, Aristotle's *Politics*, as well as Roman authors like Cicero, Livy, Marcus Aurelius and Roman law in general) this literature of moral-political guidelines and advice constitutes the basis for early modern political theory.

The political scientist Leo Strauss has argued in his book *Natural Right and History*[2] that Hobbes invented modern political science by separating political thought from faith. It is a hotly debated question whether this is true for Hobbes, and even for all those after him. But there is no question about the fact that the development of political science and theories of the political coincide with the diminishing of faith and spiritual authority and the augmentation of reason and temporal authority. As we have seen, this process is already embryonic in Luther's political-pastoral work and affects the development of not only political science but also jurisprudence, that is, the separation of civil law from ecclesiastical law. Alberico Gentili's famous statement: '*Silete theologi in munere alieno*' figuratively meaning, 'Theologians mind your own business!', made at the end of the sixteenth century, proved to be paradigmatic for the coming centuries.

To illustrate the changes in the modern theory of politics we have selected two representatives from England: King James VI/I and Thomas Hobbes. By focusing on England we want to draw attention to two competing principles in the theory of the political and in the political organization of a society in particular. Furthermore, these two principles are related to Catholicism and Protestantism and their different views on the theory of the political. The first principle is that of hierarchical order and the second is the proto-democratic principle of congregation. According to the principle of hierarchy, dominion is related to the sacred and supreme power, that is, sovereignty is concentrated in one person – the king. From this principle the Divine Right of Kings, as we will see in James' VI/I 'Speech before Parliament' (1609) and *The True Law of Free Monarchies* (1598), is established. The king 'exercises a resemblance of divine power upon earth'. The difference between the king and his subjects is an ontological one. It is not simply a difference

---

2. L. Strauss (1953), *Natural Right and History* (Chicago, IL: University of Chicago Press).

concerning duty and office. (This is the opposite of Luther's functional and anti-metaphysical understanding of vocation). The sovereignty of the king is granted by God and all other political power emanates from this sovereign source. The clearest theoretical account of this absolute monarchy is laid down in the book *Politics drawn from the Very Words of Holy Scripture*[3] by the French Catholic Bishop Jacques-Bénigne Bossuet, written between 1677 and 1679 in the court of Louis XIV. There the hierarchical principle is related to Catholicism, and the fact that Bousset was a Catholic bishop underlines this association. Conversely, the proto-democratic principle of congregation is related to Protestantism. According to this principle, sovereign power issues from an assembly and consensus of the people and not from God's gift to one king.

We have selected excerpts in which both principles are at war with each other. In the case of King James VI/I the context of his speech must be taken into consideration. It is the speech before the English parliament – the two principles of hierarchy and congregation literally meet each other in this situation. The last excerpt in this section by Thomas Hobbes demonstrates his attempt to combine both principles in a coherent theory of the political body of society. In the *Leviathan* (1651), from which the excerpt is taken, the principle of hierarchy and congregation are spelled out in terms of the sovereignty of the king and the contractual nature of the state. For early modern theories of the political the ambivalence between these two principles is fundamental. It is not by chance that the battle between parliament and king, between absolute monarchy and a collective body politic, took place in England. For the compromise of a parliamentary monarchy reflects the compromise between Protestantism and Catholicism worked out in the Anglican Church.

When we enter the eighteenth century in the next section, the proto-democratic congregational element of politics becomes dominant. There is already a fore-taste of the direction things will take in discussions concerning contract in James VI/I and Hobbes.

---

3. J.-B. Bossuet (1991), *Politics drawn from the very Words of Holy Scripture* (Cambridge: Cambridge University Press).

Chapter 5

Niccolò Machiavelli (1469–1527)

*. . . for where religion exists it is easily possible to introduce arms, but where there
are arms and not religion, religion can only be introduced there with difficulty.*

Introduction

'I have always had to labour, regardless of anything, on that which I believe to be
for the *common good*', says Machiavelli in the Preface of his book *Discourses on Livy*
(1531). In fact, Machiavelli was an active politician involved in foreign affairs as a
diplomat for Florence and his writings about politics reflect his personal experience and are informed by this political engagement.

In 1499, at age of 30, he was not only in charge of the territorial administration
of Florence but also a senior member of the diplomatic corps for foreign affairs.
This duty brought him into contact with the most powerful people of his time.
Among them were Louis XII the King of France and his enemy, the warlike Pope
Julius II – today remembered as the employer of Michelangelo – and Cesare
Borgia, the son of Pope Alexander VI and General of the papal army. Borgia's
meteoric career left a strong impression on Machiavelli and had an enormous
impact on his understanding of politics and the role of fortune in particular. With
Machiavelli we encounter a *real* politician who analyses the conditions of *realpolitik* in difficult times of war and conflict. He lived in an age prior to the establishment of nation states and international law. It is for this reason that the role
and actions of the prince, both the political and military leader, were so important.

Machiavelli's rigorous examination of political power and its exercise provoked
strong criticism, and subsequently 'Machiavellism' became a synonym for oppor-
tunism and the attitude that the aim justifies all means. But what is the *aim* of all
political action? For Machiavelli the highest good of politics, and for himself as a
politician, was the common good – the *res publica*. The maintenance and preservation of the republic superseded all other values and political ambitions, and the
Discourses on Livy outline the art of governing such a republic. Nevertheless, and this
is the ambivalence of Machiavelli's concept of politics, the republic can only flourish
and exist under the rule of a single sovereign. In his famous book *The Prince* (1532)
he outlines a set of rules and maxims whereby the political leader gains and maintains power. Thus *The Prince* was often misinterpreted as a blueprint for dictatorship and a rejection of democratic forms of government. Benito Mussolini (*Il Duce*),

81

for example, quoted a passage from *The Prince* where Machiavelli states: 'This is why all armed prophets are victorious and the unarmed destroyed. Because people are by nature fickle, it is easy to persuade them of something, but difficult to secure them in that conviction. For this reason it is worthwhile being organized in such a way that, when they no longer believe, they can be made to believe by force'. Mussolini subsequently concluded: 'Regimes based solely on consensus have never existed, do not exist and probably never will exist'.

There are many faces to Machiavelli and the interpretations of his work range from glorious admiration to ruthless condemnation. Carl Schmitt (who will be introduced in Part Four) once raised the half-ironical question concerning whether Machiavelli was a Machiavellist. Schmitt argued that if he was a Machiavellist then he would not have been very wise to write *The Prince* and *The Discourses* in such a frank manner. In fact, Machiavelli's radical examination of the immoral nature of certain necessary political actions gained him no favours. Both books were published posthumously and were put on the index of atheistic and evil works, including the person of the author. It is worth noting that Machiavelli did not write for a public audience and his intention was not to augment his reputation as a leading politician of Florence. In fact, exactly the opposite is true. Both *The Prince* and *The Discourses* were addressed to specific people. *The Discourses* was written at the behest of friends who forced him to write down his experiences in politics. When Machiavelli wrote these books he was in a miserable situation. In 1513 he was falsely accused of being a conspirator against the ruling Florentine family of the Medici. As a result of this accusation, he was removed from all of his offices and put into jail, where he was tortured. Fortunately he was released soon afterwards without any further charges. Having lost his income, he moved to his country house and there began to write *The Prince*, which is dedicated to Lorenzo de' Medici. Machiavelli hoped to gain the favour of the prince again and to be reappointed as a political advisor. However, it would take another 12 years for his reputation to be restored.

The sudden and unpredictable downfall of Machiavelli forms the biographical basis for one of the two key elements in his understanding of politics. In politics, he observed, there will always remain a certain degree of uncertainty and unpredictability about the outcome of any action. This element of the impossibility of total control can mean that the outcome of a political enterprise (such as a battle, a diplomatic negotiation or a personal decision) is in fact entirely the opposite of any original intention. Machiavelli calls this element *fortuna* (fortune). A ruler, he claims, must be a man of prudent foresight, but also needs good fortune for his political enterprises. Therefore *fortuna* is the irrational element that is inseparable from the rational qualities governing the art of politics. The personal qualities of the leader himself are summed up in what Machiavelli calls *virtú*. This term defining leadership has much wider meaning than just rational planning, technical skill, foresight, prudence and the ability to make decisions. *Virtú* also implies a certain ideal of Renaissance education. It forms the basis of good politics. Complemented by *fortuna*, good politics can become successful politics. Compared to Plato and Aristotle, the two giants of classical political theory, the awareness of and emphasis on *fortuna* makes Machiavelli's political thinking distinctive. While Plato and Aristotle are concerned with the theoretical examination of forms of governments, Machiavelli's analyses of political action provide much more practical insights. In other words, Machiavelli's understanding and examination of politics is governed by the pragmatics of success.

The first part of the excerpt chosen is taken from the first book of *The Discourses*. It illustrates Machiavelli's success-orientated examination of politics. He considers the extent to which religion is a political tool and outlines why it is important for a republic to have a religion. In a summarizing paragraph Machiavelli states:

> I conclude therefore, that the Religion introduced by Numa was among the chief reasons for the felicity of that City, for it caused good ordinances, good ordinances make good fortune, and from good fortune there arises the happy successes of the enterprises. And as the observance of divine institutions is the cause of the greatness of Republics, so the contempt of it is the cause of their ruin, for where the fear of God is lacking it will happen that that kingdom will be ruined or that it will be sustained through fear of a Prince, which may supply the want of Religion.

This quotation demonstrates how Machiavelli uses examples of Roman history in analysing contemporary politics. This disguised historical analysis is typical of *The Discourses* and explains the subtitle *The First Ten Books of Roman History by Livy*. Machiavelli composes a critical commentary on Roman history, from its foundation in 753 BCE to 293 BCE. The Numa referred to in the quotation is the mythological Numa Pompilius, the successor of Romulus.

The second part of the excerpt chosen is taken from the third book of *The Discourses* and offers not only an interesting parallel between religion and political institutions, but also a surprising account of the *virtú* of an institution. Machiavelli argues that political institutions need to be renewed from time to time. Only perpetual refreshing of the cultural memory of the origins of an institution, like a republic, can guarantee its maintenance. As is evident at the end of the excerpt, Machiavelli gains this insight from the emergence of religious sects and renewal movements within the Church at his time. In particular the charismatic preacher and condemned heretic Savonarola had an important impact on Machiavelli.

Savonarola represents the danger of conflating religion and politics at this time. He was publicly burnt at the stake after several years of moral and political criticism of the vanities of Florence. Maybe this is why for Machiavelli a politician must not always tell the truth.

Further reading

Selected English translations

Livy (1998), *The Risk of Rome*, Books 1–5, trans. T. Luct (Oxford: Oxford University Press) and Livy (1982), *History of Rome from its Foundation: Rome and Italy*, Books 6–10, trans. B. Radice (London, Penguin).

Machiavelli, N. (1998), *Discourses on Livy*, trans. H. Mansfield and N. Tascov (Chicago, IL: University of Chicago Press).

General introductions

Rahe, P. (2005), *Machiavelli's Liberal Republican Legacy* (Cambridge: Cambridge University Press).

Strauss, L. (1978), *Thoughts on Machiavelli* (Chicago, IL: University of Chicago Press).

Viroli, M. (1998), *Machiavelli, Founder of Modern Political and Social Thought* (Oxford and New York: Oxford University Press).

Reception of key ideas

Bock, G., Skinner, Q., Viroli, M. and European Culture Research Centre (1990), *Machiavelli and Republicanism, Ideas in Context* (Cambridge: Cambridge University Press).

Hörnqvist, M. (2004), *Machiavelli and Empire* (Cambridge: Cambridge University Press).

Mansfield, H. (1996), *Machiavelli's Virtue* (Chicago, IL: University of Chicago Press).

Excerpt from *Discourses on Livy**

Book I, 9: Of the religions of the Romans

Although Rome had Romulus as its original organizer and, like a daughter, owed her birth and education to him, nonetheless the heavens, judging that the institutions of Romulus were not sufficient for so great an Empire, put it into the breasts of the Roman Senate to elect Numa Pompilius as successor to Romulus, so that those things that he had omitted would be instituted by Numa. Who, finding a very ferocious people and wanting to reduce them to civil obedience by the acts of peace, *turned to religion as something completely necessary in wanting to maintain a civilization,* and he established it in such a manner that for many centuries there never was more fear of God than in that Republic, which facilitated any enterprise which the Senate or those of great Roman men should plan to do. And whoever should discuss the infinite actions of the people of Rome taken all together, and of many Romans individually by themselves, will see that those citizens feared much more the breaking of an oath than the laws, like those men who esteem more the power of God than that of man, as is manifestly seen in the examples of Scipio and of Manlius Torquatus, for after the defeat that Hannibal had inflicted on the Romans at Cannae, many citizens had gathered together and, frightened and fearful, had agreed to abandon Italy and take themselves to Sicily: when Scipio heard of this, he went to meet them, and with bared sword in hand he constrained them to swear not to abandon their country. [. . .]

---

* Italics have been added by the editors for emphasis.

And whoever considers well Roman history will see how much religion served in commanding the armies, in reuniting the plebs, both in keeping men good, and in making the wicked ashamed. So that if it were discussed as to which prince Rome should be more obligated, Romulus or Numa, I believe that Numa would rather attain the higher rank; *for where religion exists it is easily possible to introduce arms, but where there are arms and not religion, religion can only be introduced there with difficulty.* And it is seen that for Romulus to institute the Senate and to make other civil and military arrangements, the authority of God was not necessary, but it was very necessary for Numa, who *pretended* he had met with a nymph who advised him of that which he should counsel the people; and all this resulted because he wanted to introduce new ordinances and institutions in that City, and was apprehensive that his authority was not enough. And truly *there never was any extraordinary institutor of laws among a people who did not have recourse to God,* because otherwise he would not have been accepted; for these laws are very well known by prudent men, but which by themselves do not contain evident reasons capable of persuading others. Wise men who want to remove this difficulty, therefore, have recourse to God. Thus did Lycurgus, thus Solon, thus many others who had the same aims as they.

The Roman people, therefore, admiring Numa's goodness and prudence, yielded to his every decision. It is indeed true that those times were full of religion, and those men with whom Numa had to work were coarse, which gave him great facility to pursue his designs, being able easily to impress upon them any new form. And without doubt whoever should want to establish a republic in the present era, would find it more easy to do so among men of the mountains where there is no civilization, than among those who are used to living in the City, where civilization is corrupt, as a sculptor more easily extracts a beautiful statue from crude marble than of one badly sketched out by others. Considering all this I conclude therefore, that *the religion introduced by Numa was among the chief reasons for the felicity of that City,* for it caused good ordinances, *good ordinances make good fortune,* and from good fortune there arises the happy successes of the enterprises. And as the observance of divine institutions is the cause of the greatness of republics, so the contempt of it is the cause of their ruin, for where the fear of God is lacking it will happen that that kingdom will be ruined or that it will be sustained through *fear of a Prince,* which may supply the want of religion. And because Princes are shortlived, it will happen that that Kingdom will easily fall as the Prince fails in virtue. Whence it results that Kingdoms which depend solely on the virtue of one man, are not durable for long because that virtue fails with the life of that man, and it rarely happens that it is renewed in his successor, as Dante prudently says:

> Rarely there descends from the branches (father to son)
> human probity, and this is the
> will (of the one) who gives it,
> because it is asked alone from him.

The welfare of a republic or a kingdom, therefore, is not in having a Prince who governs prudently while he lives, but one who organizes it in a way that, if he should die, it will still maintain itself. And although crude men are more easily persuaded by new ordinances and opinions, yet it is not impossible because of this to persuade civilized men, and who presume themselves not to be crude. The people of Florence did not seem either crude or ignorant, nonetheless Brother Girolamo Savonarola was persuaded that he talked with God. I do not want to judge whether that was true or not, because one ought not to talk of so great a man except with reverence. But I may well say that an infinite number believed him without their having seen anything extraordinary which would make them believe, because his life, the doctrine, the subjects he took up were sufficient to make them have faith. Let no one be dismayed, therefore, if he is not able to attain that which had been attained by others, for men . . . are born, live, and die, always in the same way.

Book III, 1: To want that a sect or a republic exist for long, it is necessary to return them often to their principles

It is a most true thing that all the things of the world have to have an ending to their existence. But these only run the entire course that is generally ordained by heaven, which does not disorganize their body, but keeps it so organized that it is not changed, or if it is changed, it is for its welfare and not its injury. And as I speak here of mixed bodies, as are republics and religious sects, I say that those changes are for the better which bring them back to their original principles. And, therefore, those are better organized and have a longer existence, which through their own means *are able frequently to renew themselves*, or which through some accident outside the said organization come to that renewal. And it is something clearer than light, that these bodies which do not renew themselves, do not endure. The means of renewing them (as has been said) is to bring them back to their original principles. For all the principles of sects and republics and of kingdoms must have within themselves some goodness, by means of which they obtain their first reputation and first expansion. And as in the process of time that goodness becomes corrupted, of necessity it will kill the body, unless something intervenes to bring it back to the sign of normality. And doctors of medicine say, speaking of the bodies of men: every day something is gathered, and when it is ill, it must be cured.

This turning back to principles, speaking of republics, is caused either by an extrinsic accident or by an intrinsic prudence. As to the first, it is seen how necessary it was that Rome should be taken by the Gauls to want to be reborn, and being reborn should resume a new life and a new virtue, and should resume the observance of religion and justice, which were beginning to blemish themselves in her. This is very well known from the history of Livius, where he shows that in calling out the army against the Gauls, and in creating the tribunes with consular power, they did not observe any religious ceremony. [. . .]

It is necessary, therefore, as has been said, that men who live together in some kind of organization, often know each other either by these external incidents, or by internal ones. And as to these latter, it happens that they arise either from a law which often reviews the conduct of the men who are in that body, or truly by some good man who arises amongst them, who by his example and his deeds of virtue causes the same effect as that institution. This good then springs up in republics either from the virtue of one man or from the virtue of one institution. As to the latter, the institutions that returned the Roman republic back to its original principles were the tribunes of the plebs, and all the other laws that curbed the ambitions and insolence of men. Which institutions have need to be kept alive by the virtue of one citizen who will courageously take part in their execution against the power of those who transgress them.

The most notable examples of such execution of the laws, before the taking of Rome by the Gauls, were the death of the sons of Brutus, the death of the ten Citizens (*Decemvirs*), and that of Melius, the grain dealer; and after the taking of Rome were the death of Manlius Capitolinus, the death of the son of Manlius Torquatus, the punishment inflicted by Papirius Cursor on Fabius, his Master of Cavalry, and the accusation of Scipio. As these were the extreme and most notable examples, each time one arose, it caused the people to turn back to their principles; and when they began to be more rare, they began also to give men more latitude in becoming corrupt, and the carrying out of the laws was done with more danger and more tumults. So that from one such execution to another, no more than ten years should elapse, for beyond this time men begin to change their customs and transgress the laws; and unless something arises which recalls the punishment to their memory, and revives the fear in their minds, so many delinquents will soon come together that they cannot any longer be punished without danger.

In connection with this subject, those who governed the State of Florence, from 1434 until 1494, said that it was necessary to resume the government every five years, otherwise it would be difficult to maintain it: and they called 'the resuming of the government' *to put the same fear and terror* in men as they had done in the assuming of it, having in that time punished those who, according to that mode of living, had conducted themselves badly. But as the memory of that punishment fades, men become bold to try new things and speak ill of the government, and therefore it is necessary to provide against this, by bringing the government back to its original principles. This return of republics back to their principles also results from the simple virtue of *one man*, without depending on any law that excites him to any execution: nonetheless, they are of such influence and example that good men desire to imitate him, and the wicked are ashamed to lead a life contrary to those examples. Those particularly, who in Rome produced these good results, were Horatius Codes, Scaevola, Fabricus, the two Decii, Regulus Attilius, and some others, who by their rare examples, of virtue produced almost the same effect in Rome that laws and institutions would have done. And if the above executions, together with these particular examples, had been followed at least every ten years in that city, it would have followed of necessity that it would never have been corrupt: but as they caused both these things to become rare, corruption began to multiply, for, after Marcus Regulus, no similar example is seen: and although the two Catos had sprung up in Rome, so great was the interval between Regulus and them, and between the one and Cato, and they were so isolated instances, that they could not effect any good work by their good examples. And especially the later

Cato, who, finding the city in good part corrupt, was not able by his example to make the citizens become better. And this is enough as regards republics.

But as to the sects, such renewal is also seen to be necessary by the examples of our religion, which, if it had not been brought back to its principles by Saint Francis and Saint Dominic, would have been entirely extinguished: for by their poverty and by their example of the life of Christ, they brought it back to the minds of men where it had already been extinguished; and their new orders were so powerful, that they were the reason why the dishonesty of prelates and the heads of the religion did not ruin her; they yet continue to live in poverty and have so much credit with the people through confessions and preachings, that they were able to make them understand that it was evil to speak evil of the bad, and that it was good to live rendering them obedience, and if they had made errors to leave their punishment to God. And thus these bad rulers do as much evil as they can, because they do not fear that punishment they do not see or believe. This renewal by Saint Francis and Saint Dominic, therefore, has maintained and still maintains this religion. Kingdoms also have need to renew themselves and bring their laws back to first principles. And it is seen how much good resulted from such a renewal in the kingdom of France, which kingdom exists under laws and ordinances more than any other kingdom. The parliaments are the maintainers of these laws and ordinances, and especially that of Paris; and these are renewed by them at any time by an execution against a prince of that kingdom, and at times even by condemning the King in some of his decisions. And up to now it has maintained itself because it has been an obstinate executor against that nobility: but if at any time they should allow some disorder to go on with impunity, and which would then come to be multiplied, and without doubt there would result either that the evil-doers would be corrected with accompanying great disorders, or that the kingdom itself would be dissolved.

I conclude, therefore, that there is nothing more necessary in a community of men, either as a sect, or kingdom, or republic, than to restore it to that reputation that it had at its beginning, and to endeavour to obtain either good ordinances or good men to bring about such a result, and not to have an extrinsic force do it. For although sometimes this may be the best remedy, as it was at Rome, it is so dangerous that it is in no way desirable. But to show to anyone how much the actions of some men in particular had made Rome great and caused many good results in that city.

Chapter 6

James VI/I (1566–1625)

. . . further a king is preferred by God above all other ranks and degrees of men.

Introduction

James VI/I of Scotland was born in political turmoil amid rumours that he was the illegitimate child of Mary, Queen of Scots' secretary, David Riccio. The secretary, a Catholic like Mary and her son, was butchered. James was elevated to the throne after a Protestant coup that illegally forced his mother to abdicate in his favour. He was a baby caught up in the political and ecclesiastical machinery of a rising Scottish Protestantism; his mother struggled to regain her throne. His real father, Lord Darnley, was murdered by the man who became his mother's second husband, the fourth Earl of Bothwell. The verdict is still open as to whether Mary herself was an accomplice in this murder. She was finally imprisoned by Elizabeth in England. James was 21 when his mother was executed for treason, having been raised among warring clansmen, with continual threats upon his life and a question hanging over his head as to whether he had any right to be on the throne at all (while his mother lived). His earliest biographer, Sir Anthony Weldon, noted that all his life he wore 'padded clothes because of his fear of the assassin's knife'. And if it wasn't the assassin's knife that threatened him, it was the work of witches. In January 1591, for example, an alleged witch, one Agnes Sampson, testified that she had met with nine other witches and the devil, formed a wax image of the king and they had handed it one to the other chanting, 'This is King James the Sixth, ordered to be consumed at the instance of a nobleman, Francis Earl of Bothwell'. Francis was the fifth Earl of Bothwell and was implicated in attempts on James's life for the next four years.

The greatest of James's writings were expressions of the complexity of governing in a world where threats came from aristocrats, Church leaders or Satanists. Each of these forces had been unleashed or rejuvenated as a consequence of the Reformation. The Scottish aristocrats were divided as Catholics against Protestants, or moderate Protestants (called Erastians) against hard-line Protestants. Two of the most vociferous voices in the Scottish kirk, John Knox and Andrew Melville, attacked monarchy as an institution. It was Melville, in one of his confrontations with James, who told him: 'There is [sic] two Kings and two Kingdoms in Scotland. There is Christ Jesus the King, and his kingdom the Kirk; whose subject King James the Sixth is, and of whose kingdom not a King, nor a lord, nor a head, but a member!' Melville had come from Calvin's theocracy in Geneva. After the Reformation the older, sacral notions of kingship (given detailed exposition in Ernst Kantorowicz's *The King's Two Bodies*) could no longer be assumed. James's own first tutor, George Buchanan, in a treatise published in 1579 (when James was 13) argued that it was justifiable under the Scottish constitution to depose a king if the majority of the people found him intolerable. This sentiment, found circulating elsewhere in Europe among Catholics as wells as Calvinists, went further than any of the medieval debates on the rights or wrong of ridding a country of a tyrant. For the 'tyrant' might now only be someone who failed to defend the 'true religion'; nevertheless, this justified rebellion. As for witchcraft, though there were Scottish laws forbidding it, it was only in the 1590s that the wave of prosecutions began, following decades of Protestants using allegations of Satanism to browbeat Catholics.

James VI/I's first major work was a book on witchcraft, spirits and ghosts, *Daemonologie*, published in 1597, one year prior to *The Trew Law of Free Monarchies*. The principle it asserts is that these witches, spirits and ghosts are only given power insofar as God allows it. This becomes significant because of the role James sketches for the divinity of the king. Written with the Earl of Bothwell in mind, the practice of witchcraft in the realms of God's vice-regent was nothing less than sedition, a political crime. *The Trew Law* was published in the same year as his most famous book, a book that ran to almost 16,000 copies within a few years, *Basilikon Doron*. This book compliments *The Trew Law*, although ironically, it was the latter that was for public consumption. *Basilikon Doron* was written for James's eldest son (and heir under the law of primogeniture), Henry, and it took the form of advice on the practice of kingship. It was one of a genre of such books on advice for a prince, the most famous being Machiavelli's *The Prince*. *The Trew Law*, on the other hand, announced James's theory of kingship. Both books were written in the light of almost 18 years' first-hand experience of governing Scotland, at a time when James was beginning to see the fruits of hard-won contests with both the kirk and the clansmen. Both books are expositions of the so-called Black Acts passed in 1584, following another coup in which James was held captive. For the Black Acts asserted the 'royal power and authority over all estates as well spiritual as temporal'. The phrase is significant for the vast differences between the medieval debates over sovereignty (exemplified by Aquinas and Dante) and the post-Reformation debates. It demonstrates the new order that kings had come into and the new autonomy of nation states. *The Trew Law* is a manifesto for the new role of kings as absolute sovereigns. It was also a message to the Queen and Lords of England. For Elizabeth always refused to name James VI/I as heir to the English throne. He was the next in line, but there was much debate, which Elizabeth herself fostered, about who would succeed her. In its very clear statement about primogeniture – the hereditary right of the next in the bloodline – it clearly announced that James would press his claim irrespective of English common law, Henry VIII's will or the opinions of the English Parliament.

It is well worth inquiring into why James entitled his treatise *The Trew Law* – because with this inquiry we proceed to the heart of royal absolutism or the Divine Right of Kings. What made the law 'trew' and what kind of 'law' was it? In one of the early paragraphs of the treaty, when James outlines the threefold structure of his argument, the two ways in which truth was established are alluded to. First, the law is true because it is founded upon Scripture. As we saw with Dante, appeal to Scripture is not new, but such appeal was all the more important following the Reformation principle of *sola scriptura*. In Dante's time the ways in which Scripture was interpreted were: a) a complex appeal to a fourfold method of exegesis (the historical, tropological, anagogical and allegorical), and b) regulated by permitting only certain people access to the Bible (Luther alludes to this when he talks about the 'three walls of the Romanists' defence against a reform of the Catholic Church). Now the Bible was available much more widely, and in the vernacular, and Protestant exegesis favoured the literal meaning of the text rather than the fourfold method. There developed a view that every word of the Bible was dictated by God. James's demonstrations from Scripture are appeals to God's *revealed* law. (Though there is an interesting comparison between James VI/I's interpretation of the passage from Samuel on the appointment of kings and Thomas Paine's in the next section). The second way in which truth was established was by claiming that something accorded with the law of nature. This goes back to the impact of Aristotle. Aquinas, as we saw, establishes the natural law of government on the notions of part and whole and the ends towards which created things are made. James makes a similar move in laying down the principle of 'Unity being the perfection of all things'. Natural law related to the order of the Creator in creation as was evident to reason. Government, for Aquinas as for James, was written into the order of things. Whereas Aquinas views the *telos* of government as peace, James emphasizes unity. But both will draw arguments from analogies with the natural world. For example, James (like Dante) will employ the father to his children analogy, and, once more, we have appeal made to the body analogue. These are traditional analogies, as we have seen, but the use they are put to in the argument for royal absolutism is distinctive. The crowning analogy is, of course, the one in which God is to the king what the king is to his people.

There is one further note to be made on the use of law. As we have said, the argument rests upon appeal to God's revealed law in the Scriptures and natural law. But by 'law' James is also referring to the legislative process whereby the king *makes* laws. We can observe from the speech he delivered to the English Parliament in 1609 that the importance of these laws lies in the limitations they should impose upon the king's absolute rule. The sovereign plays many roles with respect to the law: a) he maintains the law; b) he judges when and how the law has been infringed; c) he punishes breakers of the law; and d) he *makes* the law. There are two corollaries of this situation: first, no one has any authority to judge the actions of the king but God; and, second, the king is above the laws he himself makes and interprets. But a paradox of sovereignty is opened here between the king as defender of the law and the king who is beyond the law. For James VI/I the very fact that the king was bound by no human law constituted his freedom. That is why the treatise is called *The Trew Law of Free Monarchies*. Only the king was free; everybody else was subject to that freedom. We will see this paradox – of being the condition for the law but exempt from the law – being played out in various cultural and historical contexts down to

Carl Schmitt and, more recently, Giorgio Agamben.[1] James is answering those who held to the view that kings can be resisted and overthrown. On his argument, even if the king acts wickedly, only God can judge and punish such a sovereign. James is also answering those who held that the coronation oath *made* the king and therefore promises made by the king in that oath were binding. The absolutism James advocates draws upon older, medieval debates about the king's two bodies, where the natural body of the king was distinguished from the political body of the king. In these debates, the claim was made that the royal rule was eternal. The king never died. The designated person may die, but on his or her death the next king was proclaimed. This was part of the argument for hereditary succession. The king was king, then, prior to any coronation. The coronation oath did not, then, constitute a 'contract' between the king and the people. James's thinking might be interestingly compared with Hobbes's here or with the account of sovereignty given by Jean Bodin in Book I, chapter 8 on sovereignty of the *Six livres de la république* (a copy of which was in James's library as a youth). With James there is no transfer of the rights of individuals that mandated the king to rule over them; the political power of the king was solely derived from God and birthright. It is fascinating to observe how the mercantile language of contract begins to proliferate. The duty and allegiance of the people is natural. At the coronation the king promises to discharge the office of the king. The community itself had no rights to power and so one of the great defenders of Stuart absolutism, Sir Robert Filmer, could declare democracy a blasphemy. Given that kingship was both a divine and a natural law, the only alternatives to monarchy were tyranny or anarchy.

In 1603 James VI of Scotland was crowned King James I of England. In the same year *The Trew Law of Free Monarchies* and *Basilikon Doron* were both republished in England.

Further reading

General introductions

Kenyon, J. (1977), *The Stuarts: A Study in English Kingship* (London: Severn House.)
Lee, M. (1995), *King James VI and I: Political Writings*, ed. J. Summerville (Cambridge: Cambridge University Press).

Reception of key ideas

Ferrell, L. (1998), *Government by Polemic: James I, the King's Preachers, and the Rhetorics of Conformity, 1603–1625* (Palo Alto, CA: Stanford University Press).
Fischlin, D. and Fortier, M. (2002), *Royal Subjects: Essays on the Writings of James VI and I* (Detroit, IL: Wayne State University Press).

---

1. C. Schmitt (1985 [1922]), *Political Theology* (Cambridge, MA: MIT Press); G. Agamben (1998), *Homo Sacer: Sovereign Power and Bare Life* (Palo Alto, CA: Stanford University Press); G. Agamben (2005), *State of Exception* (Chicago, IL: University of Chicago Press).

Kantorowicz, E. (1957), *The King's Two Bodies: A Study of Mediaeval Political Theology* (Princeton, NJ: Princeton University Press).

Summerville, J. P. (1991), 'James I and the Divine Right of Kings: English Politics and Continental Theory', in L. Levy (ed.), *The Mental World of the Jacobean Court* (Cambridge: Cambridge University Press), pp. 36–54.

Excerpt from *The True Law of Free Monarchies**

As there is not a thing so necessary to be known by the people of any land, next to the knowledge of their God, as the right knowledge of their allegiance, according to the form of government established among them, especially in a *Monarchy* (which form of government, as resembling the Divinity, approaches nearest to perfection, as all the learned and wise men from the beginning have agreed upon; unity being the perfection of all things, so has the ignorance, and, which is worse, the seduced opinion of the multitude blinded by them, who think themselves able to teach and instruct the ignorants, procured the wrack and overthrow of sundry flourishing commonwealths; and heaped heavy calamities, threatening utter destruction upon others. [. . .]

I have chosen then . . . to set down in this short treatise, the true grounds of the mutual duty, and allegiance between a free and absolute *Monarch,* and his people. [. . .]

First then, I will set down the true grounds, whereupon I am to build, out of the Scriptures, since *Monarchy* is the true pattern of Divinity, as I have already said: next, from the fundamental laws of our own kingdom, which nearest most concerns us: thirdly, from the law of nature, by diverse similitudes drawn out of the same: and will conclude the same by answering the most weighty and appearing incommodities that can be objected.

The princes' duty to his subjects is so clearly set down in many places of the Scriptures, and so openly confessed by all the good princes, according to their oath in their coronation, as not needing to be long therein, I shall as shortly as I can run through it.

Kings are called God's by the prophetical king David, because they sit upon God's throne in the earth, and have the account of their administration to give unto him. Their office is to administer justice and judgement to the people, as the same David says: 'to advance the good, and punish the evil'. As he likewise says: 'to establish good laws to his people, and procure obedience to the same' as diverse good kings of Judah did: 'To procure the peace of the people', as the same David says: 'To decide all controversies that can arise among them', as Solomon did. 'To be the minister of God for the welfare of them that do well, and as the minister of God, to take vengeance upon them that do evil', as St. Paul says. And finally, as a good pastor, to go out and in before his people as is said in the first of Samuel: 'That through the prince's prosperity, the peoples' peace may be procured', as Jeremiah says.

And therefore in the coronation of our own kings, as well as of every Christian

---

* Insofar as it has been necessary, we have modernized James's seventeenth-century English.

Monarchy, they give their oath, first to maintain the religion presently professed within their country, according to their laws, whereby it is established, and to punish all those that should press to alter, or disturb the profession thereof; and next to maintain all the allowable and good laws made by their predecessors: to see them put in execution, and the breakers and violaters thereof, to be punished, according to the tenor of the same: and lastly, to maintain the whole country, and every state therein, in all their ancient privileges and liberties, as well against all foreign enemies, as among themselves: and shortly to procure the welfare and flourishing of his people, not only in maintaining and putting to execution the old allowable laws of the country, and by establishing of new (as necessity and evil manners will require), but by all other means possible to foresee and prevent all dangers, that are likely to fall upon them, and to maintain concord, wealth, and civility among them, as a loving father, and careful watchman, caring for them more than for himself, knowing himself to be ordained for them, and they not for him; and therefore countable to that great God, who placed him as his lieutenant over them, upon the peril of his soul to procure the welfare of both souls and bodies, as far as in him lies, of all them that are committed to his charge. And this oath in the coronation is the clearest, civil, and fundamental law, whereby the king's office is properly defined.

By the law of nature the king becomes a natural father to all his lieges at his coronation: and as the father of his fatherly duty[2] is bound to care for the nourishing, education, and virtuous government of his children; even so is the king bound to care for all his subjects. As all the toil and pain that the father can take for his children will be thought light and well bestowed by him, so that the effect thereof redound to their profit and welfare; so ought the prince to do towards his people. As the kindly father ought to foresee all inconveniences and dangers that may arise towards his children, and though with the hazard of his own person press to prevent the same; so ought the king towards his people. As the father's wrath and correction upon any of his children that offends ought to be by a fatherly chastisement seasoned with pity, as long as there is any hope of amendment in them; so ought the king towards any of his lieges that offend in that measure. And shortly, as the father's chief joy ought to be in procuring his children's welfare, rejoicing at their welfare, sorrowing and pitying at their evil, to hazard for their safety, travail for their rest, wake for their sleep; and in a word, to think that his earthly felicity and life stands and lives more in them, nor in himself; so ought a good prince think of his people.

As to the other branch of this mutual and reciprocal band, is the duty and allegiance that the lieges owe to their king: the ground whereof, I take out of the words of Samuel cited by God's Spirit, when God had given him commandment to hear the people's voice in choosing and annointing them a king. And because that place of Scripture being well understood, is so pertinent for our purpose, I have inserted herein the very words of the text.

9 *Now therefore hearken to their voice: howbeit yet testify unto them, and show them the manner of the King, that shall reign over them.*

---

2. Compare this use of the similitude of fatherhood to that of Aquinas.

10 *So* Samuel *told all the words of the Lord unto the people that asked a King of him.*
11 *And he said, This shall be the manner of the King that shall reign over you: he will take your sons, and appoint them to his Chariots, and to be his horsemen, and some shall run before his Chariot.*
12 *Also, he will make them his captains over thousands, and captains over fifties and to care his ground, and to reap his harvest, and to make instruments of war and the things that serve for his Chariots:*
13 *He will also take your daughters, and make them Apothicaries, and Cookes, and Bakers.*
14 *And he will take your fields, and your vineyards, and your best Olive trees, and give them to his servants.*
15 *And he will take the tenth of your seed, and of your Vineyards, and give it to his Eunuchs, and to his servants.*
16 *And he will take your men-servants, and your maid-servants, and the chief of your young men, and your asses, and put them to his work.*
17 *He will take the tenth of your sheep: and ye shall be his servants.*
18 *And ye shall cry out at that day, because of your King, whom ye have chosen you: and the Lord God will not hear you at that day.*
19 *But the people would not hear the voice of Samuel, but did say: Nay, but there shall be a King over us.*
20 *And we also will be like all other Nations, and our King shall judge us and go out before us and fight our battles.*

That these words, and discourses of Samuel were dictated by God's Spirit, it needs no further probation, but that it is a place of Scripture; since the whole Scripture is dictated by that inspiration, as Paul says: which ground no good Christian will, or dare, deny. . . . And to press to dissuade them from that, which he then came to grant unto them, were a thing very impertinent in a wise man; much more in the prophet of the most high God. And likewise, it well appeared in all the course of his life after, that his so long refusing of their suit before came not of any ambition in him: which he well proved in praying, and, as it were, importuning God for the welfare of Saul. Indeed, after God had declared his reprobation unto him, yet he desisted not, while God himself was wrath at his praying, and discharged his father's suit in that errand. And that these words of Samuel were not uttered as a prophecy of Saul their first King's defection, it well appeares, as well because we hear no mention made in the Scripture of any of his tyranny and oppression . . . as likewise in respect that Saul was chosen by God for his virtue, and meet qualities to govern his people: whereas his defection sprung after-hand from the corruption of his own nature and not through any default in God, whom they that think so, would make as a step-father to his people, in making wilfully a chase of the unmeetest for governing them, since the election of that king lay absolutely and immediately in God's hand. But by the contrary, it is plain, and evident, that this speech of Samuel to the people, was to prepare their hearts before the hand to the due obedience of that king, which God was to give unto them; and therefore opened up unto them, what might be the intolerable qualities that might fall in some of their kings, thereby preparing them to patience, not to resist to God's ordinance: but as he would have said; Since God hath granted your importunate suit in giving you a king, as you have else committed an error in shaking off God's yoke, and overhasty seeking of a king; so beware you fall not into the next error, in casting off also rashly that yoke, which God at your earnest suit has laid upon you, how hard that ever it seems to be: For as you could not have obtained one without the permission and ordinance of God, so may you no more, for he who is once set over you, shake him off without the same warrant. And therefore, in time, arm yourselves with patience and humility, since he that has the only power to make him, has the only power to umake him; and you only have to obey, bearing with these straits that I now foreshow you, as with the finger of God, which lies not in you to take off. [. . .]

Now then, since the erection of this kingdom and monarchy among the Jews, and the law thereof may, and ought to be a pattern to all Christian and well founded monarchies, as being founded by God himself, who by his oracle, and out of his own mouth gave the law thereof: what liberty can broiling spirits, and rebellious minds claim justly to against any Christian monarch; since they can claim to no greater liberty on their part, nor the people of God might have done, and no greater tyranny was ever executed by any prince or tyrant, whom they can object, nor was here forewarned to the people of God, (and yet all rebellion countermanded unto them) if tyrannizing over men's persons, sons, daughters and servants; reducing noble houses, and men, and women of noble blood, to slavish and servile offices; and extortion, and spoil of their lands and goods to the prince's own private use and commodity, and of his courtiers, and servants, may be called a tyrannic? [. . .]

And the agreement of the law of nature in this our ground with the laws and constitutions of God, and man, already alledged, will by two similitudes easily appear. The king towards his people is rightly compared to a father of children, and to a head of a body composed of divers members: for as fathers, the good princes, and magistrates of the people of God acknowledged themselves to their subjects. And for all other well ruled commonwealths, the style of *Pater patriae* was ever, and is commonly used to kings. And the proper office of a king towards his subjects, agrees very well with the office of the head towards the body, and all members thereof: for from the head, being the seat of judgement, proceeds the care and fore-sight of guiding, and preventing all evil that may come to the body or any part thereof. The head cares for the body, so does the king for his people. As the discourse and direction flows from the head, and the execution according hereunto belongs to the rest of the members, everyone according to their office: so is it between a wise prince, and his people. As the lodgement coming from the head may not only employ the members, everyone in their own office as long as they are able for it; but likewise in case any of them be affected with any infirmity must care and provide for their remedy, in case it be curable, and if otherwise, cut them off for fear of infecting of the rest: even so is it between the prince and his people. And as there is ever hope of curing any diseased member by the direction of the head, as long as it is whole; but by the contrary, if it be troubled, all the members are partakers of that pain, so is it between the prince and his people.

And now first for the father's part . . . [C]onsider, I pray you, what duty his children owe to him, and whether upon any pretext whatsoever, it will not be thought monstrous and unnaturall to his sons, to rise up against him, to control him at their appetite, and when they think good to slay him, or cut him off, and adopt to themselves any other they please in his room: Or can any presence of wickedness or rigour on his part be a just excuse for his children to put hand into him? And although we see by the course of nature, that love uses to descend more than to ascend, in case it were true that the father hated and wronged the children never so much, will any man, endued with the least seed of reason, think it lawful for them to meet him with the line? Indeed, suppose the father were furiously following his sons with a drawn sword, is it lawful for them to turn and strike again, or make any resistance but by flight? I think surely, if there were no more but the example of brute beasts and unreasonable creatures, it may serve well enough to qualify and prove this my argument.

And for the similitude of the head and the body, it may very well fall out that the head will be forced to cut off some rotten member (as I have already said) to keep the rest of the body in integrity: but what state the body can be in, if the head, for any infirmity that can fall to it, be cut off, I leave it to the reader's judgement. [. . .]

And in case any doubts might arise in any part of this treatise, I will (according to my promise) with the solution of four principal and most weighty doubts, that the adversaries may object, conclude this discourse. And first it is casten up by divers, that employ their pens upon apologies for rebellions and treasons, that every man is born to carry such a natural zeal and duty to his commonwealth, as to his mother; that seeing it so rent and deadly wounded, as whiles it will be by wicked and tyrannous kings, good citizens will be forced, for the natural zeal and duty they owe to their own native country, to put their hand to work for freeing their commonwealth from such a pest.

Whereunto I give two answers: First, it is a sure axiom in *theology*, that evil should not be done, that good may come of it: the wickedness therefore of the king can never make them that are ordained to be judged by him, to become his judges. And if it be not lawful to a private man to revenge his private injury upon his private adversary (since God has only given the sword to the magistrate) how much less is it lawful to the people, or any part of them (who all are but private men, the authority being alway with the magistrate, as I have already proved) to take upon them the use of the sword, whom to it belongs not, against the public magistrate, whom to only it belongs.

Next, in place of relieving the commonwealth out of distress (which is their only excuse and colour) they shall heap double distress and desolation upon it; and so their rebellion shall procure the contrary effects that they pretend it for: for a king cannot be imagined to be so unruly and tyrannous, but the commonwealth will be kept in better order, notwithstanding thereof, by him, than it can be by his way-taking. [. . .]

And next, it is certain that a king can never be so monstrously vicious, but he will generally favour justice, and maintain some order, except in the particulars,

97

wherein his inordinate lusts and passions carry him away; whereby the contrary, no king being, nothing is unlawful to none: and so the old opinion of the philosophers proves true, that better it is to live in a commonwealth, where nothing is lawful, than where all things are lawful to all men. [. . .]

The second objection they ground upon the curse that hangs over the commonwealth, where a wicked king reigns: and, say they, there cannot be a more acceptable deed in the sight of God, nor more dutiful to their commonweal, than to free the country of such a curse, and vindicate to them their liberty, which is natural to all creatures to crave.

Whereunto for answer, I grant indeed, that a wicked king is sent by God for a curse to his people, and a plague for their sins: but that it is lawful to them to shake off that curse at their own hand, which God has laid on them, that I deny, and may so do justly. [. . .]

It is certain then (as I have already by the law of God sufficiently proved) that patience, earnest prayers to God, and amendment of their lives, are the only lawful means to move God to relieve them of that heavy curse. As for vindicating to themselves their own liberty, what lawful power have they to revoke to themselves again those priviledges, which by their own consent before were so fully put out of their hands? For if a prince cannot justly bring back again to himself the priviledges once bestowed by him or his predecessors upon any state or rank of his subjects; how much less may the subjects reave out of the prince's hand that superiority, which he and his predecessors have so long brooked over them?

But the unhappy iniquity of the time, which has oft times given over good success to their treasonable attempts, furnishes them the ground of their third objection. For, say they, the fortunate success that God has so oft given to such enterprises, proves plainly by the practice, that God favoured the justness of their quarrel.

To the which I answer, that it is true indeed, that all the success of battles, as well as other worldly things, lies only in God's hand. [. . .] As likewise by all good writers, as well theologians, as other, the duels and singular combats are disallowed; which are only made upon presence, that God will bear thereby the justice of the quarrel: for we must consider that the innocent party is not innocent before God: and therefore God will make oft times them that have the wrong side revenge justly his quarrel; and when he has done, cast his scourge in the fire; as he oft times did to his own people, stirring up and strengthening their enemies, while they were humbled in his sight, and then delivered them in their hands. So God, as the great judge may justly punish his deputy, and for his rebellion against him, stir up his rebels to meet him with the like: and when it is done, the part of the instrument is no better then the devil's part is in tempting and torturing such as God commits to him as his hangman to do: therefore, as I said in the beginning, it is oft times a very deceiveable argument, to judge of the cause by the event.

And the last objection is grounded upon the mutual paction and adstipulation (as they call it) between the king and his people, at the time of his coronation: for there, say they, there is a mutual paction, and contract bound up, and sworn between the king and the people: whereupon it follows, that if the one part of the contract or the indent be broken upon the king's side, the people are no longer bound to keep their part of it, but are thereby freed of their oath: for (say they) a contract between two parties, of all law frees the one party, if the other break unto him.

As to this contract allegedly made at the coronation of a king, although I deny any such contract to be made then, especially containing such a clause irritant as they alledge; yet I confess, that a king at his coronation, or at the entry to his kingdom, willingly promises to his people, to discharge honourably and truly the office given him by God over them: but presuming that thereafter he breaks his promise unto them never so inexcusable; the question is, who should be judge of the break, giving unto them, this contract were made unto them never so certainly, according to their allegiance. I think no man that has but the smallest entrance into the civil law, will doubt that of all law, either civil or municipal of any nation, a contract cannot be thought broken by the one party, and so the other likewise to be freed therefrom, except that first a lawful trial and cognition be had by the ordin-ary judge of the breakers thereof: or else every man may be both party and judge in his own cause; which is absurd once to be thought. Now in this contract (I say) between the king and his people, *God is doubtless the only judge, both because to him only the king must make count of his administration* (as is often said before) as like-wise by the oath in the coronation, God is made judge and revenger of the break-ers: for in his presence, as only judge of oaths, all oaths ought to be made. Then since God is the only judge between the two parties' contractors, the cognition and revenge must only appertain to him: it follows therefore of necessity, that God must first give sentence upon the king that breaks, before the people can think themselves freed of their oath. What justice then is it, that the party shall be both judge and party, usurping upon himself the office of God, may by this argument easily appear: and shall it lie in the hands of headless multitude, when they please to weary off subjection, to cast off the yoke of government that God has laid upon them, to judge and punish him, by whom they should be judged and punished; and in that case, wherein by their violence they kythe themselves to be most pas-sionate parties, to use the office of an ungracious judge or arbiter? Nay, to speak truely of that case, as it stands between the king and his people, none of them ought to judge of the other's break: for considering rightly the two parties at the time of their mutual promise, the king is the one party, and the whole people in one body are the other party. And therefore since it is certain, that a king, in case so it should fall out, that his people in one body had rebelled against him, he should not in that case, as thinking himself free of his promise and oath, become an utter enemy, and practice the wreak of his whole people and native country: although he ought justly to punish the principal authors and fellows of that universall rebellion: how much less then ought the people (that are always subject unto him, and naked of all authority on their part) press to judge and overthrow him? Otherwise the people, as the one party's contractors, shall no sooner challenge the king as breaker, but he as soon shall judge them as breakers: so as the victors making the tyners the traitors (as our proverb is) the party shall always become both judge and party in his own particular, as I have already said.

And it is here likewise to be noted, that the duty and allegiance, which the people swears to their prince, is not only bound to themselves, but likewise to their lawful heirs and posterity, the linear succession of crowns being begun among the people of God, and happily continued in divers Christian commonwealths: so as no objection either of heresy, or whatsoever private statute or law may free the people from their oath-glueing to their king, and his succession, established by the old fundamental laws of the kingdom: for, as he is their heritable overlord, and so by birth; *not by any right in the coronation, comes to his crown;* it is a like unlawful (the crown ever standing full) to displace him that succeeds thereto, as to elect the former: for at the very moment of the expiring of the king reigning, the nearest and lawful heir enters in his place: and so to refuse him, or intrude another, is not to horde out uncoming in, but to expell and put out their righteous king. [. . .]

Not that by all this former discourse of mine, and apology for kings, I mean that whatsoever errors and intolerable abominations a sovereign prince commit, he ought to escape all punishment, as if thereby the world were only ordained for kings, and they without control to turn it upside down at their pleasure: but by the contrary, by remitting them to God (who is their only ordinary judge) I remit them to the sorest and sharpest schoolmaster that can be devised for them: for the *further a king is preferred by God above all other ranks and degrees of men,* and the higher that his seat is above theirs, the greater is his obligation to his maker. And therfore in case he forget himself . . . the sadder and sharper will his correction be; and according to the greatness of the height he is in, the weight of his fall will recompense the same: for the further that any person is obliged to God, his offence becomes and grows so much the greater, than it would be in any other. . . . Neither is it ever heard that any king forgets himself towards God, or in his vocation; but God with the greatness of the plague revenges the greatness of his ingratitude: neither think I by the force and argument of this my discourse so to persuade the people, that none will hereafter be raised up, and rebell against wicked princes. But remitting to the justice and providence of God to stir up such scourges as pleases him, for punishment of wicked kings . . . my only purpose and intention in this treatise is to persuade, as far as lies in me, by these sure and infallible grounds, all such good Christian readers, as bear not only the naked name of a Christian, but bear the fruits thereof in their daily form of life, to keep their hearts and hands free from such monstrous and unnatural rebellions, whensoever the wickedness of a prince shall procure the same at God's hands. [. . .]

But craving at God, and hoping that God shall continue his blessing with us in not sending such fearful desolation, I heartily wish our king's behaviour so to be, and continue among us, as our God in earth, and loving Father, endued with such properties as I described a king in the first part of this treatise. And that you (my dear countrymen, and charitable readers) may press by all means to procure the prosperity and welfare of your king; that as he must on the one part think all his earthly felicity and happiness grounded upon your welfare, caring more for himself for your sake than for his own, thinking himself only ordained for your welfare; such holy and happy emulation may arise between him and you, as his care for your quietness, and your care for his honour and preservation, may in all your actions daily strive together, that the land may think themselves blessed with such a king, and the king may think himself most happy in ruling over so loving and obedient subjects.

Chapter 7

Thomas Hobbes (1588–1674)

For as long as every man holds this right, of doing anything he likes; so long are all men in the condition of war.

Introduction

Thomas Hobbes is the first political theorist of the modern state. In his *magnum opus*, the *Leviathan*, published in 1651 (in three different editions), Hobbes' ambitious project is to give a complete explanation of 'the matter, form and power of the commonwealth'. As we will see later on, 'commonwealth' means not only the state, but also a social community as such. In fact, in *Leviathan* the origins of society, the purpose of a state, as well as the different functions of the state as an organic body of social relations, are discussed in detail. After Plato and Aristotle, Hobbes is truly a milestone in the history of political thought and his *Leviathan* is also a key text for the study of religion and politics. This is already evident from the programmatic subtitle ('The Matter, Form and Power of a Commonwealth Ecclesiastical and Civil'), which explicitly refers to the double nature of a commonwealth. Hobbes offers a theory of the commonwealth 'ecclesiastical and civil', that is a theory that includes the secular and temporal elements of the state. Compared to the previous thinkers we have treated so far – Augustine speaking from a theological–speculative perspective, Aquinas as a systematic theologian, Dante as a humanist, Luther as primarily a pastoral-political theologian, Machiavelli as a practitioner of *realpolitik* and James as a king – Hobbes developed a theory of the political in a modern sense of the word. His systematic account of the commonwealth follows a concise methodology and offers a rational explanation of the formation and function of the state including its religious dimensions. The fact that Hobbes considers religion as important as secular politics, or using his terminology, that the civil commonwealth and the ecclesiastical commonwealth are equally essential, separates his political theory from all the political thinkers after him. For almost 200 years in the history of political thought (the work of Bodin, Locke, Hume, Montesquieu and, last but not least, in Jean-Jacques Rousseau's *Social Contract*), religion as an integral element of political theory was increasingly marginalized. Therefore, Hobbes' engagement with religious issues can either be seen as an indication that he still belongs to the pre-modern era or that his work is contemporary.

An explanation for Hobbes' interest in religion and theological matters – some commentators even speak of a theological obsession – can be found in the historical circumstances of his time. Hobbes lived most of his active life in Stuart England (1603–1714). The reign of the Stuarts was shaped and often shaken by religious controversies among Presbyterians, Anglicans and Catholics. These controversies that ranged over liturgical and doctrinal orthodoxy split the people of England into different religious parties. This split was paralleled by political debates about legitimate forms of power and increased the degree of social fragmentation. The religious and political controversies reached the level of acts of terrorism, such as the attempted assassination of King James VI/I by Catholics, known as the 'Gunpowder Plot' of 1605, and culminated in the outbreak of the Civil War. The Civil War in England (1642–9), which ended with the execution of Charles I, son of James VI/I, was followed by the dictatorial rule of Oliver Cromwell (known as the Lord Protector). This rule left an indelible impression on Hobbes and his political–philosophical work. In general, during the Stuart period two competing concepts of sovereign power were in conflict with each other. This was the long-term background of the Civil War. As we have seen, the Royalist cause was embodied in the notion of the Divine Right of Kings. Whereas the Puritan cause was embodied in the notion of parliament as the source of legitimate supreme power. (This was a continuation of the conflict principles of hierarchy and proto-democratic congregationalism that we noted with Luther). The struggle between the Puritan and Royalist causes is reflected in Hobbes' *Leviathan* on a theoretical level.

Hobbes translated the historical conflict into the language of political science and this forms the theoretical backbone of *Leviathan*. Here the struggle between Royalists and Puritans appears as two opposing conceptions of political power. On the one hand, Hobbes outlines a *contractualist* and therefore Puritan understanding of political power, and, on the other, a theory based on the doctrine of the Divine Right of Kings rooted in the emphasis upon hierarchy in the Catholic tradition. But we should not forget that these two conflicting principles of political power are already germinating in the writings of Luther and have antecedents in the history of Christianity. The competition between monocratic, hierarchical forms of government and proto-democratic, collective forms of government date back to patristic times and can be found even in biblical texts (as outlined in the General Introduction).

Before we go into the details of Hobbes' systematic analysis of these two competing principles of political power, we have to make some remarks on *Leviathan* itself, from which excerpts have been taken. The political theory developed in *Leviathan* has both its predecessors and a successor. Most prominently, Hobbes' *Elements of Law Natural and Politic* (which circulated in handwritten copies from 1640) and his Latin *Elementorum Philosophiae Sectio Tertia De Cive* (usually called *De Cive*, in circulation from 1642) anticipate the themes of *Leviathan*. Twenty-eight years after *Leviathan* was published, Hobbes' history of the English Civil War, called *Behemoth*, appeared. From the dates and the titles of these last two books it is evident that Hobbes spent more than 35 years of his life analysing the relationship between religion and politics. *Leviathan* is the exemplary expression of this analysis. It is composed of four parts, of which the two larger parts are conceived as explorations into what Hobbes calls 'a Christian Commonwealth' and 'the Kingdom of Darkness'. If we consider the frontispiece as an icon, which introduces the central theme of *Leviathan* and represents the twofold nature of the commonwealth (the civil and ecclesiastical components of the state), then the theological–political nature of *Leviathan* is even clearer. There is a continuing debate about whether Hobbes' theological reflections are relevant for understanding his political theory or they simply reflect the historical context of his times. Whatever the outcome of these discussions will be, it is undeniable that for Hobbes a theory of the political without any consideration of the religious would have been incomplete, if not impossible.

In the first part we will introduce Hobbes' anthropological assumptions on which his political theory is based. In the second part is raised the question of sovereignty in a technical and practical sense. In addition to these two main topics, we have included parts of the Introduction because at the beginning of *Leviathan* Hobbes makes reference to the body metaphor. Until Hobbes, the political use of the body metaphor was always understood theologically. The effectiveness of the body metaphor consists in the imaginary analogy between a social community and the human body, as we have with Aquinas, Dante and Luther. In St Paul's use of the body metaphor, the head represents Christ and all the organs and limbs represent the individual functions within a community. The difference is that in the Introduction to *Leviathan*, Hobbes does not refer to the Pauline context of the body metaphor, but he retains its theological sense by deploying it technically: 'Nature (the activity by which God hath made and governs the world) is by the art of man, as in many other things, so in this also imitated, that it can make an artificial animal. . . . Art goes yet further, imitating that rational and most excellent work of Nature, man. For by art is created that great LEVIATHAN called a COMMON WEALTH, or STATE (in Latin, CIVITAS), which is but an artificial man, though of greater stature and strength than the natural, for whose protection and defence it was intended'.

Hobbes has a mechanical understanding of the functions of the body. He even compares it with a machine. His task in the book is to analyse the nature of this machine and its construction. Through it Hobbes can provide a rationale for the creation of the commonwealth. Human beings create the artificial man to protect and defend each individual member. According to Hobbes' image of this 'artificial body', political science is nothing other than its anatomy. So the question of what holds this body together can be translated into an investigation of the binding forces of the social community. The nature of these binding forces is key to Hobbes' political theory. Before undertaking the investigation into the nature of these binding forces (that is, how they arise as well as how they are preserved), Hobbes offers a hypothetical reconstruction of the natural state of human beings. He imagines the condition of a 'society' prior to any form of social association between human beings in order to explain why and how these social relations came into existence. This reconstruction of a pre-societal 'society' is summoned up in Hobbes' famous formula of the *war of each man against the other*. This is expressed in the Latin phrase: *homo homini lupus* (a man is a wolf towards another man). Hobbes was frequently attacked for his negative anthropology. But why is warfare the natural condition of humankind? Hobbes' explanation is astonishing and, as we shall see, wrong. He claims that all human beings are primarily equal. Despite natural differences of physical strength and personal abilities, Hobbes is convinced that human beings are equal because anyone can theoretically kill with assistance. In his words: 'For as the strength of body, the weakest has strength enough to kill the strongest, either by secret machination or by confederation with others that are in the same danger as himself'. From this equal opportunity to kill, Hobbes infers that all humans have an equal desire for the same objects. From this arises a situation of enmity and competition among individuals. As he writes: 'From this equality of ability ariseth equality of hope in the attaining of our ends. And therefore if any two men desire the same thing, which nevertheless they cannot both enjoy, they become enemies'. The equality of humans leads inevitably to enmity and that is why the natural condition is not peace but war.

But is this really true? Two kinds of objection can be raised. First, Hobbes' reconstruction of the pre-social can be criticized. Reconstructions do not describe historical situations. They are theoretical *re*-constructions that offer explanations for reality. Thus a reconstruction where all the individuals of a 'society' are at war against each other has only a hypothetical status. Hobbes is aware of the hypothetical nature of his assumption of a social war and the difficulties in universalizing this thesis: 'It may peradventure be thought there was never such a time nor condition of war as this; and I believe it was never generally so, over all the world: but there are many places where they live so now'. A second objection can be raised, which for Hobbes is more serious. As we have seen, the basic assumption of Hobbes' negative anthropology is the equality of people. This equality results from the equal opportunity to kill either by 'secret machination' or by 'confederation with others', as Hobbes says. But this implies pre-existing forms of association. In other words, social bonds are both the precondition for a successful plot and collaboration. But the aim of this reconstruction was to provide an account of why and how sociality emerged. Technically this is called a *petitio principii*, a logically fallacious reasoning in which what has to be proved is already assumed.

So Hobbes' reconstruction of the condition of a natural society is contestable. But what about the rest of his political theory? If we accept the natural condition of war against each other, then the question is: how can we escape this situation? Is it possible to overcome the condition of war? Hobbes' answer to this question is twofold. The two conditions for the possibility of escape are: a) the existence of a common power which keeps all individual subjects in fear and awe; and b) a network of mutual contracts which fosters a community of equals. The first solution is a hierarchical or vertical one and the second is an egalitarian or horizontal one. (We have encountered this before with Martin Luther.) As we shall see later on, the horizontal cannot exist without the vertical. That is, an egalitarian network of mutual contracts between individuals cannot exist without a supreme power common to all members of this network. These two solutions define the extreme positions of a theory of the maintenance of a social community and a general theory of power. The historical struggle between Royalists and Puritans, between those who believed in the Divine Right of Kings and those who advocated proto-democratic forms of legitimate political authority is reflected in both solutions. It is worth examining both solutions in detail. Hobbes writes: '[I]t is manifest that during the time men live without a common power to keep them all in awe, they are in that condition that is called war; and such war is of every man against every man'. Furthermore, 'Whatsoever therefore is consequent to the time of war, where every man is enemy to every man, the same is consequent to the time wherein men live without other security than what their own strength and their own invention shall furnish them withal. In such a condition there is no place for industry, the fruit thereof is uncertain: and consequently no culture on earth . . .'.

Here Hobbes sees the solution to the problem of natural war as the existence of a sovereign power which keeps human beings in *awe*, forcing them to collaborate and thus constituting the basis for culture. But is a coercive power really the only possibility for peace? Is it really true that individuals are always 'selfish, nasty and brutal'? Not at all. Human beings are rational animals who are capable of communicating and are therefore able to negotiate their interests. Moreover, Hobbes has to admit that human beings prefer to live in peace rather than at war. The first step in overcoming the condition of war without the call for the coercive force of a common power is to lay aside someone's personal right: 'that a man be willing, when others are so too, as far forth as for peace and defence of himself he shall think it necessary, to lay down his right to all things and be contented with so much liberty against other men as he would allow other men against himself.' Negatively formulated: 'For as long as every man holdeth this right, of doing anything he liketh, so long are all men in the condition of war'.

This second step in overcoming the condition of war is based on a reciprocal transfer of rights. Two individuals come to an agreement which is transferring his/her personal rights to another. This mutual exchange of rights is called *contract* and is the basis for the association of people. So contract is the initial step in the process of formation of a society. Put as a principle, this can be paraphrased as: 'Whatsoever you require that others should do to you, that do ye to them'. (In the nineteenth century this principle, negatively formulated, serves as the basis for liberalism, explicitly expressed in J. S. Mill's definition of liberty: 'That the sole end for which mankind are warranted, individually or collectively, in interfering with liberty of action of any of their number, is self protection. That the only purpose for which power can be rightfully exercised over any member of a civilized community, against his will, is to prevent harm to others.'[1] It is important to stress that the contractual theory of society which, after Hobbes, became so influential in the political thinking of Locke, Hume and Rousseau, is just one element of Hobbes' theory of the commonwealth. Hobbes differs from the classical contractual theorists in that he remained sceptical about the goodwill of the people. For Hobbes, the binding force of contracts (which is merely the binding force of an exchange of words) is not strong enough to establish peace and maintain the social body.

1. J. S. Mill (1962), *Utilitarianism, Liberty, Representative Government* (London: Dent), pp. 72–3.

Once again the concept of a supreme power is needed to guarantee and safeguard the contractual bonds between people. Hobbes distinguishes two forms of supreme power. One is the 'power of spirits invisible', namely God; the other is 'the power of those men they shall therein offend'. This distinction sounds familiar and is, in fact, a reiteration of the longstanding, binary opposition of temporal and spiritual authority. Compared to the classical version of the temporal/spiritual distinction, Hobbes situates this dichotomy in a different context. The concepts of spiritual and temporal authority are now embedded in a theory of social contract. In other words, for a society based on reciprocal contracts, a common power is needed to keep people in fear so that they don't break their word. The common power is designed to safeguard the old Roman axiom: *pacta sunt servanda* ('you must not break contracts'). This common power can either be a spiritual or a temporal authority – or both. Hobbes clearly prefers the integration of spiritual and temporal authority in a single sovereign, illustrated by the frontispiece to *Leviathan*.

Further reading

General introductions

Hinnant, C. (1980), *Thomas Hobbes: A Reference Guide* (Boston, MA: G.K. Hall).
Hobbes, T., Flathman, E., Johnston, D. (1997), *Leviathan: Authoritative Text, Backgrounds, Interpretations* (London: W. W. Norton and Company).
Martinich, A. (2005), *Thomas Hobbes* (New York: Routledge).
Sorell, T. (1996), *The Cambridge Companion to Hobbes* (Cambridge: Cambridge University Press).

Reception of key ideas

Boucher, D. and Kelly P. (1994), *The Social Contract from Hobbes to Rawls* (New York: Routledge).
Oakeshott, M. (1975), *Hobbes on Civil Association* (Oxford: Blackwell).
Skinner, Q. (1996), *Reason and Rhetoric in the Philosophy of Hobbes* (Cambridge: Cambridge University Press).

Excerpt from *Leviathan**

Introduction

NATURE (the art whereby God has made and governs the world) is by the art of man, as in many other things, so in this also imitated, that it can make an artificial animal. For seeing life is but a motion of limbs, the beginning whereof is in some principal part within, why may we not say that all *automata* (engines that move themselves by springs and wheels as does a watch) have an artificial life? For what is the heart, but a spring; and the nerves, but so many strings; and the joints, but

---

* Italics have been added by the editors for emphasis.

so many wheels, giving motion to the whole body, such as was intended by the Artificer? Art goes yet further, imitating that rational and most excellent work of Nature, man. For by art is created that great LEVIATHAN called a COMMONWEALTH, or STATE (in Latin, CIVITAS), which is but an artificial man, though of greater stature and strength than the natural, for whose protection and defence it was intended; and in which the sovereignty is an artificial soul, as giving life and motion to the whole body; the magistrates and other officers of judicature and execution, artificial joints; reward and punishment (by which fastened to the seat of the sovereignty, every joint and member is moved to perform his duty) are the nerves, that do the same in the body natural; the wealth and riches of all the particular members are the strength; salus populi (the people's safety) its business; counsellors, by whom all things needful for it to know are suggested unto it, are the memory; equity and laws, an artificial reason and will; concord, health; sedition, sickness; and civil war, death. Lastly, the pacts and covenants, by which the parts of this body politic were at first made, set together, and united, resemble that fiat, or the 'Let us make man', pronounced by God in the Creation.

Chapter 13: Of the natural condition of mankind as concerning their felicity and misery

NATURE has made men so equal in the faculties of body and mind as that, though there be found one man sometimes manifestly stronger in body or of quicker mind than another, yet when all is reckoned together the difference between man and man is not so considerable as that one man can thereupon claim to himself any benefit to which another may not pretend as well as he. For as to the strength of body, the weakest has strength enough to kill the strongest, either by secret machination or by confederacy with others that are in the same danger with himself.

And as to the faculties of the mind, setting aside the arts grounded upon words, and especially that skill of proceeding upon general and infallible rules, called science, which very few have and but in few things, as being not a native faculty born with us, nor attained, as prudence, while we look after somewhat else, I find yet a greater equality amongst men than that of strength. For prudence is but experience, which equal time equally bestows on all men in those things they equally apply themselves unto. That which may perhaps make such equality incredible is but a vain conceit of one's own wisdom, which almost all men think they have in a greater degree than the vulgar; that is, than all men but themselves, and a few others, whom by fame, or for concurring with themselves, they approve. For such is the nature of men that howsoever they may acknowledge many others to be more witty, or more eloquent, or more learned, yet they will hardly believe there be many so wise as themselves; for they see their own wit at hand, and other men's at a distance. But this proves rather that men are in that point more equal, than unequal. For there is not ordinarily a greater sign of the equal distribution of anything than that every man is contented with his share.

From this equality of ability arises equality of hope in the attaining of our ends. And therefore if any two men desire the same thing, which nevertheless they cannot both enjoy, they become enemies; and in the way to their end (which is principally their own conservation, and sometimes their delectation only) endeavour to destroy or subdue one another. And from hence it comes to pass that where an invader has no more to fear than another man's single power, if one plant, sow, build, or possess a convenient seat, others may probably be expected to come prepared with forces united to dispossess and deprive him, not only of the fruit of his labour, but also of his life or liberty. And the invader again is in the like danger of another.

And from this diffidence of one another, there is no way for any man to secure himself so reasonable as anticipation; that is, by force, or wiles, to master the persons of all men he can so long till he see no other power great enough to endanger him: and this is no more than his own conservation requires, and is generally allowed. Also, because there be some that, taking pleasure in contemplating their own power in the acts of conquest, which they pursue farther than their security requires, if others, that otherwise would be glad to be at ease within modest bounds, should not by invasion increase their power, they would not be able, long time, by standing only on their defence, to subsist. And by consequence, such augmentation of dominion over men being necessary to a man's conservation, it ought to be allowed him.

Again, men have no pleasure (but on the contrary a great deal of grief) in keeping company where there is no power able to overawe them all. For every man looks that his companion should value him at the same rate he sets upon himself, and upon all signs of contempt or undervaluing naturally endeavours, as far as he dares (which amongst them that have no common power to keep them in quiet is far enough to make them destroy each other), to extort a greater value from his contemners, by damage; and from others, by the example.

So that in the nature of man, we find three principal causes of quarrel: first, competition; secondly, diffidence; thirdly, glory.

The first makes men invade for gain; the second, for safety; and the third, for reputation. The first use violence, to make themselves masters of other men's persons, wives, children, and cattle; the second, to defend them; the third, for trifles, as a word, a smile, a different opinion, and any other sign of undervalue, either direct in their persons or by reflection in their kindred, their friends, their nation, their profession, or their name.

Hereby it is manifest that during the time men live *without a common power to keep them all in awe, they are in that condition which is called war; and such a war as is of every man against every man.* For war consisteth not in battle only, or the act of fighting, but in a tract of time, wherein the will to contend by battle is sufficiently known: and therefore the notion of time is to be considered in the nature of war, as it is in the nature of weather. For as the nature of foul weather lies not in a shower or two of rain, but in an inclination thereto of many days together: so the nature of war consists not in actual fighting, but in the known disposition thereto during all the time there is no assurance to the contrary. All other time is peace.

Whatsoever therefore is consequent to a time of war, where every man is enemy to every man, the same is consequent to the time wherein men live without other security than what their own strength and their own invention shall furnish them withal. In such condition there is no place for industry, because the fruit thereof is uncertain: and consequently no culture of the earth; no navigation, nor use of the commodities that may be imported by sea; no commodious building; no instruments of moving and removing such things as require much force; no knowledge of the face of the earth; no account of time; no arts; no letters; no society; and which is worst of all, continual fear, and danger of violent death; and the *life of man, solitary, poor, nasty, brutish, and short.*

It may seem strange to some man that has not well weighed these things that nature should thus dissociate and render men apt to invade and destroy one another: and he may therefore, not trusting to this inference, made from the passions, desire perhaps to have the same confirmed by experience. Let him therefore consider with himself: when taking a journey, he arms himself and seeks to go well accompanied; when going to sleep, he locks his doors; when even in his house he locks his chests; and this when he knows there be laws and public officers, armed, to revenge all injuries shall be done him; what opinion he has of his fellow subjects, when he rides armed; of his fellow citizens, when he locks his doors; and of his children, and servants, when he locks his chests. Does he not there as much accuse mankind by his actions as I do by my words? But neither of us accuse man's nature in it. The desires, and other passions of man, are in themselves no sin. No more are the actions that proceed from those passions till they know a law that forbids them; which till laws be made they cannot know, nor can any law be made till they have agreed upon the person that shall make it.

It may peradventure be thought there was never such a time nor condition of war as this; and I believe it was never generally so, over all the world: but there are many places where they live so now. [. . .]

But though there had never been any time wherein particular men were in a condition of war one against another, yet in all times kings and persons of sovereign authority, because of their independency, are in continual jealousies, and in the state and posture of gladiators, having their weapons pointing, and their eyes fixed on one another; that is, their forts, garrisons, and guns upon the frontiers of their kingdoms, and continual spies upon their neighbours, which is a posture of war. But because they uphold thereby the industry of their subjects, there does not follow from it that misery which accompanies the liberty of particular men.

To this war of every man against every man, this also is consequent; that nothing can be unjust. The notions of right and wrong, justice and injustice, have there no place. Where there is no common power, there is no law; where no law, no injustice. Force and fraud are in war the two cardinal virtues. Justice and injustice are none of the faculties neither of the body nor mind. If they were, they might be in a man that were alone in the world, as well as his senses and passions. They are qualities that relate to men in society, not in solitude. It is consequent also to the same condition that there be no propriety, no dominion, no mine and thine distinct; but only that to be every man's that he can get, and for so long as he can keep it. And thus much for the ill condition which man by mere nature is actually placed in; though with a possibility to come out of it, consisting partly in the passions, partly in his reason.

The passions that incline men to peace are: fear of death; desire of such things as are necessary to commodious living; and a hope by their industry to obtain them. And reason suggests convenient articles of peace upon which men may be drawn to agreement. These articles are they which otherwise are called the laws of nature, whereof I shall speak more particularly in the two following chapters.

Chapter 14: Of the first and second natural laws, and of contracts

The right of nature, which writers commonly call *ius naturale*, is the liberty each man has to use his own power as he will himself for the preservation of his own nature; that is to say, of his own life; and consequently, of doing anything which, in his own judgement and reason, he shall conceive to be the aptest means thereunto.

By liberty is understood, according to the proper signification of the word, the absence of external impediments; which impediments may oft take away part of a man's power to do what he would, but cannot hinder him from using the power left him according as his judgement and reason shall dictate to him.

A law of nature, *lex naturalis*, is a precept, or general rule, found out by reason, by which a man is forbidden to do that which is destructive of his life, or takes away the means of preserving the same, and to omit that by which he thinks it may be best preserved. For though they that speak of this subject use to confound *ius* and *lex*, right and law, yet they ought to be distinguished, because right consists in liberty to do, or to forbear; whereas law determines and binds to one of them: so that law and right differ as much as obligation and liberty, which in one and the same matter are inconsistent. [. . .]

From this fundamental law of nature, by which men are commanded to endeavour peace, is derived this second law: that a man be willing, *when others are so too*, as far forth as for peace and defence of himself he shall think it necessary, to lay down this right to all things; and be contented with so much liberty against other men as he would allow other men against himself. For as long as every man holds this right, of doing anything he likes; so long are all men in the condition of war. But if other men will not lay down their right, as well as he, then there is no reason for anyone to divest himself of his: for that were to expose himself to prey, which no man is bound to, rather than to dispose himself to peace. This is that law of the gospel: Whatsoever you require that others should do to you, that do you to them. And that law of all men, *quod tibi fieri non vis, alteri ne feceris*. [. . .]

Right is laid aside, either by simply renouncing it, or by transferring it to another. By simply renouncing, when he cares not to whom the benefit thereof redounds. By transferring, when he intends the benefit thereof to some certain person or persons. And when a man has in either manner abandoned or granted away his right, then is he said to be obliged, or bound, not to hinder those to whom such right is granted, or abandoned, from the benefit of it: and that he ought, and it is duty, not to make void that voluntary act of his own: and that such hindrance is injustice, and injury, as being *sine iure*; the right being before renounced or transferred. So that injury or injustice, in the controversies of the world, is somewhat like to that which in the disputations of scholars is called absurdity. For as it is there called an absurdity to contradict what one maintained in the beginning; so in the world it is called injustice, and injury voluntarily to undo that which from the beginning he had voluntarily done. The way by which a man either simply renounces or transferres his right is a declaration, or signification, by some voluntary and sufficient sign, or signs, that he does so renounce or transfer, or has so renounced or transferred the same, to him that accepts it. And these signs are either words only, or actions only; or, as it happens most often, both words and actions. And the same are the bonds, by which men are bound and obliged: bonds that have their strength, not from their own nature (for nothing is more easily broken than a man's word), but from fear of some evil consequence upon the rupture.

Whensoever a man transfers his right, or renounces it, it is either in consideration of some right reciprocally transferred to himself, or for some other good he hopes for thereby. For it is a voluntary act: and of the voluntary acts of every man, the object is some good to himself. And therefore there be some rights which no man can be understood by any words, or other signs, to have abandoned or transferred. As first a man cannot lay down the right of resisting them that assault him by force to take away his life, because he cannot be understood to aim thereby at any good to himself. [. . .] And lastly the motive and end for which this renouncing and transferring of right is introduced is nothing else but the security of a man's person, in his life, and in the means of so preserving life as not to be weary of it. And therefore if a man by words, or other signs, seems to despoil himself of the end for which those signs were intended, he is not to be understood as if he meant it, or that it was his will, but that he was ignorant of how such words and actions were to be interpreted. *The mutual transferring of right is that which men call contract.*

There is difference between transferring of right to the thing, the thing, and transferring or tradition, that is, delivery of the thing itself. For the thing may be delivered together with the translation of the right, as in buying and selling with ready money, or exchange of goods or lands, and it may be delivered some time after.

Again, one of the contractors may deliver the thing contracted for on his part, and leave the other to perform his part at some determinate time after, and in the meantime be trusted; and then the contract on his part is called pact, or covenant: or both parts may contract now to perform hereafter, in which cases he that is to perform in time to come, being trusted, his performance is called keeping of promise, or faith, and the failing of performance, if it be voluntary, violation of faith.

When the transferring of right is not mutual, but one of the parties transfers in hope to gain thereby friendship or service from another, or from his friends; or in hope to gain the reputation of charity, or magnanimity; or to deliver his mind from the pain of compassion; or in hope of reward in heaven; this is not contract, but gift, free gift, grace: which words signify one and the same thing. [. . .]

If a covenant be made wherein neither of the parties perform presently, but trust one another, in the condition of mere nature (which is a condition of war of every man against every man) upon any reasonable suspicion, it is void: but if there be a *common power* set over them both, with right and force sufficient to compel performance, it is not void. For he that performs first has no assurance the other will perform after, because the bonds of words are too weak to bridle men's ambition, avarice, anger, and other passions, without the fear of some coercive power; which in the condition of mere nature, where all men are equal, and judges of the justness of their own fears, cannot possibly be supposed. And therefore he which performs first does but betray himself to his enemy, contrary to the right he can never abandon of defending his life and means of living.

But in a civil estate, where there is a power set up to constrain those that would otherwise violate their faith, that fear is no more reasonable; and for that cause, he which by the covenant is to perform first is obliged so to do.

The cause of fear, which makes such a covenant invalid, must be always something arising after the covenant made, as some new fact or other sign of the will not to perform, else it cannot make the covenant void. For that which could not hinder a man from promising ought not to be admitted as a hindrance of performing.

He that transfers any right transfers the means of enjoying it, as far as lies in his power. As he that sells land is understood to transfer the herbage and whatsoever grows upon it; nor can he that sells a mill turn away the stream that drives it. And they that give to a man the right of government in sovereignty are understood to give him the right of levying money to maintain soldiers, and of appointing magistrates for the administration of justice.

To make covenants with brute beasts is impossible, because not understanding our speech, they understand not, nor accept of any translation of right, nor can translate any right to another: and without mutual acceptation, there is no covenant.

To make covenant with God is impossible but by mediation of such as God speaks to, either by revelation supernatural or by His lieutenants that govern under Him and in His name: for otherwise we know not whether our covenants be accepted or not. And therefore they that vow anything contrary to any law of nature, vow in vain, as being a thing unjust to pay such vow. And if it be a thing commanded by the law of nature, it is not the vow, but the law that binds them.

The matter or subject of a covenant is always something that falls under deliberation, for to covenant is an act of the will; that is to say, an act, and the last act, of deliberation; and is therefore always understood to be something to come, and which judged possible for him that covenants to perform.

And therefore, to promise that which is known to be impossible is no covenant. But if that prove impossible afterwards, which before was thought possible, the covenant is valid and binding, though not to the thing itself, yet to the value; or, if that also be impossible, to the unfeigned endeavour of performing as much as is possible, for to more no man can be obliged.

Men are freed of their covenants two ways; by performing, or by being forgiven. For performance is the natural end of obligation, and forgiveness the restitution of liberty, as being a retransferring of that right in which the obligation consisted.

Covenants entered into by fear, in the condition of mere nature, are obligatory. For example, if I covenant to pay a ransom, or service for my life, to an enemy, I am bound by it. For it is a contract, wherein one receives the benefit of life; the other is to receive money, or service for it, and consequently, where no other law (as in the condition of mere nature) forbids the performance, the covenant is valid. Therefore prisoners of war, if trusted with the payment of their ransom, are obliged to pay it: and if a weaker prince make a disadvantageous peace with a stronger, for fear, he is bound to keep it; unless (as has been said before) there arises some new and just cause of fear to renew the war. [. . .]

A covenant not to defend myself from force, by force, is always void. For (as I have shown before) no man can transfer or lay down his right to save himself from death, wounds, and imprisonment, the avoiding whereof is the only end of laying down any right; and therefore the promise of not resisting force, in no covenant transfers any right, nor is obliging. For though a man may covenant thus, unless I do so, or so, kill me; he cannot covenant thus, unless I do so, or so, I will not resist you when you come to kill me. For man by nature chooses the lesser evil, which is danger of death in resisting, rather than the greater, which is certain and present death in not resisting. And this is granted to be true by all men, in that they lead criminals to execution, and prison, with armed men, notwithstanding that such criminals have consented to the law by which they are condemned. [. . .]

The force of words being (as I have formerly noted) too weak to hold men to the performance of their covenants, there are in man's nature but two imaginable helps to strengthen it. And those are either a *fear of the consequence of breaking their word*, or a *glory or pride in appearing not to need to break it*. This latter is a generosity too rarely found to be presumed on, especially in the pursuers of wealth, command, or sensual pleasure, which are the greatest part of mankind. The passion to be reckoned upon is fear; whereof there be two very general objects: one, the power of *spirits invisible*; the other, *the power of those men they shall therein offend*. Of these two, though the former be the greater power, yet the fear of the latter is commonly the greater fear. The fear of the former is in every man his own religion, which has place in the nature of man before civil society. The latter has not so; at least not place enough to keep men to their promises, because in the condition of mere nature, the inequality of power is not discerned, but by the event of battle. So that before the time of civil society, or in the interruption thereof by war, there is nothing can strengthen a covenant of peace agreed on against the temptations of avarice, ambition, lust, or other strong desire, but the fear of that invisible power which they every one worship as God, and fear as a revenger of their perfidy. All therefore that can be done between two men not subject to civil power is to put one another to swear by the God he fears: which swearing, or oath, is a form of speech, added to a promise, by which he that promises signifies that unless he perform he renounces the mercy of his God, or calls to him for vengeance on himself. Such was the heathen form, 'Let Jupiter kill me else, as I kill this beast'. So is our form, I shall do thus, and thus, so help me God. And this, with the rites and ceremonies which every one uses in his own religion, that the fear of breaking faith might be the greater.

By this it appears that an oath taken according to any other form, or rite, than his that swears is in vain and no oath, and that there is no swearing by anything which the swearer thinks not God. For though men have sometimes used to swear

THOMAS HOBBES (1588–1674)

by their kings, for fear, or flattery; yet they would have it thereby understood they attributed to them divine honour. And that swearing unnecessarily by God is but profaning of his name: and swearing by other things, as men do in common discourse, is not swearing, but an impious custom, gotten by too much vehemence of talking.

It appears also that the oath adds nothing to the obligation. For a covenant, if lawful, binds in the sight of God, without the oath, as much as with it; if unlawful, binds not at all, though it be confirmed with an oath.

Chapter 31: Of the Kingdom of God by nature

That the condition of mere nature, that is to say, of absolute liberty, such as is theirs that neither are sovereigns nor subjects, is anarchy and the condition of war: that the precepts, by which men are guided to avoid that condition, are the laws of nature: that a commonwealth without sovereign power is but a word without substance and cannot stand: that subjects owe to sovereigns simple obedience in all things wherein their obedience is not repugnant to the laws of God, I have sufficiently proved in that which I have already written. There wants only, for the entire knowledge of civil duty, to know what are those laws of God. For without that, a man knows not, when he is commanded anything by the civil power, whether it be contrary to the law of God or not: and so, either by too much civil obedience offends the Divine Majesty, or, through fear of offending God, transgresses the commandments of the commonwealth. To avoid both these rocks, it is necessary to know what are the laws divine. And seeing the knowledge of all law depends on the knowledge of the sovereign power. [. . .]

'God is King, let the earth rejoice,' (Psalms, 97, 1) says the psalmist. And again, 'God is King though the nations be angry; and he that sits on the cherubim, though the earth be moved' (*Ibid.*, 99, 10). Whether men will or not, they must be subject always to the divine power. By denying the existence or providence of God, men may shake off their ease, but not their yoke. But to call this power of God, which extends itself not only to man, but also to beasts, and plants, and bodies inanimate, by the name of kingdom, is but a metaphorical use of the word. For he only is properly said to reign that governs his subjects by his word and by promise of rewards to those that obey it, by threatening them with punishment that obey it not. Subjects therefore in the kingdom of God are not bodies inanimate, nor creatures irrational; because they understand no precepts as his: nor atheists, nor they that believe not that God has any care of the actions of mankind; because they acknowledge no word for his, nor have hope of his rewards, or fear of his threatenings. They therefore that believe there is a God that governs the world, and has given precepts, and propounded rewards and punishments to mankind, are God's subjects; all the rest are to be understood as enemies.

To rule by words requires that such words be manifestly made known; for else they are no laws: for to the nature of laws belongs a sufficient and clear promulgation, such as may take away the excuse of ignorance; which in the laws of men is but of one only kind, and that is, proclamation or promulgation by the voice of man. But God declares his laws three ways; by the dictates of natural reason, by revelation, and by the voice of some man to whom, by the operation of miracles, he procures credit with the rest. From hence there arises a triple word of God, rational, sensible, and prophetic; to which corresponds a triple hearing: right reason, sense supernatural, and faith. As for sense supernatural, which consists in revelation or inspiration, there have not been any universal laws so given, because God speaks not in that manner but to particular persons, and to diverse men diverse things. [. . .]

The right of nature whereby God reignes over men, and punishes those that break his laws, is to be derived, not from His creating them, as if He required obedience as of gratitude for His benefits, but from His irresistible power. I have formerly shown how *the sovereign right arises from pact*: to show how the same right may arise from nature requires no more but to show in what case it is never taken away. Seeing all men by nature had right to all things, they had right every one to reign over all the rest. But because this right could not be obtained by force, it concerned the safety of every one, laying by that right, to set up men, with sovereign authority, by *common consent*, to rule and defend them: whereas if there had been any man of power irresistible, there had been no reason why he should not by that power have ruled and defended both himself and them, according to his own discretion. To those therefore whose power is irresistible, the dominion of all men adheres naturally by their excellence of power; and consequently it is from that power that the kingdom over men, and the right of afflicting men at his pleasure, belongs naturally to God Almighty; not as Creator and gracious, but as omnipotent. [. . .]

Chapter 42: Of power ecclesiastical

And first, we are to remember that the right of judging what doctrines are fit for peace, and to be taught the subjects, is in all commonwealths inseparably annexed (as has been already proved . . .) to the sovereign power civil, whether it be in one man or in one assembly of men. For it is evident to the meanest capacity that men's actions are derived from the opinions they have of the good or evil which from those actions redound unto themselves; and consequently, men that are once possessed of an opinion that their obedience to the sovereign power will be more hurtful to them than their disobedience will disobey the laws, and thereby overthrow the commonwealth, and introduce confusion and civil war; for the avoiding whereof, all civil government was ordained. And therefore in all commonwealths of the heathen, the sovereigns have had the name of pastors of the people, because there was no subject that could lawfully teach the people, but by their permission and authority. This right of the heathen kings cannot be thought taken from them by their conversion to the faith of Christ, who never ordained that kings, for believing in him, should be deposed, that is, subjected to any but himself, or, which is all one, be deprived of the power necessary for the conservation of peace amongst their subjects and for their defence against foreign enemies. And therefore Christian *kings are still the supreme pastors of their people*, and have power to ordain what pastors they please, to teach the Church, that is, to teach the people committed to their charge.

Again, let the right of choosing them be, as before the conversion of kings, in the Church, for so it was in the time of the Apostles themselves (as has been shown already in this chapter); even so also the right will be in the civil sovereign, Christian. For in that he is a Christian, he allows the teaching; and in that he is the sovereign (which is as much as to say, the Church by representation), the teachers he elects are elected by the Church. And when an assembly of Christians choose their pastor in a Christian commonwealth, it is the sovereign that electes him, because it is done by his authority; in the same manner as when a town choose their mayor, it is the act of him that has the sovereign power: for every act done is the act of him without whose consent it is invalid. And therefore whatsoever examples may be drawn out of history concerning the election of pastors by the people or by the clergy, they are no arguments against the right of any civil sovereign, because they that elected them did it by his authority.

Seeing then in every Christian commonwealth the *civil sovereign is the supreme pastor*, to whose charge the whole flock of his subjects is committed, and consequently that it is by his authority that all other pastors are made, and have power to teach and perform all other pastoral offices, it follows also that it is from the civil sovereign that all other pastors derive their right of teaching, preaching, and other functions pertaining to that office, and that they are but his ministers; in the same manner as magistrates of towns, judges in courts of justice, and commanders of armies are all but ministers of him that is the magistrate of the whole commonwealth, judge of all causes, and commander of the whole militia, which is always the civil sovereign. And the reason hereof is not because they that teach, but because they that are to learn, are his subjects. For let it be supposed that a Christian king commit the authority of ordaining pastors in his dominions to another king (as diverse Christian kings allow that power to the Pope), he does not thereby constitute a pastor over himself, nor a sovereign pastor over his people; for that were to deprive himself of the civil power; which, depending on the opinion men have of their duty to him, and the fear they have of punishment in another world, would depend also on the skill and loyalty of doctors who are no less subject, not only to ambition, but also to ignorance, than any other sort of men. So that where a stranger has authority to appoint teachers, it is given him by the sovereign in whose dominions he teaches. Christian doctors are our schoolmasters to Christianity; but kings are fathers of families, and may receive schoolmasters for their subjects from the recommendation of a stranger, but not from the command; especially when the ill teaching them shall redound to the great and manifest profit of him that recommends them: nor can they be obliged to retain them longer than it is for the public good, the care of which they stand so long charged withal as they retain any other essential right of the sovereignty.

If a man therefore should ask a pastor, in the execution of his office, as the chief priests and elders of the people asked our Saviour, 'By what authority do you do these things, and who gave you this authority?': (Matthew, 21, 23) he can make no other just answer but that he does it by the *authority of the commonwealth, given him by the king or assembly that represents it*. All pastors, except the supreme, execute their charges in the right, that is, by the authority of the civil sovereign, that is, *iure civile*. But the king, and every other sovereign, executes his office of supreme pastor by immediate authority from God, that is to say, in God's right, or *iure divino*. And therefore none but kings can put into their titles, a mark of their submission to God only, *Dei gratia Rex*, etc. Bishops ought to say in the beginning of their mandates, 'By the favour of the King's Majesty, Bishop of such a diocese'; or as civil ministers, 'In His Majesty's name.' For in saying, *divina providentia*, which is the same with *dei gratia*, though disguised, they deny to have received their authority from the civil state, and slyly slip off the collar of their civil subjection, contrary to the unity and defence of the commonwealth.

But if *every Christian sovereign be the supreme pastor of his own subjects*, it seems that he has also the authority, not only to preach, which perhaps no man will deny, but also to baptize, and to administer sacrament of the Lord's Supper and to consecrate both temples and pastors to God's service; which most men deny, partly because they use not to do it, and partly because the administration of sacraments, and consecration of persons and places to holy uses, requires the imposition of such men's hands as by the like imposition successively from the time of the Apostles have been ordained to the like ministry. For proof therefore that Christian kings have power to baptize and to consecrate, I am to render a reason both why they use not to do it, and how, without the ordinary ceremony of imposition of hands, they are made capable of doing it when they will.

PART THREE
Religion in Democratic Culture

Prologue to Part Three

Two events in history are central to the following section. In Europe, the French Revolution in 1789 put an end to the *ancien régime* and, in 1776, the first constitution of the world was issued in the USA. In this section, which includes texts of the political writings by Jean-Jacques Rousseau, Thomas Paine, Alexis de Tocqueville and Joseph de Maistre, we shall focus on the political and religious transformations in the United States and in Europe. Both events, the Revolution and the establishment of an independent and democratic America, breathe the spirit of the Enlightenment. Even though the course of the Enlightenment differed from nation to nation (so, to be precise we have to talk of a French Enlightenment, German Enlightenment, etc.), Immanuel Kant's definition of what Enlightenment is remains. In 1784 in a popular journal called *Berlinische Monatszeitschrift*, Kant wrote:

> Enlightenment is man's emergence from his self-incurred immaturity. Immaturity is the inability to use one's own understanding without the guidance of another. This immaturity is self-incurred if its cause is not lack of understanding, but lack of resolution and courage to use it without the guidance of another. The motto of enlightenment is therefore: *Sapere aude!* Have courage to use your own understanding!

The French philosopher Michel Foucault rightly pointed out that with Kant for the first time a philosopher raised the question about the current situation in which he found himself and addressed this question to a universal audience. 'Dare to reason!' is the imperative of the Enlightenment *Zeitgeist* and everyone is entitled to use his or her own understanding. Kant suggests that everyone has the capability to reason and does not depend on external authorities or guidelines. Later we will see what effects such a self-conscious attitude and the trust in one's own capacity to reason had on religion.

Eight years before Kant published his manifesto on Enlightenment, the new consciousness of it was to be a rational human being, was given expression on

4 July 1776 in the Declaration of Independence by the United States: 'We hold these truths to be self-evident, that all men are created equal, that they are endowed by their Creator with certain unalienable Rights, that among these are Life, Liberty and the pursuit of Happiness'. The first amendment of the constitution defines the fundamental rights of every citizen: 'Congress shall make no law respecting an establishment of religion, or prohibiting the free exercise thereof; or abridging the freedom of speech, or of the press; or the right of the people peaceably to assemble, and to petition the Government for a redress of grievances'.

In a similar fashion to this American declaration of human rights, the French National Assembly declared on 26 August 1789 in the first article of its constitution: 'Men are born and remain free and equal in rights. Social distinctions may be based only on common utility'. Liberty and Equality are fundamental human rights, and the French as well as the American constitutions of human rights continue what began with the Magna Carta and other declarations concerning privileges and individual rights. What we today know as the Universal Declaration of Human Rights by the United Nations on 10 December 1948 is a further continuation of this legacy.

In both constitutional texts from 1776 and 1789, subjects were granted certain undeniable rights. In addition to that, both constitutional texts contain a democratic definition of sovereignty. The French declaration, in article 3, states: 'The principle of all sovereignty rests essentially in the nation. No body and no individual may exercise authority which does not emanate expressly from the nation'. Similarly, the US constitution declares: 'All legislative Powers herein granted shall be vested in a Congress of the United States, which shall consist of a Senate and House of Representatives'. Despite the differences between these two declarations, their common ground is the rejection of any form of sovereignty granted by the Divine Right of Kings. Compared to the political theory of Hobbes and James VI/I in Part Two, the promulgation of fundamental rights and the constitution of liberal forms of government, the eighteenth century marks the entrance into a new era of *democratic* politics. As will be illustrated by excerpts from Alexis de Tocqueville and Joseph de Maistre, this new era of liberal democracy[1] started to flourish in the United States. In Europe, on the other hand, the few glimpses of liberal democracy were overshadowed by periods of counter-revolutionary conservativism that lasted until well into the twentieth century.

There were just 15 years between the outbreak of the French Revolution and the day when Napoleon crowned himself Emperor in the presence of the Pope. As a result and reaction to the 'Reign of Terror' (see the Introduction to de Maistre) monarchy was re-established in France. But the style of monarchical government had changed throughout the eighteenth century. This new style was characterized by a combination of Enlightenment ideas and the growing awareness of national identity. Joseph II of Austria, Frederick II of Prussia and Catherine II of Russia are famous representatives of enlightened monarchs who nevertheless reigned in an

---

1. For the complex and antagonistic history of liberalism and democracy, see N. Bobbio (2005), *Liberalism and Democracy* (London: Verso).

absolutist manner. The most significant feature of these enlightened monarchs for our context here is their tolerant attitude towards religion. We have already cited the first amendment of the US constitution, where the freedom of religion and the free exercise of religion are defined as one of the fundamental rights of the people. Compared with the religious freedom of American democracy, the tolerance of religion in Europe's monarchies was less radical. The monarch in Europe *granted* the permission to worship a religion other than the official religion of the state. This permission must not be misread as a fundamental human right. At this point it is necessary to emphasize that the common view of the Enlightenment as associated with an increasing secularization and scientific atheism is a misinterpretation of the facts. The atheism viewed as being promoted by the Enlightenment is actually an accusation made by counter-revolutionary opponents of this Enlightenment, like de Maistre. If there is something like 'the religion of Enlightenment', then it is deism. Deism means the religious belief in a God who created the world and fitted human beings with a moral consciousness. For deism there is no revelation in the course of history and therefore its doctrines are few and simple. Kant expressed this minimalist theology, characteristic of deism, in his *Critique of Practical Reason* (1788): 'Two things fill the mind with increasing admiration and reverence, as I meditate more closely and steadily upon them: the starry heavens above me and the moral law within me'.[2] Creation and inner moral law are the two sources of religion, but also the twin contents of religion. As a consequence, deism excludes all other sources of revelation than those manifest in the design of the cosmos and the moral nature of human beings.

As Tocqueville observed, people in America were particularly inclined to deism and Thomas Paine is one of the most vociferous advocates of deism. In his book *The Age of Reason*, published in 1794, Paine makes an intriguing connection between deism and free forms of government:

> The only religion that has not been invented, and that has in it every evidence of divine originality, is pure and simple deism. It must have been the first and will probably be the last that man believes. But pure and simple deism does not answer the purpose of despotic governments. They cannot lay hold of religion as an engine but by mixing it with human inventions, and making their own authority a part; neither does it answer the avarice of priests, but by incorporating themselves and their functions with it, and becoming, like the government, a party in the system. It is this that forms the otherwise mysterious connection of Church and state; the Church human and the state tyrannic.[3]

Paine wrote these lines when he was imprisoned in France, because he voted against the execution of the dethroned King Louis XVI (see the Introduction to Paine). He clearly outlines an ideal type of religion which is immune from politics. His prophecy of an *apolitical deism* as the religion for democracy is tailored to his

---

2. I. Kant (1995), *Kritik der Praktischen Vernunft* (Stuttgart: Reclam), p. 253 [editors' translation].
3. D. Moncure (ed.) (1894), *The Writings of Thomas Paine*, vol. 4 (New York: G.P. Putnam's Sons), p. 190.

conception of America. But even in Jean-Jacques Rousseau's proposal for a 'civil religion' we can find a collaborative form of religion useful for a democratic state. The conviction that religion is an integral part of human life was uncontested in the eighteenth century and is far from secularization. Religion in the enlightened world, namely deism, is: first, apolitical in the sense that it is not a political player (although it still serves politics); second, privatized and therefore hostile to institutionalism; and, third, minimalistic in its system of beliefs. Two quotations by Thomas Jefferson and Thomas Paine should illustrate the understanding of enlightened deism. Jefferson declared that 'there is a strict wall of separation between the Church and the state'; and Paine, emphasizing the private nature of belief, confessed, 'I do not believe in the creed professed by the Jewish Church, by the Roman Church, by the Greek Church, by the Turkish Church, by the Protestant Church, nor by any Church that I know of. My own mind is my own Church'.

What was embryonic in the thoughts of Martin Luther starts now to become more developed in the liberal thinking of the eighteenth century. Politics becomes democratic and its religion privatized. Moreover, the eighteenth century gave birth to two fundamental poles of contemporary politics: liberalism and conservativism.

Chapter 8

Jean-Jacques Rousseau (1712–78)

The dogmas of civil religion ought to be few, simple, and exactly worded, without explanation or commentary. The existence of a mighty, intelligent and beneficent divinity, possessed of foresight and providence, the life to come, the happiness of the just, the punishment of the wicked, the sanctity of the social contract and the laws.

Introduction

What religion does democracy need? The question whether democracy needs some form of religion or the absence of all forms of religion remains a significant contemporary debate. The origins of this debate can already be found in Rousseau, as we will see. The governing question here is: To what extent does a democratic society (based on the idea of the social contract) rely on religion (as an effective social force)?

The concept of the social contract and the proposal of civil religion are the two fundamental ideas on which Rousseau's entire political theory rests. However, this interpretation of Rousseau will not go uncontested among the majority of commentators. Usually Rousseau's view on civil religion, as it is expressed in chapter 8 of the concluding fourth book of his *Social Contract* (1762), is either ignored or played down as marginal and so less important in his theory of politics. It is true that at first glance the theoretical construct of the social contract does not depend on Rousseau's demand for a civil religion, because it seems that the social contract (the political organization of a society) does not require any religion at all. This view of Rousseau's political theory is supported by the fact that the first print-version of the manuscript (from 1760) contains no chapter on civil religion. So why, then, did Rousseau add this chapter?

The excerpt from the *Social Contract* we have chosen emphasizes the idea of the social contract as the skeleton of politics and civil religion as its soul. The first part of the excerpt (taken from chapters 5, 6 and 7 of the first book) outlines the theory and conception of the social contract. The second part is a draft version of the chapter on civil religion. This introduction to Rousseau's contribution to religion and politics focuses primarily on the concepts of social contract and civil religion and we will not venture into biographical details. Nor will we discuss the socio-historical context as would be necessary for an exhaustive treatment of Rousseau's work. First-hand biographical information can be found in Rousseau's auto-biography called *Confessions*.[1] For a more comprehensive primary source on Rousseau's attitude towards religion, we recommend reading his lengthy discussion in *Emile* (his famous book on education),[2] subtitled *Professions du foi du Vicaire Savoyard*. It also needs to be mentioned that Rousseau's personal attitude towards religion was quite complex, as he himself was. Some facts illustrate this. He was born in Geneva where he was brought up as a Calvinist. But he converted to Catholicism in his youth. Later in his life, around 1754, he returned to Calvinism. But neither Calvinism nor Catholicism could really meet Rousseau's religious needs.

In the chapter on civil religion Rousseau attacked Catholicism for being a harmful dogmatism, in contrast to Calvinism which was judged positively in earlier versions of the *Social Contract*. There, Calvin is praised not only as an extraordinary theologian but also as a prudent politician. Nevertheless, Rousseau's estimation of Calvin did not last very long. After the appearance of the *Social Contract* and *Emile* (published in the same year), Rousseau condemned Calvin. It would be interesting to examine the extent to which Rousseau's understanding of the contract is informed by Calvin's theology. We would then need to question the extent to which our understanding of democracy rests on Protestant theology.

Alongside Kant, Rousseau is rightly viewed as *the* political theorist of the Enlightenment. Kant's high estimation of Rousseau's work is well known. Furthermore, almost all significant figures of the French Enlightenment (such as Diderot, d'Alembert, Voltaire) were in permanent conversation with him. Rousseau is not only *the* political theorist of the Enlightenment, but he also became the ideological cornerstone for the French Revolution. Not by accident did the young student Maximilien de Robespierre frequently visit the old Rousseau to pay tribute.

We have already seen that Hobbes and Rousseau represent two key positions in the tradition of contract theory in political science. In contrast to Hobbes, who stands at the beginning of modern political theory and thus at the beginning of a contractual theory of society, Rousseau provides an account of the origin and nature of the social contract free of the hierarchical elements evident in Hobbes. But both thinkers are still working with the same constellation of issues. Both attempt to explain how and why a mere aggregate of people forms a society. Or, expressed retrospectively, how we give a rational account of the conditions for the emergence and maintenance of society. In Rousseau's own apt words:

> The problem is to find a form of association which will defend and protect with the whole common force the person and goods of each associate, and in which each, while uniting himself with all, may still obey himself alone, and remain as free as before. This is the fundamental problem to which the *Social Contract* provides the solution.

Like Hobbes, Rousseau is convinced that the reason for the formation of a society, and the goal of any state, is the protection of its individual members. But, as

1. J.-J. Rousseau (1970), *The Confessions*, trans. J. Cohen (London: Penguin).
2. J.-J. Rousseau (1950), *Emile or Education* (London: Dent).

became evident in Hobbes, protection has its price. For both thinkers, in order to obtain protection, individuals constitute a society by giving away their personal rights. In other words, the protection offered by a collective body requires the relinquishment of one's personal freedom to a certain degree. People have to come to terms with each other, which means they have to try to find the balance between autonomous freedom and external authority.

For Rousseau, what is at stake in the constitution of a society through a network of mutual contracts between individual members is the creation of a larger and more powerful political entity. This larger entity, called 'republic' or 'body politic', differs significantly from a contractual relationship between individual members. Individuals are in contractual relations with each other, but at the same time they constitute and belong to a social body that transcends the level of interpersonal relations. Therefore, the nature of the social contract is twofold. It is both *inter*personal and *supra*personal.

In the most difficult and complex parts of the *Social Contract*, Rousseau introduces a series of binary distinctions to describe this twofold nature and its impact on the individual. He defines the republic that is formed by the social contract as follows:

> . . . it [the republic] is called by its members 'state' when passive, [but] 'sovereign' when [it is] active [. . .]. Those who associate with it take collectively the name of a *people*, and severally are called citizens, as sharing in the sovereign power, and *subjects*, as being under the laws of the state.

In fact, not all individuals forming the collective body of the republic are citizens. Only those who exercise power actively are citizens. This is to say, a political organization consists of two kinds of individuals. There are, on the one hand, citizens who are subject to the laws of the state but also actively participate in making these laws, and, on the other, there are those who are passive members of the state and merely subject to the laws. These two kinds of members of any society are interwoven through a network of individual contracts (the interpersonal nature of every society). They are both subject to the law (the law of the suprapersonal), but only one kind of membership is actively participating in sovereign power. It is important to note that the state is not identical with sovereignty. The state is the *legal* framework which incorporates the people. The sovereign is the collective body, a single entity.

The novelty of Rousseau's concept becomes evident if we compare it to Hobbes'. In Hobbes the contractual element always had to be complemented by a personal sovereign, that is sovereignty embodied in the king. Rousseau depersonalizes the concept of sovereignty. The sovereign is nothing more than the *common will* of the political body. This common will transcends the particular interests of single members and particular groups. It is the suprapersonal quality of the state in its active form and its clearest expression. Rousseau's strong notion of a sovereignty of the common will, that supersedes particular interests, associates him dangerously with totalitarianism: where the state is the people and no mediating civil society exists.

Both Rousseau's concepts of the state and the sovereignty of the common will (which results from the suprapersonal character of the social contract) remain within the realm of immanence. No appeal is made to a transcendent order. But the common will, as suprapersonal, and the collective body, as an entity which cannot be reduced to the sum of all its constituent members, give the social contract a transcendence without any notion of the divine. Human beings create this social transcendence themselves. It is a transcendence from *within* society. No external source of power, such as the divine legitimacy for kings, is needed.

Up to this point, Rousseau's *Social Contract* offers a consistent theory of politics without recourse to religion. So, why then, someone may ask, does Rousseau need to introduce the concept of civil religion? What can civil religion offer to the maintenance of a democratic society?

Rousseau starts his discussion of the role of religion in politics in a defensive way. The focus of his criticism of religion in politics is on the divisive forces of sectarian Christianity and their impact on government. The worst religion of all, he writes, is Roman Catholicism, because it brought into existence the split between the Kingdom of God and the Kingdom of this World.

> It was in these circumstances that Jesus came to set up on earth a spiritual kingdom, which by separating the theological from the political system, made the state no longer one, and brought about the internal divisions which have never been corrected to trouble Christian peoples. As the new idea of a kingdom of the other world could never have occurred to pagans, they always looked to the Christians as really rebels, who, while feigning to submit, were only waiting for the chance to make themselves independent and their masters, and to usurp by quite the authority they pretend in their weakness to respect.

Christendom is blamed, then, for having introduced a parallel society. What was, at first, merely a theological idea then became a political reality with the institution of the Church.

If we look back to Augustine, it is easy to see how Rousseau interprets Augustine's distinction between the City of God and the earthly city dualistically. As we have seen, Augustine makes the formal distinction between the City of God and the city of this world, but the material Church moves as pilgrim towards the Last Judgement. Rousseau (like Luther) simply reduces Augustine's subtle presentation to a polarity. A religion which promotes this dichotomy Rousseau called the religion of the priests and condemned it as anti-social because it destroys the unity of the people. Individuals have to obey authorities in spiritual as well as in temporal matters. A society which is divided between temporal and spiritual powers, according to Rousseau, inevitably creates conflicts of loyalty. Nevertheless, although Rousseau dismisses the religion of the priests as anti-social, he recognizes the value of religion for the stability of society. This is why that final added chapter on civil religion is significant. Nevertheless, the value of religion remains mainly a moral one:

> Now, it matters very much to the community that each citizen should have a religion. That will make him love his duty; but the dogmas of that religion concern the state

126

and its members only in so far as they have reference to morality and to the duties which he who professes them is bound to do to others.

The kind of religion which is required here for the moral education of citizens is a civil religion. Students might profitably compare this view of civil religion with Robert Bellah's celebrated essay 'Civil Religion in America'.[3]

Further reading

Selected English translations

Rousseau, J.-J. (1997), *'The Social Contract' and Other Later Political Writings*, ed. V. Gourevitch (Cambridge: Cambridge University Press).

General introductions

Bertram, C. (2003), *Routledge Philosophy Guidebook to Rousseau and the Social Contract* (London: Routledge).
Dent, N. (2005), *Rousseau* (London: Routledge).
Riley, P. (2001), *The Cambridge Companion to Rousseau* (Cambridge: Cambridge University Press).

Reception of key ideas

Rosenblatt, H. (1997), *Rousseau and Geneva: From the First Discourse to the Social Contract, 1749–1762* (Cambridge: Cambridge University Press).
Trachtenberg, Z. (1993), *Making Citizens: Rousseau's Political Theory of Culture* (New York: Routledge).
Weiss, P. (1993), *Gendered Community: Rousseau, Sex, and Politics* (New York: New York University Press).

Excerpt from *Social Contract**

Book I, 5: That we must always go back to a first convention

Even if I granted all that I have been refuting, the friends of despotism would be no better off. There will always be a great difference between subduing a multitude and ruling a society. Even if scattered individuals were successively enslaved by one man, however numerous they might be, I still see no more than a master and his slaves, and certainly not a people and its ruler; I see what may be termed an aggregation, but not an association; there is as yet neither public good nor body politic. The man in question, even if he has enslaved half the world, is still only an individual; his

---

*   Italics have been added by the editors for emphasis.
3.   R. Bellah (1991), *Beyond Belief: Essays on Religion in a Post-Traditionalist World* (Berkeley, CA: University of California Press), pp. 168ff.

interest, apart from that of others, is still a purely private interest. If this same man comes to die, his empire, after him, remains scattered and without unity, as an oak falls and dissolves into a heap of ashes when the fire has consumed it.[. . .]

Book I, 6: The social compact

I suppose men to have reached the point at which the obstacles in the way of their preservation in the state of nature show their power of resistance to be greater than the resources at the disposal of each individual for his maintenance in that state. That primitive condition can then subsist no longer; and the human race would perish unless it changed its manner of existence.

But, as men cannot engender new forces, but only unite and direct existing ones, they have no other means of preserving themselves than the formation, by aggregation, of a sum of forces great enough to overcome the resistance. These they have to bring into play by means of a single motive power, and cause *to act in concert.*

This sum of forces can arise only where several persons come together: but, as the force and liberty of each man are the chief instruments of his self-preservation, how can he pledge them without harming his own interests, and neglecting the care he owes to himself? This difficulty, in its bearing on my present subject, may be stated in the following terms:

The problem is to find a form of association which will defend and protect with the whole common force the person and goods of each associate, and in which each, while uniting himself with all, may still obey himself alone, and remain as free as before. This is the fundamental problem of which the *Social Contract* provides the solution.

The clauses of this contract are so determined by the nature of the act that the slightest modification would make them vain and ineffective; so that, although they have perhaps never been formally set forth, they are everywhere the same and everywhere tacitly admitted and recognized, until, on the violation of the social compact, each regains his original rights and resumes his natural liberty, while losing the conventional liberty in favour of which he renounced it.

These clauses, properly understood, may be reduced to one: the total alienation of each associate, together with all his rights, to the whole community; for, in the first place, as each gives himself absolutely, the conditions are the same for all; and, this being so, no one has any interest in making them burdensome to others.

Moreover, the alienation being without reserve, the union is as perfect as it can be, and no associate has anything more to demand: for, if the individuals retained certain rights, as there would be no common superior to decide between them and the public, each, being on one point his own judge, would ask to be so on all; the state of nature would thus continue, and the association would necessarily become inoperative or tyrannical.

Finally, each man, in giving himself to all, gives himself to nobody; and as there is no associate over whom he does not acquire the same right as he yields others over himself, he gains an equivalent for everything he loses, and an increase of force for the preservation of what he has.

If then we discard from the social compact what is not of its essence, we shall find that it reduces itself to the following terms:

Each of us puts his person and all his power in common under the supreme direction of the general will, and, in our corporate capacity, we receive each member as an indivisible part of the whole.

At once, in place of the individual personality of each contracting party, this act of association creates a moral and collective body, composed of as many members as the assembly contains votes, and receiving from this act its unity, its common identity, its life and its will. This public person, so formed by the union of all other persons, formerly took the name of city, and now takes that of republic or body politic; it is called by its members State when passive, Sovereign when active, and Power when compared with others like itself. Those who are associated in it take collectively the name of people, and severally are called citizens, as sharing in the sovereign power, and subjects, as being under the laws of the state. But these terms are often confused and taken one for another: it is enough to know how to distinguish them when they are being used with precision.

Book I, 7: The sovereign

This formula shows us that the *act of association comprises a mutual undertaking between the public and the individuals, and that each individual, in making a contract, as we may say, with himself, is bound in a double capacity*; as a member of the sovereign he is bound to the individuals, and as a member of the state to the sovereign. But the maxim of civil right, that no one is bound by undertakings made to himself, does not apply in this case; for there is a great difference between incurring an obligation to yourself and incurring one to a whole of which you form a part.

Attention must further be called to the fact that public deliberation, while competent to bind all the subjects to the sovereign, because of the two different capacities in which each of them may be regarded, cannot, for the opposite reason, bind the sovereign to itself; and that it is consequently against the nature of the body politic for the sovereign to impose on itself a law which it cannot infringe. Being able to regard itself in only one capacity, it is in the position of an individual who makes a contract with himself; and this makes it clear that there neither is nor can be any kind of fundamental law binding on the body of the people – not even the social contract itself. This does not mean that the body politic cannot enter into undertakings with others, provided the contract is not infringed by them; for in relation to what is external to it, it becomes a simple being, an individual.

But the body politic or the sovereign, drawing its being wholly from the sanctity of the contract, can never bind itself, even to an outsider, to do anything derogatory to the original act, for instance, to alienate any part of itself, or to submit to another sovereign. Violation of the act by which it exists would be self-annihilation; and that which is itself nothing can create nothing.

As soon as this multitude is so united in one body, it is impossible to offend against one of the members without attacking the body, and still more to offend against the body without the members resenting it. Duty and interest therefore equally oblige the two contracting parties to give each other help; and the same men should seek to combine, in their double capacity, all the advantages dependent upon that capacity. [. . .]

Book II, 7: The legislator

In order to discover the rules of society best suited to nations, a superior intelligence beholding all the passions of men without experiencing any of them would be needed. This intelligence would have to be wholly unrelated to our nature, while knowing it through and through; its happiness would have to be independent of us, and yet ready to occupy itself with ours; and lastly, it would have, in the march of time, to look forward to a distant glory, and, working in one century, to be able to enjoy in the next. It would take gods to give men laws. [. . .]

The *legislator* occupies in every respect an extraordinary position in the state. If he should do so by reason of his genius, he does so no less by reason of his office, which is neither magistracy, nor sovereignty. This office, which sets up the republic, nowhere enters into its constitution; it is an individual and superior function, which has nothing in common with human empire; for if he who holds command over men ought not to have command over the laws, he who has command over the laws ought not any more to have it over men; or else his laws would be the ministers of his passions and would often merely serve to perpetuate his injustices: his private aims would inevitably mar the sanctity of his work. [. . .]

Thus in the task of legislation we find together two things which appear to be incompatible: an enterprise too difficult for human powers, and, for its execution, an authority that is no authority. [. . .]

This sublime reason, far above the range of the common herd, is that whose decisions the legislator puts into the mouth of the immortals, in order to constrain by divine authority those whom human prudence could not move. But it is not anybody who can make the gods speak, or get himself believed when he proclaims himself their interpreter. The great soul of the legislator is the only miracle that can prove his mission. Any man may grave tablets of stone, or buy an oracle, or feign secret intercourse with some divinity, or train a bird to whisper in his ear, or find other vulgar ways of imposing on the people. He whose knowledge goes no further may perhaps gather round him a band of fools; but he will never found an empire, and his extravagances will quickly perish with him. Idle tricks form a passing tie; only wisdom can make it lasting. The Judaic law, which still subsists, and that of the child of Ishmael, which, for ten centuries, has ruled half the world, still proclaim the great men who laid them down; and, while the pride of philosophy or the blind spirit of faction sees in them no more than lucky impostures, the true political theorist admires, in the institutions they set up, the great and powerful genius which presides over things made to endure.

We should not, with Warburton, conclude from this that politics and religion have among us a common object, but that, in the first periods of nations, the one is used as an instrument for the other. [. . .]

Book IV, 8: Civil religion

At first men had no kings save the gods, and no government save theocracy. They reasoned like Caligula, and, at that period, reasoned aright. It takes a long time for feeling so to change that men can make up their minds to take their equals as masters, in the hope that they will profit by doing so.

From the mere fact that God was set over every political society, it followed that there were as many gods as peoples. Two peoples that were strangers the one to the other, and almost always enemies, could not long recognize the same master: two armies giving battle could not obey the same leader. National divisions thus led to polytheism, and this in turn gave rise to *theological and civil intolerance, which, as we shall see hereafter, are by nature the same.*

The fancy the Greeks had for rediscovering their gods among the barbarians arose from the way they had of regarding themselves as the natural sovereigns of such peoples. But there is nothing so absurd as the erudition which in our days identifies and confuses gods of different nations. As if Moloch, Saturn and Chronos could be the same god! As if the Phœnician Baal, the Greek Zeus, and the Latin Jupiter could be the same! As if there could still be anything common to imaginary beings with different names!

If it is asked how in pagan times, where each state had its cult and its gods, there were no wars of religion, I answer that *it was precisely because each state, having its own cult as well as its own government, made no distinction between its gods and its laws. Political war was also theological; the provinces of the gods were, so to speak, fixed by the boundaries of nations.* The god of one people had no right over another. The gods of the pagans were not jealous gods; they shared among themselves the empire of the world: even Moses and the Hebrews sometimes lent themselves to this view by speaking of the God of Israel. It is true, they regarded as powerless the gods of the Canaanites, a proscribed people condemned to destruction, whose place they were to take; but remember how they spoke of the divisions of the neighbouring peoples they were forbidden to attack! 'Is not the possession of what belongs to your god Chamos lawfully your due?' said Jephthah to the Ammonites. 'We have the same title to the lands our conquering God has made his own.' Here, I think, there is a recognition that the rights of Chamos and those of the God of Israel are of the same nature. [. . .]

Every religion, therefore, being attached solely to the laws of the state which prescribed it, there was no way of converting a people except by enslaving it, and there could be no missionaries save conquerors. The obligation to change cults being the law to which the vanquished yielded, it was necessary to be victorious before suggesting such a change. [. . .]

It was in these circumstances that Jesus came to set up on earth a spiritual kingdom, which, by separating the theological from the political system, made the state no longer one, and brought about the internal divisions which have never ceased to trouble Christian peoples. As the new idea of a kingdom of the other world could never have occurred to pagans, they always looked on the Christians as really rebels, who, while feigning to submit, were only waiting for the chance to make

131

themselves independent of their masters, and to usurp by guile the authority they pretended in their weakness to respect. This was the cause of the persecutions.

What the pagans had feared took place. Then everything changed its aspect: the humble Christians changed their language, and soon this so-called kingdom of the other world turned, under a visible leader, into the most violent of earthly despotisms.

However, as there have always been a prince and civil laws, this double power and conflict of jurisdiction have made all good polity impossible in Christian states; and men have never succeeded in finding out whether they were bound to obey the master or the priest.

Several peoples, however, even in Europe and its neighbourhood, have desired without success to preserve or restore the old system: but the spirit of Christianity has everywhere prevailed. The sacred cult has always remained or again become independent of the sovereign, and there has been no necessary link between it and the body of the state. Mahomet held very sane views, and linked his political system well together; and, as long as the form of his government continued under the caliphs who succeeded him, that government was indeed one, and so far good. But the Arabs, having grown prosperous, lettered, civilized, slack and cowardly, were conquered by barbarians: the division between the two powers began again; and, although it is less apparent among the Mahometans than among the Christians, it none the less exists, especially in the sect of Ali, and there are states, such as Persia, where it is continually making itself felt.

Among us, the Kings of England have made themselves heads of the Church, and the Czars have done the same: but this title has made them less its masters than its ministers; they have gained not so much the right to change it, as the power to maintain it: they are not its legislators, but only its princes. Wherever the clergy is a corporate body, it is master and legislator in its own country. There are thus two powers, two sovereigns, in England and in Russia, as well as elsewhere.

Of all Christian writers, the philosopher Hobbes alone has seen the evil and how to remedy it, and has dared to propose the reunion of the two heads of the eagle, and the restoration throughout of political unity, without which no state or government will ever be rightly constituted. But he should have seen that the masterful spirit of Christianity is incompatible with his system, and that the priestly interest would always be stronger than that of the state. It is not so much what is false and terrible in his political theory, as what is just and true, that has drawn down hatred on it.

I believe that if the study of history were developed from this point of view, it would be easy to refute the contrary opinions of Bayle and Warburton, one of whom holds that religion can be of no use to the body politic, while the other, on the contrary, maintains that Christianity is its strongest support. We should demonstrate to the former that no state has ever been founded without a religious basis, and to the latter, that the law of Christianity at bottom does more harm by weakening than good by strengthening the constitution of the state. To make myself understood, I have only to make a little more exact the too vague ideas of religion as relating to this subject.

Religion, considered in relation to society, which is either general or particular, may also be divided into two kinds: the religion of man, and that of the citizen. The first, which has neither temples, nor altars, nor rites, and is confined to the purely internal cult of the supreme God and the eternal obligations of morality, is the religion of the Gospel pure and simple, the true theism, what may be called natural divine right or law. The other, which is codified in a single country, gives it its gods, its own tutelary patrons; it has its dogmas, its rites, and its external cult prescribed by law; outside the single nation that follows it, all the world is in its sight infidel, foreign, and barbarous; the duties and rights of man extend for it only as far as its own altars. *Of this kind were all the religions of early peoples, which we may define as civil or positive divine right or law.*

There is a third sort of religion of a more singular kind, which gives men two codes of legislation, two rulers, and two countries, renders them subject to contradictory duties, and makes it impossible for them to be faithful both to religion and to citizenship. Such are the religions of the Lamas and of the Japanese, and such is Roman Christianity, which may be called the religion of the priest. It leads to a sort of mixed and anti-social code which has no name.

In their political aspect, all these three kinds of religion have their defects. The third is so clearly bad, that it is waste of time to stop to prove it such. All that destroys social unity is worthless; all institutions that set man in contradiction to himself are worthless.

The second is good in that it unites the divine cult with love of the laws, and, making country the object of the citizens' adoration, teaches them that service done to the state is service done to its tutelary god. It is a form of theocracy, in which there can be no pontiff save the prince, and no priests save the magistrates. To die for one's country then becomes martyrdom; violation of its laws, impiety; and to subject one who is guilty to public execration is to condemn him to the anger of the gods: *Sacer estod.*

On the other hand, it is bad in that, being founded on lies and error, it deceives men, makes them credulous and superstitious, and drowns the true cult of the divinity in empty ceremonial. It is bad, again, when it becomes tyrannous and exclusive, and makes a people bloodthirsty and intolerant, so that it breathes fire and slaughter, and regards as a sacred act the killing of every one who does not believe in its gods. The result is to place such a people in a natural state of war with all others, so that its security is deeply endangered.

There remains therefore *the religion of man or Christianity – not the Christianity of today, but that of the Gospel, which is entirely different.* By means of this holy, sublime and real religion all men, being children of one God, recognize one another as brothers, and the society that unites them is not dissolved even at death.

But *this religion, having no particular relation to the body politic,* leaves the laws in possession of the force they have in themselves without making any addition to it; and thus one of the great bonds that unite society considered in severalty fails to operate. Nay, more, so far from binding the hearts of the citizens to the state, it has the effect of taking them away from all earthly things. I know of nothing more contrary to the social spirit.

We are told that a people of true Christians would form the most perfect society imaginable. I see in this supposition only one great difficulty: that *a society of true Christians would not be a society of men.*

I say further that such a society, with all its perfection, would be neither the strongest nor the most lasting: the very fact that it was perfect would rob it of its bond of union; the flaw that would destroy it would lie in its very perfection.

Every one would do his duty; the people would be law-abiding, the rulers just and temperate; the magistrates upright and incorruptible; the soldiers would scorn death; there would be neither vanity nor luxury. So far, so good; but let us hear more.

Christianity as a religion is entirely spiritual, occupied solely with heavenly things; the country of the Christian is not of this world. He does his duty, indeed, but does it with profound indifference to the good or ill success of his cares. Provided he has nothing to reproach himself with, it matters little to him whether things go well or ill here on earth. If the state is prosperous, he hardly dares to share in the public happiness, for fear he may grow proud of his country's glory; if the state is languishing, he blesses the hand of God that is hard upon His people.

For the state to be peaceable and for harmony to be maintained, all the citizens without exception would have to be good Christians; if by ill hap there should be a single self-seeker or hypocrite, a Catiline or a Cromwell, for instance, he would certainly get the better of his pious compatriots. Christian charity does not readily allow a man to think hardly of his neighbours. As soon as, by some trick, he has discovered the art of imposing on them and getting hold of a share in the public authority, you have a man established in dignity; it is the will of God that he be respected: very soon you have a power; it is God's will that it be obeyed: and if the power is abused by him who wields it, it is the scourge wherewith God punishes His children. There would be scruples about driving out the usurper: public tranquillity would have to be disturbed, violence would have to be employed, and blood spilt; all this accords ill with Christian meekness; and after all, in this vale of sorrows, what does it matter whether we are free men or serfs? The essential thing is to get to heaven, and resignation is only an additional means of doing so.

If war breaks out with another state, the citizens march readily out to battle; not one of them thinks of flight; they do their duty, but they have no passion for victory; they know better how to die than how to conquer. What does it matter whether they win or lose? Does not providence know better than they what is meet for them? Only think to what account a proud, impetuous and passionate enemy could turn their stoicism! Set over against them those generous peoples who were devoured by ardent love of glory and of their country, imagine your Christian republic face to face with Sparta or Rome: the pious Christians will be beaten, crushed and destroyed, before they know where they are, or will owe their safety only to the contempt their enemy will conceive for them. It was to my mind a fine oath that was taken by the soldiers of Fabius, who swore, not to conquer or die, but to come back victorious – and kept their oath. Christians would never have taken such an oath; they would have looked on it as tempting God.

But I am mistaken in speaking of a Christian republic; the terms are mutually exclusive. Christianity preaches only servitude and dependence. Its spirit is so favourable to tyranny that it always profits by such a régime. *True Christians are made to be slaves, and they know it and do not much mind*: this short life counts for too little in their eyes.

I shall be told that Christian troops are excellent. I deny it. Show me an instance. For my part, I know of no Christian troops. I shall be told of the Crusades. Without disputing the valour of the Crusaders, I answer that, so far from being Christians, they were the priests' soldiery, citizens of the Church. They fought for their spiritual country, which the Church had, somehow or other, made temporal. Well understood, this goes back to paganism: as the Gospel sets up no national religion, a holy war is impossible among Christians.

Under the pagan emperors, the Christian soldiers were brave; every Christian writer affirms it, and I believe it: it was a case of honourable emulation of the pagan troops. As soon as the emperors were Christian, this emulation no longer existed, and, when the Cross had driven out the eagle, Roman valour wholly disappeared.

But, setting aside political considerations, let us come back to what is right, and settle our principles on this important point. The right which the social compact gives the sovereign over the subjects does not, we have seen, exceed the limits of public expediency. The subjects then owe the sovereign an account of their opinions only to such an extent as they matter to the community. Now, it matters very much to the community that each citizen should have a religion. That will make him love his duty; but the dogmas of that religion concern the state and its members only so far as they have reference to morality and to the duties which he who professes them is bound to do to others. Each man may have, over and above, what opinions he pleases, without it being the sovereign's business to take cognisance of them; for, as the sovereign has no authority in the other world, whatever the lot of its subjects may be in the life to come, that is not its business, provided they are good citizens in this life.

There is therefore a purely civil profession of faith of which the sovereign should fix the articles, not exactly as religious dogmas, but as social sentiments without which a man cannot be a good citizen or a faithful subject. While it can compel no one to believe them, it can banish from the state whoever does not believe them – it can banish him, not for impiety, but as an anti-social being, incapable of truly loving the laws and justice, and of sacrificing, at need, his life to his duty. If any one, after publicly recognizing these dogmas, behaves as if he does not believe them, let him be punished by death: he has committed the worst of all crimes, that of lying before the law.

The dogmas of civil religion ought to be few, simple, and exactly worded, without explanation or commentary. The existence of a mighty, intelligent and beneficent divinity, possessed of foresight and providence, the life to come, the happiness of the just, the punishment of the wicked, the sanctity of the social contract and the laws: these are its positive dogmas. Its negative dogmas I confine to one, intolerance, which is a part of the cults we have rejected.

Those who distinguish civil from theological intolerance are, to my mind, mistaken. The two forms are inseparable. It is impossible to live at peace with those we regard as damned; to love them would be to hate God who punishes them: we positively must either reclaim or torment them. Wherever theological intolerance is admitted, it must inevitably have some civil effect; and as soon as it has such an effect, the sovereign is no longer sovereign even in the temporal sphere: thenceforth priests are the real masters, and kings only their ministers.

Now that there is and can be no longer an exclusive national religion, tolerance should be given to all religions that tolerate others, so long as their dogmas contain nothing contrary to the duties of citizenship. But whoever dares to say: Outside the Church is no salvation, ought to be driven from the state, unless the state is the Church, and the prince the pontiff. Such a dogma is good only in a theocratic government; in any other, it is fatal. The reason for which Henry IV is said to have embraced the Roman religion ought to make every honest man leave it, and still more any prince who knows how to reason.

Chapter 9

Thomas Paine (1737–1809)

As to religion, I hold it to be the indispensable duty of all government, to protect all conscientious professors thereof, and I know of no other business which government has to do therewith.

Introduction

By the time Thomas Paine came to write *Common Sense* (in January 1776) he had already lived several lives and, following it, was to live several more. Maker of corsets, sailor, customs and excise man, tutor, shopkeeper, twice married (his first wife died and he was separated from his second), he arrived in Philadelphia, aged 37, having emigrated from England towards the end of 1774. It was then he began his career as editor and journalist. He was a man of restless energy, broad intellectual sensibilities and an acute moral sensitivity honed by a strong Quaker upbringing. An abolitionist before his time (and Lord Wilberforce's), he was a defender of women's rights, animal rights and the rights of the poor, an advocate of the redistribution of wealth and a fervent anti-colonialist. He imaginatively inhabited a future political vision that those following him (like the revolutionary English poet Shelley and the great political innovator Abraham Lincoln) never forgot. In fact, the nineteenth-century English writer William Cobbett (whom American democracy turned into a Tory patriot and the Industrial Revolution into a radical!) claimed that the day in 1774 when Paine was dismissed from the government Excise office and so began looking for where his ambitions would take him next, was the origin of the American War of Independence. For Paine went to London, befriended Benjamin Franklin and was persuaded to emigrate. The famous Boston Tea Party (where American radicals boarded ships carrying tea from England and threw it into the sea as a complaint about an imposed British tax on tea) had taken place 11 months prior to Paine's arrival in America. Nevertheless, as John Adams (who was certainly no champion of Paine) pointed out in 1805, 'Without the pen of Paine the sword of Washington would have been wielded in vain'.

Common Sense was the first of the influential writings that flowed from that pen. It sold 150,000 copies and by 4 July 1776 Congress had boldly made their Declaration of Independence. In the same month Paine enlisted in the American militia, which since April of that same year had been at war with the British. The

British army was there to protect the colonies from the Indians. In fact, the army subsequently enlisted the help of the Indians in fighting the Americans!

It was not just a matter of a tax on tea. In fact, it took many more years for the American people to be convinced that independence from Britain was a good thing. Franklin is a good example of reluctant support, because he moved between London and Boston, his family came from England, and some remained there. Many were Tory and furiously patriotic to the king (George III). What the king thought we will examine in a moment. High taxation was one issue. Britain was at war with France and making its first serious sallies into what would become a major colony, India. Taxation was high in Britain as well. But though taxed and also British citizens, the Americans had no representation in the British Parliament (which passed laws on taxation). Furthermore, the colony was not allowed to trade independently with other European countries. All goods from America had to be sent via England and likewise all goods from Europe going to America. So, prices were high, and George III was not a man who ever made concessions – to any colony or to Parliament.

Paine's thinking on monarchy has to be set alongside that of James VI/I. For in his anti-monarchalism he is attacking vestiges of what still remained of the Divine Right of Kings' doctrine and royal supremacy over the Church of England. Although, in England, the restoration of the monarchy, following the Protectorate of Oliver Cromwell, gave the British Parliament a much stronger basis for exercising its own powers, the Hannoverian King George III (whose madness is now recognized) had absolutist dreams and, from the beginning of his reign in 1760, made several attempts to curtail the rights of Parliament. When, in 1791, he wrote Part I of *Rights of Man,* Paine drew attention to Edmund Burke's defence of kingship and the national Church.[1] He critiqued this social hierarchy in the name of 'the divine origin of the rights of man at creation', with Adam. Then he outlined three political ages: a 'Government by priestcraft', a government 'by conquerors, and the third of Reason'. Of the race of conquerors, their

> Governments thus established last as long as the power to support them lasts; but that they might avail themselves of every engine in their favour, they united fraud to force, and set up an idol which they called *Divine Right,* and which, in imitation of the Pope, who affects to be spiritual and temporal, and in contradiction of the Founder of the Christian religion, twisted itself afterwards into an idol of another shape, called *Church and state.*

These political sentiments have their roots in the Radicals of the English Civil War (the Diggers, Ranters, Fifth Monarchists and Muggletonians) and the Nonconformists (Baptists, Congregationalists, Unitarians and Quakers) who, despite the Act of Tolerance (1689), were often regarded as second-class citizens in the rigidity of the British class system. Even under the Act of Tolerance Catholics were not allowed to exercise their freedom of conscience.

---

1. Both Burke and de Maistre represent a conservative re-evaluation of the ideals of the French Revolution which is paradigmatic of conservative thinking and is mirrored in the work of Carl Schmitt (see Part Four).

We have observed that the absolute sovereignty of monarchs rested on three principles related to law. We can observe with Paine how each of these principles is restated. First, the principle of divine law based upon revelation in Scripture is turned on its head. Taking the same passages concerning kingship, Paine demonstrates how kingship was a heathen notion and contrary to the will of God. It is significant for the kind of constitution he later outlines in *Common Sense* that Paine refers to the passage in Judges when Gideon refuses kingship for either himself or his sons. For the continental alliance of the 13 colonies of America at that time bears some similarities to the confederacy of the 12 tribes of Israel ruled over by a Judge. The Judge was conceived as the executor of the Mosaic law, and Paine makes explicit that in the new America 'THE LAW IS KING'. The polity he outlines is founded upon 'the divine law, the word of God', but it historically predates the institution of monarchy. This law is also given concrete expression in what he calls a charter: a written constitution. In fact, there is some slippage between divine law and the constitution itself.

The second law absolute monarchy appealed to was natural law, and once more Paine does not deny this law but restates it. His little vignette of how government arose from society points to a natural development based upon human beings 'being originally equals in the order of creation' and 'unextinguishable feelings for good and wise purposes' that the 'Almighty hath implanted'. He points out that the natural law analogy of paternity (as used to legitimate the absolute authority of the king) is not only a 'pretended title', but has also led to the most unnatural of ends: the king's slaughter of his own children. Paine even uses the geographical space between America and Britain as a natural argument demonstrating 'the design of Heaven' in favour of independence. Nevertheless, Paine differs from someone like Aristotle or Aquinas, for he does not see government itself as natural. Society is natural, but government arises because of human wickedness. Government is a fabricated form, established out of necessity 'to supply the defect of moral virtue'.

The third law of absolute monarchy was the power to make law itself, and this Paine returns to continually, arguing on the basis of reason (the laws passed in England treat English not American concerns) and the arbitrary use of power. Petitions could be sent from the colonies to Parliament, but there was no representation from America within Parliament itself. Americans had no ability to make their own laws. Paine places the power to make laws with the authority of the Continental Congress. He provides, to boot, a forceful argument against the hereditary succession of kingship.

What Paine sketches here are the lines upon which later notions of liberal democracy will be developed. An understanding of the relationship between this polity and religion is important. With the notion of the Divine Right of Kings, the king acts as mediator between God and the people. James VI/I viewed himself as a sacrament (the site of the encounter of transcendence and immanence – the visible sign of invisible grace). With Paine, the mediation between God and the people lies with nature. In his *Age of Reason*, written while he was imprisoned by the French in 1794, he defends religion based upon natural reason rather than

Scriptural revelation. The governing order of a society rests, then, upon purely immanent principles: nature, reason and law. Although he strongly supports 'religious tolerance' and even views the diversity of religious opinions as 'the will of the Almighty', there is no direct relationship between the power and authority of God and the power and authority exercised by any government. His anti-papal remarks militate against him extending religious tolerance to Roman Catholics, but when the American constitution came to be written there was no such discrimination. Tocqueville argued the case for Catholics strongly, as we will see – and de Maistre responded to it. The sacred and the secular, the private and the public are distinguished much in line with Protestant thinking after Luther. But the distinction is in law only. *De facto* they were not independent realms, as Paine's Quakerism and deism issue in a natural theology that impacts upon all his views. But this is Newton's God (Paine, like Franklin, was a fervent admirer of Isaac Newton) – withdrawn to an Archimedean point beyond creation, that now regulated itself according to its own intrinsic order. Nevertheless, it needs to be emphasized how much the origins and aspirations of modern democracy – enshrined in notions of liberty, equality and the human right for security in order to flourish – owe to Quakerism, deism and the natural theology they helped to foster. Methodism has often been seen as the vital spring of early democracy, but this needs to be qualified.

Common Sense marks a new beginning in Paine's life. The Protestant preacher's style – direct, aphoristic, witty, rich in metaphor and *exempla* – was put to a political use. In fact, from this point on, he is an early example of a professional politician. From war correspondent, to elected member of the American Congress, to diplomat for America in France, he eventually became elected to the French Convention following the revolution in that country. Outlawed from England because of sedition, he was imprisoned in France because he opposed the execution of Louis XVI, but released after the fall of Robespierre and handed over to the American ambassador. After ten years he returned to America, where he remained in retirement until his death in 1809. He was a man of many lives, but of one thing he was inordinately proud: he made no money from the enormous sales of *Common Sense*, for what money he did receive was sent to buy mittens for the American troops in Quebec.

Further reading

General introductions

Conway, M. (1974), *The Life of Thomas Paine, with a History of his Literary, Political, and Religious Career in America, France, and England. To Which Is Added a Sketch of Paine by William Cobbett* (2 vols) (Folcroft, PA: Folcroft Library Editions).

Kaye, H. (2000), *Thomas Paine: Firebrand of the Revolution* (New York: Oxford University Press).

Keane, J. (2003), *Tom Paine: A Political Life* (New York: Grove Press).

Reception of key ideas

Davidson, E. and Scheick, W. (1994), *Paine, Scripture, and Authority: The Age of Reason as Religious and Political Idea.* (Bethlehem, PA: Lehigh University Press).

Kaye, H. (2005), *Thomas J. Paine and the Promise of America* (New York: Hill & Wang).

Excerpt from *Common Sense*

Preface

The cause of America is in a great measure the cause of all mankind. Many circumstances have, and will arise, which are not local, but universal, and through which the principles of all Lovers of Mankind are affected, and in the event of which, their affections are interested. The laying of a country desolate with fire and sword, declaring war against the natural rights of all mankind, and extirpating the defenders thereof from the face of the earth, is the concern of every man to whom nature has given the power of feeling; of which class, regardless of party censures, is the author. [. . .]

Chapter 1

Some writers have so confounded society with government, as to leave little or no distinction between them; whereas they are not only different, but have different origins. Society is produced by our wants, and government by our wickedness; the former promotes our happiness positively by uniting our affections, the latter negatively by restraining our vices. The one encourages intercourse, the other creates distinctions. The first is a patron, the last a punisher.

Society in every state is a blessing, but government even in its best state is but a necessary evil, in its worst state an intolerable one; for when we suffer, or are exposed to the same miseries by a government, which we might expect in a country without government, our calamities are heightened by reflecting that we furnish the means by which we suffer! Government, like dress, is the badge of lost innocence; the palaces of kings are built on the ruins of the bowers of paradise. For were the impulses of conscience clear, uniform, and irresistibly obeyed, man would need no other lawgiver; but that not being the case, he finds it necessary to surrender up a part of his property to furnish means for the protection of the rest; and this he is induced to do by the same prudence which in every other case advises him out of two evils to choose the least. Wherefore, *security being the true design and end of government,* it unanswerably follows that whatever form thereof appears most likely to ensure it to us, with the least expense and greatest benefit, is preferable to all others.

In order to gain a clear and just idea of the design and end of government, let us suppose a small number of persons settled in some sequestered part of the earth, unconnected with the rest, they will then represent the first peopling of any country, or of the world. In this state of natural liberty, society will be their first thought. A thousand motives will excite them thereto, the strength of one man is so unequal to his wants, and his mind so unfitted for perpetual solitude, that he is soon obliged to seek assistance and relief of another, who in his turn requires the same. Four or five united would be able to raise a tolerable dwelling in the midst of a wilderness, but one man might labour out the common period of life without accomplishing any thing; when he had felled his timber he could not remove it, nor erect it after it was removed; hunger in the meantime would urge him from his work, and every different want call him a different way. Disease, nay even misfortune, would be death. For though neither might be mortal, yet either would disable him from living, and reduce him to a state in which he might rather be said to perish than to die.

Thus necessity, like a gravitating power, would soon form our newly arrived emigrants into society, the reciprocal blessings of which, would supersede, and render the obligations of law and government unnecessary while they remained perfectly just to each other; but as nothing but heaven is impregnable to vice, it will unavoidably happen, that in proportion as they surmount the first difficulties of emigration, which bound them together in a common cause, they will begin to relax in their duty and attachment to each other; and this remissness, will point out the necessity of establishing some form of government to supply the defect of moral virtue.

Some convenient tree will afford them a State-House, under the branches of which, the whole colony may assemble to deliberate on public matters. It is more than probable that their first laws will have the title only of *regulations*, and be enforced by no other penalty than public disesteem. In this first parliament every man, by natural right, will have a seat.

But as the colony increases, the public concerns will increase likewise, and the distance at which the members may be separated will render it too inconvenient for all of them to meet on every occasion as at first, when their number was small, their habitations near, and the public concerns few and trifling. This will point out the convenience of their consenting to leave the legislative part to be managed by a select number chosen from the whole body, who are supposed to have the same concerns at stake which those have who appointed them, and who will act in the same manner as the whole body would act were they present. If the colony continue increasing, it will become necessary to augment the number of the representatives, and that the interest of every part of the colony may be attended to, it will be found best to divide the whole into convenient parts, each part sending its proper number; and that the elected might never form to themselves an interest separate from the electors, prudence will point out the propriety of having elections often; because as the elected might by that means return and mix again with the general body of the electors in a few months, their fidelity to the public will be secured by the prudent reflection of not making a rod for themselves. And as this frequent interchange will establish a common interest with every part of the community, they will mutually and naturally support each other, and on this (not on the unmeaning name of king) depends the strength of government, and the happiness of the governed.

Here then is the origin and rise of government; namely, a mode rendered necessary by the inability of moral virtue to govern the world; here too is the design and end of government, viz. freedom and security. And however our eyes may be dazzled with snow, or our ears deceived by sound; however prejudice may warp our wills, or interest darken our understanding, the simple voice of nature and of reason will say, it is right.

Chapter 2

Mankind being originally equals in the order of creation, the equality could only be destroyed by some subsequent circumstance; the distinctions of rich, and poor, may in a great measure be accounted for, and that without having recourse to the harsh, ill-sounding names of oppression and avarice. Oppression is often the consequence, but seldom or never the means of riches; and though avarice will preserve a man from being necessitously poor, it generally makes him too timorous to be wealthy.

But there is another and greater distinction for which no truly natural or religious reason can be assigned, and that is, the distinction of men into *kings* and *subjects*. Male and female are the distinctions of nature, good and bad the distinctions of heaven; but how a race of men came into the world so exalted above the rest, and distinguished like some new species, is worth enquiring into, and whether they are the means of happiness or of misery to mankind.

In the early ages of the world, according to the scripture chronology, there were no kings; the consequence of which was there were no wars; it is the pride of kings which throws mankind into confusion. Holland without a king hath enjoyed more peace for this last century than any of the monarchial governments in Europe. Antiquity favours the same remark; for the quiet and rural lives of the first patriarchs hath a happy something in them, which vanishes away when we come to the history of Jewish royalty.

Government by kings was first introduced into the world by the heathens, from whom the children of Israel copied the custom. It was the most prosperous invention the devil ever set on foot for the promotion of idolatry. The heathens paid divine honours to their deceased kings, and the Christian world has improved on the plan by doing the same to their living ones. How impious is the title of sacred majesty applied to a worm, who in the midst of his splendour is crumbling into dust.

As the exalting one man so greatly above the rest cannot be justified on the equal rights of nature, so neither can it be defended on the authority of scripture; for the will of the Almighty, as declared by Gideon and the prophet Samuel, expressly disapproves of government by kings. All anti-monarchial parts of scripture have been very smoothly glossed over in monarchial governments, but they undoubtedly merit the attention of countries which have their governments yet to form. 'Render unto Caesar the things which are Caesar's' is the scriptural doctrine of courts, yet it is no support of monarchial government, for the Jews at that time were without a king, and in a state of vassalage to the Romans.

Near three thousand years passed away from the Mosaic account of the creation, till the Jews under a national delusion requested a king. Till then their form of government (except in extraordinary cases, where the Almighty interposed) was a kind of republic administered by a judge and the elders of the tribes. Kings they had none, and it was held sinful to acknowledge any being under that title but the Lords of Hosts. And when a man seriously reflects on the idolatrous homage which is paid to the persons of Kings, he need not wonder, that the Almighty, ever jealous of his honour, should disapprove of a form of government which so impiously invades the prerogative of heaven.

Monarchy is ranked in scripture as one of the sins of the Jews, for which a curse in reserve is denounced against them. The history of that transaction is worth attending to.

The children of Israel being oppressed by the Midianites, Gideon marched against them with a small army, and victory, thro' the divine interposition, decided in his favour. The Jews elate with success, and attributing it to the generalship of Gideon, proposed making him a king, saying, 'Rule thou over us, thou and thy son and thy son's son'. Here was temptation in its fullest extent; not a kingdom only, but an hereditary one, but Gideon in the piety of his soul replied, 'I will not rule over you, neither shall my son rule over you, The Lord shall rule over you.' Words need not be more explicit; Gideon does not decline the honour but denies their right to give it; neither does he compliment them with invented declarations of his thanks, but in the positive stile of a prophet charges them with disaffection to their proper sovereign, the King of Heaven.

About one hundred and thirty years after this, they fell again into the same error. The hankering which the Jews had for the idolatrous customs of the heathens, is something exceedingly unaccountable; but so it was, that laying hold of the misconduct of Samuel's two sons, who were entrusted with some secular concerns, they came in an abrupt and clamorous manner to Samuel, saying, 'Behold thou art old and thy sons walk not in thy ways, now make us a king to judge us like all the other nations'. And here we cannot but observe that their motives were bad, viz. that they might be like unto other nations, i.e. the heathens, whereas their true glory laid in being as much unlike them as possible. But the thing displeased Samuel when they said, 'Give us a king to judge us'; and Samuel prayed unto the Lord, and the Lord said unto Samuel, 'Hearken unto the voice of the people in all that they say unto thee, for they have not rejected thee, but they have rejected me, THEN I SHOULD NOT REIGN OVER THEM. According to all the works which I have done since the day; wherewith they brought them up out of Egypt, even unto this day; wherewith they have forsaken me and served other Gods; so do they also unto thee. Now therefore hearken unto their voice, howbeit, protest solemnly unto them and show them the manner of the king that shall reign over them', i.e. not of any particular king, but the general manner of the kings of the earth, whom Israel was so eagerly copying after. And notwithstanding the great distance of time and difference of manners, the character is still in fashion. And Samuel told all the words of the Lord unto the people, that asked of him a king. And he said, 'This shall be the manner of the king that shall reign over you; he will take your sons and appoint them for himself for his chariots, and to be his horsemen, and some shall run before his chariots' (this description agrees with the present mode of impressing men) 'and he will appoint him captains over thousands and captains over fifties, and will set them to ear his ground and to reap his harvest, and to make his instruments of war, and instruments of his chariots; and he will take your daughters to be confectioneries and to be cooks and to be bakers' (this describes the expense and luxury as well as the oppression of kings) 'and he will take your fields and your olive yards, even the best of them, and give them to his servants; and he will take the tenth of your seed, and of your vineyards, and give them to his officers and to his servants' (by which we see that bribery, corruption, and favouritism are the standing vices of kings) 'and he will take the tenth of your men servants, and your maid servants, and your goodliest young men and your asses, and put them to his work; and he will take the tenth of your sheep, and ye shall be his servants, and ye shall cry out in that day because of your king which ye shall have chosen, AND THE LORD WILL NOT HEAR YOU IN THAT DAY.'

This accounts for the continuation of monarchy; neither do the characters of the few good kings which have lived since, either sanctify the title, or blot out the sinfullness of the origin; the high encomium given of David takes no notice of him officially as a king, but only as a man after God's own heart. Nevertheless the people refused to obey the voice of Samuel, and they said, 'Nay, but we will have a king over us, that we may be like all the nations, and that our king may judge us, and go out before us and fight our battles.' Samuel continued to reason with them, but to no purpose; he set before them their ingratitude, but all would not avail; and seeing them fully bent on their folly, he cried out, 'I will call unto the Lord, and he shall send thunder and rain' (which then was a punishment, being the time of wheat harvest) 'that ye may perceive and see that your wickedness is great which ye have done in the sight of the Lord, IN ASKING YOU A KING.' So Samuel called unto the Lord, and the Lord sent thunder and rain that day, and all the people greatly feared the Lord and Samuel. And all the people said unto Samuel, 'Pray for thy servants unto the Lord thy God that we die not, for WE HAVE ADDED UNTO OUR SINS THIS EVIL, TO ASK A KING.' These portions of scripture are direct and positive. They admit of no equivocal construction. That the Almighty has here entered his protest against monarchial government is true, or the scripture is false. And a man has good reason to believe that there is as much of king-craft, as priest-craft in withholding the scripture from the public in Popish countries. For monarchy in every instance is the Popery of government.

To the evil of monarchy we have added that of hereditary succession; and as the first is a degradation and lessening of ourselves, so the second, claimed as a matter of right, is an insult and an imposition on posterity. *For all men being originally equals*, no one by birth could have a right to set up his own family in perpetual preference to all others for ever, and though himself might deserve some decent degree of honours of his contemporaries, yet his descendants might be far too unworthy to inherit them. One of the strongest natural proofs of the folly of hereditary right in kings is that *nature* disapproves it, otherwise she would not so frequently turn it into ridicule by giving mankind an ass for a lion.

Secondly, as no man at first could possess any other public honours than were bestowed upon him, so the givers of those honours could have no power to give away the right of posterity, and though they might say, 'We choose you for our head,' they could not, without manifest injustice to their children, say 'that your children and your children's children shall reign over ours for ever.' Because such an unwise, unjust, unnatural compact might (perhaps) in the next succession put them under the government of a rogue or a fool. Most wise men, in their private sentiments, have ever treated hereditary right with contempt; yet it is one of those evils, which when once established is not easily removed; many submit from fear, others from superstition, and the more powerful part shares with the king the plunder of the rest.

This is supposing the present race of kings in the world to have had an honourable origin; whereas it is more than probable, that could we take off the dark covering of antiquity, and trace them to their first rise, that we should find the first of them nothing better than the principal ruffian of some restless gang, whose savage manners of pre-eminence in subtlety obtained him the title of chief among plunderers; and who by increasing in power, and extending his depredations, overawed the quiet and defenceless to purchase their safety by frequent contributions. Yet his electors could have no idea of giving hereditary right to his descendants, because such a perpetual exclusion of themselves was incompatible with the free and unrestrained principles they professed to live by. Wherefore, hereditary succession in the early ages of monarchy could not take place as a matter of claim, but as something casual or complemental; but as few or no records were extant in those days, and traditionary history stuffed with fables, it was very easy, after the lapse of a few generations, to trump up some superstitious tale, conveniently timed, Mahomet like, to cram hereditary right down the throats of the vulgar. Perhaps the disorders which threatened, or seemed to threaten on the decease of a leader and the choice of a new one (for elections among ruffians could not be very orderly) induced many at first to favour hereditary pretensions; by which means it happened, as it has happened since, that what at first was submitted to as a convenience, was afterwards claimed as a right. [. . .]

Yet I should be glad to ask how they suppose kings came at first? The question admits but of three answers, viz. either by lot, by election, or by usurpation. If the first king was taken by lot, it establishes a precedent for the next, which excludes hereditary succession. Saul was by lot yet the succession was not hereditary, neither does it appear from that transaction there was any intention it ever should. If the first king of any country was by election, that likewise establishes a precedent for the next; for to say, that the right of all future generations is taken away, by the act of the first electors, in their choice not only of a king, but of a family of kings for ever, has no parallel in or out of scripture but the doctrine of original sin, which supposes the free will of all men lost in Adam; and from such comparison, and it will admit of no other, hereditary succession can derive no glory. For as in Adam all sinned, and as in the first electors all men obeyed; as in the one all mankind were subjected to Satan, and in the other to sovereignty; as our innocence was lost in the first, and our authority in the last; and as both disable us from reassuming some former state and privilege, it unanswerably follows that original sin and hereditary succession are parallels. Dishonourable rank! Inglorious connection! Yet the most subtle sophist cannot produce a juster simile.

146

Chapter 3

[. . .] Everything that is right or natural pleads for separation. The blood of the slain, the weeping voice of nature cries, 'IT IS TIME TO PART.' Even the distance at which the Almighty has placed England and America, is a strong and natural proof, that the authority of the one, over the other, was never the design of Heaven. The time likewise at which the continent was discovered, adds weight to the argument, and the manner in which it was peopled increases the force of it. The reformation was preceded by the discovery of America, as if the Almighty graciously meant to open a sanctuary to the persecuted in future years, when home should afford neither friendship nor safety.

Chapter 4

Let the assemblies be annual, with a President only. The representation more equal, their business wholly domestic, and subject to the authority of a Continental Congress.

Let each colony be divided into six, eight, or ten, convenient districts, each district to send a proper number of delegates to Congress, so that each colony send at least thirty. The whole number in Congress will be at least ninety. Each Congress to sit and to choose a president by the following method. When the delegates are met, let a colony be taken from the whole thirteen colonies by lot, after which let the whole Congress choose (by ballot) a president from out of the delegates of that province. In the next Congress, let a colony be taken by lot from twelve only, omitting that colony from which the president was taken in the former Congress, and so proceeding on till the whole thirteen shall have had their proper rotation. And in order that nothing may pass into a law but what is satisfactorily just, not less than three fifths of the Congress to be called a majority. He that will promote discord, under a government so equally formed as this, would join Lucifer in his revolt.

But as there is a peculiar delicacy, from whom, or in what manner, this business must first arise, and as it seems most agreeable and consistent, that it should come from some intermediate body between the governed and the governors, that is between the Congress and the people, let a CONTINENTAL CONFERENCE be held, in the following manner, and for the following purpose.

A committee of twenty-six members of Congress, viz. two for each colony. Two members for each house of assembly, or Provincial convention; and five representatives of the people at large, to be chosen in the capital city or town of each province, for, and on behalf of the whole province, by as many qualified voters as shall think proper to attend from all parts of the province for that purpose; or, if more convenient, the representatives may be chosen in two or three of the most populous parts thereof. In this conference, thus assembled, will be united, the two grand principles of business, knowledge and power. The members of Congress, Assemblies, or Conventions, by having had experience in national concerns, will be able and useful counsellors, and the whole, being empowered by the people will have a truly legal authority.

The conferring members being met, let their business be to frame a CONTINENTAL CHARTER, or Charter of the United Colonies; (answering to what is called the Magna Carta of England) fixing the number and manner of choosing members of Congress, members of Assembly, with their date of sitting, and drawing the line of business and jurisdiction between them: (Always remembering, that our strength is continental, not provincial.) Securing freedom and property to all men, and *above all things the free exercise of religion*, according to the dictates of conscience; with such other matter as is necessary for a charter to contain. Immediately after which, the said conference to dissolve, and the bodies which shall be chosen conformable to the said charter, to be the legislators and governors of this continent for the time being: Whose peace and happiness, may *God preserve, Amen.* [. . .]

But where says some is the King of America? I'll tell you, friend, he reigns above, and does not make havoc of mankind like the Royal of Britain. Yet that we may not appear to be defective even in earthly honours, let a day be solemnly set apart for proclaiming the charter; let it be brought forth, placed on the divine law, the word of God; let a crown be placed thereon, by which the world may know, that so far as we approve of monarchy, that in America THE LAW IS KING. For as in absolute governments the King is law, so in free countries the law ought to be King; and there ought to be no other. But lest any ill use should afterwards arise, let the crown at the conclusion of the ceremony be demolished, and scattered among the people whose right it is. [. . .]

As to religion, I hold it to be the indispensable duty of all government, to protect all conscientious professors thereof, and I know of no other business which government has to do therewith. Let a man throw aside that narrowness of soul, that selfishness of principle, which the niggards of all professions are so unwilling to part with, and he will be at once delivered of his fears on that head. Suspicion is the companion of mean souls, and the bane of all good society. For myself I fully and conscientiously believe, that it is the *will of the Almighty*, that there should be *diversity of religious opinions* among us: it affords a larger field for our Christian kindness. Were we all of one way of thinking, our religious dispositions would want matter for probation; and on this liberal principle, I look on the various denominations among us, to be like children of the same family, differing only, in what is called their Christian names.

Chapter 10

Alexis de Tocqueville 1805–59

Religion in America takes no direct part in the government of society, but it must be regarded as the first of their political institutions; for if it does not impart a taste for freedom, it facilitates the use of it.

Introduction

Alexis de Tocqueville was both a profound sociologist of American society and one of the great pioneers of democracy. This illustrates how democracy was inextricably linked to the rise of the United States of America. In contrast to the old continent, the new continent offered Tocqueville the possibility to study a democracy in its most advanced and most modern form from a sociological and a theoretical viewpoint. This double approach is also reflected in the composition of his famous book *Democracy in America,* from which the following excerpts are taken.

The first volume of the book introduces democracy in America in a much more descriptive way than the second. The second volume is written from a theoretical perspective with the intention of discussing the nature of democracy and the necessary means for its maintenance. The first volume was published in 1835, two years after the author returned from his journey to the United States. In the first volume, Tocqueville demonstrates his extraordinary sociological skills by analysing the democratic culture he has encountered. We employ the term *democratic culture* rather than democracy, because Tocqueville's sociological analysis is not restricted to a specific form of democratic government in terms of legal regulations and bureaucratic organization. He is analysing 'democracy' in a much broader sense of the word. 'Democratic culture' here encompasses a democratic way of life; a certain set of values underpinning democracy, such as equality before the law, free speech, habeas corpus, as well as a specific cultural condition that is fashioned by democracy. This democratic culture is one of the key themes in Tocqueville's oeuvre; and so this includes the phenomenon of religion.

In the second volume, published five years later in 1840, his main concern is precisely the question of religion in a democratic culture. In this volume he also draws attention in particular to the equality of conditions (*égalité des conditions*) that exist within a democratic culture. Here Tocqueville offers a remarkable critique of democracy when he warns of the perils of equality among citizens.

At a first glance Tocqueville's argument seems to be paradoxical. On the one hand, democratic culture is *based* on equality, that is, the equality of conditions, and, on the other, equality is the greatest *enemy* of a democratic culture. 'It must be acknowledged that equality, which brings great benefits into the world, nevertheless suggests to men [. . .] some dangerous propensities. It finds to isolate them from one another, to concentrate every man's attention upon himself; and it lays open the soul to an inordinate love of material gratification.' Equality has a double-negative effect. First, equality directly makes people feel independent and thus socially atomized. As a consequence, a mass of atomized individuals are not able to perform as a strong social unit and, therefore, can easily become enslaved to a tyrant. Everyone seeks to achieve his/her individual goals and material interests and this leads inevitably to a decline in solidarity and the possibility of democratic culture. We can say with Tocqueville, a loss of solidarity is directly linked to the equality of conditions among a people and is likely to give rise to tyranny. Second, in democratic cultures where everyone is equal in principle, the real exercise of power depends on public opinion. Public opinion, or common sense as Thomas Paine calls it, is the clearest expression of the will of the masses and therefore the majority of a people. But there is no guarantee that public opinion is an expression of what is morally good or that the will of the majority is in accordance with the law. This becomes evident when public opinion supersedes the personal rights of an individual or a minority.[1] Tocqueville, the French aristocrat, was always sceptical about the rule of the people in terms of the rule of the majority. He calls this danger implied in every democratic form of government 'tyranny of the majority'. In sum, the double-negative effect of equality manifests itself in the potential for two forms of tyranny. As far as the first effect is concerned, that is, the loss of solidarity, a democratic culture is always at risk of collapsing into the tyranny of dictatorial dominion. In the second case, tyranny is *de facto* exercised by the dictate of the public opinion of the majority. Throughout the history of the development of democratic cultures in the United States, Europe and, subsequently, many other countries around the world, Tocqueville's examination of democracy's inclination to become a tyrannical form of government has found its validation.

Tocqueville's contribution to sociology and the theory of democracy is also crucial for a modern understanding of the relationship between religion and politics. He is the first author who seeks to combine, or even tries to *reconcile*, the Christian religion with democracy. It is important to note here that Tocqueville, who was not hostile to monarchy at all, was still convinced that the American model of democracy would be the future form of political government in Europe. The substratum of his critical defence of democracy is its link with religion. Only a democratic culture which is impregnated with religion is sustainable because it can resist its tyrannical tendencies. To a certain extent, more obviously in the first volume of *Democracy in America*, democratic culture is portrayed ideally as the society of the freest and, at the same time, most religious people. Contrasting

---

1. See chapter 7, volume 1 of *Democracy in America*.

American society with the situation in Europe, he writes: 'The philosophers of the eighteenth century explained in a very simple manner the gradual decay of religious faith. Religious zeal, said they, must necessarily fail the more generally liberty is established and knowledge diffused. Unfortunately, the facts by no means accord with their theory. There are certain populations in Europe whose unbelief is only equalled by their ignorance and debasement; while in America, one of the freest and most enlightened nations in the world, the people fulfil with fervour all the outward duties of religion. . . . In France I had almost always seen the spirit of religion and the spirit of freedom marching in opposite directions. But in America I found they were intimately united and they reigned in common over the same country.'

It is evident from this quotation that Tocqueville prefers the American model to the secularized condition in Europe, but does not reject the Enlightenment as such. He merely juxtaposes two forms of Enlightenment or two possible results of the Enlightenment. Tocqueville's emphatic thesis is that religion is necessary for the maintenance of democratic culture and to preserve the freedom of the people. We have already encountered this idea, that democracy needs religion, in Rousseau. Rousseau proposed a civil religion to complement democratic forms of government and outlined its structure in terms of a minimalist political deism. In contrast to Rousseau, Tocqueville does not give any *a priori* criteria for a particular form of religion; rather he analyses the kind of religion which has empirically emerged in the States. 'The greatest part of British America was peopled by men who, after having shaken off the authority of the Pope, acknowledged no other supremacy: they brought with them into the New World a form of Christianity which I cannot better describe than by styling it a democratic and republican religion. This contributed powerfully to the establishment of a republic and a democracy in public affairs; and from the beginning, politics and religion contracted an alliance which has never been dissolved.' It might be expected that Tocqueville sees Protestantism as the most democratic form of religion. But in fact, he clearly draws attention to the role that Catholicism plays. In the context of what we have observed in the previous section, when the Divine Right of Kings and proto-democratic forms of governments were paralleled with Catholicism and Protestantism, Tocqueville's positive evaluation of Catholicism for the flourishing of democratic culture is strikingly original. But he envisages that it is a form of Catholicism which has 'shaken off the authority of the Pope'.

Tocqueville, who himself was rather agnostic, although a Catholic, remained a person interested in the *function* of religion, the kind of Christianity in America which supported a democratic culture. According to his sociological approach, he ensures his readers that he is 'considering religions in a purely human point of view'. This is to say that Tocqueville's account of religion in America represents another type of functionalist approach. The prevailing question is: *how* does religion, as it can be studied in America, maintain and nurture democratic culture?

In the chapters treating religion in *Democracy in America*, we can distinguish three different functions that religion plays and which the existing kinds of

Christianity fulfil. First, religion generates solidarity. This, we might say, is the fundamental argument in his functionalist approach, and it was also the main reason that Rousseau made appeal to civil religion. Second, religion provides the sources for morality and the moral education of the people. In the democratic culture of the United States, Tocqueville states, religion directly influences the public opinion: '. . . it directs the customs of the community and, by regulating domestic life, it regulates the state'. Thus, Christianity is the moral soil on which democratic government can flourish. But there is one restriction religion has to obey. Religion has to remain strictly *apolitical*; it must restrict itself to the private domain and must not interfere with the business of government. Tocqueville insists that whenever 'religion clings to the interest of the world, it becomes almost as fragile a thing as the powers of earth'. In other words, whenever religion plays a directly political role, it loses its positive effects on a democracy and will, in the long run, become insignificant. However, when religion is restricted to the domestic sphere, it can exercise an impact on society, and so Tocqueville concludes: 'Religion in America takes no direct part in the government of society, but it must be regarded as the first of their political institutions'. The apolitical nature of religion that Tocqueville demands also distinguishes him from the kind of functionalist approach taken by Machiavelli. From a Machiavellian point of view, religion is just another tool for politics and must be used if necessary to preserve political power (regardless of whether the use is moral or immoral). Tocqueville however, understands religion to be the precondition for moral politics. Third, religion has the function of counterbalancing the negative effects of social equality, because religion deals with immaterial matters and directs the desire of the people to otherworldly and eternal things. Religion functions then as an antidote for the rapacious individualism that democracy fosters.

Further reading

General introductions

Siedentop, L. (1994), *Tocqueville* (Oxford: Oxford University Press).

Zunz, O. and Kahan, A. (2002), *The Tocqueville Reader; A Life in Letters and Politics* (Oxford: Blackwell).

Welch, C. (2001), *De Tocqueville* (New York: Oxford University Press).

Reception of key ideas

Allen, B. (2005), *Tocqueville, Covenant, and the Democratic Revolution: Harmonizing Earth with Heaven* (Lanham, MD: Lexington Books).

Galston, W. (2005), *Public Matters: Essays on Politics, Policy, and Religion* (Lanham, MD: Rowman & Littlefield Publishers).

Mitchell, J. (1995), *The Fragility of Freedom: Tocqueville on Religion, Democracy, and the American Future* (Chicago, IL: University of Chicago Press).

Excerpt from *Democracy in America**

Religion considered as a political institution which powerfully contributes to the maintenance of a democratic republic among the Americans.

By the side of every religion is to be found a political opinion, which is connected with it by affinity. If the human mind be left to follow its own bent, it will regulate the temporal and spiritual institutions of society in a uniform manner, and man will endeavor, if I may so speak, to harmonize earth with heaven.

The greatest part of British America was peopled by men who, after having shaken off the authority of the Pope, acknowledged no other religious supremacy: they brought with them into the New World a form of Christianity which I cannot better describe than by styling it a *democratic and republican religion.* This contributed powerfully to the establishment of a republic and a democracy in public affairs; and from the beginning, politics and religion contracted an alliance which has never been dissolved.

About fifty years ago Ireland began to pour a Catholic population into the United States; and on their part, the Catholics of America made proselytes, so that, at the present moment more than a million Christians professing the truths of the Church of Rome are to be found in the Union. These Catholics are faithful to the observances of their religion; they are fervent and zealous in the belief of their doctrines. Yet they constitute the most republican and the most democratic class in the United States. This fact may surprise the observer at first, but the causes of it may easily be discovered upon reflection.

I think that the Catholic religion has erroneously been regarded as the natural enemy of democracy. Among the various sects of Christians, Catholicism seems to me, on the contrary, to be one of the most favorable to equality of condition among men. In the Catholic Church the religious community is composed of only two elements: the priest and the people. The priest alone rises above the rank of his flock, and all below him are equal.

On doctrinal points the Catholic faith places all human capacities upon the same level; it subjects the wise and ignorant, the man of genius and the vulgar crowd, to the details of the same creed; it imposes the same observances upon the rich and the needy, it inflicts the same austerities upon the strong and the weak; it listens to no compromise with mortal man, but, reducing all the human race to the same standard, it confounds all the distinctions of society at the foot of the same altar, even as they are confounded in the sight of God. If Catholicism predisposes the faithful to obedience, it certainly does not prepare them for inequality; but the contrary may be said of Protestantism, which generally tends to make men independent more than to render them equal. *Catholicism is like an absolute monarchy; if the sovereign be removed, all the other classes of society are more equal than in republics.*

It has not infrequently occurred that the Catholic priest has left the service of the altar to mix with the governing powers of society and to take his place among the

---

* Italics have been added by the editors for emphasis.

civil ranks of men. This religious influence has sometimes been used to secure the duration of that political state of things to which he belonged. Thus we have seen Catholics taking the side of aristocracy from a religious motive. But no sooner is the priesthood entirely separated from the government, as is the case in the United States, than it is found that no class of men is more naturally disposed than the Catholics to transfer the doctrine of the equality of condition into the political world.

If, then, the Catholic citizens of the United States are not forcibly led by the nature of their tenets to adopt democratic and republican principles, at least they are not necessarily opposed to them; and their social position, as well as their limited number, obliges them to adopt these opinions. Most of the Catholics are poor, and they have no chance of taking a part in the government unless it is open to all the citizens. They constitute a minority, and all rights must be respected in order to ensure to them the free exercise of their own privileges. These two causes induce them, even unconsciously, to adopt political doctrines which they would perhaps support with less zeal if they were rich and preponderant.

The Catholic clergy of the United States have never attempted to oppose this political tendency; but they seek rather to justify it. The Catholic priests in America have divided the intellectual world into two parts: in the one they place the doctrines of revealed religion, which they assent to without discussion, in the other they leave those political truths which they believe the Deity has left open to free inquiry. Thus the Catholics of the United States are at the same time the most submissive believers and the most independent citizens.

It may be asserted, then, that in the United States no religious doctrine displays the slightest hostility to democratic and republican institutions. The clergy of all the different sects there hold the same language; their opinions are in agreement with the laws, and the human mind flows onwards, so to speak, in one undivided current.[. . .]

Indirect influence *of religious opinions upon political society in the United States*

I have just shown what the direct influence of religion upon politics is in the United States; but its indirect influence appears to me to be still more considerable, and it never instructs the Americans more fully in the art of being free than when it says nothing of freedom.

The sects that exist in the United States are innumerable. They all differ in respect to the worship which is due to the Creator; but they all agree in respect to the duties which are due from man to man. Each sect adores the Deity in its own peculiar manner, but all sects preach the same moral law in the name of God. If it be of the highest importance to man, as an individual, that his religion should be true, it is not so to society. Society has no future life to hope for or to fear; and provided the citizens profess a religion, the peculiar tenets of that religion are of little importance to its interests. Moreover, all the sects of the United States are comprised within the great unity of Christianity, and Christian morality is everywhere the same.

It may fairly be believed that a certain number of Americans pursue a peculiar form of worship from habit more than from conviction. In the United States the sovereign authority is religious, and consequently hypocrisy must be common; but there is no country in the world where the Christian religion retains a greater influence over the souls of men than in America; and there can be no greater proof of its utility and of its conformity to human nature than that its influence is powerfully felt over the *most enlightened and free nation of the earth.*

I have remarked that the American clergy in general, without even excepting those who do not admit religious liberty, are all in favor of civil freedom; but they do not support any particular political system. They keep aloof from parties and from public affairs. In the United States religion exercises but little influence upon the laws and upon the details of public opinion; but it directs the customs of the community, and, by regulating domestic life, it regulates the state.

I do not question that the great austerity of manners that is observable in the United States arises, in the first instance, from religious faith. Religion is often unable to restrain man from the numberless temptations which chance offers; nor can it check that passion for gain which everything contributes to arouse; but its influence over the mind of woman is supreme, and women are the protectors of morals. There is certainly no country in the world where the tie of marriage is more respected than in America or where conjugal happiness is more highly or worthily appreciated. In Europe almost all the disturbances of society arise from the irregularities of domestic life. To despise the natural bonds and legitimate pleasures of home is to contract a taste for excesses, a restlessness of heart, and fluctuating desires. Agitated by the tumultuous passions that frequently disturb his dwelling, the European is galled by the obedience which the legislative powers of the state exact. But when the American retires from the turmoil of public life to the bosom of his family, he finds in it the image of order and of peace. There his pleasures are simple and natural, his joys are innocent and calm; and as he finds that an orderly life is the surest path to happiness, he accustoms himself easily to moderate his opinions as well as his tastes. While the European endeavors to forget his domestic troubles by agitating society, the American derives from his own home that love of order which he afterwards carries with him into public affairs.

In the United States the influence of religion is not confined to the manners, but it extends to the intelligence of the people. Among the Anglo-Americans some profess the doctrines of Christianity from a sincere belief in them, and others do the same because they fear to be suspected of unbelief. Christianity, therefore, reigns without obstacle, by universal consent; the consequence is, as I have before observed, that every principle of the moral world is fixed and determinate, although the political world is abandoned to the debates and the experiments of men. Thus the human mind is never left to wander over a boundless field; and whatever may be its pretensions, it is checked from time to time by barriers that it cannot surmount. Before it can innovate, certain primary principles are laid down, and the boldest conceptions are subjected to certain forms which retard and stop their completion.

[. . .] If the mind of the Americans were free from all hindrances, they would shortly become the most daring innovators and the most persistent disputants in the world. But the revolutionists of America are obliged to profess an ostensible respect for Christian morality and equity, which does not permit them to violate wantonly the laws that oppose their designs; nor would they find it easy to surmount the scruples of their partisans even if they were able to get over their own. Hitherto no one in the United States has dared to advance the maxim that everything is permissible for the interests of society, an impious adage which seems to have been invented in an age of freedom to shelter all future tyrants. Thus, while the law permits the Americans to do what they please, religion prevents them from conceiving, and forbids them to commit, what is rash or unjust.

Religion in America takes no direct part in the government of society, but it must be regarded as the first of their political institutions; for if it does not impart a taste for freedom, it facilitates the use of it. Indeed, it is in this same point of view that the inhabitants of the United States themselves look upon religious belief. I do not know whether all Americans have a sincere faith in their religion – for who can search the human heart? – but I am certain that they hold it to be indispensable to the maintenance of republican institutions. This opinion is not peculiar to a class of citizens or to a party, but it belongs to the whole nation and to every rank of society.

In the United States, if a politician attacks a sect, this may not prevent the partisans of that very sect from supporting him; but if he attacks all the sects together, everyone abandons him, and he remains alone. [. . .]

The Americans combine the notions of Christianity and of liberty so intimately in their minds that it is impossible to make them conceive the one without the other; and with them this conviction does not spring from that barren, traditionary faith which seems to vegetate rather than to live in the soul.

I have known of societies formed by Americans to send out ministers of the Gospel into the new Western states, to found schools and churches there, lest religion should be allowed to die away in those remote settlements, and the rising states be less fitted to enjoy free institutions than the people from whom they came. I met with wealthy New Englanders who abandoned the country in which they were born in order to lay the foundations of Christianity and of freedom on the banks of the Missouri or in the prairies of Illinois. Thus religious zeal is perpetually warmed in the United States by the fires of patriotism. These men do not act exclusively from a consideration of a future life; eternity is only one motive of their devotion to the cause. If you converse with these missionaries of Christian civilization, you will be surprised to hear them speak so often of the goods of this world, and to meet a politician, where you expected to find a priest. They will tell you that 'all the American republics are collectively involved with each other; if the republics of the West were to fall into anarchy, or to be mastered by a despot, the republican institutions which now flourish upon the shores of the Atlantic Ocean would be in great peril. *It is therefore our interest that the new states should be religious, in order that they may permit us to remain free*'. Such are the opinions of the Americans. [. . .]

Principal causes which render religion powerful in America

Care taken by the Americans to separate the church from the state – The laws, public opinion, and even the exertions of the clergy concur to promote this end – Influence of religion upon the mind in the United States attributable to this cause – Reason for this – What is the natural state of men with regard to religion at the present time? – What are the peculiar and incidental causes which prevent men, in certain countries, from arriving at this state?

The philosophers of the eighteenth century explained in a very simple manner the gradual decay of religious faith. Religious zeal, said they, must necessarily fail the more generally liberty is established and knowledge diffused. Unfortunately, the facts by no means accord with their theory. There are certain populations in Europe whose unbelief is only equaled by their ignorance and debasement; while in America, one of the freest and most *enlightened* nations in the world, the people fulfill with fervor all the outward duties of religion.

On my arrival in the United States the religious aspect of the country was the first thing that struck my attention; and the longer I stayed there, the more I perceived the great political consequences resulting from this new state of things. In France I had almost always seen the spirit of religion and the spirit of freedom marching in opposite directions. But in America I found they were intimately united and that they reigned in common over the same country. My desire to discover the causes of this phenomenon increased from day to day. In order to satisfy it I questioned the members of all the different sects; I sought especially the society of the clergy, who are the depositaries of the different creeds and are especially interested in their duration. As a member of the Roman Catholic Church, I was more particularly brought into contact with several of its priests, with whom I became intimately acquainted. To each of these men I expressed my astonishment and explained my doubts. I found that they differed upon matters of detail alone, and that they all attributed the peaceful dominion of religion in their country mainly to the *separation of Church and state*. I do not hesitate to affirm that during my stay in America I did not meet a single individual, of the clergy or the laity, who was not of the same opinion on this point. [. . .]

Religion, then, is simply another form of hope, and it is no less natural to the human heart than hope itself. Men cannot abandon their religious faith without a kind of aberration of intellect and a sort of violent distortion of their true nature; they are invincibly brought back to more pious sentiments. Unbelief is an accident, and faith is the only permanent state of mankind. If we consider religious institutions merely in a human point of view, they may be said to derive an inexhaustible element of strength from man himself, since they belong to one of the constituent principles of human nature.

I am aware that at certain times religion may strengthen this influence, which originates in itself, by the artificial power of the laws and by the support of those temporal institutions that direct society. Religions intimately united with the governments of the earth have been known to exercise sovereign power founded on terror and faith; but when a religion contracts an alliance of this nature, I do not hesitate to affirm that it commits the same error as a man who should sacrifice his future to his present welfare; and in obtaining a power to which it has no claim, it risks that authority which is rightfully its own. When a religion founds its empire only upon the desire of immortality that lives in every human heart, it may aspire to universal dominion; but when it connects itself with a government, it must adopt maxims which are applicable only to certain nations. Thus, in forming an alliance with a political power, religion augments its authority over a few and forfeits the hope of reigning over all.

As long as a religion rests only upon those sentiments which are the consolation of all affliction, it may attract the affections of all mankind. But if it be mixed up with the bitter passions of the world, it may be constrained to defend allies whom its interests, and not the principle of love, have given to it; or to repel as antagonists men who are still attached to it, however opposed they may be to the powers with which it is allied. The Church cannot share the temporal power of the state without being the object of a portion of that animosity which the latter excites.

The political powers which seem to be most firmly established have frequently no better guarantee for their duration than the opinions of a generation, the interests of the time, or the life of an individual. A law may modify the social condition which seems to be most fixed and determinate; and with the social condition everything else must change. The powers of society are more or less fugitive, like the years that we spend upon earth; they succeed each other with rapidity, like the fleeting cares of life; and no government has ever yet been founded upon an invariable disposition of the human heart or upon an imperishable interest.

As long as a religion is sustained by those feelings, propensities, and passions which are found to occur under the same forms at all periods of history, it may defy the efforts of time; or at least it can be destroyed only by another religion. But when religion clings to the interests of the world, it becomes almost as fragile a thing as the powers of earth. It is the only one of them all which can hope for immortality; but if it be connected with their ephemeral power, it shares their fortunes and may fall with those transient passions which alone supported them. The alliance which religion contracts with political powers must needs be onerous to itself, since it does not require their assistance to live, and by giving them its assistance it may be exposed to decay. [. . .]

In proportion as a nation assumes a democratic condition of society and as communities display democratic propensities, *it becomes more and more dangerous to connect religion with political institutions;* for the time is coming when authority will be bandied from hand to hand, when political theories will succeed one another, and when men, laws, and constitutions will disappear or be modified from day to day, and this not for a season only, but unceasingly. *Agitation and mutability are inherent in the nature of democratic republics, just as stagnation and sleepiness are the law of absolute monarchies.*

If the Americans, who change the head of the government once in four years, who elect new legislators every two years, and renew the state officers every twelve months; if the Americans, who have given up the political world to the attempts of innovators, had not placed religion beyond their reach, where could it take firm hold in the ebb and flow of human opinions? Where would be that respect which belongs to it, amid the struggles of faction? And what would become of its immortality, in the midst of universal decay? The American clergy were the first to perceive this truth and to act in conformity with it. They saw that they must renounce their religious influence if they were to strive for political power, and they chose to give up the support of the state rather than to share its vicissitudes.

In America religion is perhaps less powerful than it has been at certain periods and among certain nations; but its influence is more lasting. It restricts itself to its own resources, but of these none can deprive it; its circle is limited, but it pervades it and holds it under undisputed control. [. . .]

I am fully convinced that this extraordinary and incidental cause is the close connection of politics and religion. The unbelievers of Europe attack the Christians as their political opponents rather than as their religious adversaries; they hate the Christian religion as the opinion of a party much more than as an error of belief; and they reject the clergy less because they are the representatives of the Deity than because they are the allies of government.

In Europe, Christianity has been intimately united to the powers of the earth. Those powers are now in decay, and it is, as it were, buried under their ruins. The living body of religion has been bound down to the dead corpse of superannuated polity; cut by the bonds that restrain it, and it will rise once more. I do not know what could restore the Christian Church of Europe to the energy of its earlier days; that power belongs to God alone; but it may be for human policy to leave to faith the full exercise of the strength which it still retains. [. . .]

How religion in the United States avails itself of democratic tendencies

I have shown in a preceding chapter that men cannot do without dogmatic belief, and even that it is much to be desired that such belief should exist among them. I now add that, of all the kinds of dogmatic belief, the most desirable appears to me to be dogmatic belief in matters of religion; and this is a clear inference, even from no higher consideration than the interests of this world. [. . .]

For my own part, *I doubt whether man can ever support at the same time complete religious independence and entire political freedom.* And I am inclined to think that if faith be wanting in him, he must be subject; and if he be free, he must believe.

Perhaps, however, this great utility of religions is still more obvious among nations where equality of conditions prevails than among others. It must be acknowledged that equality, which brings great benefits into the world, nevertheless suggests to men (as will be shown hereafter) some very dangerous propensities. It tends to isolate them from one another, to concentrate every man's attention upon himself; and it lays open the soul to an inordinate love of material gratification.

The greatest advantage of religion is to inspire diametrically contrary principles. There is no religion that does not place the object of man's desires above and beyond the treasures of earth and that does not naturally raise his soul to regions far above those of the senses. Nor is there any which does not impose on man some duties towards his kind and thus draw him at times from the contemplation of himself. This is found in the most false and dangerous religions.

Religious nations are therefore naturally strong on the very point on which democratic nations are weak; this shows of what importance it is for men to preserve their religion as their conditions become more equal.

159

I have neither the right nor the intention of examining the supernatural means that God employs to infuse religious belief into the heart of man. I am at this moment considering religions in a purely human point of view; my object is to inquire by what means they may most easily retain their sway in the democratic ages upon which we are entering.

It has been shown that at times of general culture and equality the human mind consents only with reluctance to adopt dogmatic opinions and feels their necessity acutely only in spiritual matters. This proves, in the first place, that at such times religions ought more cautiously than at any other to confine themselves within their own precincts; for in seeking to extend their power beyond religious matters, they incur a risk of not being believed at all. The circle within which they seek to restrict the human intellect ought therefore to be carefully traced, and beyond its verge the mind should be left entirely free to its own guidance.

Mohammed professed to derive from Heaven, and has inserted in the Koran, not only religious doctrines, but political maxims, civil and criminal laws, and theories of science. The Gospel, on the contrary, speaks only of the general relations of men to God and to each other, beyond which it inculcates and imposes no point of faith. This alone, besides a thousand other reasons, would suffice to prove that the former of these religions will never long predominate in a cultivated and democratic age, while the latter is destined to retain its sway at these as at all other periods.

In continuation of this same inquiry I find that for religions to maintain their authority, humanly speaking, in democratic ages, not only must they confine themselves strictly within the circle of spiritual matters, but their power also will depend very much on the nature of the belief they inculcate, on the external forms they assume, and on the obligations they impose.

The preceding observation, that equality leads men to very general and very vast ideas, is principally to be understood in respect to religion. Men who are similar and equal in the world readily conceive the idea of the one God, governing every man by the same laws and granting to every man future happiness on the same conditions. The idea of the unity of mankind constantly leads them back to the idea of the unity of the Creator; while on the contrary in a state of society where men are broken up into very unequal ranks, they are apt to devise as many deities as there are nations, castes, classes, or families, and to trace a thousand private roads to heaven.

It cannot be denied that Christianity itself has felt, to some extent, the influence that social and political conditions exercise on religious opinions. [. . .]

It seems evident that the more the barriers are removed which separate one nation from another and one citizen from another, the stronger is the bent of the human mind, as if by its own impulse, towards the idea of a single and all-powerful Being, dispensing equal laws in the same manner to every man. In democratic ages, then, it is particularly important not to allow the homage paid to secondary agents to be confused with the worship due to the Creator alone. Another truth is no less clear, that religions ought to have fewer external observances in democratic periods than at any others. [. . .]

Chapter 11

Joseph de Maistre (1753–1821)

*. . . it seems to me that every true philosophy must choose between two assumptions,
either that it is going to fashion a new religion or that Christianity will be revived
in some miraculous way.*

Introduction

Can we take de Maistre seriously? Reading Joseph de Maistre today confronts us
with the question of whether his reactionary thinking would be better ignored or
whether we should listen to him. Almost every author dealing with de Maistre raises
this question. It is not surprising that introductory comments on the work of the
ultraconservative de Maistre often start with a peculiar mixture of critical evaluation and apology.[1] Referring to de Maistre seems to be controversial today.
De Maistre prefers polemical attacks to rational arguments; his statements are bold
and written with anger and hatred. This hatred relates to everything we today would
normally regard as valuable. For de Maistre hates democracy, he ridicules the idea
of a constitution as the basis for a state, and he denies the possibility of the progress
of humankind. In short, de Maistre attacks and seeks to destroy everything that we
regard as the fruits of the French Revolution and liberal politics, including human
rights. De Maistre is an anti-liberal Catholic, a reactionary monarchist and a bom-
bastic polemicist. So, can we take de Maistre seriously? The answer to this question
is closely linked with the fate of liberalism. It is more than likely that de Maistre's
work will resurface again in times of a crisis of liberalism and liberal democracy.
Despite all the difficulties with his style, arrogance and almost bigoted religiosity,
the inchoate rediscovery of de Maistre has already begun, hand in hand with the
increasing number of critics of liberalism. Interestingly enough, the contemporary
rediscovery of de Maistre was not only initiated by conservative thinkers like Carl
Schmitt (see Part Four), but also by liberals like Isaiah Berlin.

In this collection de Maistre represents the counterpart *par excellence* to
Rousseau. Rousseau's *Social Contract* and de Maistre's book *On Sovereignty* are
divided historically and ideologically by the French Revolution. Rousseau and his
political theory predates but also constitutes a prelude to the events of 1789 and its

---

1. See, for example, I. Berlin (2002), *Freedom and its Betrayal: Six Enemies of Human Liberty* (Princeton,
    NJ: Princeton University Press).

aftermath. De Maistre's work, on the other hand, provides a critical reflection on the outcomes of the Revolution. His *counter*-revolutionary ambitions literally negate Rousseau's idea of any social contract made by man and through man. The events of the French Revolution, the subversion of the *ancien régime* and the subsequent Reign of Terror create a gulf between these two thinkers. On the one side stands Rousseau's optimistic portrait of a free society of equals, and on the other stands de Maistre's reactionary petition for a return to absolute monarchy and divine sovereignty. De Maistre is the antipode of Rousseau. This symmetrical and inverted relation is illustrated by the subtitle of de Maistre's unfinished manuscript on sovereignty (1794–5) entitled *Anti-social Contract*. De Maistre inverts all the ideas of the social contract.

The following excerpt is taken from his book *Considerations on France* (1796) and introduces three key themes in de Maistre's thought. These are: a) the divine nature of the Revolution, b) the religious foundation of institutions, and, closely related to that foundation, c) the false legitimacy of man-made institutions. All three topics are held together by one fundamental distinction which, simultaneously, defines what is at stake between Rousseau and de Maistre. That is, what is at stake between pre-revolutionary and counter-revolutionary thought. In the opening paragraph of *Considerations on France,* the author deploys this fundamental distinction: 'We are all bound to the throne of the Supreme Being by a flexible chain which restrains without enslaving us. The most wonderful aspect of the universal scheme of things is the action of free beings under divine guidance'. According to de Maistre, the human condition before God is to be 'free slaves'. Human beings depend on God's guidance and providence. To ignore this dependency is hubris. Consequently, he says: 'In the works of man, everything is as poor as its author; vision is confined, means are limited, scope is restricted, movements are laboured, and results are humdrum'.

It is the question of *authorship* which divides de Maistre from Rousseau. For de Maistre, nothing can be achieved without divine assistance. He is utterly sceptical about the unassisted abilities of human beings and whether a society can be achieved by simply a social contract. This scepticism becomes even more evident when comparing the quotation above (in particular the notion of human beings as free slaves) with Rousseau's anthropological assumption for the social contract: 'Man is born free, but everywhere he is in chains. One sees himself as the master of the other and still remains more slave than they are'.

The difference between de Maistre and Rousseau is that for the latter human beings are *naturally* born free, but as a consequence of the social condition subject to others. For Rousseau, the evolution of a society is simultaneously the process of enslaving those who are naturally free. Contrary to this, de Maistre presents a far more pessimistic view of human nature. Human beings are always subject to an authority, though the ultimate authority is not human but *divine.* That is, humans *are enslaved by nature* and were never intended to be 'liberated' entirely. This eternal dependence is not negative, according to de Maistre. Exactly the opposite is true. De Maistre uses a paradoxical phrase to characterize the natural condition of human beings when he calls them *free slaves*. This paradox only holds for the relation between God and human beings. It does not hold for the relation *between human beings*. De Maistre is convinced that real slavery begins when humans beings empower themselves to be masters of their own destiny, liberating themselves from the divine chains. This idea is crucial to de Maistre's criticism of the Revolution as a human transformation of the social order, and his criticism of constitutions as social norms constructed by human beings. Nothing made by human beings will last without the imprimatur of divine authorship.

De Maistre's insistence on God's divine guidance in all matters sometimes takes a strange direction. This is certainly the case in his interpretation of the French Revolution and its divine nature. Despite its anti-religious character, de Maistre insists that the French Revolution *reveals* most clearly God's providence. He argues: 'It has been said with good reason that the French Revolution leads men more than men lead it. . . . Never did Robespierre, Collot, or Barere think of establishing the revolutionary government or the Reign of Terror; they were led imperceptibly by circumstances . . . It cannot be too often repeated that men do not at all guide the Revolution; it is the Revolution that uses men. It is well said that it has its own impetus. This phrase shows that never has the Divinity revealed itself so clearly in any human event. If it employs the vilest instruments, it is to regenerate by punishment'.

This was written in 1796, two years after Robespierre was beheaded and the Reign of Terror ended. The Reign of Terror arbitrarily persecuted and executed nearly 40,000 people. For all that, according to de Maistre, this was part of God's providence and happened for the sake of social regeneration. Regeneration here means the return to theocratic monarchy. In de Maistre's view, the Revolution and its bloody aftermath only confirmed and fulfilled God's plan to regenerate society and restore the *ancien régime*. Today, such an interpretation of the French Revolution seems to be naive and theologically unsupportable. But for all monarchs at that time, who were threatened by the outcome of the Revolution, such an interpretation was clearly positive and to be embraced.

Prior to the period of the Restoration, between the Revolution of 1789 and the return of the Bourbon monarch Louis-Philippe in 1830, de Maistre's work reached the climax of its popularity and was widely translated. One might say that de Maistre therefore is of purely historical interest. But in the quotation above we also find a remarkable observation. De Maistre recognizes the autonomous impetus of the Revolution. It was started by people and, initially, designed to realize clearly defined intentions, but it took its own unpredictable direction. This illustrates the fact that great social changes like revolutions or wars have a life of their own. To put it more abstractly, de Maistre discovered the *autopoetic* nature of great social changes. It is true that de Maistre's interpretation of the French Revolution is ideologically fashioned, but nevertheless it contains an interesting observation on the dynamics of social transformation.

This is also true for his discussion of social institutions. For de Maistre's conviction is that: 'Every conceivable institution either rests on a religious idea or is ephemeral. Institutions are strong and durable to the degree that they partake of the Divinity'. If institutions are only human constructs and bear no divine

163

character, they are founded on a vacuum and will disappear as quickly as they emerged. In de Maistre's polemical words: 'I do not believe in the fecundity of a vacuum'. As far as politics is concerned, political institutions cannot exist very long without a religious basis. And if the political institution at stake is a form of government, only those governments will last which combine the political and the religious. In other words, only the unity of throne and altar can guarantee a durable government. Once again this bold statement seems to be utterly outdated. But de Maistre's argument has also something remarkable to offer when he draws his conclusion from this: all institutions founded merely on 'philosophy' (a secular political theory of the Enlightenment like Rousseau's social contract) have to make a choice 'either that they are going to fashion a new religion or that Christianity will be revived in some miraculous way'. If we take de Maistre's argument seriously, then we can say that every lasting institution either *integrates* the religious or *invents* the religious. This view sheds some interesting light on the nature of secular forms of political government today. Are there any forms of *invented religion* involved in maintaining contemporary political institutions? And if there are, what forms do these religions take? De Maistre gives us one concrete example. Constitutional forms of government like those advanced by the Enlightenment are based on the invented religion of rationality. This is why de Maistre attacks all constitutions which are the result of rational agreement. They all, as he puts it, worship 'the goddess of reason'.

This leads us to the last key topic of de Maistre's work, namely, the criticism of the *legitimacy* of institutions or constitutional acts in general. By reiterating his reservations against *promethean* human activity, he points out that 'man can modify everything in the sphere of his activity, but creates nothing'. The inability of human beings to create makes a constitution or any constitutional acts a naïve enterprise. A constitution in terms of a binding norm for social living and fundamental for law can never be the outcome of rational discussion or the product of a single human author. All constitutions are blasphemous and hubristic. Paine's catchy phrase that for him a constitution is nothing unless he can put it into his pockets is, for de Maistre, the epitome of wickedness. In the last part of the excerpt below, de Maistre lists the criteria for the limits of constitutional authority. This list of criteria is a draft version of his critique of constitution as it is elaborated in his *Essai sur le principe générateur des constitutions politiques et des autres institutions humaines*. Prior to Carl Schmitt, with Joseph de Maistre, liberal democracy and secularism meet their foremost critic.

Further reading

General introductions

Bradley, O. (1999), *A Modern Maistre: The Social and Political Thought of Joseph de Maistre* (Lincoln, NA: University of Nebraska Press).
Lebrun, R. (1965), *Throne and Altar; the Political and Religious Thought of Joseph de Maistre* (Ottawa: University of Ottawa Press).

Lebrun, R. (2001), *Joseph de Maistre's Life, Thought and Influence: Selected Studies* (Montreal and Ithaca, NY: McGill-Queen's University Press).

Reception of key ideas

Berlin, I. and Hardy, H. (2002), *Freedom and Its Betrayal: Six Enemies of Human Liberty* (Princeton, NJ: Princeton University Press).

Davies, P. (2002), *The Extreme Right in France, 1789 to the Present: From de Maistre to Le Pen* (New York: Routledge).

Goldhammer, J. (2005), *The Headless Republic: Sacrificial Violence in Modern French Thought* (Ithaca, NY: Cornell University Press).

Excerpt from *Considerations on France**

Chapter 1: Of Revolutions

We are all bound to the throne of the Supreme Being by a flexible *chain which restrains without enslaving us*. The most wonderful aspect of the universal scheme of things is the action of free beings under divine guidance. *Freely slaves*, they act at once of their own will and under necessity: they actually do what they wish without being able to disrupt general plans. Each of them stands at the center of a sphere of activity whose diameter varies according to the decision of the *Eternal Geometer*, which can extend, restrict, check, or direct the will without altering its nature.

In the works of man, everything is as poor as its author; vision is confined, means are limited, scope is restricted, movements are labored, and results are humdrum. In divine works, boundless riches reveal themselves even in the smallest component; its power operates effortlessly: in its hands everything is pliant, nothing can resist it; everything is a means, nothing an obstacle: and the irregularities produced by the work of free agents come to fall into place in the general order.

If one imagines a watch all of whose springs continually vary in power, weight, dimension, form, and position, and which nevertheless invariably shows the right time, one can get some idea of the action of free beings in relation to the plans of the Creator.

In the political and moral world, as in the physical, there is a usual order and there are exceptions to this order. Normally, we see a series of effects following the same causes; but in certain ages we see usual effects suspended, causes paralyzed and new consequences emerging.

A *miracle* is an effect produced by a divine or superhuman cause which suspends or is inconsistent with an ordinary cause. [. . .]

But in revolutionary times, the chain that binds man is shortened abruptly, his field of action is cut down, and his means deceive him. Carried along by an unknown force, he rails against it, and instead of kissing the hand that clasps him, he ignores or insults it.

---

* Italics have been added by the editors for emphasis.

'I don't understand anything' is the popular catchphrase. The phrase is very sensible if it leads us to the root cause of the great sight now presented to men; it is stupid if it expresses only spleen or sterile despondency. The cry is raised on all sides, 'How then can the guiltiest men in the world triumph over the world?' A hideous regicide has all the success for which its perpetrators could have hoped. *Monarchy is dormant all over Europe.* Its enemies find allies even on thrones themselves. The wicked are successful in everything. They carry through the most immense projects without difficulty, while the righteous are unfortunate and ridiculous in everything they undertake. Opinion runs against faith throughout Europe. The foremost statesmen continually fall into error. The greatest generals are humiliated. And so on.

Doubtless, because its primary condition lays it down, there are no means of preventing a revolution, and no success can attend those who wish to impede it. But never is purpose more apparent, never is Providence more palpable, than when divine replaces human action and works alone. That is what we see at this moment.

The most striking aspect of the French Revolution is this overwhelming force which turns aside all obstacles. Its current carries away like a straw everything human power has opposed to it. No one has run counter to it unpunished. [. . .]

It has been said with good reason that *the French Revolution leads men more than men lead it.* This observation is completely justified; and, although it can be applied more or less to all great revolutions, yet it has never been more strikingly illustrated than at the present time. The very villains who appear to guide the Revolution take part in it only as simple instruments; and as soon as they aspire to dominate it, they fall ingloriously. Those who established the Republic did so without wishing it and without realizing what they were creating; they have been led by events: no plan has achieved its intended end.

Never did Robespierre, Collot, or Barere think of establishing the revolutionary government or the Reign of Terror; they were led imperceptibly by circumstances, and such a sight will never be seen again. Extremely mediocre men are exercising over a culpable nation the most heavy despotism history has seen, and, of everyone in the kingdom, they are certainly the most astonished at their power.

But at the very moment when these tyrants have committed every crime necessary to this phase of the Revolution, a breath of wind topples them. This gigantic power, before which France and Europe trembled, could not stand before the first gust; and because there could be no possible trace of greatness or dignity in such an entirely criminal revolution, providence decreed that the first blow should be struck by the Septembrists, so that justice itself might be degraded.

It is often astonishing that the most mediocre men have judged the French Revolution better than the most talented, that they have believed in it strongly while skilled men of affairs were still unbelievers. This conviction was one of the foremost elements of the Revolution, which could succeed only because of the extent and vigor of the revolutionary spirit or, if one can so express it, because of the revolutionary faith. So untalented and ignorant men have ably driven what they call *the revolutionary chariot*; they have all ventured without fear of counter-revolution; they have always driven on without looking behind them; and everything has fallen into their lap because they were only the instruments of a force more far-sighted than themselves. They have taken no false steps in their revolutionary career, for the same reason that the flutist of Vaucanson[2] never played a false note.

The revolutionary current has taken successively different courses; and the most prominent revolutionary leaders have acquired the kind of power and renown appropriate to them only by following the demands of the moment. Once they attempted to oppose it or even to turn it from its predestined course, by isolating themselves and following their own bent, they disappeared from the scene. [. . .]

In short, the more one examines the apparently more active personalities of the Revolution, the more one finds something passive and mechanical about them. It cannot be too often repeated that men do not at all guide the Revolution; it is the Revolution that uses men. It is well said that it has its own impetus. This phrase shows that never has the *Divinity revealed itself so clearly* in any human event. If it employs the most vile instruments, it is to *regenerate by punishment*.

Chapter 5: On the French Revolution considered in its antireligious character

There is a *satanic* element in the French Revolution which distinguishes it from any other revolution known or perhaps that will be known. Remember the great occasions – Robespierre's speech against the priesthood, the solemn apostasy of the priests, the desecration of objects of worship, the inauguration of the *goddess of Reason*, and the many outrageous acts by which the provinces tried to surpass Paris: these all leave the ordinary sphere of crimes and seem to belong to a different world.

Now that the Revolution has lost its force, the grossest abuses have disappeared, yet the principles still remain. Have not the *legislators* (to make use of their term) made the historically unique claim that *the nation will not pay for any form of worship*? Some men of this age seem to me to raise themselves at certain moments to a hatred for the Divinity, but this frightful act is not needed to make useless the most strenuous creative efforts: the neglect of, let alone scorn for, the great Being brings an irrevocable curse on the human works stained by it. *Every conceivable institution either rests on a religious idea or is ephemeral.* Institutions are strong and durable to the degree that they partake of the Divinity. Not only is human reason, or what is ignorantly called philosophy, unable to replace those foundations ignorantly called superstitions, but philosophy is, on the contrary, an essentially destructive force. [. . .]

These reflections apply to everyone, to the believer as well as the skeptic, for I am advancing a fact and not an argument. It does not matter whether these ideas are laughed at or respected; true or false, they no less form the only base for every stable institution.

Rousseau, perhaps the most mistaken of men, has nevertheless hit on this truth, without wanting to draw the full consequences from it.

---

2. In 1737 Jacques de Vaucanson built an automata of a life-size shepherd which played the flute. Vaucanson's invention of an artificial man is indicative of the fascination of the Enlightenment for technical progress. De Maistre attacks this belief in technological progress, because it is for him an expression of the hubris of humans and overestimation of human capabilities. [Eds]

'The Judaic law, he says, which is still in existence, and that of the child of Ishmael, which for ten centuries ruled half the world, still proclaim the great men who laid them down. . . . Pride-ridden philosophy or the blind spirit of faction sees in them no more than lucky impostors.' [*Social Contract*, Book ii, Chap. vii.]

He ought to have drawn the conclusion, instead of talking about *the great and powerful genius which watches over durable institutions*, as if this high-flown language explained anything.

When one reflects on the facts attested by the whole of history, when one grasps that the whole range of human institutions from those that have shaped world history to the smallest social organization, from empires to monasteries, have a divine basis, and that human power, whenever it stands alone, can create only faulty and ephemeral works, what are we to think of the new French system and the power that has produced it? For my own part, I will never believe in the *fecundity of a vacuum*.

It would be interesting to go thoroughly through our European institutions and to show how they are all *christianized*, how religion, touching on everything, animates and sustains everything. Human passions can well pollute or even pervert primitive institutions, but if the principle is divine, this is enough to ensure them a long life. [. . .]

This is a divine law as certain and as palpable as the laws of gravitation.

Every time a man puts himself, according to his ability, in harmony with the Creator and produces any institution whatever in the name of God, he participates in some way in the omnipotence of which he has made himself the instrument, however great his individual weakness, his ignorance and poverty, the obscurity of his birth, in a word his absolute lack of any ordinary means of influence; he produces works whose power and durability confound reason. [. . .]

I am so convinced of the truths I am defending that, when I consider the general decline of moral principles, the anarchy of opinions, the weakness of sovereignties lacking any foundations, the immensity of our needs and the poverty of our means, it seems to me that every true philosophy must choose between two assumptions, either that it is going *to fashion a new religion* or that *Christianity will be revived* in some miraculous way. One of these suppositions must be chosen, according to the view that is held about the truth of Christianity.

This conjecture will not be rejected disdainfully except by the shortsighted who believe that nothing is possible except what they see before their eyes. Who in the ancient world could have foreseen Christianity? And who outside this religion could, in its beginnings, have foreseen its future success? How do we know that a great moral revolution is not in progress? [. . .]

But a host of ideas crowd in on me at this point and push me to the widest of considerations.

The present generation is witnessing one of the most dramatic sights humanity has ever seen; it is the fight to the death between Christianity and the cult of philosophy. The lists are open, the two enemies have come to grips, and the world looks on.

As in Homer, *the father of gods and men* is holding the scales in which these two great forces are being weighed; soon one of the scales must tilt.

To the biased man, whose heart is master of his head, events prove nothing; having chosen sides irrevocably either for or against, observation and reasoning are equally useless. But for all men of goodwill, who deny or doubt perhaps, let the great history of Christianity settle their doubts. For eighteen centuries, it has ruled over a great part of the globe, and particularly the most enlightened part. This religion does not go back just to this age; going back to before its founder came to earth, it links up with another order of things, a prophetic religion that preceded it. The one cannot be true without the other being so: the one prides itself on promising what the other prides itself on having; so that this religion, by a visible sequence, goes back to the origin of the world. *It was born on the day that days were born.*

There is no other example of such durability; and, to confine one-self just to Christianity, no institution in the world can be compared to it. Any comparison with other religions can only be misleading, for several striking characteristics exclude it. It is not the place here to detail them; one word only must suffice. Can anyone show me another religion founded on miraculous facts and revealing incomprehensible dogmas, yet believed for eighteen centuries by a good part of humanity and defended in every age by the best men of the time, from Origen to Pascal, in spite of every effort of a rival sect which, from Celsus to Condorcet, has ceaselessly fulminated against it?

It is a wonderful thing that, when one reflects on this great institution, the most natural hypothesis, that which all the probabilities point to, is that of a divine creation. If it were a human artifact, there would no longer be any means of explaining its success; by excluding the idea of a miracle, an explanation can be given.

Every nation, it is said, has mistaken copper for gold. Very well, but has this copper been thrown into the European crucible and tested for eighteen centuries by chemical observation? Or, if submitted to this test, has it emerged from it with honor? Newton believed in the incarnation, but Plato, I think, had very little belief in the miraculous birth of Bacchus.

Christianity has been preached by the ignorant and believed by the learned, and in this it resembles no other known thing. [. . .]

Today, finally, the experiment is being repeated in still more favorable circumstances, since they all conspire to make it decisive. All those who have not learned thoroughly the lessons of history pay particular attention. You have said that the Crown propped up the Papacy; well, the *Crown no longer plays any part on the world's stage*; it has been smashed and the pieces thrown into the mud. You suspected that the influence of a rich and powerful priest could enforce the dogmas he preached. I do not think that there is any power that can make men believe, but let that pass. There are no longer any priests; they have been exiled, slaughtered, and degraded; they have been deprived of everything, and those who have escaped the guillotine, the stake, daggers, fusillades, drowning, and deportation receive the alms that formerly they themselves gave. You feared the force of custom, the ascendancy of authority, the illusions of imagination: there is no longer any of that, no longer custom and no longer masters; *each man's mind is his own*. Philosophy having corroded the cement binding man to man, there are no longer any moral ties. The civil authority, promoting with all its resources the overthrow of the old system, gives to the enemies of Christianity all the aid which it formerly gave to Christianity itself: the human mind uses every imaginable means to combat the old national religion.[3] These efforts are applauded and paid for, while anything against them is a crime. You have no longer anything to fear from visual delights, always the most deceiving; displays of pomp and vain ceremonies no longer impress the people before whom everything has been mocked for seven years. The churches are closed, or are opened only for the noisy discussions and drunken revels of a frenzied people. The altars are overthrown; filthy animals have been led through the streets in bishops' vestments; chalices have been used in disgraceful orgies; and around the altar that the old faith surrounded with dazzling cherubims, nude prostitutes have been painted. The *cult of philosophy* has therefore no longer any room for complaint; fortune is completely in its favor; everything is working for it and against its rival. If it is victorious, it will not say like Caesar, *I came, I saw, and I conquered*, but in the end it will have won: it can applaud and sit proudly on an overturned cross. But if Christianity emerges from this terrible test purer and more virile; if the Christian Hercules, strong in his own vigor, lifts *the son of the earth* and crushes him in his arms *patuit Deus*. – Frenchmen, give place to the Christian King, place him yourselves on his old throne; raise once more his oriflamme, and let his coinage, traveling again from one pole to the other, carry to every part of the world the triumphant device:

CHRIST COMMANDS, HE REIGNS, HE IS THE VICTOR.

Chapter 6: Of the Divine influence in political constitutions

Man can modify everything in the sphere of his activity, but he creates nothing: such is the law binding him in the physical as in the moral world. No doubt a man can plant a seed, raise a tree, perfect it by grafting, and prune it in a hundred ways, but never has he imagined that he can make a tree. How has he thought that he has the power to make a constitution? Was it through experience? See what it can teach us.

All free constitutions known to the world took form in one of two ways. Sometimes they *germinated*, as it were, in an imperceptible way by the combination of a host of circumstances that we call fortuitous, and sometimes they have a single author who appears like a freak of nature and enforces obedience. In these two assumptions can be seen the signs by which God warns us of our weakness and of the right he has reserved to himself in the formation of governments.

1. No government results from a deliberation; popular rights are never written, or at least constitutive acts or written fundamental laws are always only declaratory statements of anterior rights, of which nothing can be said other than that they exist because they exist.

2. God, not having judged it proper to employ supernatural means in this field, has limited himself to human means of action, so that in the formation of consti-

---

3. This is Roman Catholicism. [Eds]

tutions circumstances are all and men are only part of the circumstances. Fairly often, even, in pursuing one object they achieve another, as we have seen in the English constitution.

3. The rights of the *people*, properly speaking, start fairly often from a concession by sovereigns, and in this case they can be established historically; but the rights of the sovereign and of the aristocracy, at least their essential rights, those that are constitutive and basic, have neither *date nor author*.

4. Even the concessions of the sovereign have always been preceded by a state of affairs that made them necessary and that did not depend on him.

5. Although written laws are always only declarations of anterior rights, yet it is very far from true that everything that can be written is written; there is even in every constitution always something that cannot be written, and that must be left behind a dark and impenetrable cloud on pain of overturning the state.

6. The more that is written, the weaker is the institution, the reason being clear. Laws are only declarations of rights, and rights are not declared except when they are attacked, so that the multiplicity of written constitutional laws shows only the multiplicity of conflicts and the danger of destruction. This is why the most vigorous political system in the ancient world was that of Sparta, in which nothing was written.

7. *No nation can give itself liberty if it has not it already*. Its laws are made when it begins to reflect on itself. Human influence does not extend beyond the development of rights already in existence but disregarded or disputed. If imprudent men step beyond these limits by foolhardy reforms, the nation loses what it had without gaining what it hopes for. In consequence, it is necessary to innovate only rarely and always moderately and cautiously.

8. When providence has decreed the more rapid formation of a political constitution, a man appears invested with indefinable powers: he speaks and exacts obedience: but these heroes belong perhaps only to the ancient world and the youth of nations. However that may be, the distinctive characteristic of these legislators is that they are kings or high nobles; there is and can be no exception to this . . .

9. Even these legislators with their exceptional powers simply bring together preexisting elements in the customs and character of a people; but this gathering together and rapid formation which seem to be creative are carried out only in the name of the Divinity. Politics and religion start together: it is difficult to separate the legislator from the priest, and his public institutions consist principally *in ceremonies and religious holidays*.

10. In one sense, *liberty has always been a gift of kings*, since all free nations have been constituted by kings. This is the general rule, under which the apparent exceptions that could be pointed out will fall if they were argued out.

11. No free nation has existed which has not had in its natural constitution germs of liberty as old as itself, and no nation has ever succeeded in developing by written constitutional laws rights other than those present in its natural constitution.

12. No assembly of men whatever can create a nation; all the *Bedlams*[4] in the world could not produce anything more absurd or extravagant than such an enterprise.

To prove this proposition in detail, after what I have said, would, it seems to me, be disrespectful to the wise and over-respectful to the foolish.

13. I have spoken of the basic characteristic of true legislators; another very striking feature, on which it would be easy to write a whole book, is that they are never what are called *intellectuals*; they do not write; they act on instinct and impulse more than on reasoning, and they have no means of acting other than a certain moral force that bends men's wills as the wind bends a field of corn. [. . .]

The 1795 constitution, like its predecessors, was made for *man*. But there is no such thing as *man* in the world. During my life, I have seen Frenchmen, Italians, Russians, and so on; thanks to Montesquieu, I even know that one can be *Persian*; but I must say, as for *man*, I have never come across him anywhere; if he exists, he is completely unknown to me. [. . .]

Is not a constitution a solution to the following problem: *Given the population, customs, religion, geographical situation, political relations, wealth, good and bad qualities of a particular nation, to find the laws which suit it?* Yet this problem is not even approached in the 1795 constitution, which was aimed solely at *man*. Thus every imaginable reason combines to show that this enterprise has not the divine blessing. It is no more than a schoolboy's exercise.

Already at this moment, how many signs of decay does it reveal!

---

4. *Bedlams* means 'mad, lunatic people' and is derived from the name of a sanatory in London. The Oxford English Dictionary explains: 'The Hospital of St. Mary of Bethlehem, used as an asylum for the reception and cure of mentally deranged persons; originally situated in Bishopsgate, in 1676 rebuilt near London Wall, and in 1815 transferred to Lambeth. Jack or Tom o' Bedlam: a madman'. [Eds]

PART FOUR
Politics after Religion

Prologue to Part Four

What is significant reading the writings compiled in this section is a dramatic change in the relationship between religion and politics. The Enlightenment thinkers worked within an operative deism. However remote God might be, however detached from the immanent self-regulating work of nature, their political thinking was developed within the purview of a religious horizon. What is evident when we move into the nineteenth century is a profound secularization.

In the second half of the nineteenth century, Nietzsche (through his figure Zarathustra) will proclaim that 'God is dead' and, furthermore, it is mankind who has killed him. We can take Nietzsche's proclamation as one symptom of a complex process in which the structures of believing in what Max Weber termed an *enchanted world* were transformed. It was not simply that Enlightenment rationalism fostered increases in religious scepticism and a decline in religious conviction – such that explanations were sought for miracles and sacred texts examined as literary genres. This kind of rationalization and critique went on, in fact 'critique' (practised and emphasized by Kant) became a major mode of intellectual enquiry in the nineteenth century. But secularization defined a cultural change in social, not just intellectual, values. At the end of the nineteenth century, Emile Durkheim reflected upon the profound relationship between religious ideas about community and belonging and the values any society invests in. This society, over the course of the nineteenth century, was transformed dramatically with the rise of industrial activity and the vast movement of people towards the city.

In 1845, Engels, living in Manchester began to describe the new social conditions of urban life as they were experienced by a new class of people, the masses:

> Passing along a steep bank, among stakes and washing-lines, one penetrates into this chaos of small, one-storied, one-roomed hovels, in most of which there is no artificial floor; kitchen, living and sleeping-room all in one. In such a hole, scarcely five feet long by six broad, I found two beds – and such bedsteads and beds! – which, with a staircase

and a chimney-place, entirely filled the room. In several others I found absolutely nothing, while the door stood open, and the inhabitants leaned against it. Everywhere before the doors refuse and offal; that any sort of pavement lay underneath could not be seen but only felt, here and there, with the feet. This whole collection of cattle-sheds for human beings was surrounded on two sides by houses and a factory, and on the third by the river, and besides the narrow bank, a narrow doorway alone led out into another almost equally ill-built, ill-kept labyrinth of dwellings.[1]

Following the introduction of the word into modern French first by Montesquieu and then Rousseau, Engels and Marx called this new class of people the *proletariat*. What they were defining by this term (unlike Montesquieu and Rousseau) was a class born of the Industrial Revolution (and therefore a class that were more clearly visible in England at the time than anywhere else in Europe). The Industrial Revolution introduced into the social realm new alienations, new inequalities and new experiences of utilitarian thinking. New responses to these social conditions arose – most notably for this volume, *socialism*, and the rise of a new political consciousness among a class that previously were excluded from the public sphere, the workers.

The development of the proletariat is inconceivable outside the bludgeoning of the middle classes. These had been gaining in strength and self-confidence since the early stages of world trade began in the fifteenth and sixteenth centuries, but in the nineteenth century their financial and political power was as immense as the new territories for trade they were opening up. The colonial expansion of nation states brought an increasing demand for trained officials, educated professionals and civil servants. The *bourgeoisie* became conscious of themselves as the bearers of culture, of progress away from the traditionalisms of the *ancien régime*. At the turn into the twentieth century, in the Introduction to his famous *The Protestant Ethic and the Spirit of Capitalism*,[2] Weber reflects upon the superiority of Western civilization and its bourgeois class; it is a civilization that had now become a benchmark of universal significance and value.

But new social and economic conditions need not change human habits. In fact, the decline in church attendance (often taken as the sign of a deepening secularization) only occurs in Britain, France and Germany in the last two decades of the nineteenth century. Whatever the pronouncements in the US about the necessary gulf between Church and state, in practice there remained many institutional and customary bridges that spanned the dichotomy between the private and the public in Europe. The division was a constitutional fiction – and it remains so in the US today. The evidence in late-eighteenth- and nineteenth-century England shows religion as one of the main forces in the fostering of a new political consciousness, and not only among the working people. From the preaching of the Wesleys and the social welfare programmes inaugurated by the Quakers, to the establishment of the Christian Socialist's Office for Promoting Working Men's Associations by F. D. Maurice and Charles Kingsley in December 1850, religious conviction is

1. F. Engels (1993), *The Condition of the Working Class in England* (Oxford: Oxford University Press).
2. M. Weber (2001), *Protestant Ethic and the Spirit of Capitalism* (London: Routledge).

manifestly not divorced from social and political action. Even with Marx, whatever he thought of the truth of religion, religion remained a dominant social force that required examination before extirpation. Weber took this task of examining the social function of religion further, developing, by the early twentieth century, a sociology of religion. But the new social and economic conditions of the nineteenth century accompanied a mindset that had been developing since the time of Luther: that inner certainty was infinitely superior to outward conformity. What was being preached from the pulpits to rich and poor alike was matched by what was being taught in the classrooms of grammar schools, boarding schools and the lecture halls of new universities (like Manchester) – the importance of coming to one's own beliefs, of assessing the evidence, of developing informed judgements. Contemporary pluralism has its roots in the free market of opinion encouraged by religious appeals to toleration and *laissez-faire* liberalism. One cannot evade the conclusion that modern Christian theologians like Johann Baptist Metz and Harvey Cox celebrate: that the origins of secularism, and the early processes of secularization, owe everything to elements within the Christian faith itself that Protestantism foregrounded. One cannot evade what history makes so manifest in the nineteenth century, that the expansion of the franchise and the development of democracy is associated with a notion of the right of the freedom of the individual that is prior to any religious conviction, tradition or creed. 'Liberty is not a means to a higher political end. It is itself the highest political end . . . [L]iberty is the only object which benefits all alike, and promotes no sincere opposition', the great nineteenth-century historian, Lord Acton, wrote.[3] No wonder then one finds, most notably among Catholics of this period, the stark recognition of the relationship between secularization, liberal humanism and democracy. And, consequently, the need in attacking one to attack the others. Already in 1841, John Henry Newman, prior to his conversion from Anglicanism to Roman Catholicism could write: 'The more serious among us are used . . . to regard the spirit of liberalism as characteristic of the destined AntiChrist'.[4] The statement accords with later papal statements that saw in the rise of liberal democracies (that by definition must be secular in order to safeguard the freedom of an individual's conscience and minimize state intervention) a profound threat to a consensus founded upon authority.[5]

Because of lack of space we have not included any of F. D. Maurice's Christian socialist lectures or anything from John Stuart Mill's essays on religion or Lord Acton's famous address on 'The history of freedom in Christianity'. Our selection begins where the new appeals to the material, the historical and the secular assert their polemics against religion and their political agendas. In tracing the socialist arc from Marx to Lenin we attend to the divorce of religion and politics that the

---

3. See O. Chadwick (1975), *The Secularization of the European Mind in the Nineteenth Century*. (Cambridge: Cambridge University Press).
4. Ibid.
5. Catholic anti-modernism developed between Pius IX and Pius XII and it was the latter who made the first positive statement about democracy in his speech to the *collegium* of cardinals on Christmas Day 1944.

secularization of the European mind promoted. With Weber polemics give way to systematic enquiry, historically informed, of types of ecclesial and political power and their relationship to each other. His work represents a more liberal, academic voice. But even while he was bringing his oeuvre to a close, the undertow of a more conservative thinking (both religious and political) was surfacing again in the wake of the First World War. This thinking finds expression in the work of Charles Maurras and *Action Française*, but it finds its most notorious form in the political theology of Carl Schmitt because of his relationship later with National Socialism. Both Maurras and Schmitt were Catholic, though conservative Protestants like Karl Barth also inveighed against the liberal belief in self-realization; a Prometheanism that militated against religious authority and led politically to either totalitarianism or anarchy.

If the French Revolution permeated the political thought of Paine, Tocqueville and de Maistre, it is the Russian Revolution that permeated the political thought of the post First World War generation. Between them both Lord Acton could speak of 'the red spectre of social revolution [that] arose in the track of democracy'.[6] The spectre of revolution raised the twin threats of totalitarianism and anarchy to the secular liberal minds of what were now destabilized democracies. These European democracies had expanded their franchise and shed, in the Great War, the last remnants of monarchic power. But with the recession of royal power in the Austro-Hungarian Empire, in Germany, Spain and England as well as Russia, the sovereignty of the people was revealing its darker side. The fear of mob revolt invoked tremors of social panic throughout the middle-nineteenth to the middle-twentieth century. They spread across Europe in 1848; they erupted in the wake of the Paris Communes of 1871; they coursed through the *Gassen* of Weimar and Zurich in the 1920s; and they rattled the major cities of England in the General Strike of 1926. If some sought to mobilize the fear, and the mob itself (Communists and National Socialists alike), Conservatives and Monarchists sought to suppress it and Socialists and Liberals sought to understand its grievances and legislate to resolve them. Simone Weil is not a lone expression of the workers' plight in the inter-war years and the need to recover a spirituality deeper than the optimisms of liberal humanism in order to address it. Other religious and political voices readily presented themselves – Jacques Maritan in France and William Temple in Britain. But we chose Weil because the sheer complex tensions in her position – between Judaism and Christianity, Communism and classical Greek hierarchy, self-hatred and love for one's country – represent the outworking of nineteenth-century, bourgeois, secular individualism. With Marx and Engels, religion needs to be divorced from politics and the butt of critique for the sake of the liberation of the poor and oppressed. With Weil (Maritan and Temple, to say nothing of the Liberation theologians after Vatican II) the poor and oppressed become the new focus for rethinking the relationship between religion and politics.

---

6. O. Chadwick (1975), *The Secularisation of the European Mind in the Nineteenth Century* (Cambridge: Cambridge University Press).

Chapter 12

Karl Marx (1818–83)

Thus, the criticism of Heaven turns into the criticism of Earth, the criticism of religion into the criticism of law, and the criticism of theology into the criticism of politics.

Introduction

At the height of a cholera epidemic that raged through the overcrowded city of Berlin, on 14 November 1831, Georg Wilhelm Friedrich Hegel died unexpectedly. He was 61 with much work still in preparation, and for the previous ten years his philosophy had dominated German culture. A few months later seven of his closest friends and brilliant students came together to ensure the continuing dissemination of the master's ideas and to prepare the first complete edition of his works. These constituted the core of what became known as the Old Hegelians. Bruno Bauer was listed among these Old Hegelians until 1839. But among Hegel's other students and disciples were a group of men who would become some of the most prominent German intellectuals of the nineteenth century: Arnold Ruge, Ludwig Feuerbach, Max Stirner and David Strauss. Marx was only 13 at the time; Engels 11. These would become known as the Young Hegelians, though there was much debate among themselves, and they never really formed a coherent school of thought (except in the minds of those who vilified them). Ten years later one of the Old Hegelians remarked that 'if Marx, Bruno Bauer and Feuerbach come together to found a theological-philosophical review, God would do well to surround Himself with all His angels and indulge in self-pity, for these three will certainly drive him out of His heaven'.[1] To understand this comment is to understand why the critique of religion was so central, not only to the essay by Marx we have chosen, but for all the Young Hegelians.

There are two main reasons why religion played such an important role in the formulation of the radical political thinking that characterized the writings of most of the Young Hegelians. The first reason lies with Hegel himself and the way the Old Hegelians promoted his work immediately after his death. Hegel was a Lutheran; in fact, he considered himself an orthodox Lutheran. In his late *Lectures on the Philosophy of Religion* he outlined a historical logic that viewed Christianity as the

---

1. L. S. Stepelevich (ed.) (1997), *The Young Hegelians: An Anthology* (New Jersey: Humanities Press).

absolute religion. It was religion in its most perfect expression or representation. Speculative philosophy, for Hegel, articulated the form and logic of this representation. So philosophy and religion had, for Hegel, the same content. Nevertheless, from his early work, philosophy had a higher task than religion because religion treated ideas pictorially. Philosophy's task was more abstract and therefore more essential. The death of God in Christ, for Hegel, represented the giving over of God's self to the world; his resurrection was in and as the community. We will trace the significance of this politically in a moment. The important point is that all the major Young Hegelians were trained in theology first and took up philosophy under the aegis of Hegel who integrated them. Furthermore, the critique of religion by the Young Hegelians began with Hegel's own ideas. This critique was first given expression in the early and infamous work of David Strauss *The Life of Jesus* (1833). Strauss examined the representation of Jesus's life in terms of an elaborate understanding of myth, in which the incarnation of the Logos was not solely limited to Jesus but was, through him distributed 'among the multiplicity of individuals'. The incarnation is therefore a continual unfolding of God. This notion, embryonic in Hegel, but never fully developed, was taken further by Feuerbach who, in his 1841 book *The Essence of Christianity*, viewed God as a projection of the highest possible aspirations for being human; collapsing theology into anthropology, religious piety into humanism. The language and thesis of this book resonate in the major premise of Marx's critique of religion in the excerpt we have chosen: that 'Man who looked for a superman in the fantastic reality of heaven found nothing there but a *reflection* of himself'. It was also in 1841 that Bauer, a one-time critic of Strauss and now a leader of a group of Young Hegelians in Berlin, published his ironic *Trumpet of the Last Judgement Against Hegel the Atheist and Anti-Christ*. There had often been remarks about the orthodoxy of Hegel's Lutheranism even when he was alive, but the full consequences of Hegel's thought now became apparent. It is these works which lie behind Marx's own aphoristic declaration at the opening of his *Towards a Critique of Hegel's Philosophy of Right* that 'For Germany, the critique of religion is essentially completed'.

But Hegel's *Philosophy of Right*, although inseparable from the ideas expounded in his *Lectures on the Philosophy of Religion*, is actually concerned with the state. And it is here that we can develop the second reason why the critique of religion was so important a step for the Young Hegelians on their way to furthering their own radical politics. Strauss, as a consequence of his book, lost his job in the university. Teachers at all levels were appointed by the state, they were understood to be civil servants – and published works on religion and politics were submitted to the censors. The reason for this is made apparent in an article Marx published in July 1842 in the *Kölnische Zeitung*. He is answering another earlier leading article which had claimed: 'Religion is the foundation of the state, as it is the most necessary condition for every social association.' The Church and state worked hand in hand in Prussia. To critique religion was one way of drawing attention to the illiberal elements in the state itself, and the years that followed Hegel's death saw the rise of a pietist distrust of philosophy allied to a highly conservative Prussian nobility. Bauer's shift in position towards the Young Hegelians in 1839 followed the

178

withdrawal of his own state-given license to teach. In 1840 the old Prussian king, Friedrich Wilhelm III, died and the new king, Friedrich Wilhelm IV began by relaxing censorship of the press. It was at this time that the Young Hegelians, Marx and Engels now among them, began to be openly political. Again the move from religion to politics was already traced out by Hegel, but the implications of Hegel's speculative philosophy was the development of a philosophy of action concerned not with concepts but material practices. But before the end of 1841, the new king was taking up the old absolutist powers (and the Divine Right of Kings' doctrine), imprisoning dissidents and imposing strict censorship of the press. An article Marx wrote at the time inveighing against the new censorship laws was itself not only censored but, later, the journal he had sent it to (*Deutsche Jahrbücher*, run by Arnold Ruge and a vehicle for the ideas of the Young Hegelians) was also forced to close.

Ruge decided to set up another journal, with Marx as its editor – the *Deutsch-Französische Jahrbücher*. It was in this review that Marx published *Towards a Critique of Hegel's Philosophy of Right* in spring 1844. The title of the journal is significant. Increasingly, French radical ideas (from Saint-Simon, who was greatly admired by Marx's father-in-law, and Fourier, for example) had been filtering into German intellectual circles. Particularly, following the revolution of 1830 when the restored Bourbon monarchy of Charles X was ousted, and the constitution elected Louis-Philippe as the 'citizen-king', to reign. As Marx commented laconically in the summer of 1843: 'the law makes the king (new monarchy)'. The journal was to be run from Paris, beyond the pressures of Prussian censorship, and it was hoped that a number of the French radicals would contribute to it. They in fact declined, and interestingly declined mainly on the grounds that the German radicals had gone too far in their anti-religious stance. It was in the weeks before leaving for Paris that Marx composed two articles that would appear in the new journal: *The Jewish Question* and *Towards a Critique of Hegel's Philosophy of Right*. The appeal to the French association is strong in the excerpt selected, especially with its talk of the *ancien régime*, revolutions and counter-revolutions.

The two essays should be read together, and only lack of space determined the selection here. But before commenting upon both of them it is important to realize how little, at this point, Marx knew about political science. The political views of the Young Hegelians were not particularly well developed or coherent – the differences between Bruno Bauer and Marx on the Jewish question makes this evident. In general, they were against absolutism, against Church-state ideology and saw no future in the liberal *via media*. But they had no alternative polity, and Marx saw Communism at the time as just a 'dogmatic abstraction'. So we must not read back into either of these texts Marx's more developed understanding of socialism, capitalism, labour, productivity and commodification. Historical materialism was in its infancy and the possibilities of revolution only just being scented. From *The Jewish Question*, what Marx is desiring politically, at this point, is a democracy with a constitution (along American lines, where religion is not brought into the public sphere), a free-state (which in German is *Freistaat*, a republic), universal franchise (the vote not tied to having property) and the freedom of the press. In the last few pages of his article he discusses money, but it was not until he had read Engel's attack on capitalism in his own contribution to the first and only edition of *Deutsch-Französische Jahrbücher* ('Outline for a Critique of the Political Economy') that Marx recognized the importance of economics. In fact, it was Engel's article that persuaded him to give up the idea of a more sustained *Critique of Hegel's Philosophy of Right* and concentrate on more immediate and material tasks.

'The Critique' was the second essay to be written for Ruge's new journal. It is not insignificant that Ruge had himself written an essay on 'Hegel's philosophy of right' published in 1842 in his first journal, *Deutsche Jahrbücher*. What remains visionary in this article (which actually brought to an end his relationship with Ruge) was Marx's perception that the future emancipation of Germany lay in the hands of the proletariat, those outside participating civil society because they owned no property and therefore were not part of the establishment. Marx defined here a class of historical agents, and a struggle that was coming, that previously had been ignored or not considered. Other than Engels, the other Young Hegelians (and Ruge is representative here) viewed the proletariat as backward. It was a class that increasingly both Marx and Engels realized only came to be conscious of itself through the social crisis of the Industrial Revolution. England was at the vanguard of this new class consciousness. Hence the importance to Marx of Engels' book *The Condition of the Working Class in England* (written between 1844 and 1845).

What is important for the relationship between religion and politics in Marx's work is not their divorce (advanced now much further than the divorce announced by Luther, as Marx's own observations on Luther make apparent), but in fact the new way in which they are related. For despite Marx's trenchant critique of religion, religion remains (and appears time and time again both in his writings and those of Engels). True, religion has nothing to do with the transcendent any more. But Marx's new myth of historical progress towards emancipation is only the secularization of a Christian eschatology – as Marx's own use of 'resurrection' in the final sentence makes plain. Marx, after Feuerbach, recognized religion was an expression of something authentic about the human condition. But this expression alienated human beings from understanding the truth of that condition. His political programme uses the language of religion while reorientating it towards a material and immanent project: the just society. There is a visionary Promethean humanism here but it depended upon what the concluding statement of the *Communist Manifesto* (1848) demanded – that the workers of the world unite. And this ran counter, as he saw in *The Jewish Question*, to the self-interest and egotism behind the language of human rights.

Further reading

English translations

Marx, K. (1978), *Critique of Hegel's 'Philosophy of Right'* (Cambridge: Cambridge University Press).

General introductions

Carver, T. (1991), *The Cambridge Companion to Marx* (Cambridge: Cambridge University Press).

McLellan, D. (1980), *The Thought of Karl Marx: An Introduction* (London: Macmillan).

Wheene, F. (1999), *Karl Marx* (London: Fourth Estate).

Reception of key ideas

Harris, C. (1988), *Karl Marx, Socialism as Secular Theology: A Philosophic Study* (St Louis, MO: W. H. Green).

Lash, N. (1982), *A Matter of Hope: A Theologian's Reflections on the Thought of Karl Marx* (Notre Dame, IN: University of Notre Dame Press).

McKown, D. (1975), *The Classical Marxist Critiques of Religion : Marx, Engels, Lenin, Kautsky* (The Hague: Martinus Nijhoff).

Thomson, E. (2004), *The Discovery of the Materialist Conception of History in the Writings of the Young Karl Marx* (Lewiston, NY: Edwin Mellen Press).

Excerpt from the Introduction to the *Critique of Hegel's 'Philosophy of Right'*

For Germany, the *criticism of religion* has been essentially completed, and the criticism of religion is the prerequisite of all criticism.

The *profane* existence of error is compromised as soon as its *heavenly oratio pro aris et focis* i.e. 'speech for the altars and hearths' has been refuted. Man, who has found only the *reflection* of himself in the fantastic reality of heaven, where he sought a superman, will no longer feel disposed to find the *mere appearance* of himself, the non-man [*Unmensch*], where he seeks and must seek his true reality.

The foundation of irreligious criticism is: *Man makes religion*, religion does not make man. Religion is, indeed, the self-consciousness and self-esteem of man who has either not yet won through to himself, or has already lost himself again. But *man* is no abstract being squatting outside the world. Man is *the world of man* – state, society. This state and this society produce religion, which is an *inverted consciousness of the world*, because they are an *inverted world*. Religion is the general theory of this world, its encyclopaedic compendium, its logic in popular form, its spiritual *point d'honneur*, its enthusiasm, its moral sanction, its solemn complement, and its universal basis of consolation and justification. It is the *fantastic realization* of the human essence since the *human essence* has not acquired any true reality. The struggle against religion is, therefore, indirectly the struggle *against that world* whose spiritual *aroma* is religion.

Religious suffering is, at one and the same time, the *expression* of real suffering and a *protest* against real suffering. Religion is the sigh of the oppressed creature, the heart of a heartless world, and the soul of soulless conditions. It is the *opium* of the people.

The abolition of religion as the *illusory* happiness of the people is the demand for their *real* happiness. To call on them to give up their illusions about their condition is to call on them to *give up a condition that requires illusions.* The criticism of religion is, therefore, *in embryo, the criticism of that vale of tears* of which religion is the *halo.*

Criticism has plucked the imaginary flowers on the chain not in order that man shall continue to bear that chain without fantasy or consolation, but so that he shall throw off the chain and pluck the living flower. The criticism of religion disillusions man, so that he will think, act, and fashion his reality like a man who has discarded his illusions and regained his senses, so that he will move around himself as his own true sun. Religion is only the illusory sun which revolves around man as long as he does not revolve around himself.

It is, therefore, the *task of history*, once the *other-world of truth* has vanished, to establish the *truth of this world*. It is the immediate *task of philosophy*, which is in the service of history, to unmask self-estrangement in its *unholy forms* once the *holy form* of human self-estrangement has been unmasked. Thus, the criticism of Heaven turns into the criticism of Earth, the *criticism of religion* into the *criticism of law*, and the *criticism of theology* into the *criticism of politics.* [. . .]

Indeed, German history prides itself on having travelled a road which no other nation in the whole of history has ever travelled before, or ever will again. We have shared the restorations of modern nations without ever having shared their revolutions. We have been restored, firstly, because other nations dared to make revolutions, and, secondly, because other nations suffered counter-revolutions; on the one hand, because our masters were afraid, and, on the other, because they were not afraid. With our shepherds to the fore, we only once kept company with freedom, on the day of its internment.

One school of thought that legitimizes the infamy of today with the infamy of yesterday, a school that stigmatizes every cry of the serf against the knout as mere rebelliousness once the knout has aged a little and acquired a hereditary significance and a history, a school to which history shows nothing but its *a posteriori*, as did the God of Israel to his servant Moses, the *historical school of law* – this school would have invented German history were it not itself an invention of that history. A Shylock, but a cringing Shylock, that swears by its bond, its historical bond, its Christian-Germanic bond, for every pound of flesh cut from the heart of the people.

Good-natured enthusiasts, Germanomaniacs by extraction and free-thinkers by reflexion, on the contrary, seek our history of freedom beyond our history in the ancient Teutonic forests. But, what difference is there between the history of our freedom and the history of the boar's freedom if it can be found only in the forests? Besides, it is common knowledge that the forest echoes back what you shout into it. So peace to the ancient Teutonic forests!

War on the German state of affairs! By all means! They are *below the level of history, they are beneath any criticism*, but they are still an object of criticism like the criminal who is below the level of humanity but still an object for the *executioner*. In the struggle against that state of affairs, criticism is no passion of the head, it is the head of passion. It is not a lancet, it is a weapon. Its object is its *enemy*, which it wants not to refute but to *exterminate*. For the spirit of that state of affairs is refuted. In itself, it is no object *worthy of thought*, it is an existence which is as despicable as it is despised. Criticism does not need to make things clear to itself as regards this object, for it has already settled accounts with it. It no longer assumes the quality of an *end-in-itself*, but only of a *means*. Its essential pathos is *indignation*, its essential work is *denunciation*. [. . .]

What a sight! This infinitely proceeding division of society into the most mani-fold races opposed to one another by petty antipathies, uneasy consciences, and brutal mediocrity, and which, precisely because of their reciprocal ambiguous and distrustful attitude, are all, without exception although with various formalities, treated by their *rulers* as *conceded existences*. And they must recognize and acknowledge as a concession of heaven the very fact that they are *mastered, ruled, possessed*! And, on the other side, are the rulers themselves, whose greatness is in inverse proportion to their number!

Criticism dealing with this content is criticism in a *hand-to-hand* fight, and in such a fight the point is not whether the opponent is a noble, equal, *interesting* opponent, the point is to *strike* him. The point is not to let the Germans have a minute for self-deception and resignation. The actual pressure must be made more pressing by adding to it consciousness of pressure, the shame must be made more shameful by publicizing it. Every sphere of German society must be shown as the *partie honteuse* of German society: these petrified relations must be forced to dance by singing their own tune to them! The people must be taught to *be terrified* at itself in order to give it *courage*. This will be fulfilling an imperative need of the German nation, and the needs of the nations are in themselves the ultimate reason for their satisfaction.

This struggle against the limited content of the German *status quo* cannot be without interest even for the *modern* nations, for the German *status quo* is the *open completion of the ancien régime* and the *ancien régime* is the *concealed deficiency of the modern state*. The struggle against the German political present is the struggle against the past of the modern nations, and they are still burdened with reminders of that past. It is instructive for them to see the *ancien régime*, which has been through its *tragedy* with them, playing its *comedy* as a German revenant. *Tragic* indeed was the pre-existing power of the world, and freedom, on the other hand, was a personal notion; in short, as long as it believed and had to believe in its own justification. As long as the *ancien régime*, as an existing world order, struggled against a world that was only coming into being, there was on its side a historical error, not a personal one. That is why its downfall was tragic.

On the other hand, the present German regime, an anachronism, a flagrant con-tradiction of generally recognized axioms, the nothingness of the *ancien régime* exhibited to the world, only imagines that it believes in itself and demands that the world should imagine the same thing. If it believed in its own *essence*, would it try to hide that essence under the *semblance* of an alien essence and seek refuge in hypocrisy and sophism? The modern *ancien régime* is rather only the *comedian* of a world order whose *true heroes* are dead. History is thorough and goes through many phases when carrying an old form to the grave. The last phases of a world-historical form is its *comedy*. [. . .]

Meanwhile, once *modern* politico-social reality itself is subjected to criticism, once criticism rises to truly human problems, it finds itself outside the German *status quo*, or else it would reach out for its object *below* its object. An example. The relation of industry, of the world of wealth generally, to the political world is one of the major problems of modern times. In what form is this problem beginning to engage the attention of the Germans? In the form of *protective duties*, of the *prohibitive system*, or *national economy*. Germanomania has passed out of man into matter, and thus one morning our cotton barons and iron heroes saw themselves turned into patriots. People are, therefore, beginning in Germany to acknowledge the sovereignty of monopoly on the inside through lending it *sovereignty on the outside*. People are, therefore, now about to begin, in Germany, what people in France and England are about to end. The old corrupt condition against which these countries are revolting in theory, and which they only bear as one bears chains, is greeted in Germany as the dawn of a beautiful future which still hardly dares to pass from *crafty* theory to the most ruthless practice. Whereas the problem in France and England is: *Political economy*, or the *rule of society over wealth*; in Germany, it is: National economy, or the *mastery of private property over nationality*. In France and England, then, it is a case of abolishing monopoly that has proceeded to its last consequences; in Germany, it is a case of proceeding to the last consequences of monopoly. There is an adequate example of the *German* form of modern problems, an example of how our history, like a clumsy recruit, still has to do extra drill on things that are old and hackneyed in history. [. . .]

As the ancient peoples went through their pre-history in imagination, in *mythology*, so we Germans have gone through our post-history in thought, in *philosophy*. We are philosophical contemporaries of the present without being its historical contemporaries. German philosophy is the *ideal prolongation* of German history. If therefore, instead of of the *œuvres incomplètes* of our real history, we criticize the *œuvres posthumes* of our ideal history, *philosophy*, our criticism is in the midst of the questions of which the present says: *that is the question*. What, in progressive nations, is a *practical* break with modern state conditions, is, in Germany, where even those conditions do not yet exist, at first a critical break with the philosophical reflexion of those conditions.

German philosophy of right and state is the only *German history* which is *al pari* ['on a level'] with the *official* modern present. The German nation must therefore join this, its dream-history, to its present conditions and subject to criticism not only these existing conditions, but at the same time their abstract continuation. Its future cannot be *limited* either to the immediate negation of its real conditions of state and right, or to the immediate implementation of its ideal state and right conditions, for it has the immediate negation of its real conditions in its ideal conditions, and it has almost *outlived* the immediate implementation of its ideal conditions in the contemplation of neighboring nations. Hence, it is with good reason that the *practical* political part in Germany demands the *negation of philosophy*. [. . .]

The criticism of the *German philosophy of state and right*, which attained its most consistent, richest, and last formulation through *Hegel*, is both a critical analysis of the modern state and of the reality connected with it, and the resolute negation of the whole manner of the *German consciousness in politics and right* as *practiced* hereto, the most distinguished, most universal expression of which, raised to the level of *science*, is the *speculative philosophy* of right itself. If the speculative philosophy of right, that abstract extravagant *thinking* on the modern state, the reality of which remains a thing of the beyond, if only beyond the Rhine, was possible only in Germany, inversely the German thought-image of the modern state which makes abstraction of *real man* was possible only because and insofar as the modern state itself makes abstraction of *real man*, or satisfies the whole of man only in imagination. In politics, the Germans *thought* what other nations *did*. Germany was their *theoretical conscience*. The abstraction and presumption of its thought was always in step with the one-sidedness and lowliness of its reality. If, therefore, the *status quo of German statehood* expresses the *completion* of the *ancien régime*, the completion of the thorn in the flesh of the modern state, the *status quo* of German state science expresses the *incompletion of the modern state*, the defectiveness of its flesh itself.

Already as the resolute opponent of the previous form of *German* political consciousness the criticism of speculative philosophy of right strays, not into itself, but into *problems* which there is only one means of solving – *practice*.

It is asked: can Germany attain a practice *à la hauteur des principles* – i.e., a *revolution* which will raise it not only to the *official level* of modern nations, but to the *height of humanity* which will be the near future of those nations?

The weapon of criticism cannot, of course, replace criticism of the weapon, material force must be overthrown by material force; but theory also becomes a material force as soon as it has gripped the masses. Theory is capable of gripping the masses as soon as it demonstrates *ad hominem*, and it demonstrates *ad hominem* as soon as it becomes radical. To be radical is to grasp the root of the matter. But, for man, the root is man himself. The evident proof of the radicalism of German theory, and hence of its practical energy, is that it proceeds from a resolute *positive* abolition of religion. The criticism of religion ends with the teaching that *man is the highest essence for man* – hence, with the *categoric imperative to overthrow all relations* in which man is a debased, enslaved, abandoned, despicable essence, relations which cannot be better described than by the cry of a Frenchman when it was planned to introduce a tax on dogs: Poor dogs! They want to treat you as human beings!

Even historically, theoretical emancipation has specific practical significance for Germany. For Germany's *revolutionary* past is theoretical, it is the *Reformation*. As the revolution then began in the brain of the *monk*, so now it begins in the brain of the *philosopher*.

Luther, we grant, overcame bondage out of *devotion* by replacing it by bondage out of *conviction*. He shattered faith in authority because he restored the authority of faith. He turned priests into laymen because he turned laymen into priests. He freed man from outer religiosity because he made religiosity the inner man. He freed the body from chains because he enchained the heart.

185

But, if Protestantism was not the true solution of the problem, it was at least the true setting of it. It was no longer a case of the layman's struggle against the *priest outside himself* but of his struggle against his *own priest inside himself*, his priestly nature. And if the Protestant transformation of the German layman into priests emancipated the lay popes, the *princes*, with the whole of their priestly clique, the privileged and philistines, the philosophical transformation of priestly Germans into men will emancipate the *people*. But, *secularization* will not stop at the *confiscation of Church estates* set in motion mainly by hypocritical Prussia any more than emancipation stops at princes. The Peasant War, the most radical fact of German history, came to grief because of theology. Today, when theology itself has come to grief, the most unfree fact of German history, our *status quo*, will be shattered against philosophy. On the eve of the Reformation, official Germany was the most unconditional slave of Rome. On the eve of its revolution, it is the unconditional slave of less than Rome, of Prussia and Austria, of country junkers and philistines.

Meanwhile, a major difficulty seems to stand in the way of a *radical* German revolution.

For revolutions require a *passive* element, a material basis. Theory is fulfilled in a people only insofar as it is the fulfilment of the needs of that people. But will the monstrous discrepancy between the demands of German thought and the answers of German reality find a corresponding discrepancy between civil society and the state, and between civil society and itself? Will the theoretical needs be immediate practical needs? It is not enough for thought to strive for realization, reality must itself strive towards thought.

But Germany did not rise to the intermediary stage of political emancipation at the same time as the modern nations. It has not yet reached in practice the stages which it has surpassed in theory. How can it do a *somersault*, not only over its own limitations, but at the same time over the limitations of the modern nations, over limitations which it must in reality feel and strive for as for emancipation from its real limitations? Only a revolution of radical needs can be a radical revolution and it seems that precisely the preconditions and ground for such needs are lacking.

If Germany has accompanied the development of the modern nations only with the abstract activity of thought without taking an effective share in the real struggle of that development, it has, on the other hand, shared the *sufferings* of that development, without sharing in its enjoyment, or its partial satisfaction. To the abstract activity on the one hand corresponds the abstract suffering on the other. That is why Germany will one day find itself on the level of European decadence before ever having been on the level of European emancipation. It will be comparable to a *fetish worshipper* pining away with the diseases of Christianity.

If we now consider the *German governments*, we find that because of the circumstances of the time, because of Germany's condition, because of the standpoint of German education, and, finally, under the impulse of its own fortunate instinct, they are driven to combine the *civilized shortcomings of the modern state world*, the advantages of which we do not enjoy, with the *barbaric deficiencies of the ancien régime*, which we enjoy in full; hence, Germany must share more and more, if not in the reasonableness, at least in the unreasonableness of those state formations which are beyond the bounds of its *status quo*. Is there in the world, for example, a country which shares so naively in all the illusions of constitutional statehood without sharing in its realities as so-called constitutional Germany? And was it not perforce the notion of a German government to combine the tortures of censorship with the tortures of the French September laws [1835 anti-press laws] which provide for freedom of the press? As you could find the gods of all nations in the Roman Pantheon, so you will find in the Germans' Holy Roman Empire all the sins of all state forms. That this eclecticism will reach a so far unprecedented height is guaranteed in particular by the *political-aesthetic gourmanderie* of a German king [Frederick William IV] who intended to play all the roles of monarchy, whether feudal or democratic, if not in the person of the people, at least in his *own* person, and if not for the people, at least for *himself*. *Germany, as the deficiency of the political present constituted a world of its ow*n, will not be able to throw down the specific German limitations without throwing down the general limitation of the political present.

It is not the *radical* revolution, not the *general human* emancipation which is a utopian dream for Germany, but rather the partial, the *merely* political revolution, the revolution which leaves the pillars of the house standing. On what is a partial, a merely political revolution based? On *part of civil society* emancipating itself and attaining *general* domination; on a definite class, proceeding from its *particular situation*; undertaking the general emancipation of society. This class emancipates the whole of society, but only provided the whole of society is in the same situation as this class – e.g., possesses money and education or can acquire them at will.

No class of civil society can play this role without arousing a moment of enthusiasm in itself and in the masses, a moment in which it fraternizes and merges with society in general, becomes confused with it and is perceived and acknowledged as its *general representative*, a moment in which its claims and rights are truly the claims and rights of society itself, a moment in which it is truly the social head and the social heart. Only in the name of the general rights of society can a particular class vindicate for itself general domination. For the storming of this emancipatory position, and hence for the political exploitation of all sections of society in the interests of its own section, revolutionary energy and spiritual self-feeling alone are not sufficient. For the *revolution of a nation*, and the *emancipation of a particular class* of civil society to coincide, for one estate to be acknowledged as the estate of the whole society, all the defects of society must conversely be concentrated in another class, a particular estate must be the estate of the general stumbling-block, the incorporation of the general limitation, a particular social sphere must be recognized as the notorious crime of the whole of society, so that liberation from that sphere appears as general self-liberation. For one estate to be *par excellence* the estate of liberation, another estate must conversely be the obvious estate of oppression. The negative general significance of the French nobility and the French clergy determined the positive general significance of the nearest neighboring and opposed class of the *bourgeoisie*.

But no particular class in Germany has the constituency, the penetration, the courage, or the ruthlessness that could mark it out as the negative representative of society. No more has any estate the breadth of soul that identifies itself, even for a moment, with the soul of the nation, the geniality that inspires material might to political violence, or that revolutionary daring which flings at the adversary the defiant words: *I am nothing but I must be everything*. The main stem of German morals and honesty, of the classes as well as of individuals, is rather that *modest egoism* which asserts its limitedness and allows it to be asserted against itself. The relation of the various sections of German society is therefore not dramatic but epic. Each of them begins to be aware of itself and begins to camp beside the others with all its particular claims not as soon as it is oppressed, but as soon as the circumstances of the time, without the section's own participation, creates a social substratum on which it can in turn exert pressure. Even the *moral self-feeling of the German middle class* rests only on the consciousness that it is the common representative of the philistine mediocrity of all the other classes. It is therefore not only the German kings who accede to the throne *mal à propos*, it is every section of civil society which goes through a defeat before it celebrates victory and develops its own limitations before it overcomes the limitations facing it, asserts its narrow-hearted essence before it has been able to assert its magnanimous essence; thus the very opportunity of a great role has passed away before it is to hand, and every class, once it begins the struggle against the class opposed to it, is involved in the struggle against the class below it. Hence, the higher nobility is struggling against the monarchy, the bureaucrat against the nobility, and the bourgeois against them all, while the proletariat is already beginning to find itself struggling against the bourgeoisie. The middle class hardly dares to grasp the thought of emancipation from its own standpoint when the development of the social conditions and the progress of political theory already declare that standpoint antiquated or at least problematic.

In France, it is enough for somebody to be something for him to want to be everything; in Germany, nobody can be anything if he is not prepared to renounce everything. In France, partial emancipation is the basis of universal emancipation; in Germany, universal emancipation is the *conditio sine qua non* of any partial emancipation. In France, it is the reality of gradual liberation that must give birth to complete freedom, in Germany, the impossibility of gradual liberation. In France, every class of the nation is a *political idealist* and becomes aware of itself at first not as a particular class but as a representative of social requirements generally. The role of *emancipator* therefore passes in dramatic motion to the various classes of the French nation one after the other until it finally comes to the class which implements social freedom no longer with the provision of certain conditions lying outside man and yet created by human society, but rather organizes all conditions of human existence on the premises of social freedom. On the contrary, in Germany, where practical life is as spiritless as spiritual life is unpractical, no class in civil society has any need or capacity for general emancipation until it is forced by its *immediate* condition, by *material* necessity, by its *very chains*.

Where, then, is the *positive* possibility of a German emancipation?

Answer: In the formulation of a class with *radical chains*, a class of civil society which is not a class of civil society, an estate which is the dissolution of all estates, a sphere which has a universal character by its universal suffering and claims no *particular right* because no *particular wrong*, but *wrong generally*, is perpetuated against it; which can invoke no *historical*, but only *human*, title; which does not stand in any one-sided antithesis to the consequences but in all-round antithesis to the premises of German statehood; a sphere, finally, which cannot emancipate itself without emancipating itself from all other spheres of society and thereby emancipating all other spheres of society, which, in a word, is the *complete loss* of man and hence can win itself only through the *complete re-winning of man*. This dissolution of society as a particular estate is the *proletariat*.

The proletariat is beginning to appear in Germany as a result of the rising *industrial* movement. For, it is not the *naturally arising* poor but the *artificially impoverished*, not the human masses mechanically oppressed by the gravity of society, but the masses resulting from the *drastic dissolution* of society, mainly of the middle estate, that form the proletariat, although, as is easily understood, the naturally arising poor and the Christian-Germanic serfs gradually join its ranks.

By heralding the *dissolution of the hereto existing world order*, the proletariat merely proclaims the *secret of its own existence*, for it is the factual dissolution of that world order. By demanding the *negation of private property*, the proletariat merely raises to the rank of a principle of society what society has raised to the rank of *its* principle, what is already incorporated in *it* as the negative result of society without its own participation. The proletarian then finds himself possessing the same right in regard to the world which is coming into being as the *German king* in regard to the world which has come into being when he calls the people *his* people, as he calls the horse *his* horse. By declaring the people his private property, the king merely proclaims that the private owner is king.

As philosophy finds its material weapon in the proletariat, so the proletariat finds its *spiritual* weapon in philosophy. And once the lightning of thought has squarely struck this ingenuous soil of the people, the emancipation of the *Germans* into *men* will be accomplished.

Let us sum up the result:

The only liberation of Germany which is *practically* possible is liberation from the point of view of *that* theory which declares man to be the supreme being for man. Germany can emancipate itself from the Middle Ages only if it emancipates itself at the same time from the *partial* victories over the *Middle Ages*. In Germany, *no* form of bondage can be broken without breaking *all* forms of bondage. Germany, which is renowned for its *thoroughness*, cannot make a revolution unless it is a *thorough* one. The *emancipation of the German* is the *emancipation of man*. The *head* of this emancipation is *philosophy*, its *heart* the *proletariat*. Philosophy cannot realize itself without the transcendence [*Aufhebung*] of the proletariat, and the proletariat cannot transcend itself without the realization [*Verwirklichung*] of philosophy.

When all the inner conditions are met, the *day of the German resurrection* will be heralded by the *crowing of the cock of Gaul*.

Chapter 13

Carl Schmitt (1888–1985)

All significant concepts of the modern theory of the state are secularized theological concepts . . .

Introduction

Money and philosophical concepts have something in common. Both are subject to inflation. The more a currency is circulated the less its value. The same is true for philosophical concepts and especially for the term 'Political Theology'. What is Political Theology? The term was coined by Carl Schmitt in 1922 when he published his book, *Politische Theologie. Vier Kapitel zur Lehre von der Souveränität*. But Schmitt's understanding of Political Theology has little to do with its current use. Today Political Theology is used synonymously with critical theology, public theology or theology in the public sphere. Political Theology functions as an umbrella term for various types of an ecumenical theology closely related to pastoral theology and the Western reception of Liberation Theology. The *Blackwell Companion to Political Theology*, published in 2004, and the essay in this volume by Jürgen Manemann, illustrates this. Political Theology in this sense is *public* theology because according to its proponents theology is itself political and plays a role in the public sphere. The origins of this meaning of Political Theology lie in the work of Johann Baptist Metz and his 'new political theology'. Metz, a liberal Catholic and former student of Karl Rahner, combined in his new political theology liberal Catholic theology (in the wake of the Second Vatican Council) and the critical theory of the *Frankfurter Schule*. This new coinage of Schmitt's term is inextricably related to the socio-historical context in Germany in the 1970s. For this generation of theologians, two things were important. First, the Second Vatican Council promised a reform of the Catholic Church and to make the boundaries between Church and society permeable. Secondly, from the 1960s on a new generation of students started to revolt against the taboo of the years after the Second World War and the denial of the German collective past. In other words, new political theology was informed by an awakening from a political slumber and the spirit of liberation. From Metz to the *Blackwell Companion* this new political theology or public theology understands itself as a critical force in society with a political voice. It speaks on behalf of the powerless, on the basis of Christian charity, responsibility and compassion. It is a theology of goodwill.

Carl Schmitt's understanding of the term is contradistinctive to these liberal notions of political theology. Its original meaning causes some discontent and this is related to Schmitt's political conservatism and his engagement with the National Socialist Party. In this introduction to the excerpt from Schmitt's *Politische Theologie* two topics become fundamental. First, the ambiguity of the person Carl Schmitt; and, secondly, the concept of Political Theology outlined in his publication of 1922 (Schmitt published a *Politische Theologie II* in 1970 where he seems to support the new liberal theology of that time). As far as the second topic is concerned, as we shall see, Political Theology is not designed as a theological programme. Rather it is linked to a specific methodology called 'the sociology of juridical concepts' that has similarities to Max Weber's type of sociological analysis. We have then to distinguish between the author and his work. The question of whether one has to be interpreted by the other is, in the case of Schmitt, extremely important and difficult. In the context of this reader it is sufficient only to point out these difficulties.

Despite his political ambivalent engagement with the Nazi regime, Carl Schmitt has contributed classical concepts to political science, like the 'state of exception', the definition of the political as the differentiation between friend and enemy, 'political theology', 'the safeguard of the constitution'. Furthermore his historical and juridical investigations into the political ideology of romanticism, the genesis of dictatorship, the ideological conditions of parliamentarism and his commentary on the constitution of the Weimar Republic are cornerstones in the twentieth-century history of political thought. Recently, Schmitt's work has become popular again through Giorgio Agamben and his work.[1] In fact, Schmitt is more attractive than ever before and the list of secondary literature is growing fast. But this was not always the case.

In 1969 when the students were rioting across Europe, Hans Barion edited a *Festschrift* to celebrate Schmitt's eightieth birthday. This *Festschrift* is truly one of the most peculiar of its genre, and documents the ambiguous reputation of Carl Schmitt. Usually a *Festschrift* is designed to commemorate the groundbreaking contributions of the person to whom it is dedicated. The reader would expect an introduction or foreword in which these contributions are praised and situated in the academic field to demonstrate how the person being celebrated influenced the academic discipline and scientific discourse. Nothing of this can be found in the *Festschrift* for Schmitt. There is no *laudatio* and no emphatic appraisal of Schmitt's work. Moreover, the *Festschrift*, bearing the enigmatic title *Epirrhosis*, is divided into two volumes which distinguish between those academics who had contact with Carl Schmitt *after 1945* and those whom he knew personally or academically *before 1945*. The *Festschrift* for Carl Schmitt is a unique document *for* insiders *by* insiders. The title *Epirrhosis* sheds some light on this. For the Greek word means the action of coming to someone's aid in difficult times. In fact, after the Second World War Schmitt was in difficulties. He was accused in 1945 of collaborating with the Nazi

---

1. G. Agamben (1998), *Homo Sacer: Sovereign Power and Bare Life* (Palo Alto, CA: Stanford University Press); G. Agamben (2005), *State of Exception* (Chicago, IL: University of Chicago Press).

regime, of which he was the chief legal theorist until 1936, and subsequently he was imprisoned. When he was released from prison he was not allowed to take up his academic position again, his library was confiscated and he was forced to retire without any pension. Even though Schmitt was among the leading intellectuals of the Weimar years, everyone avoided him, except some ultraconservatives and persons regarded as politically suspect like Hans Barion (he was a Catholic priest who was disciplined by Rome for his positive views on eugenics).

Let us turn to the texts and examine Schmitt's understanding of political theology. The excerpt in this volume, introducing the concept of political theology, is taken from chapter three of *Politische Theologie*. It is preceded by a definition of sovereignty and a legal discussion about the implications of this definition. In these foregoing chapters, Schmitt advocates his own political decisionism. This is immediately evident in the opening sentence of the book, defining sovereignty by his famous formula: 'The sovereign is he who decides on the state *of exception (Ausnahmezustand)*'. The German word *Ausnahmezustand* means both a state of exception and a state of emergency. It is a state of exception because it leads to the suspension of common law and a state of emergency because martial law is implemented in such situations. For example, the decision to suspend the right of habeas corpus as a necessary means to protect people from terrorism illustrates how 'the state of exception' nullifies a fundamental right of an individual in the legal state. According to Schmitt, the sovereign is the one who has the power to decide whether a situation is exceptional and is therefore declared to be a 'state of emergency'. This is to say that the sovereign has to decide whether a crisis can be handled by normal means or requires exceptional decision-taking and actions. The point here is that these actions are normally illegal and only justified by the exceptional conditions of a state of emergency. The power to decide on the state of exception puts the sovereign *above* the law. In the second chapter of *Political Theology* Schmitt explores the difficult question of the legal status of the state of exception and how the decision to suspend the law can be justified on legal grounds.

In the first part of the book Schmitt focuses on the state of exception in terms of legal theory and in the second half the modern concept of the State is examined in terms of a history of ideas. Despite the differences between these two parts of the book the notion of sovereignty is the central issue for both. Sovereignty is not only linked with the state of *emergency* but also with the *emergence* of the modern concept of the state. To borrow a phrase from Thomas Hobbes, for whom the state can be seen as an artificial body: 'sovereignty is an artificial soul, as giving life and motion to the whole body'. Thus the analysis of the concept of sovereignty is, at the same time an analysis of the principle of life for the state. Therefore, to understand the concept of sovereignty is to understand what makes the state a *living unity* and to understand how that state can exist. This is the context in which the term political theology is embedded.

In order to give a preliminary definition of political theology, we can say political theology is *that kind of ideology* which makes a specific form of political organization (like absolute monarchy, or parliamentary democracy) possible. Thus the analysis of the concept of sovereignty is, at the same time, an analysis of the principle of life for the state. For to understand the concept of sovereignty is to understand what makes the state a *living unity*, a body. It is in the context of the state as a body that the term 'Political Theology' is embedded. It is an offspring of seventeenth-century theology. The state and subsequently the notion of sovereignty are both initially theological concepts. Thus it becomes clear why Schmitt can summerize the meaning of political theology by saying: 'All significant concepts of the modern theory of the state are secularized theological concepts'. For Schmitt all the key terms of political theory (such as the state, sovereignty, authority, the people or even the idea of the state of exception) have their theological equivalents. In the excerpt we have chosen, he points out, for example, the parallel between the state of exception in politics and the idea of a miracle in theology. Another more graphic example is the analogy between the idea of God's omnipotence and the will of the people as the ultimate source of political power. The theological idea of God's omnipotence has been secularized and incorporated into a theory of the state, where this idea appears again either as the omnipotence of the legislator (in Rousseau) or the tyranny of the majority (in Tocqueville's critique of radical democracy).

Furthermore, we can observe from the excerpt below how Schmitt outlines a wider methodological framework, called 'sociology of juridical concepts'. This sociology of juridical concepts, he writes, 'transcends juridical conceptualization oriented to immediate practical interest. It aims to discover the basic, radically systematic structure and to compare this conceptual structure with the conceptually represented social structure of a certain epoch. There is no question here of whether the ideas produced by radical conceptualization are a reflex of social reality, or whether social reality is conceived as the result of a particular kind of thinking and therefore also of acting. Rather this sociology of concepts is concerned with establishing proof of two spiritual but at the same time substantial identities'.

Schmitt, as we have already mentioned in the introduction to Joseph de Maistre, represents the conservative strand of modern Catholic political theory. But his concept of Political Theology must also be seen in the sociological context for which it was designed. This aligns Schmitt with the sociological approaches offered by Karl Marx and Max Weber.

Further reading

Selected English translations

Schmitt, Carl (2005), *Political Theology: Four Chapters on the Concept of Sovereignty* (Chicago, IL: University of Chicago Press).

General introductions

Balakrishnan, G. (2000), *The Enemy: An Intellectual Portrait of Carl Schmitt* (New York: Verso).

Meier, H. (1998), *The Lesson of Carl Schmitt: Four Chapters on the Distinction between Political Theology and Political Philosophy* (Chicago, IL: University of Chicago Press).

Schwab, G. (1989), *The Challenge of the Exception: An Introduction to the Political Ideas of Carl Schmitt Between 1921 and 1936* (Westport, CT: Greenwood Press).

Reception of key ideas

McCormick, J. (1997), *Carl Schmitt's Critique of Liberalism: Against Politics as Technology* (New York: Cambridge University Press).

Meier, H. (1995), *Carl Schmitt & Leo Strauss: The Hidden Dialogue* (Chicago, IL: University of Chicago Press).

Mouffe, C. (1999), *The Challenge of Carl Schmitt* (London: Verso).

Excerpt from *Political Theology**

All significant concepts of the modern theory of the state are secularized theological concepts not only because of their historical development – in which they were transferred from theology to the theory of the state, whereby, for example, the omnipotent God became the omnipotent lawgiver – but also because of their systematic structure, the recognition of which is necessary for a sociological consideration of these concepts. The state of exception in jurisprudence is analogous to the miracle in theology. Only by being aware of this analogy can we appreciate the manner in which the philosophical ideas of the state developed in the last centuries.

The idea of the modern constitutional state triumphed together with *deism*, a theology and metaphysics that banished the miracle from the world. This theology and metaphysics rejected not only the transgression of the laws of nature through an exception brought about by direct intervention, as is found in the idea of a miracle, but also the sovereign's direct intervention in a valid *legal* order. The rationalism of the Enlightenment rejected the exception in every form. Conservative authors of the counter-revolution who were *theists* could thus attempt to support the personal sovereignty of the monarch ideologically, with the aid of analogies from a theistic theology.

I have for a long time referred to the significance of such fundamentally systematic and methodical analogy.[2] A detailed presentation of the meaning of the concept of the miracle in this context will have to be left to another time. What is relevant here is only the extent to which this connection is appropriate for a *sociology of juristic concepts*. The most interesting political application of such analogies is found in the Catholic philosophers of the counterrevolution, in Bonald, de Maistre, and Donoso Cortes. What we immediately recognize in them is a conceptually clear and *systematic analogy*, and not merely that kind of playing with ideas, whether mystical,

---

*   Italics have been added by the editors for emphasis.

2.   *Der Wert des Staates*, 1951; *Politische Romantik*, 1919; *Die Diktatur*, 1921.

natural-philosophical, or even romantic, which, as with everything else, so also with state and society, yields colourful symbols and pictures.

The clearest philosophical statement of that analogy is found in Leibniz.[3] Emphasizing the systematic relationship between *jurisprudence and theology*, he rejected a comparison of jurisprudence with medicine and mathematics: 'We have deservedly transferred the model of our division from theology to jurisprudence because the similarity of these two disciplines is astonishing.' Both have a double principle, reason (hence there is a natural theology and a natural jurisprudence) and scripture, which means a book with positive revelations and directives.

Adolf Menzel noted in an essay[4] that today sociology has assumed functions that were exercised in the seventeenth and eighteenth centuries by natural law, namely, to other demands for justice and to enunciate philosophical-historical constructions or ideals. He seems to believe that sociology is inferior to jurisprudence, which is supposed to have become positive. He attempts to show that all heretofore sociological systems end up by making 'political tendencies appear scientific.' But whoever takes the trouble of examining the public law literature of positive jurisprudence for its basic concepts and arguments will see that the state intervenes everywhere. At times it does so as *a deus ex machina*,[5] to decide according to positive statute a controversy that the independent act of juristic perception failed to bring to a generally plausible solution; at other times it does so as the graceful and merciful lord who proves by pardons and amnesties supremacy over his own laws. There always exists the same inexplicable identity: lawgiver, executive power, police, pardoner, welfare institution. Thus to an observer who takes the trouble to look at the total picture of contemporary jurisprudence, there appears a huge cloak-and-dagger drama, in which the state acts in many disguises but always as the same invisible person. The 'omnipotence' of the modern lawgiver, of which one reads in every textbook on public law, is not *only* linguistically derived from theology.

Many reminiscences of theology also appear in the details of the argumentation, most of course with polemical intent. In a positivistic age it is easy to reproach an intellectual opponent with the charge of indulging in theology or metaphysics. If the reproach were intended as more than mere insult, at least the following question could suggest itself: What is the source of this inclination for such theological and metaphysical derailments? One would have had to investigate whether they may be explained historically, perhaps as an aftereffect of monarchical public law, which identified the theistic God with the king, or whether they are underpinned by systematic or methodical necessities. I readily admit that because of an inability to master intellectually contradictory arguments or objections, some jurists introduce the state in their works by a mental short circuit, just as certain metaphysicians misuse the name of God. But this does not yet resolve the substantive problem. [. . .]

---

3. Leibniz, G. W. *Nova Methodus*, 1684, §§ 4, 5.
4. Menzel, A. *Naturrecht und Soziologie*, 1912.
5. *Deus ex machine* figuratively means the intervention of the state as an external and omnipotent force. The metaphor originates in ancient Greek theatres where a kind of mechanical crane was used to introduce (from above) in a dramatic scene a god or goddess who would then solve a difficult and dangerous situation [Eds].

Kelsen has the merit of having stressed since 1920 the methodical relationship of theology and jurisprudence. In his last work on the sociological and the juristic concepts of the state[6] he introduced many analogies. Although diffuse, these analogies make it possible for those with a deeper understanding of the history of ideas to discern the inner heterogeneity between his neo-Kantian epistemological point of departure and his ideological and democratic results. At the foundation of his identification of state and legal order rests a metaphysics that identifies the lawfullness of nature and normative lawfullness. This pattern of thinking is characteristic of the natural sciences. It is based on the rejection of all 'arbitrariness' and attempts to banish from the realm of the human mind every exception. In the history of the parallel of theology and jurisprudence, such a conviction finds its place most appropriately probably in J.S. Mill. In the interest of objectivity and because of his fear of arbitrariness, he too emphasized the validity without exception of every kind of law. But he probably did not assume, as did Kelsen, that the free deed of legal perception could shape just any mass of positive laws into the cosmos of its system, because this would nullify the objectivity already achieved. For a metaphysics that suddenly falls into the pathos of objectivity, it should make no difference whether an unconditional positivism directly adheres to the law that presents itself, or whether it bothers to first establish a system.

Kelsen, as soon as he goes one step beyond his methodological criticism, operates with a concept of causation that is entirely natural-scientific. This is most clearly demonstrated by his belief that Hume's and Kant's critique of the concept of substance can be transferred to the theory of the state.[7] But he fails thereby to see that the concept of substance in scholastic thought is entirely different from that in mathematical and natural-scientific thinking. The distinction between the *substance* and the *practice of law*, which is of fundamental significance in the history of the concept of sovereignty,[8] cannot be grasped with concepts rooted in the natural sciences and yet is an essential element of legal argumentation. When Kelsen gives the reasons for opting for democracy, he openly reveals the mathematical and natural-scientific character of his thinking:[9] 'Democracy is the expression of a political relativism and a scientific orientation that are liberated from miracles and dogmas and based on human understanding and critical doubt.'

For the sociology of the concept of sovereignty it is altogether vital to be clear about the sociology of legal concepts as such. The aforementioned systematic analogy between theological and juristic concepts is stressed here precisely because a sociology of legal concepts presupposes a consistent and *radical ideology*.[10] Yet it would be erroneous to believe that therein resides a spiritualist philosophy of history as opposed to a materialist one.

6. Kelsen, H. *Der Soziologische und juristische Staatsbegriff,* 1922.
7. Ibid., 208.
8. Schmitt, C. *Die Diktatur,* 1919, pp. 44, 105, 194.
9. Kelsen, H. 'Vom Wesen und Wert der Demokratie', *Archiv für Sozialwissenschaft and Sozialpolitik* 47 (1920–21): 84.
10. Schmitt uses the word radical here in the sense of 'thought out to the end'.

The *political theology* of the Restoration offers an exemplary illustration of the sentence Max Weber articulated in his critique of Rudolf Stammler's philosophy of right, namely, that it is possible to confront irrefutably a radical materialist philosophy of history with a similarly radical spiritualist philosophy of history. The authors of the counterrevolution explained political change as a result of change in outlook, and traced the French Revolution to the philosophy of the Enlightenment. It was nothing more than a clear antithesis when radical revolutionaries conversely attributed a change in thought to a change in the political and social conditions. That religious, philosophical, artistic, and literary changes are closely linked with political and social conditions was already a widespread dogma in Western Europe, especially in France, in the 1820s.

In the Marxist philosophy of history this interdependence is *radicalized to an economic dependence*; it is given a systematic basis by seeking a point of ascription also for political and social changes and by finding it in the economic sphere. This materialist explanation makes a separate consideration of ideology impossible, because everywhere it sees only 'reflexes', 'reflections', and 'disguises' of economic relations. Consequently, it looks with suspicion at psychological explanations and interpretations, at least in their vulgar form. Precisely because of its massive rationalism, this philosophy can easily turn into an irrationalist conception of history, since it conceives all thought as being a function and an emanation of vital processes. The anarchic-syndicalist socialism of Georges Sorel thus linked in this fashion Henri Bergson's philosophy of life with Marx's economic conception of history.

Both the spiritualist explanation of material processes and the materialist explanation of spiritual phenomena seek causal relations: At first they construct a contrast between two spheres, and then they dissolve this contrast into nothing by reducing one to the other. This method must necessarily culminate in a caricature. Just as Engels saw the Calvinist dogma of predestination as a reflection of capitalist competition in terms of its senselessness and incalculability, it would be just as easy to reduce the modern theory of relativity and its success to currency relations in today's world market, and thus to find the economic basis of that theory. Some would call such a procedure the *sociology of a concept or a theory*. This, however, is of no concern to us.

It is otherwise with the sociological method, which, with a view to certain ideas and intellectual constructions, seeks the typical group of persons who arrive at certain ideological results from the peculiarity of their sociological situations. In this sense one can speak of a sociology of juristic concepts, in the case of Max Weber, who traced the differentiation of the various legal fields to the development of trained jurists, civil servants who administer justice, or legal dignitaries.[11] The sociological 'peculiarity of the group of persons who professionally concern themselves with forming law' necessitates definite methods and views of juristic thinking. But this is still *not a sociology of a legal concept*. To trace a conceptual result back to a sociological carrier is *psychology*; it involves the determination of a certain kind of motivation of human action. This is a sociological problem, but not a problem

11. Weber, M. *Rechtssoziologie*, II, §1.

of the sociology of a concept. If this method is applied to intellectual accomplishments, it leads to explanations in terms of the milieu, or even to the ingenious 'psychology' that is known as the sociology of specific types, that is, of the bureaucrat, the attorney, or the professor who is employed by the state. The Hegelian system, for example, if investigated by applying this method, would have to be characterized as the philosophy of the professional lecturer, who by his economic and social situation is enabled to become, with contemplative superiority, aware of absolute consciousness, which means to practice his profession as a lecturer of philosophy; or it would be possible to view Kelsen's jurisprudence as the ideology of the lawyer-bureaucrat practicing in changing political circumstances, who, under the most diverse forms of authority and with a relativistic superiority over the momentary political authority, seeks to order systematically the positive decrees and regulations that are handed down to him. In its consequent manner this type of sociology is best assigned to *belles-lettres*; it provides a socio-psychological 'portrait' produced by a method that cannot be distinguished from the brilliant literary criticism of a Sainte-Beuve, for example.

Altogether different is the sociology of concepts, which is advanced here and alone has the possibility of achieving a scientific result for a concept such as sovereignty. *This sociology of concepts transcends juridical conceptualization oriented to immediate practical interest. It aims to discover the basic, radically systematic structure and to compare this conceptual structure with the conceptually represented social structure of a certain epoch.* There is no question here of whether the idealities produced by radical conceptualization are a reflex of sociological reality, or whether social reality is conceived of as the result of a particular kind of thinking and therefore also of acting. Rather this sociology of concepts is concerned with establishing proof of *two spiritual but at the same time substantial identities.* It is thus not a sociology of the concept of sovereignty when, for example, the monarchy of the seventeenth century is characterized as the real that is 'mirrored' in the Cartesian concept of God. But it is a sociology of the concept of sovereignty when the historical-political status of the monarchy of that epoch is shown to correspond to the general state of consciousness that was characteristic of Western Europeans at that time, and when the juristic construction of the historical-political reality can find a concept whose structure is in accord with the structure of metaphysical concepts. *Monarchy* thus becomes as self-evident in the consciousness of that period as *democracy* does in a later epoch.

The presupposition of this kind of sociology of juristic concepts is thus a *radical conceptualization*, a consistent thinking that is pushed into *metaphysics and theology*. The metaphysical image that a definite epoch forges of the world has the same structure as what the world immediately understands to be appropriate as a form of its political organization. The determination of such an identity is the sociology of the concept of sovereignty. It proves that in fact, as Edward Caird said in his book on Auguste Comte, *metaphysics* is the most intensive and the clearest expression of an epoch.

'Imitate the immutable decrees of the divinity.' This was the ideal of the legal life of the state that was immediately evident to the rationalism of the eighteenth century. This utterance is found in Rousseau's essay *Political Economy*. The politicization of theological concepts, especially with respect to the concept of sovereignty, is so striking that it has not escaped any true expert on his writings. Said Emile Boutmy, 'Rousseau applies to the sovereign the idea that the *philosophes* hold of God: He may do anything that he wills but he may not will evil.'[12] In the theory of the state of the seventeenth century, the *monarch is identified with God* and has in the state a position exactly *analogous* to that attributed to God in the Cartesian system of the world. According to Atger, 'The prince develops all the inherent characteristics of the state by a sort of continual creation. The prince is the Cartesian god transposed to the political world.'[13]

There is psychologically (and, from the point of view of a phenomenologist, phenomenologically as well) a *complete identity*. A continuous thread runs through the metaphysical, political, and sociological conceptions that postulate the sovereign as a personal unit and primeval creator. The fine tale of the *Discours de la méthode* provides an extraordinarily instructive example. It is a document of the new rationalist spirit. In the depth of doubt, it finds consolation by using reason unswervingly: 'J'étais assuré d'user en tout de ma raison.' But what is it that becomes clear in the first place to the mind suddenly forced to reason? That the works created by several masters are *not as perfect* as those created by one. 'One sole architect' must construct a house and a town; the best constitutions are those that are the work of a sole wise legislator, they are 'devised by only one'; and finally, a sole God governs the world. As Descartes once wrote to Mersenne, 'It is God who established these laws in nature just as a king establishes laws in his kingdom.'

The seventeenth and eighteenth centuries were dominated by this idea of the sole sovereign, which is one of the reasons why, in addition to the decisionist cast of his thinking, Hobbes remained personalistic and postulated an ultimate concrete deciding instance, and why he also heightened his state, the *Leviathan*, into an immense person and thus point-blank straight into mythology. This he did despite his nominalism and natural-scientific approach and his reduction of the individual to the atom. For him this was no anthropomorphism – from which he was truly free – but a *methodical and systematic postulate* of his juristic thinking. But the image of the architect and master builder of the work reflects a confusion that is characteristic of the concept of causality. The world architect is *simultaneously* the *creator and the legislator*, which means the legitimizing authority. Throughout the Enlightenment period until the French Revolution, such an architect of world and state was called the legislator.

Since then the consistency of exclusively scientific thinking has also permeated political ideas, repressing the essentially juristic-ethical thinking that had predominated in the age of the Enlightenment. The general validity of a legal prescription has become *identified* with the lawfulness of nature, which applies without exception. The sovereign, who in the deistic view of the world, even if conceived as

12. Boutmy, E. *Annales des sciences politiques* 4 (1902), p. 418.
13. Atger, *Essai sur l'histoire des doctrines du contract social* (1906), p. 136.

residing outside the world, had remained the engineer of the great machine, has been radically pushed aside. The machine now runs by itself. The metaphysical proposition that God enunciates only general and not particular declarations of will governed the metaphysics of Leibniz and Nicolas Malebranche. The *general will* of Rousseau became identical with the *will of the sovereign*; but simultaneously the concept of the general also contained a quantitative determination with regard to its subject, which means that the *people became the sovereign*. The decisionistic and personalistic element in the concept of sovereignty was thus lost. The will of the people is always good: 'The people are always virtuous.' Said Emmanuel Sieyès, 'In whatever manner a nation expresses its wishes, it is enough that it wishes; all forms are good but its will is always the supreme law.' But the necessity by which the people always will what is right is not identical with the rightness that emanated from the commands of the personal sovereign. In the struggle of opposing interests and coalitions, absolute monarchy made the decision and thereby created the unity of the state. The unity that a people represents does not possess this decisionist character; it is an organic unity, and with rational consciousness the ideas of the state originated as an organic whole. The theistic as well as the deistic concepts of God become thus unintelligible for political metaphysics.

It is true nevertheless that for some time the aftereffects of the idea of God remained recognizable. In America this manifested itself in the reasonable and pragmatic belief that the voice of the people is the voice of God – a belief that is at the foundation of Jefferson's victory of 1801. Tocqueville in his account of American democracy observed that in democratic thought the people hover above the entire political life of the state, just as God does above the world, as the cause and the end of all things, as the point from which everything emanates and to which everything returns. Today, on the contrary such a well-known legal and political philosopher of the state as Kelsen can conceive of democracy as the expression of a relativistic and impersonal scientism. This notion is in accord with the development of political theology and metaphysics in the nineteenth century.

To the conception of God in the seventeenth and eighteenth centuries belongs the idea of his transcendence *vis-à-vis the world*, just as to that period's philosophy of state belongs the notion of the transcendence of the sovereign *vis-à-vis the state*. Everything in the nineteenth century was increasingly governed by conceptions of *immanence*. All the identities that recur in the political ideas and in the state doctrines of the nineteenth century rest on such conceptions of immanence: the democratic thesis of the *identity of the ruler and the ruled*, the organic theory of the state with the identity of the state and sovereignty, the constitutional theory of Krabbe with the identity of sovereignty and the legal order, and finally Kelsen's theory of the *identity of the state and the legal order*.

After the writers of the Restoration developed a political theology, the radicals who opposed all existing order directed, with heightened awareness, their ideological efforts against the belief in God altogether, fighting that belief as if it were the most fundamental expression of the belief in any authority and unity. The battle against God was taken up by Proudhon under the clear influence of Auguste Comte. Bakunin continued it with Scythian fury. The battle against traditional religiosity can be traced naturally to many different political and sociological motives: the conservative posture of ecclesiastical Christianity, the alliance of throne and altar, the number of prominent authors who were 'déclassé', the appearance of an art and literature in the nineteenth century whose genial representatives, at least in the decisive periods of their lives, had been spat out by the bourgeois order – all this is still largely unrecognized and unappreciated in its sociological detail.

The main line of development will undoubtedly unfold as follows: conceptions of transcendence will *no longer be credible* to most educated people, who will settle for either a more or less clear immanence-pantheism or a positivist indifference toward any metaphysics. Insofar as it retains the concept of God, the immanence philosophy, which found its greatest systematic architect in Hegel, draws God into the world and permits law and the state to emanate from the immanence of the objective. But among the most extreme radicals, a consequent atheism began to prevail. The German left-Hegelians were most conscious of this tendency. They were no less vehement than Proudhon in proclaiming that mankind had to be substituted for God. Marx and Engels never failed to recognize that this ideal of an unfolding self-conscious mankind must end in anarchic freedom. Precisely because of his youthful intuition, the utterance of the young Engels in the years 1842–1844 is of the greatest significance: 'The essence of the state, as that of religion, is mankind's fear of itself.'[14]

If viewed from this perspective of the history of ideas, the development of the nineteenth-century theory of the state displays two characteristic moments: the elimination of all theistic and transcendental conceptions and the formation of a new concept of legitimacy. The traditional principle of legitimacy obviously lost all validity. Neither the version of the Restoration based on private law and patrimony nor the one founded on a sentimental and reverent attachment was able to resist this development. Since 1848 the theory of public law has become 'positive', and behind this word is usually hidden its dilemma; or the theory has propounded in different paraphrases the idea that all power resides in the *pouvoir constituant* of the people, which means that the democratic notion of legitimacy has replaced the monarchical. It was therefore an occurrence of utmost significance that Donoso Cortes, one of the foremost representatives of *decisionist thinking* and a *Catholic* philosopher of the state, one who was intensely conscious of the metaphysical kernel of all politics, concluded in reference to the revolution of 1848, that the epoch of royalism was at an end. Royalism is no longer because there are no kings. Therefore legitimacy no longer exists in the traditional sense. For him there was one solution: *dictatorship*. It is the solution that Hobbes also reached by the same kind of decisionist thinking, though mixed with mathematical relativism. *Autoritas, non veritas facit legem*. A detailed presentation of this kind of decisionism and a thorough appreciation of Donoso Cortes are not yet available. Here it can only be pointed out that the theological mode of thought of the Spaniard was in complete accord with the thought of the Middle Ages, whose

14. Friedrich Engels, *Schriften aus der Frühzeit*, ed. G. Mayer (Berlin, 1920), p. 281.

construction was juristic. All his perceptions, all his arguments, down to the last atom, were juristic; his lack of understanding of the mathematical natural-scientific thinking of the nineteenth century mirrored the outlook of natural-scientific thinking toward decisionism and the specific logic of the juristic thinking that culminates in a personal decision.

Chapter 14

Vladimir I. Lenin (1870–1924)
and Simone Weil (1909–43)

Introduction

As noted in the Introduction to Karl Marx, in his early essay *The Jewish Question* (when his understanding of socialism and communism was not yet developed) Marx approved of religious tolerance as it was being practised in the United States. What he inveighed against was the institutional employment of religion for State purposes. For himself, Feuerbach had advanced Hegel's understanding of the 'death of God' and the object of Marx's own religion from this point on was humanity. But through Engels' discussions with the Chartists and the Owenites in England, his own involvement with workers' associations and the Communist League, both in London and on the Continent, and his debates with the French radicals, Marx became increasingly aware of Christian socialism. In England, Christian socialism developed in the wake of the revolutionary fevers of 1848. Its central figures were F. D. Maurice, Charles Kingsley and John Ludlow. Marx's blast against Christian socialism in *The Communist Manifesto* came only months before, in February 1848, printed, ironically, in London though written in German:

> Nothing is easier than to give Christian asceticism a socialist tinge. Has not Christianity declaimed against private property, against marriage, against the state? Has it not preached, in the place of these, charity and poverty, celibacy and mortification of the flesh, monastic life and Mother Church? Christian socialism is but the holy water with which the priest consecrates the heartburnings of the aristocrat.

Given Engels' pietist and Marx's Lutheran background, this polemic is decidedly anti-Catholic. But this suited the 'feudalist socialism' he outlines in Book III.1 of *The Communist Manifesto*.

Even so, Marx's recognition that socialism has profoundly Christian roots in the West accounts for the number of books written trying to relate or completely disassociate Marxism from Christianity. The debates arose in the early days of socialism, particularly between the French utopian thinkers, like Proudhon, and German atheists, like Marx and Ruge. But the debates have not gone away – as the work of Liberation theologians in Latin America make manifest; and they constitute an important body of theoretical work in which religion and politics are intertwined. From that work we have chosen two extracts, both by Communists, who are sharply divided on this matter: the atheist Vladimir Illyich Ulyanov (Lenin) and the woman whom André Gide called the best spiritual writer of the twentieth century and T. S. Eliot a saint, Simone Weil. These extracts open up a conversation between secular and mystic Marxism.

In 1920, following the Russian Revolution of 1917 and the establishment of the Soviet Union, Lenin (1870–1923), like everyone else, had to complete a Party questionnaire. In it he stated that he retained his Orthodox religious beliefs until he was 16. Between that age and 35 (when he wrote the paper we have selected) much was to happen to him that would, eventually, change the shape of world politics. It was his older brother, Alexander, who was the first radical and revolutionary in the family. As a result of a botched assassination attempt on Emperor Alexander III, he was hanged in St Petersburg at the age of 21. Lenin was 17 at the time. The Emperor was a late example of an absolutist ruler committed to the Divine Right of Kings. But it was not until Lenin was expelled from the university of Kazan in 1887 for involvement in a demonstration, and forced to live with his mother in their country villa for three years, that he began to read his brother's books and develop his own radical stance. This stance was to be unique at the time because it centred on Lenin's idolization of Marx and Russian radicalism at that time was not Marxist. But for Lenin, Marx and Engels uncovered the 'scientific' and material principles of economic and class history.

In the excerpt selected, a paper Lenin delivered at the Second Congress of the Social Democratic Workers Party (held in London in April 1905), both the influence of Marx and Lenin's commitment to a scientific materialism are evident. But Lenin goes further than Marx, and more in the direction of Engels. First, he has none of Marx's Hegelian heritage. Lenin's materialism is empirical and positivist and it is on these bases that he can espouse Marxist analysis as scientific. Secondly, while following Marx in wishing to critique all forms of social ideology, and allowing private religious devotion, Lenin is more aggressive in wishing to promote atheism as part of a specific political and educational programme.

No doubt this had something to do with the situation Lenin and the other radical revolutionaries faced in 1905. Most of Marx's (and Engel's) political thinking was done following the failure of the 1848 Revolution – in France and Germany. Lenin, on the other hand, now leader of the Bolsheviks, was speaking in the midst of events that became known as the 1905 Revolution. Significant for the relationship between religion and political life at this time in Russia, this Revolution was organized initially by an Orthodox priest (Father Gapon), who was a fervent believer in the traditional relationship between the Tsar and his people. On Sunday 9 January, a peaceful march of over 120,000 insurgents moved towards the gates of the Winter Palace to petition the Tsar to be the father of his oppressed people. The guards mowed them down with sabres and artillery fire. Father Gapon left for Geneva. Workers strikes across the country followed the massacre – but the main Socialist leaders (e.g. Lenin) were in exile. By February, the government had been forced to close nearly all the universities. In April, when Lenin delivered his paper, the possibility of the collapse of the Russian Empire was extremely high. Peasant uprisings took place in a myriad different locations and the army was called in 2,700 times.

In June, the most vicious counterattack was launched in Odessa with the battleship *Potemkin* at its centre resulting in 2,000 deaths and a further 3,000 being wounded. By October, millions of workers were on strike and the country was at a standstill. But when Lenin's paper was published in December, the Revolution was over and the Emperor had been forced to promulgate a manifesto in which major political reforms were promised. A further twelve years was to pass before conditions were ripe for another radical *coup d'état*.

Simone Weil knew the work of Lenin well. In the 1930s she was a militant activist for the trade unions, and although never a member of a political party, such as the *Partie Communiste Français*, she knew the literature emerging after the Russian Revolution. In an attack written in the last months of 1933, she submitted Lenin's most well-known philosophical treatise, *Materialism and Empiriocriticism* to a scathing critique:

> He does not say: such and such a conception distorts the true relationship between man and the world, therefore it is reactionary; but, such and such a conception deviates from materialism, leads to idealism, furnishes religion with arguments; it is reactionary, therefore false. He was not at all concerned with seeing clearly his own thought, but solely with maintaining intact the philosophical traditions on which the Party lived.

Ironically, Lenin had written the book in London at the British Library (in 1908) and it is his most vigorous defence of Marx. Three points can be discerned in Weil's critique: first, Lenin's materialism is reductive; secondly, it is an ideology for a party that will eventually lead to 'the stifling regime which weighs at present on the Russian people'; and thirdly, it misreads Marx, for whom what is at stake *is* the 'relationship between man and the world'. Weil's own political and spiritual writings issue from a profound affinity with the poor and the oppressed worker, and a total rejection of her own bourgeois upbringing. Long essays, such as *The Causes of Liberty and Social Oppression* (1934) and, eight years later, *The Need for Roots*, seek to detail the servile conditions under which so many people labour (not in spite of but actually because of advancing technology) and expose the mechanisms of power that perpetuate it. Inspired by the heroic traditions of Ancient Greece, she eschewed utopianism and social day-dreaming, calling even Marx's communism 'an opium'. The aim of her political work is summed up in an early essay *Prospects* (1933): 'If we are to perish in the battles of the future, let us do our best to prepare ourselves to perish with a clear vision of the world we shall be leaving behind'. The battles were not in the far-off future; they were already being prepared in Italy, Germany and Spain. Weil herself fought for an anarchist Republican group in the Spanish Civil War, in the French Resistance and died while working in a London being pounded by the Blitz. She died of starvation which, in all likelihood, was self-induced.

An emotionally complex woman, Weil was born in France of Jewish parents, raised in a climate of agnosticism and embraced Christianity following a series of conversion experiences in 1938. But though she flirted with Roman Catholicism, she was never able to be part of a church, always wishing to remain staunchly independent and free-thinking. Her understanding of Christianity was profoundly related to her understanding of suffering and oppression. Echoing Nietzsche and yet inverting him, she wrote: 'Christianity is pre-eminently the religion of the slaves, so that slaves cannot help belonging to it, and I among others'. But the only collective she was able to give herself to was France herself. Her patriotism (despite denunciations of French nationalism!) was as intense and mystical as that of Joan of Arc.

Her spirituality, socialism and patriotism find unique expression in *L'Enracinement* [rootedness], translated as *The Need for Roots*. It was written in the dark winter nights of 1942–3, following the fall of France to the Germans and the occupation of Paris in 1940. Weil herself had just returned to Europe from America, where her parents had emigrated to avoid Nazi persecution. The book was commissioned by the Resistance who asked her to draft projects for the revitalization of France and the re-establishment of the French government that would follow the defeat of Germany.

In the extract we have chosen, the guiding principle of Weil's vision throughout her book receives clear expression: a 'Man's dignity in his work . . . is a value of a spiritual order'. In fact, the first section of the book is a catalogue of what she defines as 'the needs of the soul'. Without these needs being met the spiritual and moral well-being of the social body is jeopardized. Weil views meeting these needs as the highest of human obligations. She will even claim that 'the notion of obligation comes before that of rights, which is subordinate and relative to the former'. The obligation one human being has towards meeting the needs (body and soul) of another is independent of all social conditions and universal. It is a moral *a priori*. The spiritual needs that require satisfaction are: order, liberty, obedience, responsibility, equality, hierarchism, honour, punishment, freedom of opinion, security, risk, private property, collective property and, finally, truth. Human beings 'must become accustomed to love truth'.

This is the intellectual context within which Weil sets out her agenda for working people. It becomes evident why, then, she found Lenin's materialism reductive – for it could only speak to the human being as an organism. Her own 'socialism' – which she distinguishes from previous socialisms – is concerned with the moral capacity of human beings and the day-to-day practicalities of the working life. To some extent it looks back to the humanism of Kant, for it does not state that religion is necessary for socialism, only ethics. But in her conviction that there 'is no possible chance of satisfying people's need, unless men can be found for this purpose who love truth', she is appealing to a transcendent notion of truth which, while owing much to Plato and her love of classical literature, is fundamentally religious.

Further reading

Selected English translations

Vladimir Ilyich Lenin: The Essential Works, trans. and ed. H. Christman (Toronto: Dover Publications, 1987).

Lenin: Collected Works, vol. 10 (Moscow: Progress Publishers, 1965), pp. 83–7.

Weil, S., *The Need for Roots: Prelude to a Declaration of Duties towards Mankind* (London: Routledge and Kegan Paul, 1978).

Weil, S., *Oppression and Liberty* (London: Routledge, 2001).

General introductions

Abosch, H. (1994), *Simone Weil: An Introduction* (New York: Pennbridge Books).

Fiori, G. (1989), *Simone Weil, an Intellectual Biography* (Athens, GA: University of Georgia Press).

Weber, G. (1980), *Lenin: Life and Works* (London: Macmillan).

Williams, B. (2000), *Lenin* (Harlow: Longman).

Reception of key ideas

Bell, R. (1998), *Simone Weil: The Way of Justice as Compassion*, (Lanham, MD: Rowman and Littlefield Publishers).

Dietz, M. (1998), *Between the Human and the Divine: The Political Thought of Simone Weil* (Totowa, NJ: Rowman and Littlefield).

LeBlanc, J. (2004), *Ethics and Creativity in the Political Thought of Simone Weil and Albert Camus* (Lewiston, NY: Edwin Mellen Press).

Patsouras, L. (1992), *Simone Weil and the Socialist Tradition* (San Francisco, CA: EMText).

Polan, A. (1985), *Lenin and the End of Politics* (London: Methuen).

'Socialism and Religion' by Lenin

Present-day society is wholly based on the exploitation of the vast masses of the working class by a tiny minority of the population, the class of the landowners and that of the capitalists. It is a slave society, since the 'free' workers, who all their life work for the capitalists, are 'entitled' only to such means of subsistence as are essential for the maintenance of slaves who produce profit, for the safeguarding and perpetuation of capitalist slavery.

The economic oppression of the workers inevitably calls forth and engenders every kind of political oppression and social humiliation, the coarsening and darkening of the spiritual and moral life of the masses. The workers may secure a greater or lesser degree of political liberty to fight for their economic emancipation, but no amount of liberty will rid them of poverty, unemployment, and oppression until the power of capital is overthrown. Religion is one of the forms of spiritual oppression which everywhere weighs down heavily upon the masses of the people, overburdened by their perpetual work for others, by want and isolation. Impotence of the exploited classes in their struggle against the exploiters just as inevitably gives rise to the belief in a better life after death as impotence of the savage in his battle with nature gives rise to belief in gods, devils, miracles, and the like. Those who toil and live in want all their lives are taught by religion to be submissive and patient while here on earth, and to take comfort in the hope of a heavenly reward. But those who live by the labour of others are taught by religion to practise charity while on earth, thus offering them a very cheap way of justifying their entire existence as exploiters and selling them at a moderate price tickets to well-being in heaven. Religion is opium for the people. Religion is a sort of spiritual booze, in which the slaves of capital drown their human image, their demand for a life more or less worthy of man.

But a slave who has become conscious of his slavery and has risen to struggle for his emancipation has already half ceased to be a slave. The modern class-conscious worker, reared by large-scale factory industry and enlightened by urban life, contemptuously casts aside religious prejudices, leaves heaven to the priests and bourgeois bigots, and tries to win a better life for himself here on earth. The proletariat of today takes the side of socialism, which enlists science in the battle against the fog of religion, and frees the workers from their belief in life after death by welding them together to fight in the present for a better life on earth.

Religion must be declared a private affair. In these words socialists usually express their attitude towards religion. But the meaning of these words should be accurately defined to prevent any misunderstanding. We demand that religion be held a private affair so far as the state is concerned. But by no means can we consider religion a private affair so far as our Party is concerned. Religion must be of no concern to the state, and religious societies must have no connection with governmental authority. Everyone must be absolutely free to profess any religion he pleases, or no religion whatever, i.e., to be an atheist, which every socialist is, as a rule. Discrimination among citizens on account of their religious convictions is wholly intolerable. Even the bare mention of a citizen's religion in official documents should unquestionably be eliminated. No subsidies should be granted to the established Church nor state allowances made to ecclesiastical and religious societies. These should become absolutely free associations of like-minded citizens, associations independent of the state. Only the complete fulfilment of these demands can put an end to the shameful and accursed past when the Church lived in feudal dependence on the state, and Russian citizens lived in feudal dependence on the established Church, when mediaeval, inquisitorial laws (to this day remaining in our criminal codes and on our statute-books) were in existence and were applied, persecuting men for their belief or disbelief, violating men's consciences, and linking cosy government jobs and government-derived incomes with the dispensation of this or that dope by the established Church. Complete separation of Church and State is what the socialist proletariat demands of the modern state and the modern Church.

The Russian Revolution must put this demand into effect as a necessary component of political freedom. In this respect, the Russian revolution is in a particularly favourable position, since the revolting officialism of the police-ridden feudal autocracy has called forth discontent, unrest and indignation even among the clergy. However abject, however ignorant Russian Orthodox clergymen may have been, even they have now been awakened by the thunder of the downfall of the old, mediaeval order in Russia. Even they are joining in the demand for freedom, are protesting against bureaucratic practices and officialism, against the spying for the police imposed on the 'servants of God'. We socialists must lend this movement our support, carrying the demands of honest and sincere members of the clergy to their conclusion, making them stick to their words about freedom, demanding that they should resolutely break all ties between religion and the police. Either you are sincere, in which case you must stand for the complete separation of Church and State and of School and Church, for religion to be declared wholly and absolutely a private affair. Or you do not accept these consistent demands for freedom, in which case you evidently are still held captive by the traditions of the inquisition, in which case you evidently still cling to your cosy government jobs and government-derived incomes, in which case you evidently do not believe in the spiritual power of your weapon and continue to take bribes from the state. And in that case the class-conscious workers of all Russia declare merciless war on you.

So far as the party of the socialist proletariat is concerned, religion is not a private affair. Our Party is an association of class-conscious, advanced fighters for the emancipation of the working class. Such an association cannot and must not be indifferent to lack of class-consciousness, ignorance or obscurantism in the shape of religious beliefs. We demand complete disestablishment of the Church so as to be able to combat the religious fog with purely ideological and solely ideological weapons, by means of our press and by word of mouth. But we founded our association, the Russian Social-Democratic Labour Party, precisely for such a struggle against every religious bamboozling of the workers. And to us the ideological struggle is not a private affair, but the affair of the whole Party, of the whole proletariat.

If that is so, why do we not declare in our Programme that we are atheists? Why do we not forbid Christians and other believers in God to join our Party?

The answer to this question will serve to explain the very important difference in the way the question of religion is presented by the bourgeois democrats and the Social-Democrats.

Our Programme is based entirely on the scientific, and moreover the materialist, world-outlook. An explanation of our Programme, therefore, necessarily includes an explanation of the true historical and economic roots of the religious fog. Our propaganda necessarily includes the propaganda of atheism; the publication of the appropriate scientific literature, which the autocratic feudal government has hitherto strictly forbidden and persecuted, must now form one of the fields of our Party work. We shall now probably have to follow the advice Engels once gave to the German Socialists: to translate and widely disseminate the literature of the eighteenth-century French Enlighteners and atheists.[1]

But under no circumstances ought we to fall into the error of posing the religious question in an abstract, idealistic fashion, as an 'intellectual' question unconnected with the class struggle, as is not infrequently done by the radical-democrats from among the bourgeoisie. It would be stupid to think that, in a society based on the endless oppression and coarsening of the worker masses, religious prejudices could be dispelled by purely propaganda methods. It would be

1. See Frederick Engels, 'Flüchtlings-Literatur', *Volksstaat*, Nr 73 vom 22.6 (1874).

bourgeois narrow-mindedness to forget that the yoke of religion that weighs upon mankind is merely a product and reflection of the economic yoke within society. No number of pamphlets and no amount of preaching can enlighten the proletariat, if it is not enlightened by its own struggle against the dark forces of capitalism. Unity in this really revolutionary struggle of the oppressed class for the creation of a paradise on earth is more important to us than unity of proletarian opinion on paradise in heaven.

That is the reason why we do not and should not set forth our atheism in our Programme; that is why we do not and should not prohibit proletarians who still retain vestiges of their old prejudices from associating themselves with our Party. We shall always preach the scientific world-outlook, and it is essential for us to combat the inconsistency of various 'Christians'. But that does not mean in the least that the religious question ought to be advanced to first place, where it does not belong at all; nor does it mean that we should allow the forces of the really revolutionary economic and political struggle to be split up on account of third-rate opinions or senseless ideas, rapidly losing all political importance, rapidly being swept out as rubbish by the very course of economic development.

Everywhere the reactionary bourgeoisie has concerned itself, and is now beginning to concern itself in Russia, with the fomenting of religious strife – in order thereby to divert the attention of the masses from the really important and fundamental economic and political problems, now being solved in practice by the all-Russian proletariat uniting in revolutionary struggle. This reactionary policy of splitting up the proletarian forces, which today manifests itself mainly in Black-Hundred pogroms, may tomorrow conceive some more subtle forms. We, at any rate, shall oppose it by calmly, consistently and patiently preaching proletarian solidarity and the scientific world-outlook – a preaching alien to any stirring up of secondary differences.

The revolutionary proletariat will succeed in making religion a really private affair, so far as the state is concerned. And in this political system, cleansed of mediaeval mildew, the proletariat will wage a broad and open struggle for the elimination of economic slavery, the true source of the religious humbugging of mankind.

Excerpt from *The Need for Roots* by Weil

We shall never put an end to the proletarian lot by passing laws, whether these be concerned with the nationalization of key industries, the abolition of private property, powers granted to the trade-unions to negotiate collective agreements, representation by factory delegates or the control of engagement. All the measures that are proposed, be they given a revolutionary or a reformist label, are purely legal, and it is not on a legal plane that working-class distress is situated, nor the remedy for this distress. Marx would perfectly well have understood this if he had been intellectually honest with himself, for it is a truth which bursts forth in the best pages of his *Capital*.

It is no use attempting to discover in the demands put forward by the workers the cure for their misfortune. Plunged in misfortune body and soul, including the imagination, how should they be able to imagine anything which didn't bear misfortune's mark? If they make a violent effort to extricate themselves therefrom, they fall into apocalyptic reverie, or seek compensation in a working-class imperialism which is no more to be encouraged than a national imperialism.

What one *can* look out for in their demands is the sign and token of their sufferings. Now, all, or nearly all, of these demands express the suffering caused by uprootedness. If they want control of engagement and nationalization, it is because they are obsessed by the fear of total uprootedness – that is, of unemployment. If they want the abolition of private property, it is because they have had enough of being admitted into wherever it is they work as immigrants allowed to enter on sufferance. This was also the psychological mainspring behind the workers' occupation of the factories in June 1936. For some days they experienced a pure, unmixed joy at finding themselves at home there where they spent their working-day; the joy of a child who doesn't want to think of tomorrow. Nobody could reasonably expect that tomorrow was going to be a particularly happy one.

The French working-class movement which came out of the Revolution was essentially a cry, less one of revolt than one of protest, in face of the pitiless hardship of the lot reserved for all the oppressed. Considering what can be expected from *any* kind of collective movement, this one certainly contained a relatively very high degree of purity of motive. It came to an end in 1914; ever since, there have been only echoes of it, the toxins generated by society in general having even corrupted the sense of misfortune. We must endeavour to recover its tradition; but nobody could wish to see it revived. However beautiful the sound of a cry of woe may be, one cannot wish to hear it again; it is more human to wish to cure the woe.

The actual list of workmen's woes supplies us with a list of the things that need changing. First of all, we must do away with the shock experienced by a lad who at twelve or thirteen leaves school and enters a factory. There are some workmen who could feel happy enough, had this shock not left behind it an ever-open wound; but they don't realize themselves that their suffering comes to them from the past. The child while at school, whether a good or a bad pupil, was a being whose existence was recognized, whose development was a matter of concern, whose best motives were appealed to. From one day to the next, he finds himself an extra cog in a machine, rather less than a thing, and nobody cares any more whether he obeys from the lowest motives or not, provided he obeys. The majority of workmen have at any rate at this stage of their lives experienced the sensation of no longer existing, accompanied by a sort of inner vertigo, such as intellectuals or *bourgeois,* even in their greatest sufferings, have very rarely had the opportunity of knowing. This first shock, received at so early an age, often leaves an indelible mark. It can rule out all love of work once and for all.

We must change the system concerning concentration of attention during working hours, the type of stimulants which make for the overcoming of laziness or exhaustion – and which at present are merely fear and extra pay – the type of obedience necessary, the far too small amount of initiative, skill and thought demanded of workmen, their present exclusion from any imaginative share in the work of the enterprise as a whole, their sometimes total ignorance of the value, social utility and destination of the things they manufacture, and the complete divorce between working life and family life. The list could well be extended. [. . .]

Speaking in general terms, a reform of an infinitely greater social importance than all the measures arrayed under the title of Socialism would be a transformation in the very conception of technical research. So far, no one has ever imagined that an engineer occupied in technical research on new types of machinery could have anything other than the following double objective in view: first, to increase the profits of the firm which has ordered the research, and secondly, to serve the interests of the consumer. For in such a case, when we talk about the interests of production, we mean producing more and at a cheaper rate; that is to say, these interests are really identical with those of the consumer. Thus, these two words are constantly being used the one for the other.

As for the workmen who will be spending their energies on this machine, nobody thinks twice about them. Nobody even thinks it possible to think about them. The most that ever happens is that from time to time some vague security apparatus is provided, although, in fact, severed fingers and factory stairs daily splashed with fresh human blood are such a common feature.

But this feeble show of interest is the only one. Not only does nobody consider the moral well-being of the workmen, which would demand too great an effort of the imagination; but nobody even considers the possibility of not injuring them in the flesh. Otherwise one might perhaps have found something else for the mines than that appalling automatic drill worked by compressed air, which sends an uninterrupted series of shocks for eight hours through the body of the man manipulating it.

No one thinks either of asking himself whether some new type of machine, by making capital less fluid and production more rigid, will not aggravate the general danger of unemployment.

What is the use of workmen obtaining as a result of their struggles an increase in wages and a relaxation of discipline, if meanwhile engineers in a few research departments invent, without the slightest evil intent, machines which reduce their souls and bodies to a state of exhaustion, or aggravate their economic difficulties? What use can the partial or total nationalization of economic production be to them, if the spirit of these research departments hasn't changed? And so far, as far as one can tell, it hasn't changed in places where nationalization has been introduced. Even Soviet propaganda has never claimed that Russia had discovered a radically new type of machine, worthy of being handled by an all-powerful proletariat.

And yet, if there is one conviction which stands out with irresistible force in the works of Marx, it is this one: that any change in the relationship between the classes must remain a pure illusion, if it be not accompanied by a transformation in technical processes, expressing itself in entirely new types of machinery. From the workman's point of view, a machine needs to possess three qualities. First, it should be able to be worked without exhausting the muscles, or the nerves, or any organ whatever – and also without cutting or lacerating the flesh, save under very exceptional circumstances.

LENIN (1870–1924) AND WEIL (1909–43)

Secondly, in relation to the general danger of unemployment, the productive apparatus as a whole should be as flexible as possible, so as to be able to follow the fluctuations in demand. Consequently, the same machine ought to serve a variety of purposes, the more the better, and even to a certain extent indeterminate ones. This also forms a military requirement, for the greater ease in transferring from a peacetime to a war-time footing. Lastly, it is a factor which makes for happiness during working-hours, for it is thus possible to avoid that monotony so much feared by workmen because of the boredom and disgust it engenders.

Thirdly, it should normally be in keeping with the work of which a fully qualified man is capable. This again is a military necessity, and it is, furthermore, indispensable to the dignity and moral well-being of the workmen. A working-class composed almost entirely of competent professionals is not a proletariat.

A considerable development of the adjustable automatic machine, serving a variety of purposes, would go far to satisfy these needs. The first models of this type are already in existence, and it is certain that in this direction lie very great possibilities. Such machines make the work of a machine-minder obsolete. In a huge concern like Renault, few of the workmen look happy as they stand at work; amongst these few privileged beings are those in charge of automatic turrets with movable cam adjustment.

But what is essential is the idea itself of posing in technical terms problems concerning the effect of machines upon the moral well-being of the workmen. Once posed, the technicians have only to resolve them; just as they have resolved countless others. All that is necessary is that they should want to do so. For this reason, the places where new machinery is devised should no longer fall entirely within the network of capitalist interests. It would be natural for the State to exercise some control over them by means of grants. And why shouldn't the workers' organizations do the same by giving bonuses? – without mentioning other means of bringing influence and pressure to bear. If the workers' unions could become really alive, they would be in perpetual contact with the research departments where new technical processes were being studied. Such a contact could be prepared in advance by fomenting a sympathetic atmosphere towards workmen in engineering schools.

Up to now, technicians have never had anything else in mind than the requirements of manufacture. If they were to start having always present before them the needs of those who do the manufacturing, the whole technique of production would be slowly transformed.

This ought to become a part of the instruction given in engineering schools and technical schools generally – but a part with some real substance to it.

There would no doubt be everything to be gained in putting in hand right away investigations concerning this type of problem.

The subject of such investigations would be easy enough to define. A pope once said: 'Material comes out of the factory ennobled, the workers come out of it debased.' Marx made exactly the same observation in still more vigorous terms. What is wanted is that all those who endeavour to carry out technical improvements should have continually present in their minds the conviction that among all the deficiencies of all kinds it is possible to detect in the present state of manufacturing, the one for which it is by far the most indispensably urgent to find a remedy is this one: that nothing must be done to make it worse; that everything must be done to make it less. This conception should henceforth form part of the sense of professional obligation, the sense of professional honour, with whosoever holds a responsible position in industry. One of the principal tasks before the workmen's trade-unions, if they were capable of carrying it out, would be to make this conception sink deep into the universal consciousness. [. . .]

To sum up, the abolition of the proletarian lot, chiefly characterized by uprootedness, depends upon the creation of forms of industrial production and culture of the mind in which workmen can be, and be made to feel themselves to be, at home. Of course, in any such reconstruction, a major part would have to be played by the workmen themselves. But, in the nature of things, this part would go on increasing in proportion as their actual liberation began to take effect. Inevitably, only the minimum participation can be expected of them whilst they remain in the grip of distress.

This problem of the building of entirely new working-class conditions of existence is an urgent one, and needs to be examined without delay. A policy should at once be decided upon. For as soon as the war is over, we shall be busy building in the literal sense of the word – that is, constructing houses, buildings. What is built this time will not be demolished again, unless there is another war, and life will become adapted to it. It would be paradoxical if the stones which will, maybe for several generations, determine the whole of our social life, were allowed to be thrown together just anyhow. For this reason, we shall have to have a clear idea beforehand of the form industrial enterprise is to take in the immediate future.

If by any chance we failed to face up to this necessity, through fear of possible divisions in our midst, this would merely mean that we were not qualified to take a hand in shaping the destinies of France.

It is urgent, therefore, to consider a plan for re-establishing the working-class by the roots. Tentative proposals for such are summarized below.

Large factories would be abolished. A big concern would be composed of an assembly shop connected with a number of little workshops, each containing one or more workmen, dispersed throughout the country. It would be these same workmen, and not specialists, who would take it in turns to go and work for a time in the central assembly shop, and there ought to be a holiday atmosphere about such occasions. Only half a day's work would be required, the rest of the time being taken up with hob-nobbing with others similarly engaged, the development of feelings of loyalty to the concern, technical demonstrations showing each workman the exact function of the parts he makes and the various difficulties overcome by the work of others, geography lectures pointing out where the products they help to manufacture go to, the sort of human beings who use them, and the type of social surroundings, daily existence or human atmosphere in which these products have a part to play, and how big this part is. To this could be added general cultural information. A workman's university would be in the vicinity of each central assembly shop. It would act in close liaison with the management of the concern, but would not form part of the latter's property.

The machines would not belong to the concern. They would belong to the minute workshops scattered about everywhere, and these would, in their turn, be the property of the workmen, either individually or collectively. Every workman would, besides, own a house and a bit of land.

This triple proprietorship comprising machine, house and land would be bestowed on him by the State as a gift on his marriage, and provided he had successfully passed a difficult technical examination, accompanied by a test to check the level of his intelligence and general culture.

The choice of a machine would be made to depend in the first place on the individual workman's tastes and natural abilities, and secondly on very general requirements from the point of view of production. It should be, of course, as far as possible, an adjustable automatic machine with a variety of uses.

This triple proprietorship could be neither transmitted by inheritance, nor sold, nor alienated in any way whatever. (The machine alone could, under certain circumstances, be exchanged.) The individual having the use of it would only be able to relinquish it purely and simply. In that event, it should be made difficult, but not impossible, for him later on to obtain an equivalent one elsewhere.

On a workman's death, this property would return to the State, which would, of course, if need be, be bound to maintain the well-being of the wife and children at the same level as before. If the woman was capable of doing the work, she could keep the property.

All such gifts would be financed out of taxes, either levied directly on business profits or indirectly on the sale of business products. They would be administered by a board composed of government officials, owners of business undertakings, trade-unionists and representatives of the Chamber of Deputies.

This right to property could be withdrawn on account of professional incapacity after sentence by a court of law. This, of course, presupposes the adoption of analogous penal measures for punishing, if necessary, professional incapacity on the part of the owner of a business undertaking.

A workman who wanted to become the owner of a small workshop would first have to obtain permission from a professional organization authorized to grant the same with discretion, and would then be given facilities for the purchase of two or three extra machines; but no more than that.

A workman unable to pass the technical examination would remain in the position of a wage-earner. But he would be able throughout the whole of his life, at whatever age, to make fresh attempts to satisfy the conditions. He would also at any age, and on several occasions, be able to ask to be sent on a free course of some months at a training-school.

These wage-earners through incapacity would work either in little workshops not run on a co-operative basis, as assistants to a man working on his own, or as hands in the assembly shops. But only a small number of them should be allowed to stay in industry. The majority should be sent to fill jobs as manual labourers and pen-pushers, which are indispensable to the carrying on of the public services and trade.

Up to the time he gets married and settles down somewhere for the remainder of his life – that is to say, depending on the individual character, up to the age of twenty-two, twenty-five or thirty – a young man would be regarded as being still in a state of apprenticeship.

During childhood, enough time should be left out of school to enable children to spend many, many hours pottering about in their father's company whilst at work. Semi-attendance at school – a few hours' study followed by a few hours' work – should then go on for some considerable time. Later, a very varied existence is what is needed: journeys of the *Tour de France* type, working courses spent, now with artisans working on their own, now in little co-operative workshops, now in assembly shops belonging to different concerns, now in youth associations of the *Chantiers* or *Compagnons* type; working courses which, according to individual tastes and capacities, could be several times repeated and further prolonged by attendance at workmen's colleges for periods varying between a few weeks and two years. The ability to go on such working courses should, moreover, under certain conditions, be made possible at any age. They should be entirely free of charge, and not carry with them any sort of social advantages.

When the young workman, gorged and glutted with variety, begin to think of settling down, he would be ripe for planting his roots. A wife, children, a garden supplying him with a great part of his food, work associating him with an enterprise he could love, be proud of, and which was to him as a window opened wide on to the outside world – all this is surely enough for the earthly happiness of any human being.

Naturally, such a conception of the young working-man's development implies a complete recasting of the present prison-like system.

As for wages, it would be necessary to avoid, in the first place, of course, that they were so low as to cause actual distress – though there would scarcely be any fear of that under such conditions – since they absorb the workman's attention and prevent his attachment to the concern.

Corporative bodies, for purposes of arbitration, etc., ought to be created solely with this purpose in view: to function in such a way that no workman has hardly ever to think about money matters.

The profession of manager, like that of medical practitioner, is one whose practice the State, acting in the public interest, should license only after certain conditions have been fulfilled. Such conditions should concern not only capacity, but also moral character.

Capital sums involved would be much smaller than at present. A credit system could easily make it possible for any young man without capital who had the necessary capacity and vocation for such a post to become a manager.

Business enterprise could thus be made again an individual thing. As for incorporated joint-stock companies, perhaps it would be just as well, while arranging for a suitable method of transition, to abolish them and declare them illegal.

Naturally, the variety of business undertakings would involve the consideration of very varied forms of administration. The plan sketched here is only presented as the final stage reached after long efforts, amongst which advances in technical invention would be indispensable.

At all events, such a form of social existence would be neither capitalist nor socialist.

It would put an end to the proletarian condition, whereas what is called Socialism tends, in fact, to force everybody without distinction into that condition.

Its goal would be, not, according to the expression now inclined to become popular, the interest of the consumer – such an interest can only be a grossly material one – but Man's dignity in his work, which is a value of a spiritual order.

The difficulty about such a social conception *is* that there is no possible chance of its emerging from the domain of theory unless a certain number of men can be found who are fired by a burning and unquenchable resolve to make it a reality. It is not at all certain that such men can be found or called into being.

Yet, otherwise, it really seems the only choice left is one between different, and almost equally abominable, forms of wretchedness.

Although such a conception can only become a reality over a long period of time, post-war reconstruction should at once adopt as its rule the dispersion of industrial activity.

PART FIVE

The Contemporary Debates

Prologue to Part Five

Why does this book appear now? For it would not have appeared even ten years ago. To ask this question, and to attempt to answer it, involves analysing how the relationship between religion and politics has changed. As we have seen throughout, the relationship between religion and politics, even the meaning of 'religion' and 'politics' itself, has never been stable. The essays in this section all reflect the character of this *contemporary change*. Europe's radical understanding of secularization was mainly informed by Max Weber's idea of the process of rationalization, resulting in the disenchantment of the world.[1] The change reflected in the essays below respond to a *re-evaluation* of this process of secularization.

What are the changes in the relationship between religion and politics from a European perspective?[2] First of all, intellectuals are admitting that secularization has to be rethought because religion has *not* disappeared and still shapes society. Some strong advocates of the Weberian thesis in the past (Peter Berger, Jürgen Habermas and David Martin among others) are speaking now about a cultural 'turn' towards religion. So that to some extent 'religion' is academically fashionable again. Of course this still begs the question of what is meant by 'religion'. For religion takes many different guises today, from traditional and institutionally organized religions to individual spiritualities and eclectic syncretisms. There is, furthermore, an interest in religion again by those who make reference to classical theological sources (such as the letters of St Paul)[3] in order to point out the shortcomings of

---

1. See his unfinished *magnum opus*: M. Weber (1975), *Economy and Society. An Outline of Interpretative Sociology*, 2 vols, eds G. Roth and C. Wittich (Berkeley, CA: University of California Press).
2. For the US perspective see Robert Bellah's (1967) celebrated essay on 'Civil Religion in America' in *Daedalus, Journal of the American Academy of Arts and Sciences*, 96 (Boston, MA), pp. 1–21 and R. Wuthnow (ed.) (1998), *The Encylopedia of Politics and Religion*, 2 vols (Washington, DC: Congressional Quarterly).
3. For instance, G. Agamben (2005), *The Time that Remains: A Commentary on the Letter to the Romans*, trans. Patricia Daley (Stanford, CA: Stanford University Press); A. Badiou (2003), *St Paul: The Foundation of Universalism*, trans. Brassies (Stanford, CA: Stanford University Press); and S. Žižek (2003), *The Puppet and the Dwarf: The Perverse Love of Christianity* (Boston, MA: MIT Press).

democracy and make suggestions about how religion might address these. Their interest in religion is rooted in a serious concern about basic social principles, such as the decline of solidarity and the knowledge of what it means to be a member of a community. Their turn towards religion is beyond confessionalism (which can simply be sectarian and counter-cultural); for they recognize religion as part of everyday life and an important facet of politics. Politics here is understood as the art of organizing, maintaining and enhancing social living. Religion is viewed by these people as providing values, world-views and goals for such living. In short, the resources of religion facilitate both a critique of the social and a therapy for the individual.

Theologians, those involved with the analysis of specific religious traditions, have not altogether been silent in the face of this 'turn'. Used to the therapeutical nature of religion (even its tranquillizing nature, as Marx observes – see Chapter 12), these intellectuals have also rediscovered the *critical potential* of religion. Alongside philosophical figures such as Walter Benjamin, Jacques Derrida and Emmanuel Levinas, to name a few, the eminently critical character of religion has fostered new forms of political theology. We came across the description 'political theology' with Carl Schmitt (see Chapter 13) and we observed that from the 1960s Johann Baptist Metz developed this is a new liberal and secularizing direction. But the contemporary rethinking of such a political theology is represented in this volume by his pupil Jürgen Manneman. The critical impetus is not restricted to a certain legacy of German Catholic theology, as is evident in the contributions here by John Milbank and Marcella Althaus-Reid. Critique is a tool also being employed with respect to the anti-liberal politics of Radical Orthodoxy and the gender politics of Queer theology.

Facing the political changes today, theology, understood as an investigation into the rational discourse of a specific religion, can be best characterized as *being impatient*. Theologians, not only those of the Christian faith, share this impatience with intellectuals in political science and social theory more generally. The impatience arises from wishing to speak out once more, and to be heard in the public arena. As we saw in Part Two, by the sixteenth century theologians were already being taught the adage *silete theologii in munera alieni*. By the eighteen century religion was well on the way to being privatized, and with no right to speak in civic debates. But more recently, political, social and legal theorists have also experienced a silencing – by economics in its neo-liberal guise. For where economics governs (even drives) policy these social scientists are relegated to providing comments on what has passed rather than pioneering new ways of understanding and thinking about the social body. The economics of global market capitalism is not essentially rational in itself because, as Marx pointed out in the first volume of *Das Kapital*, commodities and their value are governed by a fetishism that dazzles and seduces the consumer. Fetishism is clearly a religious term. If mathematics is the rational language *par excellence* (as in the later parts of *Das Kapital*), what Marx demonstrates in this appeal to religious language is an ineradicable irrationality of a culture in the sway of market forces. The impatience of both theologians and social scientists to speak out concerns what is at stake here. It is not the economic order such that an old-fashioned Marxist critique of capitalism will suffice to remedy the situation. What is at stake is *liberty* itself.

Moreover, the impatience in the West is not simply a Judaeo-Christian phenomenon as evidenced in the prophets and Jesus' preaching of the realization of an inchoate kingdom. Islam too has its impatience. Perhaps this is because monotheistic religions are by nature eschatological – they conceive themselves as one further step towards or to an epoch within an absolute fulfilment of time. Even the vision of a return to the golden age is eschatological. This eschatological understanding of history became inherent to the Western conception of time (certainly after Hegel). Nowadays in the shadow of Hegel, postmodern thinkers like Emmanel Levinas and Jacques Derrida reiterate the eschatological quality of time. This brings us back to our first observation which is paradigmatic of social scientists today – i.e. the new awareness of the religious as a constitutive element of society and its cultural foundations. One of the clearest examples of this new awareness is a critical voice like Slavoj Žižek's, and his ironical re-evaluation of orthodoxy. Žižek is mesmerized by the fact of orthodoxy and does not hesitate to parallel it to absolute submission to a form of political ideology like Leninism. In his work, the parallel between Lenin and St Paul seems to be omnipresent whenever he talks about politics. For Žižek, 'efficient' polity (evident in both St Paul and Lenin) involves political decisionism. Such decisionism requires strong notions of leadership. But one must never forget the irony and rhetoric with which Žižek advocates his position. He has no alternative politics to offer, while nevertheless feeling enjoined to critique, polemically, the present possibilities. He represents what might be termed 'left-wing conservatives' – that is left-wing thinkers who have discovered that the only option for the effective critique of liberal polity is to adopt or simulate conservative views on both religion and politics. We see this again in the essay by John Milbank.[4]

There is no doubt that Michel Foucault's late work on sexuality, religion and governmentality marks the beginning of this shift in left-wing intellectualism. His work on biopolitics (the *technologies of the self* and the *hermeneutics of the self*),[5] that owes a debt to Louis Althusser on 'state apparatuses',[6] drew attention to a new concept of politics and the multiple fields of political operations. Politics after Foucault, as is evident in the essay by Marcella Althaus-Reid, is understood on a *micro* level as it is experienced by marginalized groups like transvestites, transsexuals and the gay-lesbian movement. The thinking of these groups became the *avant-garde* in the 1980s and 1990s. The manner in which Althaus-Reid's essay moves between Liberation Theology, queer theory and this new understanding of politics is indicative of the new hybrid discourses in which the contemporary relationship between religion and politics is framed. While these hybrid discourses reflect the way in

4. A striking illustration of this trend can be found in C. Davis (ed.) (2005), *Theology and the Political. The New Debate.* (Durham, NC: Duke University Press).
5. M. Foucault (2000), *The Essential Works of Foucault 1954–1984,* vol. 3, ed. James D. Faubion, trans. Robert Hurley et al. (New York: The New Press).
6. L. Althusser (2001), *Lenin and Philosophy and Other Essays,* trans. Ben Brewster (New York: Monthly Review Press), pp. 85–132. Althusser also uses Christianity as a paradigm for the cultural production of subjectivities.

which religion has become visible in the public sphere today, they also have a lobbying force to engage the political arena and affect the current debates. They have then a polemical character – albeit not ironically cast in the way Žižek's is.

We have also included an essay in this section whose tone is not polemical, but measured and weighed with historical analysis. Without being a defender of Enlightenment liberalism, Charles Taylor is a proponent of a philosophical school of political science (sometimes called communitarianism) which values religion for social politics. Taylor's essay wishes to uncover the social imaginaries that make possible material forms of government. In undertaking a genealogy of modern social imaginaries from the seventeenth century onwards, he is also providing a *thick description*[7] of the processes of secularization. In his more recent attention to the contemporary situation Taylor also observes the need to review Weber's prognosis.[8] After Weber's scenario of the *disenchantment* of the world through the processes of rationalization, Taylor among others draws attention to emergence of a new re-enchantment. To summarize, while sociologists of religion[9] still demonstrate the decline in institutional religions (e.g. church attendance), spiritualities and a diffused notion of the sacred flourishes. This goes hand in hand with what theologians point out concerning the loss of a common theological vernacular.

The contemporary scene is characterized then by a new *blurring* of the lines between the temporal and the spiritual. In the classical texts from Augustine to Lenin, the categories of *temporal and spiritual* (politics and religion) were, at least formally, distinct. The struggles between temporal and spiritual authority can be analysed in terms of the relationships between them. Regardless of whether the spiritual claims to have priority over the temporal (Boniface VIII – see Chapter 3, Introduction) or the spiritual is subordinate to the temporal (Marx – see Chapter 12), the binary categories structured inquiries into the field of religion and politics. What is evident today is the way the dichotomy can no longer be used as an appropriate tool for examining the relationship between religion and politics. Religion *is* political and the political *is* infused with religion. The two social elements *cannot* be separated and reduced to a binary formula. There is a new phenomenon in the amalgamation of religion and politics. How is it possible to understand the lobbying power of certain religious groups with respect to, say, stem cell research or abortion? How can we conceive contemporary terrorism, and the politics of fear it has fostered, without taking into account its religious basis? How are we able to investigate the contemporary debates about European unity without consideration of the waves of immigration, religious diversity and the complex historical layers of belief, heresy, persecution and assimilation?

What is evident with these questions is the opening of a new field of intellectual enquiry and research, the importance of which cannot be underestimated for future policy-making and decision-taking. Because of the complex weave of issues and the very ambiguities of both religion and politics, one is tempted to shy away

7. See also C. Taylor (2002), *Varieties of Religion Today: William James Revisited* (Cambridge, MA: Harvard University Press).
8. C. Geertz (1993), *The Interpretation of Cultures* (London: Fontana Press), pp. 3–30.
9. S. Bruce (2002), *God is Dead: Secularization in the West* (Oxford: Blackwell).

from working through the new social and international challenges. But the current relationship between religion and politics will not go away. In fact, on the contrary, in the decades ahead, there will be new global constellations and new distributions of power in which religion will play a dominant role. What liberty means, concretely, will be 'renegotiated'. But because so much has been forgotten, knowledge of what has passed will govern any understanding of the possibilities for the future. If this book can provide a resource for the history of religion and politics, and a motivation for current research into the new field of intellectual enquiry, it will have served its purpose. And so, with the essays that follow, we move from the classical texts to the contemporary debates.

Chapter 15

John Milbank
Liberality versus Liberalism

Today we live in very peculiar circumstances indeed. The welfare of this world is being wrecked by the ideology of neo-liberalism and yet its historic challengers – conservatism and socialism – are in total disarray. Socialism, in particular, appears to be wrong-footed by the discovery that liberalism and not socialism is the bearer of 'modernity' and 'progress'. If the suspicion then arises that perhaps modernity and progress are themselves by no means on the side of justice, then socialists today characteristically begin to half-realize that their own traditions in their Marxist, Social Democratic and Fabian forms have been themselves too grounded in modes of thought that celebrate only utility and the supposedly 'natural' desires, goods and needs of isolated individuals.

For these reasons, there is no merit whatsoever in the contention of the ageing left (Habermas, Hobsbawm, etc.) that we are faced with an abandonment of progress and the enlightenment by a postmodern era. To the contrary, it is clear that what we are now faced with is rampant enlightenment, after the failure of secular ideologies derived from the nineteenth century – socialism, positivism, communism – that sought to some degree to *qualify* enlightenment, individualism and formalism with organicism, distributive justice and socio-historical substance.

Instead, in the face of a very peculiar situation, we need to take the risk of thinking in an altogether new way that will take up the traditions of socialism less wedded to progress, historical inevitability, materialism and the State, and put them into debate with conservative anti-capitalist thematics and classical and Biblical political thought which may allow us to see the inherent restrictions of the parameters of modern social, political and economic reflection. Our perspective may remain basically a 'Left' one, but we need to consider the possibility that only a re-alignment of the Left with more primordial, 'classical' modes of thinking will now allow it to criticize currently emerging tyranny.

This must include at its centre an openness to religion and to the question of whether a just politics must refer beyond itself to transcendent norms. For this reason, in what follows I have undertaken the experiment of thinking through a Catholic Christian approach to the social sphere in the light of current reality, in the hope that this will have something to offer not just to Christians, but to a degree also to Jews, Muslims and people of no religious persuasion whatsoever. I do not choose to insult the latter by concealing in any way the religious grounds of what I wish to say, nor my view that a predominantly secular culture will only sustain the neo-liberal catastrophe.

The documents of Vatican II, especially *Gaudium et Spes*, appear in retrospect to have been in some ways over-accepting of modern liberal democracy and market economics. This is historically understandable – since the Church needed to move beyond a previous endorsement of reactionary and sometimes absolutist monarchy, and static and hierarchical economic systems linked to unequal landholding.

Today though, we need to recognize that we are in a very different situation. First of all, recent events demonstrate that liberal democracy can itself devolve into a mode of tyranny. One can suggest that this is for a concatenation of reasons: an intrinsic indifference to truth as opposed to majority opinion, means in practice that the manipulation of opinion will usually carry the day. Then governments tend to discover that the manipulation of fear is more effective than the manipulation of promise, and this is in keeping with the central premises of liberalism which, as Pierre Manent says, are based in Manichean fashion upon the ontological primacy of evil and violence: at the beginning is a threatened individual, piece of property or racial terrain. This is *not* the same as an Augustinian acknowledgement of original sin, perversity and frailty – a hopeful doctrine since it affirms that all-pervasive evil for which we cannot really account (by saying for example with Rousseau that it is the fault of private property or social association as such) is yet all the same a contingent intrusion upon reality, which can one day be fully overcome through the lure of the truly desirable which is transcendent goodness (and that itself, in the mode of grace, now aids us). Liberalism instead begins with a disguised naturalization of original sin as original egotism: our own egotism which we seek to nurture, and still more the egotism of the other against which we need protection.

Thus increasingly, a specifically liberal politics (and not, as so many journalists fondly think, its perversion) revolves round a supposed guarding against alien elements: the terrorist, the refugee, the person of another race, the foreigner, the criminal. Populism seems more and more to be an inevitable drift of unqualified liberal democracy. A purported defence of the latter is itself deployed in order to justify the suspending of democratic decision-making and civil liberties. For the reasons just seen, this is not just an extrinsic and reactionary threat to liberal values: to the contrary it is liberalism itself that tends to cancel those values of liberality (fair trial, right to a defence, assumed innocence, *habeas corpus*, a measure of free speech and free enquiry, good treatment of the convicted) which it has *taken over*, but which as a matter of historical record it did not invent, since they derive rather from Roman and Germanic law transformed by the infusion of the Christian notion of charity, which in certain dimensions means a generous giving of the benefit of the doubt, as well as succour even to the accused or wicked. For if the ultimate thing to be respected is simply individual security and freedom of choice (which is not to say that these should not be accorded penultimate respect) then almost any suspensions of normal legality can tend to be legitimated in the name of these values. In the end, liberalism takes this sinister turn when all that it endorses is the free market along with the nation-state as a competitive unit. Government will then tend to become entirely a policing and military function as J G Fichte (favourably!) anticipated. For with the decay of all tacit constraints embedded in family, locality and mediating institutions between the individual and the State, it is inevitable that the operation of economic and civil rules that no individual has any longer any interest in enforcing (since she is socially defined only as a lone chooser and self-seeker) will be ruthlessly and ever-more exhaustively imposed by a State that will become totalitarian in a new mode. Moreover, the obsessive pursuit of security against terror and crime will only ensure that terror and crime become more sophisticated and subtly effective: we have entered a vicious global spiral.

In the face of this neo-liberal slide into despotism, Catholic Christianity needs once more to proclaim with the classical tradition it carries – and which tended to predict just such a slide of a 'democratic' ethos – that government is properly mixed. Democracy can only function without manipulation of opinion if it is balanced by an 'aristocratic' element of the pursuit of truth and virtue for their own sake and by a 'monarchic' sense of an architectonic imposition of intrinsic justice that is unmoved by either the prejudices of the few or those of the many. In addition, the Church needs boldly to teach that the only justification for democracy is theological: since the people is potentially the *ecclesia*, and since nature always anticipates grace, truth lies finally dispersed amongst the people (although they need the initial guidance of the virtuous) because the Holy Spirit speaks through the voice of all.

But to say this is to ask that we subordinate contract to gift. A government may be contractually legitimate as elected and its laws may be legitimate as proceeding from sovereign power, but such arrangements can be formally correct and yet lead to tyranny – as the Nazi example and now the Bush example so clearly show. So beyond this it needs to be supposed that the truth lies with the people somewhat in the way that truth lies in the Church for St Paul: namely that the body of Christ receives from the Holy Spirit, who is life and gift, a life of circulation which is the exchange of gifts. Different people and groups have different talents and insights – these they share for the good of the whole body. The people give their goods to the head of the Church who is Christ: in like manner the people should give their gifts of insight and talent to the sovereign representative who acts in their name.

Inversely the sovereign power must think of itself as distributing gifts – gifts of good governance and ordering, not simply as imposing a fiat in order to expand the utility and productiveness of a nation-state. This is an outrageous notion – for example Blair's racist view that Britain should only accept 'skilled' immigrants and refugees who can increase the gross national product. A government that gives must pursue the intrinsic fulfilment of its citizens. To rule in this way means that the subjects of rule can participate in this ruling, can appropriate its task to themselves. To be ruled renders them indeed 'subjects' even in the ontological sense, since thereby something is proposed to them that can form their own good if they respond to it. And no-one is self-originated.

This means that to be a subject of a 'crown' (in an extended sense) is actually a more radical idea than to be a citizen of a republic in the contractualist sense of Rousseau (not necessarily in the ancient Roman sense). For the citizen is a natural individual before the state comes into being and only a citizen as co-composing the state. This means that he is always implicitly threatened by what Giorgio Agamben calls 'the state of the exception': if he lapses back into being a natural individual like the denizens of Guantanamo Bay, he now lacks all human dignity. This will only be granted to him as long as the contractual co-composition of the State holds good. By contrast, if one has what one may metaphorically describe as 'constitutional monarchy' (I am not necessarily advocating it in the literal sense) then according to natural law and not just natural right, the sovereign authority is only 'subjecting' men because it is obliged to offer them the gift of good co-ordination of diverse talents and needs. St Paul desacralized and redefined human rule as only concerned with justice and not with the protection of religious power or a domain – hence no human animal can fall outside this beneficent subjecting (in principle) which is in excess of contract. For this reason, the Christian princi-ples of polity stand totally opposed to any idea of the 'nation-state' as the ultimate unit and rather favour at once the natural pre-given 'region' on the one hand, and the universal human cosmopolis on the other.

This positive feature of 'monarchy' does not of course mean that the 'monar-chic' power should not be elected. To the contrary, it should be regarded as able to give rule because it has first been constituted by the mass donation of varied talents and points of view.

This perspective, however, should encourage us to revisit notions of 'corporate' authority that are characteristic of Catholic thought and linked with the principle of subsidiarity. Not all bonding and grouping happens at the central level and there is not first of all an aggregate of isolated individuals. To the contrary, people forever form micro-social bodies, and governments should treat people not according to formal abstraction but as they are – in regions, metiers, local cultures, religious bodies, etc. We will not be able peaceably to accommodate Islam within Europe if we do not treat Islam as a 'political' body and not just as a mass of indi-vidual believers – a notion which is foreign to Islam itself.

To re-insist on monarchic, aristocratic and corporate dimensions is in one sense conservative. Yet I am in fact a socialist of some sort. My case is rather that democ-racy will collapse into sophistic manipulation as Plato taught, if it is not balanced by the element of 'education in time' which requires a certain constantly self-cancelling hierarchy. The hierarchies of liberalism are in fact absolute spatial hier-archies of fixed power: one can climb up the ladder of power but only to displace someone else. The purpose of control here is simply utility and not the sharing of excellence. By contrast, the genuine spiritual hierarchy (after Dionysius the Areopagite) is a hierarchy that for human spiritual beings is endemic to time: in which pupil may overtake master and yet there should be no jealousy of the hier-arch for the temporarily subordinate because excellence is intrinsically shareable. Today, especially in Britain, all education is being subordinated to politics and eco-nomics. But a Catholic view should teach just the reverse: all politics and eco-nomics should be only for the sake of *paideia*.

This means: make time equal to space or even primary. Unqualified democracy has a kind of spatial bias – it supposes that we are all contracting individuals within a sort of eternalized *agora*. But this is to deny *life* – indeed it is part of the culture of death of which the Pope speaks – for life flows as a perpetual *glissando* through time. Life is not democratic, because it is both spontaneously creative and giving: with the arrived child, something new emerges. We must give to this child nurture, but from the outset the child reverses this hierarchy by revealing his unique creative power of response. No democratic contract can be involved here: pure democracy tends to deny the sanctity of life, the importance of the child, the procedure beyond mere political participation to old age and death – its 'normal' person is rather the freely choosing and contracting autonomous 31 year old. But *no* human person is forever like this; it is rather only a moment in a coming to be and passing away.

Politics subordinate to education – and so to the various traditions of wisdom, including religious traditions which can alone undertake a real *paideia* – can be truer to life as such, and also will be bound to ask questions about the final end of life. For only if life is deemed to have such a final end can every moment of life in fact be granted value. At this point it is not, after all, that one is advocating the temporal dimension over the spatial one. Nor an aristocracy of *paideia* over a democracy of the *agora*. Instead, the point is that pure spatialization will *also* tend to subordinate every given spatial form to the process of time leading towards the future. But not the time of gift: rather the empty time of pointless accumulation of a new spatial hoard of 'wealth'. By contrast, time can only be the time of gift where time is providing gradually the way to eternity beyond time. From this perspective every formed spatial stage of the way has an aesthetic value in itself and is not subordinate to future production.

Hence pure contractual democracy is spatial and yet in fact it nihilistically evacuates material space in favour of an abstract time always to come. On the other hand, a mixed government grounded in eternal law actually sanctifies space in its actual temporality and does not subordinate it to the pure *glissando* of mere process.

So in the face of the crisis of liberal democracy, Catholic Christian thought (including Roman Catholic, Anglican, Orthodox and even some Reformed strands) needs to return to certain older themes of its critique of liberalism, but for radical and not conservative reasons. The 'modernity' of liberalism has only delivered mass poverty, inequality, erosion of freely associating bodies beneath the level of the State and ecological dereliction of the earth – and now, without the compensating threat of communism, it has abolished the rights and dignity of the worker, ensured that women are workplace as well as domestic and erotic slaves, and finally started to remove the ancient rights of the individual which long precede the creed of liberalism itself (such as *habeas corpus* in Anglo-Saxon law) and are grounded in the dignity of the person rather than the 'self-ownership' of autonomous liberal man (sic).

The only creed which tried, often valiantly, to challenge this multiple impoverishment – communism – did so only in the name of the subordination of all to the future productivity of the nation, and ignored people's need for an aesthetic and religious relationship to each other and to nature. What must rather challenge liberalism is a truer 'liberality' in the literal sense of a creed of generosity which would suppose, indeed, that societies are more fundamentally bound together by mutual

RELIGION AND POLITICAL THOUGHT

generosity than by contract – this being a thesis anciently investigated by Seneca in his *De Beneficiis* and in modernity again reinstated by Marcel Mauss.

But considerations about gift are relevant also to a second context for contemporary social reflection. This concerns the economic realm. Today we live under the tyranny of an unrestricted capitalist market. We have abandoned the Marxist view that this market must inevitably collapse and evolve into socialism. So we have thereby abandoned immanent, secular, historicist hope. But we have also largely abandoned the social democratic idea that the capitalist market can be mitigated: here a Marxist analysis still largely holds good. Social democracy was in the capitalistic interest for a phase which required a Keynesian promotion of demand; but it was abandoned when labour demanded too much and when the generation of profits became problematic. It is true that neo-liberalism has scarcely solved the problems of slow productive growth since the 1950's, but nevertheless the inherent logic of capital accumulation seems to prevent any return to social democratic solutions.

Here again, Catholic social thought needs to remain true to its own genius which has always insisted that solutions do not lie either in the purely capitalist market nor with the centralized state. There is in fact no 'pure' capitalism, only degrees of this. Small-scale local capitalist economies are only in truth semi-capitalist, because they often exhibit a competition for excellence but not a mutually-abolishing drive of companies towards monopoly (as was rightly argued by Fernand Braudel). This is because in such cases – e.g. parts of North Italy and of Germany – a certain local culture of design excellence ensures that there is *no* pursuit of production *only* to make money nor any exchange of commodities *only* determined by supply and demand and not also by a shared recognition of quality such that supply and demand plus the accumulation of capital for future and offering of loans at interest for reasonable social benefit themselves are involved in an exchange in what is taken to be inherent value and not just formal, market-determined value. (This is not at all to deny that there will always be a never foreclosed *debate* as to what constitutes intrinsic value.)

Given such a consideration, one can see that an element of 'gift-exchange' can remain even within the modern market economy. Producers of well-designed things do not just contract with consumers. The latter give them effectively counter-gifts of sustenance in return for the gifts of intrinsically good things, even though this is mediated by money.

From this example one can suggest that more of the economy could be like this. This requires indeed that local production is favoured of locally suitable things linked to local skills. We should import and export only what we have to or what truly can only come from elsewhere – for I am not advocating asceticism! Rather the true hedonism of the genuine and its interchange. But if we receive only the exotic from elsewhere, then here too there can be a form of gift-exchange in operation. In actual fact global communications and transport favour this: within a global village those in Europe wishing to receive the good gift of organically-farmed coffee can in exchange pay a fair price for this which is a counter-gift ensuring that producers should not be exploited.

It is also likely that Islam and Judaism will be sympathetic to this way of looking at things and in fact the best hope for Europe is the re-emergence, beyond the dominance of a worn-out *Aufklärung*, of a certain religiously informed but shared philosophic culture built around a wisdom tradition that re-awakens the old Western fusion of Biblical with neoplatonic (Platonic plus Aristotelian and Stoic elements) tradition. This alone will be able to ground the possibility of a future achievement of social participation that is a real consensus (rather than the liberal semi-suspended warfare of plural co-existence) in a belief in ontological participation of the temporal in eternal peace and the hope for a final eschatological disclosure of this peace here on earth.

Things like the economy of fair-trade coffee may not sound dramatic or decisive and indeed they remain pathetically marginal, but nevertheless the extension of such gift-exchange bit by bit is the sure way forward rather than revolution, government action or capitalistic solutions. Groups linking across the globe can ensure that something is given back to the earth and that genuine goods go into planetary circulation. We need once again to form systematic links between producer and consumer cooperatives and we need to see an emergence of cooperative banking (perhaps supervised by Church, Islamic and Jewish bodies) to regulate and adjudicate the interactions between many different modes of cooperative endeavour. Only this will correct the mistake of all our current politics: namely to suppose that the 'free market' is a given which should be either extended or inhibited and balanced. For if the upshots of the free-market are intrinsically unjust, then 'correcting' this through another welfare economy is only a mode of resignation; moreover its task is sysyphean and periodically doomed to go under with every economic downturn (British Chancellor of the Exchequer Gordon Brown as Sisyphus, always expostulating, puffing and blowing).

Instead we need a different sort of market: a re-subordination of money transaction to a new mode of universal gift-exchange. This requires that in every economic exchange of labour or commodity there is always a negotiation of ethical value at issue. Indeed, economic value should only be ethical value, while inversely ethical value should be seen as emerging from the supply and demand of intrinsic gifts.

For ethical value is not for Christianity just 'virtue': rather it is charity and therefore it is the forging of bonds through giving and receiving. Virtue is here ecstasized and therefore its context ceases to be simply as for Aristotle, political, but rather becomes, as for St Paul also economic – the virtue of a new 'social' in the middle realm between *polis* and *oikos* that is equally concerned with political just distribution and with domestic care and nurture (the equality of women which stems from Paul, even though he could not see how far this must go, has profoundly to do with this). St Paul does not mention *arete* though he does talk of the person who is *phronimos*. The latter though, is now more a giver and receiver of gifts as *Philippians* especially shows. For St Paul, in speaking of *ecclesia*, proposes a new sort of *polis* which can counteract and even eventually subsume the Roman Empire – as the heirs of Abraham, Moses and Plato must today subsume the American one. This new *polis*, as Bruno Blumenfeld shows, as with Philo, is at once monarchic, headed by Christ, and drastically democratic in a participatory sense – the people are the body of the King; the King can only act through the people. Since virtue is now newly to do with the wisdom of love, virtue with Christianity gets democratized and is indeed dispersed amongst the diverse gifts of the body of Christ which as talents also need to be constantly exchanged to realize the solidarity of the whole. As much later in Christian history (the seventeenth century) Pierre Bérulle suggested (though too much in the sense of Royal absolutism) human kingly rule is entirely Christological, since it echoes the kenotic and deificatory exchange of worshipping and worshipped (the King manifesting in a faint degree the glory of divine rule as such) that is fused in one corpus by the Incarnation.

The latter event creates a new paracosmic reality – a new order somehow embracing both God and the Creation and a new order which abolishes the previous dominance and semi-universality of the law, of *torah, lex* and *nomos* and so of all political process as such. The participation of the creation in God through the newly realized cosmic body of Christ ruled by the new order of love is utterly self-abandoning toward the good of the community of *esse* (as for Aquinas, there is only one divine *esse* in Christ for Bérulle). And it meets all the time with an equivalent divine kenosis: such that God now is – or is also and so is even in himself – simply a sharing of himself with the Creation, and yet this by free gift of love and not by inexorable fate of imminent pantheistic process which would tend always to appropriate the beings of the Creation. No. As created, things exceed both temporal process and fixed form, out of these they constantly weave the exchange of *relation*, and relation persists all the way down, because the created thing is at bottom outside itself as relation to another, namely God who gives it to be. But the God who creates affirms this within himself as generation of the *Logos*, and affirms also the worshipping response of the Creation within himself as the procession of the Holy Spirit.

Yet to this infinite good within the Trinity is added the ecstatic mysterious 'extra' of finite dependence and finite worship. God, as both Philo and Bérulle in different eras said, lacks worship of himself, since he does not, as ontological rather than ontic, depend even on himself anymore than he causes himself. Yet in the Incarnation, suggests Bérulle, God ceases to lack even this and in coming to share God's life we are returned by God in Christ always back to specifically finite excellence. The invisible points back to the visible as well as the other way round, as Maximus the Confessor says in his *Mystagogy*.

So with the Incarnation, for all that God, it seems, can receive nothing, it happens that God comes to receive our worship of himself by joining to the personhood of the *Logos* our human worship. Thus in some mysterious way, it is not just that the finite receives in a unilateral way the infinite, nor that the finite returns to the infinite a unilateral praise. It is now rather true that there is an infinite-finite exchange of gifts – as St John of the Cross affirmed was the case in his experience of deification. And in this way Christ is now King upon the earth and so it follows that there should be always a fusion of democratic dispersal with monarchic liberality and objectivity. Indeed this should run almost in the direction of monarchic anarchy, as clearly recommended by Tolkien in the *Lord of the Rings* (no law in the Shire but the orderly echo of remote kingship). Property, as Hilaire Belloc taught, needs to be as widely and equally dispersed as possible in order to ensure that people have real creative liberty, little interest in greed and a tendency to spontaneously form self-regulating mechanisms of exchange of benefits. Today very few people, even middle-class 'well-off' people, possess any real property as opposed to a mass of temporary commodities that they have been more or less constrained into buying. For all the neo-liberal talk of freedom, it is not an accident that so few are allowed the kind of property that permits one to leave a creative mark in the world. This is above all true of land – but we are made to pay most dearly of all and on almost life-time lease for the very space in which it is possible to sleep, make love, be born, die, prepare food, engage in play and in the arts. We should instead provide people as widely as possible with real property, commencing with landed property itself. As I have just indicated, property that is to do with self-fulfilment rather than accumulation is the foundation for a free giving and receiving that begins to compose a wider social household. But here gift-exchange is not just a mode of economy, but also a mode of politics. Its spontaneous formation of an ethos and of tacit conventions restricts, without entirely removing, the need for the operation of codified and enforceable law – though this is still somewhat required, especially to prevent any breaking of the norms of wide dispersal. Monarchy in some sense, as Belloc like Tolkien taught, enters into the picture here, because mass popular movements along with the centralizing ambitions of the few can – as in fact occurred in the early modern period – tend to subvert the more genuine operation of local participatory democracy that is linked to the dispersal of property whether in town or countryside (in the Mediaeval case, especially in the towns).

What is the *ecclesia*? For St Paul it seems to be a kind of universal tribalism of gift-exchange over against both local polis and universal empire. But how can this be? Gift-exchange is normally of sacred things amongst friends. With strangers one needs formal rules of contract to ensure mutual benefit. Things exchanged here get secularized. How can one return to tribalism and exchange gifts with strangers? Well, I have already indicated that there may be a virtuous dialectic at work here: the more we become strangers also the more potentially at least we become universal neighbours. We cannot achieve this as isolated individuals, but we can achieve this if across the globe localities and kinship groups still retain identity – as they tend to do, to assert themselves against anonymity – and yet ceaselessly exchange this with other groups: the way for example different folk musics remain themselves and yet constantly borrow from other folk musics – like English Elizabethan folk music from Celtic and Iberian sources. And today this goes on of course far more.

But there is another and specifically theological point. Christianity renders all objects sacred: everything is a sign of God and of his love. Moreover, in Christ this is *shown again*, and he provides the *idiom* for rendering all sacred. Hence there need be no more neutral commodities just as there are no more strangers – not because we are citizens, even of *cosmopolis*, but because we are sons, daughters, and brothers in Adam and now in the new Adam who is Christ. We are literally one kin, as the Middle Ages saw it – one kin both physical and spiritual; one kin under Christ. Thus we live by an exchange of blood and charity as just this exchanging.

But is it? Is not charity the free one-way gift? But this makes love always sacrifice. But what is sacrifice, the ultimate free one-way gesture of love for? Surely to re-establish exchange. In this way sacrifice by no means escapes an economy, nor should it. And yet in gift-exchange, though there is equivalent return, the same thing does not come back. Something passes never to return at all. And for this reason no counter-gift ever cancels a debt but always inaugurates a new one. In the New Testament one finds both repeated unease (in both the gospels and the epistles) about gift-exchange as something pursued for the power of the benefactor, unlike the grace of God, and yet at the same time a continued insistence that God's grace must be actively received and responded to and that the mediators of this grace, like St Paul himself, deserve acknowledgement and support. The tension between these two stresses underlies many tortured passages in his writings.

For this reason the gift is not a straight line, but nor is it a closed circle. Rather it is a spiral or a strange loop. Beyond the law of non-contradiction it is both unilateral and reciprocal. It spirals on and on, and there is no first free gift because to give to another one must have received at least her presence. Likewise one cannot be grateful without a gesture which is already a counter-gift.

And when one gives, for that unilateral instance, one is a monarch. One stands, as it were, hierarchically above the one who cannot choose what you are going to give to him, say to him, etc. No contractual liberalism can ever bind the oscillating aristocracy of mere conversation. Likewise when one receives, for that instance one is a monarch receiving tribute, even if the roles will be reversed in the next instance. Thus to give, or to receive, is hierarchically and unilaterally to help continue a process that is nonetheless fundamentally democratic and reciprocal. Indeed charity as welfare and equity have always been the prerogative of kings and empires rather than city-states all the way from Babylon to Elizabethan England. But charity is not just welfare, it is also, as the Middle Ages taught, the festive 'between' that binds people, like the state of grace between the beggar who blesses you and you who give your coin to the beggar.

We today have totally divided reciprocal market contract from private free giving. And yet the latter remains secretly a contract and the former is also like the crossing of two unilateral gifts whose objects in no way mingle. Our situation therefore has crazy undercurrents that go unrecognized. Giving is, by contrast, only really free and liberal where it respects and helps further to create reciprocal norms. Contract is only really fair where there is a judged equivalence of objects and also a free mutual promotion by donation of the welfare of the exchanging parties.

If all objects are sacred then, as for primitives, they possess a kind of animated force. Objects or their equivalents must return because they have in some sense personality. And this is the ecological dimension of gift-exchange. Humans identify themselves through the production and exchange of things. Marx was right. So inversely things are imbued with the story of human comings and goings. Objects naturally carry memories and tell stories. Only commodified ones don't – or they tell shameful tales which they also conceal. In a modest way even the packet of fair-trade coffee can start again to be a mythical object with personality.

For Catholic Christians, this is as it should be. Everything is sacramental; every-thing tells of the glory of Christ and therefore every economy is part of the economy of salvation and every process of production and exchange prepares the elements of the cosmic Eucharist. This was true for St Paul. His thought about grace is indisso-ciable from his thought about the human exchange of talents and of material benefits. But the latter can only be a just exchange where there are constantly re-negotiated and agreed upon standards concerning the human common good: of what should be produced and with what standards; of what should be rewarded and to what degree for the sake of further beneficial (to herself and the community) action by individuals. 'To each according to his needs and from each according to his means' should still be our aim, but outside a completely crass materialism the question is about legitimate and desirable needs and means and the ordering of diverse needs and means. Here the crucial paradox so often ignored by socialists (but not by John Ruskin) is that only where there is an agreed hierarchy of values, sus-tained by the constantly self-cancelling hierarchy of education, can there actually be an equal sharing (according to a continuous social judgement as to who will most benefit from such and such a gift, etc.) of what is agreed to be valuable. Without such an agreement, sustained through the operation of professional guilds and associa-tions as well as cooperative credit unions and banks, there can only be market medi-ation of an anarchy of desires – of course ensuring the triumph of a hierarchy of sheer power and the secret commanding of people's desires by manipulation.

For where there is no public recognition of the primacy of absolute good as grounded in something super-human, then democracy becomes impossible, for it is no longer supposed that one should even *search* for the intrinsically desirable. It then follows that people can only find out what they 'should' desire, or even about the possible objects of desire from the very 'mass' processes that are supposed to represent only the general desires of the people. Liberal democracy is then doomed to specularity: the represented themselves only represent to themselves the spec-tacle of representation. This is why there is no truth in the Marxist assumption that freed from the shackles of oppression people will 'by reason' choose equality and justice. To the contrary, in the light of a mere reason that is not also vision, *eros* and faith, people may well choose to prefer the petty triumphs and superiorities of a brutally hierarchic *agon* of power or the sheer excitement of a social spectacle in which they may potentially be exhibited in triumph. This is exactly why the vast numbers of the American poor are not waiting to rise up in revolt.

For the same reason, 'pure' democracy would be a *mise en abîme*. One would have to have endless 'primaries' before 'primaries'. Instead, in reality, at the end of the line always, someone puts herself forward as a 'candidate' (in some sense), someone stands up and says something that no-one has voted on or contractually agreed that she should say. Gift always precedes both choice and contract because no formal pre-arrangements can entirely control the content of what we impose upon others in our words and symbolic actions which inevitably sway them in a certain fashion. In the United States part of the problem is that there is a yearning for the madness of pure democracy: thus there is no 'monarchic' body that organizes boundaries of voting districts, because this would be considered 'undemocratic'. In consequence this task is left to the reigning political party and the resultant gerrymandering is seen as just a fact of life. In this way the lure of the democratic abyss abolishes democracy, whereas some admission of aristocratic and monarchic principles (as in Canada, for example) actually secures the space of the possibility of democracy.

We need, then, in the Europe and the World of the future, a new conception of the economy as exchange of gifts in the sense of both talents and valued objects that blend material benefit with sacramental significance. We need also to encourage a new post-liberal participatory democracy that is enabled by the aristocracy of an education that seeks after the common good and absolute transcendent truth. Finally, we need to see that it is equally enabled by a monarchic principle which permits a unified power at the limit to intervene in the name of non-codifiable equity – the liberal alternative to this being the brutal exclusion of those, like the inmates of Guantanamo Bay, who escape the nets of codes and are therefore deemed to be sub-human.

Does all this sound fantastic? No, the fantastic is what we have: an economy that destroys life, babies, childhood, adventure, locality, beauty, the exotic, the erotic, people and the planet itself.

Moreover, if we refuse a profound and subtle theological social carapace, we will not necessarily recover secularity in the future. Instead, we may witness the effective triumph (in power if not in numbers) of religious fundamentalism – and especially Protestant fundamentalism – in cynical alliance with a liberal nihilism. For the formal emptiness of the liberal market and bureaucracy is now apparent to all. Its heart will be filled with something, and especially with a neo-Calvinistic creed that justifies this emptiness because cumulative success in the reckoning to oneself of its void sums is seen as a sign of favour with another eternal world that alone really matters – although that too is conceived in terms of preferential absolute success in contrast with absolute failure.

Most, including myself, have hitherto supposed that the religious conflicts in Ireland are an anachronistic echo, in a remote corner of Europe, of ancient European conflicts. But then why have they flared up again so recently (the latter half of the twentieth century) and persisted so long? Is not Ireland somewhat like the United States, where a 'belated' avoidance of secular ideologies has turned imperceptibly into a foreshadowing of a time when those ideologies are exhausted? Here again, there is no progressive plot to history. What one has seen in the province of Ulster has often been a conflict between a bigoted, puritanical and hyper-evangelical neo-Calvinism on the one hand, and a largely reasonable, socially and politically aspiring Catholicism on the other – the fanatics on this side have tended to be so for socio-political rather than religious reasons. Certainly not in any simple fashion, but nonetheless in a real one, it could be that the Irish conflict is in fact a harbinger of a wider, future and much more complex and many-faceted new struggle for the soul of Christianity itself which may yet dictate the future of Europe and even of the world.

Chapter 16

Slavoj Žižek
Passion in the Era of Decaffeinated Belief

The credentials of those who, even prior to its release, virulently criticize Mel Gibson's new film on the last 12 hours of Christ's life, seem impeccable: are they not fully justified in their worry that the film, made by a fanatic Catholic trad-itionalist with occasional anti-Semitic outbursts, may ignite anti-Semitic senti-ments? More general, is *Passion* not a kind of manifesto of our own (Western, Christian) fundamentalists and anti-secularists? Is it, then, not the duty of every Western secularist to reject it? Is such an unambiguous attack not a *sine qua non* if we want to make it clear that we are not covert racists attacking only the funda-mentalism of *other* (Muslim) cultures?

The Pope's ambiguous reaction to the film is well known: immediately after seeing it, deeply moved, he muttered 'It is as it was!' – and this statement was quickly withdrawn by the official Vatican speakers. A glimpse into the Pope's spon-taneous reaction was thus quickly replaced by the 'official' neutral stance, corrected in order not to hurt anyone. This shift is the best exemplification of what is wrong with liberal tolerance, with the politically correct fear that anyone's specific reli-gious sensibility may be hurt: even if it says in the Bible that the Jewish mob demanded the death of Christ, one should not stage this scene directly, but play it down and contextualize it to make it clear that Jews are collectively not to be blamed for the Crucifixion . . . The problem of such a stance is that, in this way, the aggressive religious passion is merely repressed: it remains there, smouldering beneath the surface and, finding no release, gets stronger and stronger.

In November 2002, George Bush came under attack by the right-wing members of his own party for what was perceived as too soft a stance on Islam: he was reproached for repeating the mantra that terrorism has nothing to do with Islam, this great and tolerant religion. As a column in the *Wall Street Journal* put it, the true enemy of the United States is not terrorism, but militant Islam. Consequently, one should gather the courage and proclaim the politically incorrect (but, nonetheless, obvious) fact that there is a deep strain of violence and intolerance in Islam – that, to put it bluntly, something in Islam resists the acceptance of the liberal–capitalist world order. It is here that a truly radical analysis should break with the standard liberal attitude: no, one should NOT defend Bush here – his atti-tude is ultimately no better than that of Cohen, Buchanan, Pat Robertson and

237

other anti-Islamists – both sides of this coin are equally wrong. It is against this background that one should approach Oriana Fallaci's *The Rage and the Pride*, this passionate defence of the West against the Muslim threat, this open assertion of the superiority of the West, this denigration of Islam not even as a different culture, but as barbarism (entailing that we are not even dealing with a clash of civilizations, but with a clash of our civilization and Muslim barbarism). The book is *stricto sensu* the obverse of politically correct tolerance: its lively passion is the truth of lifeless PC tolerance.

Within this horizon, the only 'passionate' response to the fundamentalist passion is aggressive secularism of the kind displayed recently by the French state where the government prohibited wearing all too conspicuous religious symbols and dresses in schools (not only the scarves of Muslim women, but also the Jewish caps and too-large Christian crosses). It is not difficult to predict what the final result of this measure will be: excluded from the public space, the Muslims will be directly pushed to constitute themselves as non-integrated fundamentalist communities. This is what Lacan meant when he emphasized the link between the rule of post-revolutionary *fraternité* and the logic of segregation.

And, perhaps, the prohibition to embrace a belief with a full passion explains why, today, 'culture' is emerging as the central life-world category. Religion is permitted – not as a substantial way of life, but as a particular 'culture' or, rather, lifestyle phenomenon: what legitimizes it is not its immanent truth-claim but the way it allows us to express out innermost feelings and attitudes. We no longer 'really believe', we just follow (some of the) religious rituals and mores as part of the respect for the 'lifestyle' of the community to which we belong (recall the proverbial non-believing Jew who obeys kosher rules 'out of respect for tradition'). 'I do not really believe in it, it is just part of my culture' effectively seems to be the predominant mode of the disavowed/displaced belief characteristic of our times: what is a 'cultural lifestyle' if not the fact that, although we do not believe in Santa Claus, there is a Christmas tree in every house and even in public places every December? Perhaps, then, 'culture' is the name for all those things we practise without really believing in them, without 'taking them seriously'. Is this not also the reason why science is not part of this notion of culture – it is all too real? And is this also not why we dismiss fundamentalist believers as 'barbarians', as anti-cultural, as a threat to culture – they dare to *take seriously* their beliefs? Today, we ultimately perceive as a threat to culture those who immediately live their culture, those who lack a distance towards it. Recall the outrage when, three years ago, the Taliban forces in Afghanistan dynamited the ancient Buddhist statues at Bamiyan: although none of us, enlightened Westerners, believed in the divinity of Buddha, we were so outraged because the Taliban Muslims did not show the appropriate respect for the 'cultural heritage' of their own country and the entire humanity. Instead of believing through the other like all people of culture, they really believed in their own religion and thus had no great sensitivity for the cultural value of the monuments of other religions – for them, the Buddha statues were just fake idols, not 'cultural treasures'. (And, incidentally, is this outrage not the same as that of today's enlightened anti-Semite who, although he does not believe in Christ's divinity, nonetheless blames Jews for killing our Lord Jesus? Or as the typical secular Jew who, although he does not believe in Jehova and Moses as his prophet, nonetheless thinks that Jews have a divine right to the land of Israel?)

Jacques Lacan's definition of love is 'giving something one doesn't have' – what one often forgets is to add the other half which completes the sentence: '. . . to someone who *doesn't want it*.' This is confirmed by our most elementary experience when somebody unexpectedly declares passionate love to us – is not the first reaction, preceding the possible positive reply, that something obscene, intrusive, is being forced upon us? This is why, ultimately, passion as such is 'politically incorrect': although everything seems permitted, prohibitions are merely displaced. Recall the deadlock of sexuality or art today: is there anything more dull, opportunistic and sterile than to succumb to the superego injunction of incessantly inventing new artistic transgressions and provocations (the performance artist masturbating on stage or masochistically cutting himself, the sculptor displaying decaying animal corpses or human excrements), or to the parallel injunction to engage in more and more 'daring' forms of sexuality. In some 'radical' circles in the USA, there came recently a proposal to 'rethink' the rights of necrophiliacs (those who desire to have sex with dead bodies) – why should they be deprived of it? So the idea was formulated that, in the same way people sign permission for their organs to be used for medical purposes in the case of their sudden death, one should also allow them to sign the permission for their bodies to be given to necrophiliacs to play with them. Is this proposal not the perfect exemplification of how the PC stance realizes Kierkegaard's old insight into how the only good neighbour is a dead neighbour? A dead neighbour – a corpse – is the ideal sexual partner of a 'tolerant' subject trying to avoid any harassment: by definition, a corpse cannot be harassed.

On today's market, we find a whole series of products deprived of their malignant property: coffee without caffeine, cream without fat, beer without alcohol . . . And the list goes on: what about virtual sex as sex without sex, the Colin Powell doctrine of warfare with no casualties (on our side, of course), as warfare without warfare, the contemporary redefinition of politics as the art of expert administration, as politics without politics, up to today's tolerant liberal multiculturalism as an experience of Other deprived of its Otherness (the idealized Other who dances fascinating dances and has an ecologically sound holistic approach to reality, while features like wife-beating remain out of sight . . .)? Along the same lines, what the politically correct tolerance is giving us is a decaffeinated belief: a belief which does not hurt anyone and does not fully commit even ourselves.

Everything is permitted to today's hedonistic Last Man – you can enjoy everything, BUT deprived of its substance which makes it dangerous. This is why Lacan was right to turn around Dostoyevski's well-known motto: 'If God doesn't exist, everything is prohibited!' God is dead, we live in a permissive universe, you should strive for pleasures and happiness – but, in order to have a life full of happiness and pleasures, you should avoid dangerous excesses, be fit, live a healthy life, not harass others . . . so everything is prohibited if it is not deprived of its substance, and you end up leading a totally regulated life. And the opposite also holds: if there is God, then *everything is permitted* – to those who claim to act directly on behalf of God, as the instruments of His will. Clearly, a direct link to God justifies our violation of any 'merely human' constraints and considerations (as in Stalinism, where the reference to the big Other of historical Necessity justifies absolute ruthlessness).

Today's hedonism combines pleasure with constraint – it is no longer the old notion of the 'right measure' between pleasure and constraint, but a kind of pseudo-Hegelian immediate coincidence of the opposites: action and reaction should coincide, the very thing which causes damage should already be the medicine. It is no longer 'Drink coffee, but with moderation!'; it is rather 'Drink all the coffee you want, because it is already decaffeinated.' The ultimate example of this stance is *chocolate laxative*, available in the US, with the paradoxical injunction 'Do you have constipation? Eat more of this chocolate!' – i.e., of the very thing which causes constipation. And is not a negative proof of the hegemony of this stance the fact that true unconstrained consumption (in all its main forms: drugs, free sex, smoking) is emerging as the main danger? The fight against these dangers is one of the main investments of today's 'biopolitics'. Solutions are here desperately sought which would reproduce the paradox of the chocolate laxative. The main contender is 'safe sex' – a term which makes one appreciative of the truth of the old saying 'Is having sex with a condom not like taking a shower with a raincoat on?' The ultimate goal would be here, along the lines of decaf coffee, to invent 'opium without opium': no wonder marijuana is so popular among liberals who want to legalize it – it already IS a kind of 'opium without opium'.

The structure of the 'chocolate laxative', of a product containing the agent of its own containment, can be discerned throughout today's ideological landscape. There are two topics which determine today's liberal tolerant attitude towards Others: the respect of Otherness, openness towards it AND the obsessive fear of harassment – in short, the Other is OK insofar as its presence is not intrusive, insofar as the Other is not really Other. This is what is more and more emerging as the central 'human right' in late-capitalist society: *the right not to be harassed*, i.e., to be kept at a safe distance from the others. A similar structure is clearly present in how we relate to capitalist profiteering: it is OK IF it is counteracted with charitable activities – first you amass billions, then you return (part of) them to the needy. And the same goes for war, for the emerging logic of humanitarian or pacifist militarism: war is OK insofar as it really serves to bring about peace, democracy, or to create conditions for distributing humanitarian help. And does the same not hold more and more even for democracy and human rights? It is OK if human rights are 'rethought' to include torture and a permanent emergency state, if democracy is cleansed of its populist 'excesses' . . .

In our era of over-sensitivity for 'harassment' by the Other, every ethical pressure is experienced as a false front of the violence of power. This stance gives rise to the effort to 'rewrite' religious injunctions, making them adequate to our specific condition. Is some command too severe? Let us reformulate it in accordance with our sensitivities! 'Thou shalt not commit adultery!' – *except if it is emotionally sincere and serves the goal of your profound self-realization* . . . Exemplary here is Donald Spoto's *The Hidden Jesus*, a New Age tainted 'liberal' reading of Christianity, where we can read apropos of divorce: 'Jesus clearly denounced divorce and remarriage. /. . . / But

Jesus did not go further and say that marriages cannot be broken /. . . / nowhere else in his teaching is there any situation when he renders a person forever chained to the consequences of sin. His entire treatment of people was to liberate, not to legislate. /. . . / It is self-evident that in fact some marriages simply do break down, that commitments are abandoned, that promises are violated and love betrayed.' Sympathetic and 'liberal' as these lines are, they involve the fatal confusion between emotional ups and downs and an unconditional symbolic commitment which is supposed to hold precisely when it is no longer supported by direct emotions. What Spoto is effectively saying is: 'Thou shalt not divorce – except when your marriage "in fact" breaks down, when it is experienced as an unbearable emotional burden that frustrates your full life' – in short, except when the prohibition to divorce would have regained its full meaning (since who would divorce when his/her marriage still blossoms?)!

Does this mean that, against the false tolerance of the liberal multiculturalism, we should return to religious fundamentalism? The very ridicule of Gibson's film makes clear the impossibility of such a solution. Gibson first wanted to shoot the film in Latin and Arameic and to show it without subtitles; under the pressure of distributors, he later decided to allow English (or other) subtitles. However, this compromise on his part is not just a concession to the commercial pressure; sticking to the original plan would have rather directly displayed the self-refuting nature of Gibson's project. That is to say, let us imagine the film without subtitles shown in a large American suburban mall: the intended fidelity to the original would turn it into its opposite, into an incomprehensible exotic spectacle.

But there is a third position, beyond religious fundamentalism and liberal tolerance. Let us return to the 'politically correct' distinction between Islamic fundamentalism and Islam: Bush and Blair (and even Sharon) never forget to praise Islam as a great religion of love and tolerance which has nothing to do with the disgusting terrorist acts. In the same way that this distinction between 'good' Islam and 'bad' Islamic terrorism is a fake, one should also render problematic the typical 'radical-liberal' distinction between Jews and the State of Israel or Zionism, i.e., the effort to open up the space in which Jews and Jewish citizens of Israel will be able to criticize the State of Israel's politics and Zionist ideology not only without being accused of anti-Semitism, but also, even more, formulating their critique as based on their very passionate attachment to Jewishness, on what they see as worth saving in the Jewish legacy. However, is this enough? Marx said about the *petit-bourgeois* that he saw in every object two aspects, bad and good, and tried to keep the good and fight the bad. One should avoid the same mistake in dealing with Judaism: the 'good' Levinasian Judaism of justice, respect for and responsibility towards the other, against the 'bad' tradition of Jehova, his fits of vengeance and genocidal violence against the neighbouring people. One should gather the courage to transpose the gap, the tension, into the very core of Judaism: it is no longer the question of defending the pure Jewish tradition of justice and love for the neighbour against the Zionist aggressive assertion of the Nation-State. Along the same lines, instead of celebrating the greatness of true Islam against its misuse by fundamentalist terrorists, or of bemoaning the fact that, of all great religions,

Islam is the one most resistent to modernization, one should rather conceive this resistance as an open chance: it does not necessarily lead to 'Islamo-Fascism'; it can also be articulated into a Socialist project. Precisely because Islam harbours the 'worst' potentials of the Fascist answer to our present predicament, it can also turn out to be the site for the 'best'.

Instead of trying to redeem the pure ethical core of a religion against it political instrumentalizations, one should thus ruthlessly criticize this very core – in ALL religions. Today, when religions themselves (from the New Age spirituality to the cheap spiritualist hedonism of Dalai Lama) are more than ready to serve the post-modern pleasure-seeking, it is paradoxically only a consequent materialism which is able to sustain a truly ascetic militant ethical stance.

Chapter 17

Marcella María Althaus-Reid
Graffiti on the Walls of the Cathedral of Buenos Aires: Doing Theology, Love and Politics at the Margins

. . . It happens that I'm not stable
And it happens that I'm changing!
If I were the one who suffered most,
And was a humiliated angel,
[Then I was] Dead, (the ideal victim) . . .
[But] at other times I surprised myself as an executioner,
Or as 'The Centre of Light.'
Because what happens is that there are days when I burn to a crisp
    and on others,
I'm a fridge with a freezer; a 'Kelvinator'
    with a three year guarantee.

Graffiti found on the wall in Buenos Aires, January 1999

A Counter-guide to Liberation Theology

It may be that, after all, love has ceased to haunt theology, and all we have been left with in these times of neo-liberalism is a theology that has replaced love by melancholy. To the sense of history as heritage, 'package and sanitized,'[1] we should add liberation theologies as part of an increasingly nostalgic sentimental journey to an imaginary past. Today, Latin American Liberation Theology struggles against the market which makes commodities of theological praxis, by replacing creativity and dissent by repetitions without subversion. In market theologies, reproductions have succeeded resurrections. We are living at a time when theological dictionaries fail to produce reflection beyond the self centred vision of a Church which only considers its own property interests (Church gatherings and documents) and cannot deal with unprofitable love, an important dimension of the liberationist movement.[2] Paradoxically, it is in popular art or in films, such as those from Almodovar, that we find something that conveys the feeling of Liberation Theology, in a way that many

1. T. Gorriage (2004), *Furthering Humanity: A Theology of Culture* (London: Ashgate), p. 260.
2. For a recent critique of Liberation Theology from a Latin-American perspective, see, for instance, I. Petrella (2004), *The Future of Liberation Theology* (London: Ashgate).

articles cannot do. At least they can bring back something of love to theology by reminding us of the creative spirituality and the pleasure to be found in a praxis of solidarity, in the context of failure and struggles of people at the margins. Loving alliances at the margins have been and still are the sustainers of liberationist theological practices.

If I were ever to compose a counter-guide to Liberation Theology, that is to uncover non-archaeological sites where the layers of historiographic claims with which the West has surrounded the liberationist movement could be disputed, I would not start with the episcopal conferences of Medellín or Puebla. Instead, I would start by taking an option for the unprofitable sites of love present in current liberationist praxis, sites of the unproductive, wasteful, gratuitous, rebellious love found at the margins of the religious authoritative discourse of power. These are sites of grace (or unprofitable love) to be found outside of the economic metaphors of redemption, metaphors more suited to global capitalist societies than to poor economies such as that of my country, Argentina. In Argentina, where banks have collapsed and whole sectors of the population are excluded from economic exchanges based on currency, the excluded are outside redemptive economic systems. We should need to consult other theological archives and to redefine what is the archive of the poor and persecuted, searching for their historical experience as recorded in other types of documents and monuments. Take, for instance, the graffiti that people have been writing for decades on the walls of the cathedral of Buenos Aires. Are they not archives of the counter-theological discourses from the margins, in a more effective way than the documents produced by Ecclesial Basic Communities? While the Basic Communities have contributed enormously to a general theological debate with the Church (even if from only a sector of the Church), other people have been writing and establishing in the fragile memory of a nation, many political and theological disputes of the time. Graffiti written on the walls of Buenos Aires and preserved in the collective memory by photographs, media and popular stories constitute the love archive from the poor or the 'messianic files' of Liberation Theology. For it so happened that during those years when the military regime in Argentina burnt books, burning bibles and the love poems from Pablo Neruda on the same pyre, the official political discourse was centred on a theological concept: *mesianismo* (messianism) was considered to be subversive. Any political or religious challenge to the fascist government of the times (such as political graffiti) was denounced as 'messianic', that is, politically subversive of the institutional order. The fact that a theological term could be used in official discourses highlights the fact that the North Atlantic concept of secularism has been completely inappropriate when applied to Liberation Theology. It is significant that the English term 'secular' has no equivalent in Spanish. To appreciate the extent to which the life of the nation is saturated by the ethos of the Roman Catholic Church we need only recall that, only a few years ago, a Muslim had to renounce his Islamic faith before he could take the oath of office and become president of Argentina. It is a perspective which divides the world into religious and non-religious institutions. In the Latin American universe, constructed by the dialectical forces of discourses about lay and ordained people, the word *secular* is only used to refer to diocesan priests, in contrast to the 'religious' who are members of monastic orders.[3] In a similar way, to those in power, society is divided into civilians and the military, who have been invested (ordained) with authority from the state. Symbols such as uniforms, religious or military, reinforce the world-view. By contrast, those without uniforms, the civilian, lay population, possess no authority and receive no respect. In that atmosphere, where priests and military share a common vocabulary and world-view, any criticism of the institutional Church or the state, is routinely described as 'messianic'.[4] Guerrillas and trade unionists were called messianic. Paradoxically, as if following an accelerated Althusserian process of interpellation, messianism, as a derisory term, was appropriated by the discourses of the Church.[5] From the pulpits and in the media, priests of the religion of the Jesus the Messiah used the term 'messianic' as an insult or a threat. In Argentina, Liberation theologians were denounced as 'messianic' from barracks and churches alike. Their persecution was therefore justified in this universe through a theological grammatical pact.

Yet it is part of my counter-archaeological project to call to mind documents, monuments and symbolic works, such as graffiti, of a Liberation Theology which disputes the reification of the vocation of Jesus, which was true Messianism. This Liberation Theology comes from love stories which were written on the walls of the city, including the walls of the cathedral. These were not only expressions of the struggles and the protests on behalf of ordinary people, but on behalf of God, as if our love stories and the story of God's love belonged together, the fragile hearts of people and the vulnerable heart of the Messiah. The relevance of theological graffiti is here borderline with what Derrida calls 'architectonic thought'. The architectonic metaphor, which does not separate between theory and practice,[6] is present in the theology of liberation as innovation and invention, while continuing the paths of deconstruction and of Marxist thought from the different locations of the praxis of the poor in Buenos Aires.

Excluded love: Theology of AIDS on a Derelict Wall

... It happens that I'm not stable
And it happens that I'm changing!
If I was the one who suffered most,
And was a humiliated angel,
[Then I was] Dead, (the ideal victim) ...

3. See, for instance, Graham Ward's discussion on the term 'secular', a part of his cultural hermeneutical project. Ward makes the point that the word *saeculum* has been 'exchanged and circulates in specific cultural and historic contexts', and needs to be understood in that way. G. Ward (2003), *True Religion* (Oxford: Blackwell), p. 3.
4. Heinrich Heine in his poem *Memorials of Krahwinkel's Days of Terror* makes the point that the Prussian police preferred people to believe in God since 'whoever tears himself away from his God will sooner or later break with his earthly superiors too'. Quoted in S. Korner (1955), *Kant* (London: Penguin), p. 129.
5. For this point see F. Graziano (1992), *Divine Violence, Spectacle, Psychosexuality and Radical Christianity in the Argentine Dirty War* (Boulder, CO: Westview Press).
6. J. Derrida (1999), *No Escribo sin Luz Artificial* (Valladolid: Custro Editiones), p. 133.

One day, some years ago, written on a wall opposite my mother's house in Buenos Aires I found this graffiti-poem, transient and anonymous. I am not referring here to 'high grade' graffiti, but to humble graffiti: not the artistic graffiti from the New York or London subcultures: not the famous tags (signatures) which may confer fame and respect to the authors, and which come from carefully designed sketch books, the so-called 'black books' of the graffiti writer. I am referring here to crayon or chalk graffiti, graffiti written not with an aerosol, but scribbled on the walls with pencils, the kind of cheap wax colourful bars used by children, or even charcoal. Its aims are also different from the graffiti art which attracts the interest of ethnologists and researchers in cultural studies and urban youth. That is the graffiti of neo-liberalism, where even transgression obeys certain basic laws concerning profit: it may not bring money but it gives status amongst peers, or a subcultural type of fame and affirmation. The graffiti of the excluded in Argentina obeys a different logic. Most of the time it is a political or existential text, a mobile and fragile text, a kind of sacred scripture of the poor which preserves a different memory of the times and sometimes functions as a site for strange theological revelations.

This graffiti-poem I am reflecting upon was written on the wall of a derelict house, opposite my mother's house in *Montserrat*, which is one of the oldest *barrios* of Buenos Aires. The wall was painted black resembling either two school blackboards side by side or perhaps an open book. The purpose seems to have been to create a space for graffiti, a kind of 'book of graffiti' on the wall, containing the writing of the *Other* from our neighbourhood. It was a place where people could write their thoughts with chalk or crayon, a community writing board for humble, marginal poets and dissidents of the city. Graffiti poems appeared there every so often, in an unpredictable way. Sometimes a poem was written, but then by the intrusion of someone else's words the original poem was changed, challenged and became another poem. Or there could be a new poem arising from 'a tradition', that is previous modified poems. As in all truly 'community' texts, sometimes all the graffiti disappeared from the 'book on the wall' for months, and the street was decorated by a simple simulation of two empty black open pages. This graffiti poem I am referring to did not disappear so quickly but it was transformed by that process of inner intertextuality. The first version I read started with the words: 'And I also exist!' That in itself could have been a clue to its authorship. Any poor neighbourhood of Buenos Aires is full of destitute migrant workers from the provinces but also from other countries at the frontiers, such as Perú or Bolivia. Now, 'I still exist!' is a verb in the *Quechua Chanka* language. The verbal expression is *Kach ka ni raq mi* and it is used when someone wants to express the fact that in spite of adversity, she or he still exists, full of hope and possibilities for the future.[7] In other words, it is an expression of human survival. Such is the ontological grammatical heritage of the nations who survived the invasion of the Americas in the fifteenth century.

Let me say now why to reflect on Liberation Theology we need to consider love at the bottom of the pile. An indigenous *Aymara* person could have written that

---

7. J. Arguedas (1962), *Tupac Amaru Kamaq Taytanchisman. Haylli Taki* (To Our Creator Father Tupac Amaru. A Hymm) (Lima: Salqanday), p. 7.

poem, as homage to migrant survivors. The house opposite my mother's, where I found that graffiti, was a cheap boarding house. Boarding houses are the homes of the poor in big cities such as Buenos Aires, the last stop before ending up in the slums or sleeping on the streets. The hearts at the bottom of the pile in my neighbourhood (and in theology) were in this story, those of two men dressed in black with strange haircuts and old-fashioned shoes, whose presence was not immediately identified. As it happens, they were priests or rather, ex-priests, priests who had been asked to leave the Church because they were suffering from AIDS. They were slightly older men, impoverished and without a place to go and so they came to rent rooms in the boarding house opposite my mother's. As the poem was about fallen angels, struggling between passionate love and icy hearts, frozen in the struggle of those who might have preferred not to be still living, it could have contained a whole theology of AIDS and the Church.

The point is that I have never come across a hermeneutical circle of theological action and reflection starting from the community of poor as it is, rather than as pastoral documents would prefer to imagine it. In Liberation Theology we are supposed to start our reflections from the experience of people and not from theological documents from the Church. By the experience of people we mean the life of the poor, their cultural expectations and their religious world, but including also their loving relationships, needs and desires. Theology knows so little about love and writes about love so badly that it ends up missing the best stories of love. It misses also the dignity of the praxis of justice, which is a praxis of rebellious, transgressive love. And that love is not the legally permitted love envisaged in ecclesiastical encyclicals on the family. It is the encounter of love and justice at the margins of lawful and hegemonic systems. Theology seldom remembers that those margins are also sexual margins. It is from these margins that graffiti-poems are written, poems which claim that our existence is linked to a sense of becoming. The graffiti poem reminds us that angels (and priests) may also fall and somehow die unless they recognize that they can still be at the centre of light, that life is to be invented and not just represented.

What can we then say about love in Liberation Theology? Unless the theological *caminata* follows the path of a kind of graffiti-theology and stops using its theological common sense to produce repetitions without critical differences, then hearts are always going to be crushed. Curiously, it is not only a sentimental journey in theology which we should consider here, but also the fact that economic systems too are forms of human relationship which can be called loving. Take for instance the three characteristics of neo-liberal processes: exclusion, objectification and mutation in terms of private and common interests. They express values concerning loving and relating. Love is a theme in theology as it is in politics and economic orders. You cannot challenge one without the other. But love is also a knowledge, a praxis, and it is to that that a graffiti-inspired theology of liberation might contribute. At the end, it is about making theology more indecent, less limiting, less blind to the reality of people's lives at the margins of the Church and the economic system, a theology which is more messianic.

Schizzo-Theologies of Resistance

The French philosopher Gilles Deleuze distinguished various ways of thinking in a manner which relates to Liberation Theology. Graffiti is an interesting type of thinking which goes beyond the written message. In Buenos Aires during the Cold War the distinction was blurred between what constituted a religious and a political dispute. Disputes on the virginity of Mary occurred at the same time as discussions on genocide. To have been found daubing graffiti could cost writers dear, perhaps even their lives.[8] Acts of political and theological defiance also constitute the Liberationist genre of graffiti: some were left unfinished, sometimes because either the primary author or the secondary authors (those who overwrote the graffiti) were no longer alive. To this complex intertextuality, should be added the fact that there is a sense of national identity attached to such buildings as the cathedral of Buenos Aires, the House of Bishops, or the Parliament, which is linked to the history of the city, thus adding extra meaning to the writing on its walls.[9] The important thing to reflect on, though, is that these graffiti have left open for us as a different way of thinking about the sacred. Deleuze would call graffiti-thinking 'schizophrenic' or 'schizzo thinking.' For Deleuze there were two main types of thinking, a fascist, totalitarian form, and a more fragmentary and free form, linked to poetic creativity. He called that latter 'schizophrenic', meaning by that a way of thinking 'in flux', becoming, not stemming from a fixed identity a thinking that changes and mutates, like our graffiti-poem.

Let us consider this in more detail. It is related to the core of theology of liberation, the struggle between a theology of becoming against a destiny of fixity. This is about the rebelliousness of Liberation Theology and not about the domesticity of theological thinking. What the popular reading of the Bible wanted to attempt was precisely to provide an element of instability and dynamism to the false sense of 'closure' produced by the prescriptive reading of the Scriptures. As in Deleuze's idea of fascist thinking, it prevents invention, divergences and it closes up the site of revelations as a 'rebellious' kind of sacred knowledge. I am acquainted with the popular reading of the Bible, as I have been part of many community readings in this style. I consider that its contribution cannot be underestimated in the history of Liberation Theology and theology in general. It allows divine revelation to come out from its historical closets with a blessing of abundance in understanding and transformative

8. For instance, in the mid-1980s, the Roman Catholic Church disputed the public view of Jean-Luc Godard's film *Je vous salue, Marie* (1985), claiming that it did not uphold the doctrine on Mary's virginity. At the same time, the Church was proposing a process of reconciliation which allowed the perpetrators of crimes against humanity committed during the 1970s to be forgiven. I have seen a photograph of the Catholic central cathedral of Buenos Aires pasted with dozens of posters against the proposed indult and with graffiti on the film's dispute. The posters say: 'Not to the indults (*No al Punto Final*). Jail to the genocides' and the graffiti reads: 'Godard is a virgin. Mary.' (The photograph shows a priest walking by the cathedral with a background of the posters and the graffiti. See *Crisis*, July 1986, p. 6.)
9. See, for instance, R. Young (2003), 'Buenos Aires and the narration of urban spaces and practices' in S. Hart and R. Young (eds), *Contemporary Latin American Cultural Studies* (London: Arnold), pp. 300–13, where the author reflects on the milieu of the city monuments and buildings as sites for contested and changing identities.

praxis of love and justice. However, the process must continue. The doing of a Liberation Theology requires us to add depth and suspicion to our questioning, and also to our questioning of love. We need to think of justice and love at the margins. We need to challenge a historiography of Liberation Theology, comprising clichés and a dangerous self-centrism from the Church. I have already considered the possibility of doing a popular Christology from the starting point of a 'graffiti Jesus'. A graffiti Jesus or a Christology from graffiti could be the starting point for a theology which would like to take seriously marginalization, using a strategy of 'theological dislocation'.[10] Theological dislocation, or 'kenotic dislocation', is a self-emptying process produced by putting theological (Western)[11] logics out of place. That displacement or marginalization process then becomes in itself a site of revelation. So in Liberation Theology we are putting the Logos out of place; that is, the word and the Word. If Jesus is the Word of God amongst people, then we need a different understanding of what constitutes a translation process. Moreover, we may need to do a theology which interferes with the theological translation process of God and, metaphorically speaking, the Scriptures. Graffiti gives us a clue for such a move. The aim of graffiti is not representation but invention. In fact, graffiti also requires an inventive reading, not just writing. How can we then do an inventive reading of God? An invention is always a discovery: an invention of God would need to recognize different desires and values. It would need to find a breakthrough for theology, not just to be able to tell different love stories but also to find a different love knowledge.

If we follow Gutiérrez in the understanding that the poor are the sacrament of God amongst us, as the visible sign of God's presence in our communities, then the poor as a sacrament do not need to correspond to a theology which never grounds love when speaking about poverty. It is interesting here to recall how Gutiérrez mentions the fact that the poor have been made 'insignificant', that is, they do not count. In other words, the poor do not point us towards meaning in society, since they are excluded from the system of production which confers meaning on people in capitalist systems. But neither do they refer to any transcendental meaning in theology. Is that true? Somehow yes. The poor signify theologically in Liberation Theology only by the fact that theology adds its own meaning to the presence of the poor. Theology becomes a tour guide taking God to the margins of the representation system of Christianity. Using Deleuze again, I should say that theology applies its common sense (that is, non-reflective) to the life of the poor. This ignores the fact that there is a substantial difference between

10. I have reflected already on the possibility of a 'graffiti-Jesus' as a deconstructive Liberation Theology project which takes serioulsy an epistemology of the margins. M. Althaus-Reid (2004), 'El Tocado. Sexual irregularities in the translation of God the Word in Jesus' in K. Hart and I. Sherwood, *Other Testaments, Derrida and Religion* (London: Routledge).
11. All theology in Latin America is 'Western' theology in the sense of the strangeness of Christianity amongst the Original Nations. Latin America had developed sophisticated religious systems before the arrival of Christianity but Christian theology is conceptually untranslatable. Christianity requires the use of theological concepts without equivalent in the original religions. Even Liberation Theology needed to recognize that there are limits to be 'authentically Latin American', unless it engages with a postcolonial theological questioning of key disputed concepts such as, for instance, monotheism. See G. Chamorro (2004), *Teología Guaraní* (Ecuador: Quito).

being a marginal God, and being an authentic God from the margins. Margins include transvestites and sexual dissidents from heteronormativity, messianic people still struggling against the commodification of messianism, and for an alternative order of social and loving justice. As the graffiti said, many were fallen angels who once thought they were at the 'centre of the Light'. Now the guarantee is over. But they existed and yet their identities could not be fixed. 'A variable' (unstable) identity is claimed by the fallen angel.

Love – gratuitous, unprofitable or promiscuous (freely given) – has much to do with Liberation Theology, because it may give it its sense of becoming; made of 'schizzos' (or disjointed) parts; made of conflicting fragments and sometimes made of pieces from an almost unintelligible theology, like graffiti. But is it in the encounter of theology and art and the art of the poor, as the scriptures on the walls of a poor city, that God may have the capacity to rupture life, to transform life?

Dissenting praxis. How to do a Queer Liberation Theology

'God never made Love.'

A graffiti written on the wall of a monument opposite the Parliament building of Buenos Aires, at the time when gay marriage was being debated.

Is that true? Can we say that God never made love when we have Jesus? Should we not know better? The 'God never made love' graffiti started to appear at the time of debates about sexuality. These were bitterly opposed by the Church and the message should perhaps be understood in that context. The graffiti might have been saying that the Church does not know about love. This is a sweeping statement, but it might for the most part be true. And love is the site of Queer reflections, that is, a site of contradictions and surprises which tend to overflow theological discourse that mentions love, without displaying any knowledge of love. Real love is a site of dislocations for theology, including Liberation Theology.

I have been reflecting on Queer theory and theology without ever clarifying the word 'Queer', because I have been discussing issues concerning theological dislocations. By theological dislocations I mean a way of doing theology which introduces new subjects and different experiences into our praxis. Any theology done from the margins necessarily needs to dislocate a theological discourse from the centre. And this is what doing theology from a Queer perspective achieves. By focusing on the life and experience of the poor, it changes the context, dislocating the assumed theological site of reflections about sexuality. It also brings some instability, but also invention and discovery, to our theological reflections. And this is what a *Queering* process brings to theology: something that we could call a practice of Christian becoming which welcomes challenges and shifts in theology. We can now begin to consider the path of Queer Liberation Theology. First of all, it is necessary to move in a direction that I should call 'to the Queer via Liberation Theology.' We can do that because, surprisingly, there are points of coincidence between Queer Theory and Liberationists. In fact, Judith Butler and Paulo Freire have something to say to each other.

Liberation Theology was a theology of 'dislocations'. It did that by devising a geographical theological model around the political centre and periphery understanding of the time. This model of centre–periphery does not apply in our times of the global expansion of capitalism as it did previously. At that time it promoted an understanding of the conditions of dependency under which Latin Americans were living and tried to produce a strategy of dislocation. This praxis had profound consequences in the context of Latin American theology, theological methods and also in ecclesiology, that is, the attempt to understand the meaning of the Church and its organization. Liberation Theology not only exposed a centre–periphery dynamic of power and constituency in politics, but also denounced that model of dependency in the Church and theology. In this it was not completely original, but the criticism was sustained. It was even taken up at the higher levels of the Churches, where such challenges and changes, welcomed by Liberation Theology, were beginning to appear, producing several dislocations.

First of all, liberationists dislocated the traditional view of who is the subject of theology, that is, who is the implicit believer in theology. The new subjects of theology were the poor. It was not that the poor had not been part of the implicit body of believers in theology before, but the difference was now that the poor became the implicit readers of, believers in and even producers of theology. That produced important challenges and changes to theology and to the Church. The poor brought their own problematic and cultural world to Latin American theology.

Second, and as a consequence of this, a dislocation was produced in theology and in the organization of the Churches. The Basic Ecclesial Communities are an example of this dislocation of the Church, the Church no longer in its familiar position because the life of the community was organized literally at the margins of parishes and congregations, spatially but also structurally. With Liberation Theology the Churches did not increase their membership, precisely because their membership was to be found at the margins and remained marginal: if anything it was the militant but middle-class Churches which declined in membership. Systematic theology also encountered challenges which arose from reflection on contextual sites. For instance, during the years of dictatorial repression there was much discussion on the sacramental presence of Christ during the Lord's Supper or communion. The immediate context was the real presence of survivors who reappeared out of the concentration camps in Argentina. 'Transcendence' as a theological category started to be considered in relation to the category of *lo cotidiano* ('everyday life'), that is, not just the being of the God of the Heavens, but the presence of God here on earth, the presence of Christ among the suffering people.

A third important dislocation was the dislocation of the theologian. That has been a major contribution of Liberation Theology to theology worldwide, to question the identity and role of the theologian. The liberation theologian is not an objective neutral observer but someone who takes sides, someone who, while not a representative of any community, has a relationship with the community and articulates their concerns. This was the 'theologian at the margins' and the concept of the margins in theology was elaborated at this time. The margins became not a distant place to be pointed to as an illustration, but rather the new location for a theological praxis. The criteria of orthodoxy (right dogma) were contrasted with the criteria of orthopraxis (right action). Not that dogmas were discarded. No one who reads Gustavo Gutiérrez's *Towards a Liberation Theology* at the beginning of the twenty-first century can fail to be struck by just how conservative was Gutiérrez on matters of doctrine. And yet, it was controversial in one important respect, that he required that Christian dogmas were verified in action, in action related to critical reality. In this a para-dogma was created, which does not mean 'a parallel dogma' but a discerning dogma which emerged from an understanding of the processes of ideological formation responsible for the construction of truth in theology.

Let us consider now a (Queer) Liberation Theology. As hinted above, it would be productive to put Judith Butler, whose work has been foundational for Queer Theory, together with Paulo Freire, the Brazilian educator for liberation. Let us reflect on Queer theory and theology via Paulo Freire. What is Queer? In a philosophical sense, Queer as a concept is visual. Imagine a transverse movement, a crossing or twisting of ideas which produces a breakdown of fixed societal identities, or more concretely sexual identities with which we now normally associate the word Queer. We have already spoken of dislocations and the dynamic of dislocation produced by Liberation Theology. There is a Queer dynamic in Liberation Theology, a transgressive, destabilizing and anti-iconic[12] style of thinking which aims to show the political interests and historiography of theology and theological truths. Now it might be objected that Queer refers only to sexual identities, while in Liberation Theology the aim is to unveil political identities and that consequently the two do not correspond. But the point is that we cannot so easily separate sexual and political identities. In that sense a Queer thinking is at the base of any unveiling of ideologies in Churches and theology.

Let us pursue this point in more detail. Queer theory implies a hermeneutics of suspicion and a distrust of fixed identities. Those are sexual identities, but Queer theory considers them foundational to epistemological processes, foundational to our way of knowing and understanding life. For Judith Butler the foundational ideology of any society is a sexual understanding of life and order which is represented in a heterosexual system. Succinctly, Butler says that it is in the construction of heterosexuality that the three elements of sexuality (a practice), gender (a behaviour) and sex (a biological given) are supposed to combine in a biological destiny. Certain gender behaviour is supposed to correspond to male or female sexuality, in which certain desires have been predetermined by the biological sex of the person at birth. Yet Queer theory would argue with this and claim that in reality, gender, sexuality and sex seldom match each other and that the 'matching' that we see comes via enforcement by educational or religious legislation. Considering that Butler's performativity does not mean that a subject can produce

---

12. This anti-iconism is manifested in popular theology by graffiti. For instance, there is a graffiti-Mariology done with the silhouettes of disappeared mothers and children, drawn beside the Virgin Mary in the cathedral. The drawings may have an intrinsic meaning coinciding with that of Christian theology: the suffering of Mary and the injustice of the punishment of the innocent son. Yet the anti-iconism is of a political (ideological) nature.

a gender reality by only naming it, it does mean that there is a gender expectation which precludes the horizon of the subject and requires repetitions (rituals or sexual liturgies) to be internalized.[13]

Desires, practices and identities do not line up according to expectations. Butler takes the example and paradigm of transsexualism to demonstrate how these three elements are to be found at the point of their intersection. For example, the sex of a drag queen may stand in opposition to her sexuality and her gendered behaviour. But the key here is the role of gender. Gender is perceived to have a teaching role in sexuality: gender disciplines sexualities. The transvestite and the drag queen are proofs that gendered behaviour can be acquired and imitated, as in a theatrical performance. Gender may have, then, a more profound meaning in relation to sexuality than previously thought.

Heterosexuality is an ideology and it is produced by the system of gender. It is a fragile ideology, though, which needs to be affirmed through various ways, but basically, according to Butler, through gender performances or repetitions. According to Butler, that element of repetition demonstrates the instability of heterosexuality which is also affirmed in a negative way, that is, by affirming itself against what it is not. In that sense the homosexual as a category of the immoral is important and fulfils an affirmative function in a heterosexual system.

Freire, who once stood up in a Feminist Congress and controversially said 'I am also a woman' was not very far away from Butler in this style of thinking (especially since both had read Althusser). Freire was trying to make a point about sexually fixed identities in relation to issues of justice. He saw theology as ideology and as such, fragile, unstable and arbitrary, but reinforced liturgically, as, for instance, in the annual religious processions that Latin American people have carried out for centuries. In one of the early books used for leaders of *conscientisacion* processes in my country, I found a note from Freire precisely about processions (*proseciones*). Freire saw them as processes of indoctrination where people were taught a theology of submissiveness and resignation to political powers of exploitation. Also a theology of oppression used a negative style of reaffirming its own virtues. That is, by the way, a postcolonial analysis, which highlights how in colonial Christianity the vices of the natives were necessary to build the virtues of the colonizers. The more the natives were constructed as part of a theological discourse which represented them as more depraved, more idolatrous and more prone to break the ten commandments, the more Christian missionaries were able to construct by contrast their self-righteous, Christian and Western civilized identity. I have elaborated on this negative affirmation of colonial theology already in relation to the doctrine of grace, as ideologically constructed as a heuristic device of colonial self-affirmation. The disgrace of the natives highlighted the grace poured upon the missionaries.

Is Liberation Theology unstable? As Butler would say, heterosexuality is an unstable category, but so is God. Can we see, then, how Butler and Freire can talk Queer? Both in Liberation Theology and Queer theory, Queer represents the path

<hr>

13. Butler's concept of performativity needs to be understood in the context of the subject simultaneously 'subjected and generated'. See J. Butler (2003), *Bodies that Matter* (New York: Routledge).

of abnormality, and its opposite is by definition reached by the path of ideologies of normalization. Butler even considered that one of the main culprits in the propagation of the heterosexual ideology lies in ourselves, in the way we have accepted without questioning and thus naturalized what is no more than a sexual construct. Butler takes that from Althusser, who developed the concept of 'interpellation' to explain this phenomenon. It is the idea of being interpreted and defined by others while we think that we are acting according to our free will. Althusser says that an indoctrination process succeeds when the individual feels an emotional response which identifies her or him with the ideological imposition. Freire put it in other words. He spoke of the 'internalization of oppression'. A member of my congregation in Buenos Aires during the time of the political repression used to explain this as: 'what happens to a person when that person does not need control from the police, because the police are inside his heart'. The ideology has succeeded in creating an emotional mechanism of control and annulled possibilities of rebellion or questioning.

Liberation Theology, like Queer theory, is constructivist, although not completely. Its task is to unveil ideologies of power working within theology. Liberation Theology may not have followed Butler, but it did follow Gramsci in his understanding of how the construction of the 'common sense' or everyday practice can in reality be uncritical consciousness. But how can this false consciousness be challenged? How can the oppressed be liberated against themselves? That was one of Freire's preoccupations when trying to organize a praxis of liberation around people who, theologically, had been made to believe for generations that their poverty was a product of their sins.

So even here, Butler and Freire can talk. For Butler the key is to pinpoint the processes of gender repetition in order to disrupt them. Gender is the matrix of sexualities and therefore gender chaos produces the contradictions to the heterosexual system of heteronormativity which will unmask its natural pretences. Similarly, Freire sought to disrupt oppressive theological repetitions which create false consciousness and identities. He wanted an end to religious processions as indoctrination for resignation and wanted people to problematize their faith.

Butler has used the example of drag queens as a pedagogical device, because they show us the performance of gender and the making of sexuality. What Butler means by the localization and denunciation of repetitions is to be able to see mechanisms of the formation of sexual ideologies in action – that is, to see how gender is created and how sexuality is created or affirmed after that. That, according to Butler, would show us many other things; for instance, that there are as many sexualities as there are gender performances. But Freire was not so far from that when he saw that Church organizations were the tool to perpetuate theological ideologies. The repetitions of Church structures tend to show a false, constructed identity, already criticized before Freire by many indigenous Christians who were dismayed that Christianity would not use some of their traditional and tested forms of organization in the Church.

Mechanisms of power and control repeated through Church structures and in alliance with the state produced many things, including an image of God in Latin

America as inaccessible and remote as an absentee landlord in Brazil. For that reason amongst others, Mariology had a privileged place in Latin America. People could not connect to the Church nor with God or Jesus. Mary was the one whom they understood and who could speak in their names to the higher deities. Therefore Freire introduced the idea of disrupting repetitions. He was a key figure in the organization of the Basic Ecclesial Communities. Basic Ecclesial Communities disrupted and dislocated Churches by creating alternative centres of reflection and decision making. They dislocated the Church but they were creative centres too, not only liturgically but also theologically, where many important issues were discussed by the people. More importantly, by dislocating the identity of 'the believer', the way of thinking also changed.

Disrupting 'The Sacred Believer'. *Genderization* Processes in Theology

Some years ago there was a beggar from my home town of Rosario named Cachilo, known for his characteristic newspaper-style graffiti. At the time of a heavy censorship, Cachilo, thanks to the fact that he was considered insane, was able to initiate a messianic project in which he asked the bishops to be accountable to their people. He wrote on the walls of the House of Bishops, 'After so many years, you should not be receiving any payment to preach the Gospel.' He also wrote a series of graffiti under the *nom de plume* identity he called the 'sacred believer'. One of them read, 'You have been brought up as a sacred believer. With the surety of truth. But if you disagree, you'll disappear (get locked up) in jail.' Somehow he seemed to have anticipated the issue of bodies in theology, characteristic of Liberation Theology. Liberation Theology is, after all, a *habeas corpus* theology, a theology which denounces the disappearance of a body and demands resurrection. It denounces the existence of the hungered body, the tortured body, the denied existence of thousands of disappeared people from the years of political repression. Cachilo questioned the construction of the identity of the 'sacred believer' on the walls of the House of Bishops from a political perspective.

However, there is a difference here. In Queer Theory sexuality is the ideology to uncover and to subvert. Liberation Theology has been primarily focused on class structures, although race and gender now occupy some space. Gender in Liberation Theology is still gender at the level which Butler calls 'performance'. It is the superficiality of gender codes which has been considered and not sexuality. Can Queer and Liberationist walk together? The sex, sexuality and gender crossroads, which are the core of identity formation (including political identity), are constitutive of other sustaining orders such as theology. Theology is a sexual act: that has been one of my premises. Theology deals with sacred sexual narratives and understands the role of gender in keeping under control the heteronormalization of God and humanity. Genderization processes are very important in theology. Sexuality is unstable and so is God. Therefore it is through a genderization process that theology keeps people and concepts in place. For instance, it keeps in place a reproductive theology, authorized by legitimate connections and the logic of arguments. But it also keeps in place the given-ness of the understanding of what is humanity and what is God. We have yet to consider the genderization of theology as a way to ensure the reproductive system of theological reflections and an understanding of humanity and God. In indecent theology the liberation theological insights which challenge some of these formations are highlighted, while providing new forms of disruptions to the sexual and economic base of Western theology.

To queer, then, is to facilitate a process of leaving an assigned space of belonging. Although this is a sexual space, it is also a political space. Queer theory politicized sexuality and identity by mixing the realm of the private with the public and by placing 'love' as a category to contest the 'regimes of the normal'. Queering theology needs to be a dissenting praxis, a praxis for transformation of structures of oppression which have been normalized by ideologies in power, in alliance with Christian theology. Although Liberation Theology understands how theology can be de-ideologized, unfortunately it has ignored how sexuality contributes as an epistemological foundation, not only to our conception of God but also to the way that society works. Global regimes are gendered. The formation of gender and the core heterosexual ideological processes of formation which are sustained by it pervade societies. A Queer theology is, then, an interdisciplinary task, with a multilevel framework of suspicion. Here theory is put into practice. While heterosexual theological frameworks tend to be disembodied, a Queer theology is not void of desire and corporeality. In this we must say that queering Liberation Theology has given back sexuality to the poor, at more than one level. It functions at the level of political and social analysis and at the level of thinking about what a theology, which incorporates a sexuality from the margins, can tell us about ourselves and God.

The Return of the Queer God

'The Pope comes to Argentina: Jesus comes to our Country'
'Jesus cannot come: He is a disappeared one.'

Let me consider another significant series of graffiti on God as 'a disappeared'. During the first visit of Pope John Paul II to Argentina in 1982 the Church produced a welcoming campaign with the slogan, 'The Pope comes to Argentina: Jesus comes to our Country.' The walls of the cathedral of Buenos Aires were covered with banners with these words. At the same time, a graffiti campaign also started up which modified the text of the banners. The first part was not modified but the second part of the graffiti read 'Jesus (cannot) come. He is a disappeared one (*desaparecido*)'. To the bodies of the disappeared and the 'body of knowledge and experience' which also suffered at that time under the military regime in Argentina, that graffiti has added the disappearance of Jesus. God Godself had disappeared in some concentration camp but the Church had not realized it as yet.

That may have been true. That was a time when people searched for the real face of God which was hidden under discourses of ecclesial and dictatorial power. However, if we are talking about Indecent Theology as a Queer and Liberation Theology, we are still talking about the rediscovery of the face of God among us. The search has not finished yet. Interestingly, that was the premise of the liberationists at the beginning. They even spoke about the conflicts amongst 'gods' in the Scriptures and in theology. Gustavo Gutiérrez, who took inspiration for his theology from José Maria Arguedas, the indigenist writer who reflected on the life of the indigenous people from Perú, referred to this. In his first edition of *Liberation Theology*, Gutiérrez dedicated his book to Arguedas and used a text from him.[14] The text was about a dialogue between an indigenous man and a Roman Catholic priest. When the priest mentions 'God', the indigenous man asks, '*Qué Dios Padrecito?*' 'Which God, dear Father (are you talking about?) . . . God of the masters or God of the people? . . . God of the masters is not the same God. That one makes you suffer without consolation.'[15] The question 'Which God?' is an old one in Latin American religious life.

In the queering of Liberation Theology, or what I have called 'Indecent Theology', we also may be asking 'Which God?' The process of calling into question the sexual ideology of theology may produce a crisis in the understanding of God when linked to those sexual ideological constructions. This is a more difficult process than it was for Feminists of the first wave, who realized that God the Father and Son required some theological reflection in order to produce an inclusive theology. As I have said before, gender identities are not as problematic in the understanding of the sacred as sexual identities.

In addition to all that, we are trying to do a theology from the perspective of both poor and Queer communities. I am using the term 'Queer communities' to demystify the theological construction of the love imaginary and traditions of economic exchange amongst poor communities. This requires a hermeneutical circle of permutations which allows us to begin at the place where people are. The hermeneutical circle of Liberation Theology did that, but in order to deal with contradictions to ecclesial orthodoxy, it tended to assume as the starting point, not the experiences from the people themselves, but the theologized experiences of the people. By that we mean the experiences of the people after they had been processed through the theological framework of reference of the Church. This is a crucial point, one which Freire also considered in his work of conscientization. I remember him saying that the problem with the Churches was that they never took people as they were. People had to be modified and interpreted, according to the understanding of the Church, before they were allowed to be part of the community. Because of this, Freire concluded that the Church would have problems being a community, because that honest dialogue in community which requires acceptance and respect was precluded. But if we take on board the amatory experiences of the Latin American people, as, for example, in the institution of *tenderness,* or the solidarity amongst the poor which comes from patterns of so called 'promiscuity' (the extended family of the poor), we can enter the hermeneutical circle of suspicion from a different place. This is a departure from the imposed

---

14. The text from Arguedas, which comes from his novel *Todas las Sangres* and is considered to be the cornerstone of Gutiérrez's thesis, was surprisingly omitted from the first and subsequent English translations as the text in Spanish was considered to be 'difficult'. See J. Nikoloff (ed.) (2000), *Gustavo Gutiérrez: Essential Writings* (New York: Orbis) p. 15.
15. Gutiérrez, G. (1971), *Teologia de la Liberacion* (Lima: CEP).

Western medieval notions of family in Christianity and the imposition of forms of loving exchanges that even culturally do not represent people's lives. What we have here is a different subject, a non-theologized subject in her/his community. It is the beginning of a hermeneutical circle with the excluded bodies of theology, that is, the non-productive bodies. This is because in the theological economy of the Church there are also margins of productivity. Those who do not have anything to add to what is already in place are somehow unproductive and therefore ignored. The poor nuclear family may receive attention because it adds to the Church's theological production, but not two gay priests with AIDS, even if they have been a loving family too in many ways. Taking a different starting point, from a non-productive marginal subject, we are then confronted with a path which leads towards a non-reproductive theology, leading in turn to the discovery of a hidden face of God. That may be God the stranger amongst us, a queer God of the margins.

This is an important point, with consequences, namely the location of God (and Christ Jesus) in the margins. We must consider what are the conditions of such a location. Do the margins provide a temporary location for a God who graciously visits the poor but, like a married minister working in a slum, goes back to his wife and kids after the day's work? Or to the contrary, is it that we do not have a God at the margins but a God from the margins, distributing God's presence from that location outside the centres of power of Church and theology? If an Indecent, Queer Theology can cast theology into crisis, it means that the location of God also becomes critical. That critical location of God in our communities and in theology is a Queer one, and constitutes a process of sexual decolonization of our Christian discourses. And beyond that, a Queer God, whose face we have intuitively seen appearing and disappearing from the walls of the cathedral of Buenos Aires, embodies the second coming of a Stranger God at the margins of political, sexual and religious exclusion.

Chapter 18

Charles Taylor
The Moral Order:
The Transition to Political Modernity

Enlightened modernity puts forward a new understanding of society. We might say better, a new idea of the moral order underlying society. This was most clearly stated in the new theories of Natural Law which emerged in the seventeenth century, largely as a response to the domestic and international disorder wrought by the Wars of Religion. Grotius and Locke are the most important theorists of reference for our purposes here.

Grotius derives the normative order underlying political society from the nature of its constitutive members. Human beings are rational, sociable agents who are meant to collaborate in peace to their mutual benefit.

Starting from the seventeenth century, this idea has come more and more to dominate our political thinking, and the way we imagine our society. It starts off in Grotius' version as a theory of what political society is, that is, what it is in aid of, and how it comes to be. But any theory of this kind also offers inescapably an idea of moral order. It tells us something about how we ought to live together in society.

The picture of society is that of individuals who come together to form a political entity, against a certain pre-existing moral background, and with certain ends in view. The moral background is one of natural rights; these people already have certain moral obligations towards each other. The ends sought are certain common benefits, of which security is the most important.

The underlying idea of moral order stresses the rights and obligations which we have as individuals in regard to each other, even prior to or outside of the political bond. Political obligations are seen as an extension or application of these more fundamental moral ties. Political authority itself is legitimate only because it was consented to by individuals (the original contract), and this contract creates binding obligations in virtue of the pre-existing principle that promises ought to be kept.

In the light of what has later been made of this 'contract' theory, even later in the same century by Locke, it is astonishing to us how tame the moral-political conclusions are which Grotius draws from it. The grounding of political legitimacy in consent is not put forward in order to question the credentials of existing governments. The aim of the exercise is rather to undercut the reasons for rebellion being

259

all too irresponsibly urged by confessional zealots; the assumption being that existing legitimate regimes were ultimately founded on some consent of this kind. Grotius also seeks to give a firm foundation, beyond confessional cavil, to the basic rules of war and peace. In the context of the early seventeenth century, with its continuing bitterly fought Wars of Religion, this emphasis was entirely understandable.

It is Locke who first uses this theory as a justification of 'revolution', and as a ground for limited government. Rights can now be seriously pleaded against power. Consent is not just an original agreement to set up government, but a continuing right to agree to taxation.

In the next three centuries, from Locke to our day, although the contract language may fall away, and be used only by a minority of theorists, the underlying idea of society as existing for the (mutual) benefit of individuals, and the defence of their rights, takes on more and more importance. That is, it both comes to be the dominant view, pushing older theories of society, or newer rivals to the margins of political life and discourse; and it also generates more and more far-reaching claims on political life. The requirement of original consent, via the half-way house of Locke's consent to taxation, becomes the fully-fledged doctrine of popular sovereignty under which we now live. The theory of natural rights ends up spawning a dense web of limits to legislative and executive action, via the entrenched charters which have become an important feature of contemporary government. The presumption of equality, implicit in the starting point of the State of Nature, where people stand outside of all relations of superiority and inferiority,[1] has been applied in more and more contexts, ending with the multiple equal treatment or non-discrimination provisions, which are an integral part of most entrenched charters.

In other words, during these last three centuries, the idea of moral order implicit in this view of society has undergone a double expansion: in extension, on one hand (more people live by it, it has become dominant), and in intensity, on the other (the demands it makes are heavier and more ramified). The idea has gone, as it were, through a series of 'redactions', each richer and more demanding than the previous one, up to the present day.

A crucial point which ought to be evident from the foregoing is that the notion of moral order I am using here goes beyond some proposed schedule of norms which ought to govern our mutual relations and/or political life. What an understanding of moral order adds to an awareness and acceptance of norms is an identification of features of the world, or divine action, or human life which make certain norms both right and (up to the point indicated) realizable. In other words, the image of order carries a definition not only of what is right, but also of the context in which it makes sense to strive for, and hope to realize the right (at least partially).

1. John Locke, in the *Second Treatise on Government*, ch. II, defines the state of Nature as a condition 'wherein all the Power and Jurisdiction is reciprocal, no one having more than another: there being nothing more evident, than that Creatures of the same species and rank promiscuously born to all the same advantages of Nature, and the use of the same faculties, should be equal one amongst another without Subordination or Subjection, unless the Lord and Master of them all, should by any manifest Declaration of his Will set one above another, and confer on him by evident and clear appointment an undoubted Right to Dominion and Sovereignty.' See P. Laslett (ed.) (1967), *Two Treatises of Government* (Cambridge: Cambridge University Press), p. 287.

Now it is clear that the images of moral order which descend through a series of transformations from that inscribed in the Natural Law theories of Grotius and Locke are rather different from those embedded in the social imaginary of the pre-modern age.

Two important types of pre-modern moral order are worth singling out here, because we can see them being gradually taken over, displaced or marginalized by the Grotian–Lockean strand during the transition to political modernity. One is based on the idea of the law of a people, which has governed this people since time out of mind, and which in a sense defines it as a people. This idea seems to have been widespread among the Indo-European tribes who at various stages erupted into Europe. It was very powerful in seventeenth-century England, under the guise of the Ancient Constitution, and became one of the key justifying ideas of the rebellion against the king.[2]

This case should be enough to show that these notions are not always conservative in import; but we should also include in this category the sense of normative order which seems to have been carried on through generations in peasant communities, and out of which they developed a picture of the 'moral economy', from which they could criticize the burdens laid on them by landlords, or the exactions levied on them by state and Church.[3] Here again, the recurring idea seems to have been that an original acceptable distribution of burdens had been displaced by usurpation, and ought to be rolled back. The other type is organized around a notion of a hierarchy in society which expresses and corresponds to a hierarchy in the cosmos. These were often theorized in language drawn from the Platonic–Aristotelian concept of Form, but the underlying notion also emerges strongly in theories of correspondence: e.g., the king is in his kingdom, as the lion among animals, the eagle among birds, etc. It is out of this outlook that the idea emerges that disorders in the human realm will resonate in nature, because the very order of things is threatened. The night on which Duncan was murdered was disturbed by 'lamenting heard i' the air; strange screams of death', and it remained dark even though day should have started. On the previous Tuesday a falcon had been killed by a mousing owl; and Duncan's horses turned wild in the night, 'Contending against obedience, as they would / Make war with mankind'.[4]

In both these cases, and particularly in the second, we have an order which tends to impose itself by the course of things; violations are met with backlash which transcends the merely human realm. This seems to be a very common feature in pre-modern ideas of moral order. Anaximander likens any deviation from the course of nature to injustice, and says that things which resist it must eventually 'pay penalty and retribution to each other for their injustice according to the assessment of time'.[5] Heraclitus speaks of the order of things in similar terms,

2. See J. G. A. Pocock (1987), *The Ancient Constitution and the Feudal Law* (Cambridge: Cambridge University Press).
3. The term 'moral economy' is borrowed from E. Thompson (1971), 'The Moral Economy of the English Crowd in the Eighteenth Century' in *Past and Present*, 50, pp. 76–136.
4. W. Shakespeare, *Macbeth*, 2.3.56; 2.4.17–18.
5. Quoted in L. Dupré (1993), *Passage to Modernity* (New Haven, CT: Yale University Press), p. 1.

when he says that if ever the sun should deviate from its appointed course, the Furies would seize it and drag it back.[6] And, of course, the Platonic forms are active in shaping the things and events in the world of change.

In these cases, it is very clear that a moral order is more than just a set of norms; that it also contains what we might call an 'ontic' component, identifying features of the world which make the norms realizable. Now the modern order which descends from Grotius and Locke is not self-realizing in the sense invoked by Hesiod or Plato, or the cosmic reactions to Duncan's murder. It is therefore tempting to think that our modern notions of moral order lack altogether an ontic component. But this would be a mistake, as I hope to show later. There is an important difference, but it lies in the fact that this component is now a feature about us humans, rather than one touching God or the cosmos, and not in the supposed absence altogether of an ontic dimension.

Now what is peculiar to our modern understanding of order stands out most clearly if we focus on how the idealizations of Natural Law theory differ from those which were dominant before. Pre-modern social imaginaries, especially those of the second type mentioned above, were structured by various modes of hierarchical complementarity. Society was seen as made up of different orders. These needed and complemented each other. But this didn't mean that their relations were truly mutual, because they didn't exist on the same level. They formed rather a hierarchy in which some had greater dignity and value than the others. An example is the often repeated medieval idealization of the society of three orders, *oratores*, *bellatores*, *laboratores*: those who pray, those who fight, and those who work. It was clear that each needed the others, but there was no doubt that we have here a descending scale of dignity; some functions were in their essence higher than others.

It is crucial to this kind of ideal that the distribution of functions is itself a key part of the normative order. It is not just that each order ought to perform its characteristic function for the others, granted they have entered these relations of exchange, while we keep the possibility open that things might be arranged rather differently, e.g., in a world where everyone does some praying, some fighting and some working. No, the hierarchical differentiation itself is seen as the proper order of things. It was part of the nature, or form, of society. In the Platonic and neo-Platonic traditions, as I have just mentioned, this form was already at work in the world, and any attempt to deviate from it turned reality against itself. Society would be denatured in the attempt. Hence the tremendous power of the organic metaphor in these earlier theories. The organism seems the paradigm locus of forms at work, striving to heal its wounds and cure its maladies. And at the same time, the arrangement of functions which it exhibits is not simply contingent; it is 'normal' and right. That the feet are below the head is how it should be.

The modern idealization of order departs radically from this. It is not just that there is no place for a Platonic-type form at work; but, connected to this, whatever

6. 'The sun will not overstep his measures; if he does, the Erinyes, the handmaids of Justice, will find him out.' Quoted in G. Sabine (1961), *A History of Political Theory* (New York: Holt Rinehart & Winston), p. 26.

distribution of functions a society might develop is deemed contingent; it will be justified or not instrumentally; it cannot itself define the good. The basic normative principle is, indeed, that the members of society serve each other's needs, help each other – in short, behave like the rational and sociable creatures that they are. In this way, they complement each other. But the particular functional differentiation which they need to take on to do this most effectively is endowed with no essential worth. It is adventitious, and potentially changeable. In some cases, it may be merely temporary, as with the principle of the ancient *polis*, that we may be rulers and ruled in turn. In other cases, it requires lifetime specialization, but there is no inherent value in this, and all callings are equal in the sight of God. In one way or the other, the modern order gives no ontological status to hierarchy, or any particular structure of differentiation.

In other words, the basic point of the new normative order was the mutual respect and mutual service of the individuals who make up society. The actual structures were meant to serve these ends, and were judged instrumentally in this light. The difference might be obscured by the fact that the older orders also ensured a kind of mutual service; the clergy prays for the laity, and the laity defend/work for the clergy. But the crucial point is just this division into types in their hierarchical ordering; whereas on the new understanding we start with individuals and their debt of mutual service, and the divisions fall out as they can most effectively discharge this debt.

Thus Plato, in Book II of the *Republic*, starts out by reasoning from the non-self-sufficiency of the individual to the need for an order of mutual service. But quite rapidly it becomes clear that it is the structure of this order which is the basic point. And the last doubt is removed when we see that this order is meant to stand in analogy and interaction with the normative order in the soul. By contrast, in the modern ideal, the whole point is the mutual respect and service, however achieved.

I have mentioned two differences which distinguish this ideal from the earlier, Platonic-modelled orders of hierarchical complementarities: the Form is no longer at work in reality, and the distribution of functions is not itself normative. A third difference goes along with this. For the Platonic-derived theories, the mutual service which the classes render to each other when they stand in the right relation includes bringing them to the condition of their highest virtue; indeed, this is the service which the whole order, as it were, renders to all its members. But in the modern ideal, the mutual respect and service is directed towards serving our ordinary goals, life, liberty, sustenance of self and family. The organization of society, as I said above, is judged not on its inherent form, but instrumentally. But now we can add that what this organization is instrumental to concerns the very basic conditions of existence as free agents, rather than the excellence of virtue – although we may judge that we need a high degree of virtue to play our proper part in this.

Our primary service to each other was thus (to use the language of a later age) the provision of collective security, to render our lives and property safe under law. But we also serve each other in practising economic exchange. These two main ends, security and prosperity, are now the principal goals of organized society, which itself can come to be seen as something in the nature of a profitable exchange between its constituent members. The ideal social order is one in which our purposes mesh, and each in furthering him/herself helps the others.

This ideal order was not thought to be a mere human invention. Rather it was designed by God, an order in which everything coheres according to God's purposes. Later in the eighteenth century, the same model is projected on the cosmos, in a vision of the universe as a set of perfectly interlocking parts, in which the purposes of each kind of creature mesh with those of all the others.

This order sets the goal for our constructive activity, insofar as it lies within our power to upset it, or realize it. Of course, when we look at the whole, we see how much the order is already realized; but when we cast our eye on human affairs, we see how much we have deviated from it and upset it; it becomes the norm to which we should strive to return.

This order was thought to be evident in the nature of things. Of course, if we consult the book of Revelation, we will also find the demand formulated there that we abide by it. But reason alone can tell us God's purposes. Living things, including ourselves, strive to preserve themselves. This is God's doing. Being endowed with reason, we see that not only our lives but also those of all humans are to be preserved. And in addition, God made us sociable beings. So that 'every one as he is bound to preserve himself, and not quit his Station willfully; so by the like reason when his Preservation comes not in competition, ought he, as much as he can, to preserve the rest of Mankind.'[7]

Similarly Locke reasons that God gave us our powers of reason and discipline so that we could most effectively go about the business of preserving ourselves. It follows that we ought to be 'Industrious and Rational'.[8] The ethic of discipline and improvement is itself a requirement of the natural order that God had designed. The imposition of order by human will is itself called for by his scheme.

We can see in Locke's formulation how much he sees mutual service in terms of profitable exchange. 'Economic' (that is, ordered, peaceful, productive) activity has become the model for human behaviour, and the key for harmonious co-existence. In contrast to the theories of hierarchical complementarity, we meet in a zone of concord and mutual service, not to the extent that we transcend our ordinary goals and purposes, but on the contrary, in the process of carrying them out according to God's design . . .

[W]e tend to read the march of this new principle of order, and its displacing of traditional modes of complementarity, as the rise of 'individualism' at the expense of 'community'. Whereas the new understanding of the individual has as its inevitable flip-side a new understanding of sociality, the society of mutual benefit, whose functional differentiations are ultimately contingent, and whose members are fundamentally equal. This is what I have been insisting on in these pages, just because it generally gets lost from view. The individual seems primary, because we read the displacement of older forms of complementarity as the

---

7. Locke's *Two Treatises*, I. ch. XI, para 6, p. 289; see also chap XI, para 135, p. 376; and *Some Thoughts Concerning Education*, para 116.
8. Ibid., p. 309.

erosion of community as such. We seem to be left with a standing problem of how to induce or force the individual into some kind of social order, make him conform and obey the rules.

This recurrent experience of breakdown is real enough. But it shouldn't mask from us the fact that modernity is also the rise of new principles of sociality. Breakdown occurs, as we can see with the case of the French Revolution because people are often expelled from their old forms, through war, revolution or rapid economic change, before they can find their feet in the new structures, that is, connect some transformed practices to the new principles to form a viable social imaginary. But this doesn't show that modern individualism is by its very essence a solvent of community. Nor that the modern political predicament is that defined by Hobbes: how do we rescue atomic individuals from the prisoners' dilemma? The real, recurring problem has been better defined by Tocqueville, or in our day, François Furet.

The second distortion is the familiar one. The modern principle seems to us so self-evident: are we not by nature and essence individuals such that we are tempted by a 'subtraction' account of the rise of modernity? We just needed to liberate ourselves from the old horizons, and then the mutual service conception of order was the obvious alternative left. It needed no inventive insight or constructive effort. Individualism and mutual benefit are the evident residual ideas which remain after you have sloughed off the older religions and metaphysics.

But the reverse is the case. Humans have lived for most of their history in modes of complementarity, mixed with a greater or lesser degree of hierarchy. There have been islands of equality, like that of the citizens of the *polis*, but they are set in a sea of hierarchy, once you replace them in the bigger picture. Not to speak of how alien these societies were to modern individualism. What is rather surprising is that it was possible to win through to modern individualism; not just on the level of theory, but also transforming and penetrating the social imaginary. Now that this imaginary has become linked with societies of unprecedented power in human history, it seems impossible and mad to try to resist. But we must not fall into the anachronism of thinking that this was always the case.

The best antidote to this error is to bring to mind again some of the phases of the long and often conflictual march by which this theory has ended up achieving such a hold on our imagination.

I haven't space to do that here. Rather at this stage, I want to pull together the preceding discussion and outline the main features of this modern understanding of moral order.

This can be sketched in two points:

1) The original idealization of this order of mutual benefit comes in a theory of rights and of legitimate rule. It starts with individuals, and conceives society as established for their sake. Political society is seen as an instrument for something pre-political.

This individualism signifies a rejection of the previously dominant notion of hierarchy, according to which a human being can only be a proper moral agent embedded in a larger social whole, whose very nature is to exhibit a hierarchical complementarity. In its original form, the Grotian–Lockean theory stands against all those views, of which Aristotle's is the most prominent, which deny that one can be a fully competent human subject outside of society.

As this idea of order advances, and generates new 'redactions', it becomes connected again with a philosophical anthropology which once again defines humans as social beings, incapable of functioning morally on their own. Rousseau, Hegel and Marx provide earlier examples, and they are followed by a host of thinkers in our day. But I see these still as redactions of the modern idea, because what they posit as a well-ordered society incorporates relations of mutual service between equal individuals as a crucial element. This is the goal, even for those who think that the 'bourgeois individual' is a fiction, and that the goal can only be achieved in a communist society. Even connected to ethical concepts antithetical to those of the Natural Law theorists, and indeed, closer to the Aristotle they rejected, the kernel of the modern idea remains an idée-force in our world.

As an instrument, political society enables these individuals to serve each other for mutual benefit; both in providing security, and in fostering exchange and prosperity. Any differentiations within it are to be justified by this *telos*; no hierarchical or other form is intrinsically good.

The significance of this, as we saw above, is that the mutual service centres on the needs of ordinary life, rather than aiming to secure for them the highest virtue. It aims to secure their conditions of existence as free agents. Now here, too, later redactions involve a revision. With Rousseau, for instance, freedom itself becomes the basis for a new definition of virtue, and an order of true mutual benefit becomes inseparable from one which secures the virtue of self-dependence. But Rousseau and those who followed him still put the central emphasis on securing freedom, equality and the needs of ordinary life.

2) The theory starts with individuals, which political society must serve. More importantly, this service is defined in terms of the defence of individuals' rights. And freedom is central to these rights. The importance of freedom is attested in the requirement that political society be founded on the consent of those bound by it.

If we reflect on the context in which this theory was operative, we can see that the crucial emphasis on freedom was overdetermined. The order of mutual benefit is an ideal to be constructed. It serves as a guide for those who want to establish a stable peace, and then remake society to bring it closer to its norms. The proponents of the theory already see themselves as agents who through disengaged, disciplined action can reform their own lives, as well as the larger social order. They are buffered, disciplined selves. Free agency is central to their self-understanding. The emphasis on rights, and the primacy of freedom among them, doesn't just stem from the principle that society should exist for the sake of its members; it also reflects the holders' sense of their own agency, and of the situation which that agency normatively demands in the world, viz. freedom.

Thus the ethic at work here should be defined just as much in terms of this condition of agency, as in terms of the demands of the ideal order. We should best think of it as an ethic of freedom and mutual benefit. Both terms in this expression are essential. And that is why consent plays such an important role in the political theories which derive from this ethic. [. . .]

Summing up, we can say that (1) the order of mutual benefit holds between individuals (or at least moral agents who are independent of larger hierarchical orders); (2) the benefits crucially include life and the means to life, however securing these relates to the practice of virtue; (3) it is meant to secure freedom, and easily finds expression in terms of rights. To these we can add a fourth point: (4) these rights, this freedom, this mutual benefit is to be secured to all participants equally. Exactly what is meant by equality will vary, but that it must be affirmed in some form follows from the rejection of hierarchical order. These are the crucial features, the constants that recur in the modern idea of moral order, through its varying 'redactions'.

(i) This understanding is atomistic. Society is understood as constituted by its component individuals. (ii) Artifice plays an important role here, and on two levels. The social reality is seen as built by artifice, in the theory of origins through social contract, and in the continuing invitation to restructure things, which ends up being constitutive of modern political understanding. At the same time, society is to be properly understood as made up of individuals; the proper method involves reconceptualizing it in this way. That is what proper method involves.

(iii) The contrast to this mode of being/understanding of society, against which it defines itself, is the older notion(s) of order. These cannot be atomistically understood; they have to be understood as whole, as encompassing patterns. They are, moreover, prior to the individuals; they lay out roles, and we can only be properly human beings by assuming one or other role. The idea that a full human being could stand outside all such was seen by Aristotle as a kind of absurdity; we would either have to be beasts or Gods.

In keeping with these three features, the modern understanding of society involves objectifying it in a new way. This may seem strange, because the new model also greatly expands human agency. Society is created by its members. But curiously these two features belong together. We can see this duality, if we look at the three major forms of modern social imaginary which emanate from this idea of order: the economy, the public sphere, and the citizen state. What I want to say comes to light when we contrast the economy with the other two forms. Both of these – the public sphere and the self-ruling 'people' – imagine us as collective agencies. And it is these new modes of collective agency which are among the most striking feature of Western modernity and beyond; we understand ourselves, after all, to be living in a democratic age.

Chapter 19

Jürgen Manemann
The Depoliticization of God as a Challenge for Political Theology[1]

I Desecularization: The Return of Religions

Today, we are living in a 'global society' of crisis. Everything indicates that a storm is arising. The term 'crisis' increasingly becomes an appropriate signature for our times, ideologically and politically. We are familiar with words like 'crisis of employment', 'moral crisis', 'political crisis' and 'ecological crisis'. There is even the crisis of the Church and the crisis of God. Everywhere a crisis is apparent, except with religion. There is no crisis of religion. Religion flourishes, sociologists are already talking about a religious surplus.

After the Second World War the political ambition of the Enlightenment Movement seemed to be fulfilled, as politics itself finally had emancipated itself from religion. Religion was not banned, but considered first and foremost as a private or family affair. Some analysts believed economical and social modernization led to a degradation of religion as a main factor of human existence. Their belief was unwarranted. 'The economical and social modernization was a global one and simultaneously led to a worldwide renaissance of religion.'[2] Yet, it is not the return of private forms of religion, but of public forms which irritates and threatens. It destroys all harmonic visions of an 'end of history' which were promulgated everywhere after the fall of the Berlin Wall. The numbers of voices which advocate a rethinking of a failed modernity are on the increase. They are criticizing modernity for they believe agnosticism is the cause of modernity's shortcomings. These commentators demand a desecularization, which means to found society upon a religious basis. This proposal is common, particularly among those who belong to monotheistic faiths.

Since 9/11 this development has become more dramatic. In the process of a return and reinvention of the political, religion (and Christianity in particular) has become more important. This is because now Christianity serves as an identifying

1. . Translated from the German by the editors.
2. S. P. Huntington (1998), *Kampf der Kulturen. Die Neugestaltung der Weltpolitik im 21. Jahrhundert* (München/Wien: Siedler), p. 144.

label and as a tool of distinction. A neopoliticization of religion is looming which abuses religion as a weapon in the fight for creating collective identities. This is to say that the return of religions is more than just unproblematic. In short, the *homo christianus* should be alerted whenever the *homo religiosus* becomes popular.

The question of the relation between religion and modernity, religion and the secular states and also religion and a pluralist society becomes more and more problematic. The increased return of public religions today threatens the basis of a democratic society and democratic culture. At the same time, there is a danger of the emergence of new totalitarianisms. Whoever is seriously interested in examining this phenomenon is well advised to avoid the contradictory dichotomy of religion and politics, modernity and fundamentalism and to perceive the dialectics of secularization. Those working with these dichotomies are in danger of forgetting their own ideological standpoint. This is the reason why we have to remember that these phenomena are not a reappearance of a premodern 'medieval' obscurantism. They have emerged from within the project of modernity itself. Thus the return of religion is a modern phenomenon. This becomes evident if we realize that the members of these religious movements are embedded in and the result of the process of modernity.

The awareness of the intrinsic modern character of the process of desecularization makes us sensitive to hidden connections between democracy and totalitarianism, or even between modernity and fundamentalism. This connection might be a causal one. Therefore it is not surprising that the process of desecularization is not just a phenomenon that occurs in undemocratic 'societies of fear', if we call to mind G. W. Bush's neo-conservatism. It also occurs in democratic 'societies of freedom'.[3] Bush declares that the Americans have the task of ruling the world and, at the same time, sees himself as a divine instrument of God. He combines theological ideas of the Last Judgement and its final decision on good and evil with a real political institution. The danger is evident when a particular political institution empowers itself to be the 'subject of history'.[4] Subsequently, this political institution will produce executors of the Judgement Day of history. At the basis of this self-empowerment there is a polemical dualistic distinction between friend and enemy which goes hand in hand with a polity grounded on the notion of radical enmity.

II Secularization: The Demand for Depoliticizing God

How can we face these challenges? Adressing these difficulties with religions like Islam and Christianity it is more than understandable that more and more intellectual voices plea for a total secularization. All those who advocate this total secularization are not just demanding the separation between Church and state but they

3. For this terminology see, N. Sharansky and R. Dremer (2004), *The Case of Democracy. The Power of Freedom to overcome Terror and Tyranny* (New York: Public Affairs).
4. See D. Junker (1995), 'Auf dem Weg zur imperialen Hypermacht? Die manichäische Falle ist besetzt. U.S.-Außenpolitik nach dem 11. September', in M. Brocker (ed.), *God bless America. Politik und Religion in den USA* (Darmstadt: Prima), pp. 208–23.

intend to disconnect entirely religion from politics and want to ban religion from the public sphere. According to these people, religion should only be practised in the mosque, in the Church, in the synagogue or private domain. Along with these claims for privatizing religion, the question arises whether all religions due to their absolute convictions are naturally antidemocratic. Is it not obvious after the events of 9/11 that it is impossible to break the intrinsic relationship between monotheistic religions and violence? Does 9/11 not prove that with God everything is permitted, even the annihilation of thousands of people? Consequently morality would not be rooted in the concept of God but the belief in the one God would be the cause of immorality. Dostoyevsky's famous phrase 'without God everything is permitted' should have been reformulated to: 'with God everything is permitted'!

Would not it not be quite timely to depoliticize religion in general and Christendom in particular? The biblical God could claim his rights of residence at best only in the private domain.

Now, what position will take up the 'New Political Theology', itself, regarding on the one hand the call for neopoliticization, and a strict depoliticization of Christendom on the other? To answer this question I want to sum up the key features of the 'New Political Theology'.

III Political Theology: Speaking of God in Our Time

It was the Catholic theologian Johan Baptist Metz who, after the Second World War, introduced the concept 'New Political Theology' to the theological discourse. However, Metz did not coin the term,[5] it was coined by Carl Schmitt, the so-called 'crown-jurist of Adolf Hitler' (W. Gurian),[6] who brought 'Political Theology' to the fore at the very beginning of the twentieth century. Metz, for his part, transposed theology from a transcendental idealist discourse to a political one through a positive interpretation of secularization. This being understood as both the becoming world of the world (*Weltwerdung*) and the means whereby people are challenged to participate responsibly and accountably in public affairs (*Mündigkeit des Menschen*).

Metz developed this understanding of secularization from Aquinas's idea of '*conversio ad phanasmata*', Karl Rahner's combination of theology and anthropology[7] and Bonhoeffer's work on the conscientious majority (*Mündigkeit*). It was Dietrich Bonhoeffer who argued in his *Letters from Prison* to think of God in secular terms. His verdict focused not on secularization but on the enfeeblement of human beings by both Christendom and theology. According to Bonhoeffer, theology reluctantly realized that while the world had become more autonomous there remain ultimate questions that human beings cannot answer themselves. Here theology had secured

5. B. Wacker and J. Manemann (2006), 'Political Theology' in J. Downey, J. Manemann and St Ostovich (eds), *Missing God?* (Münster: Lit Verlag).
6. See J. Manemann (2002), *Carl Schmitt und die Politische Theologie. Politischer Anti-Monotheismus* (Münster: Aschendorff Verlag).
7. See T. Peters (1998), *Johann Baptist Metz. Theologie des vermissten Gottes* (Mainz: Theoligische Profile).

a position in which it could not be replaced by other disciplines. Bonhoeffer very clearly pointed out that such a theology 'is an exploitation of the weakness of a human being for ends that were different from his own goals'. The task of theology is to seek God in concrete situations, not in some other world. 'Diminishing the world and what is human is not honouring God and, conversely, the augmentation of the world is not a limitation of God.'[8]

This was the stimulus for Metz to propose a 'theology of the world'[9] or to put it more precisely a theology 'with its face toward the world'[10] committed to contributing to the becoming world of the world (*Weltwerdung*). This theology was designed as a contribution to the project of making life more human, and maintaining it. This is already politics since, according to Aristotle, political action is orientated towards the common good. Consequently, God's action is politics too. This becomes very important for preventing *Gottesrede* (God-talk) from shifting to *Gottesgerede* (gossip-talk about God). Theology therefore tends to become political. Actual political life indicates whether we really believe in God or just in our believing in our belief in God. Because whenever we use the word 'God' this must change our life.

Johan Baptist Metz is not, and this is significant, advocating a bourgeois attitude towards religion. He is not trapped by a bourgeois and secular understanding of religion which reduces religion to a tool for a culture of the bourgeois subject. In this bourgeois understanding of religion, religion is just used but not necessary for becoming a subject.[11] Against this bourgeois instrumentalization of religion as a cultural label, political theology is arguing for a deprivatization of religion and theology. This was, and still is, its genuine theological intention. Political theology is fighting against the substitution of the political 'I' by a decontextualized individual, in society as well as in the Church and theology.

On the basis of a 'productive eschatology', which prevented compromising the hope of a universal justice for the living and the dead, the New Political Theology was a critical theory from its beginnings. Aggravated by the memory on the 'eschatological deferral', the relation to modernity was always a dialectical one. Initially this dialectical relation was a reaction to the tension between an increasing hominization of the world and a decreasing humanization. 'The modern world and its scientific and technological civilization is not simply a "rational universe."'[12] Evolution is its myth, a fiction of time as an empty and unsurprising eternity in which everything is mercilessly imprisoned. This evolution is driven by the command 'keep going!' which implies two unquestioned assumptions. First, the belief in an optimistic future and, second, since this belief did not last very long, it

8. D. Bonhoeffer (1983), *Widerstand und Ergebung. Briefe und Aufzeichnungen aus der Haft* (Gütersloh: Gütersloh Verlagshaus), p. 379.
9. See J. Metz (1985), *Zur Theologie der Welt* (Mainz : Grünewald).
10. J. Metz (2006), 'Cultural amnesia', in: J. Downey, J. Manemann, and St Ostovich (eds), *Missing God?* (Münster: Lit Verlag).
11. J. Metz (1984), *Glaube in Geschichte und Gesellschaft. Studien zu einer praktischen Fundamentaltheologie* (Mainz: Grünewald), p. 32.
12. J. Metz (1999), Der Kampf um die verlorene Zeit. Thesen zur Apokalpytik', in J. Manemann (ed.), *Jahrbuch Politische Theologie. Bd. 3: Befristete Zeit* (Munster: LIT.), 212–21.

271

was followed by 'procedural melancholy'.[13] Expectations were diminished, utopias and visions destroyed. The social consequences can hardly be ignored. On one side, there is a tremendous apathy; on the other, an unfettered hatred; fatalism here, fanaticism there.

This criticism of modernity was apocalyptically radicalized when the catastrophe of Auschwitz was faced. Metz writes in his 'Thesis on Apocalypse': 'Catastrophies are broadcast in between two songs – the music continues like the heard flow of time which unmercifully overruns everything and cannot be interrupted. "When the criminal deed occurs like the rain falls, nobody will interfere, shouting: Stop it!" (B. Brecht)'.[14] Benjamin had summarized this critique in his own apt words: 'The fact that everything "continues as usual" is the catastrophe.'[15]

Throughout the last decades, the catastrophe of Auschwitz has become more and more the *locus theologicus* of Political Theology. In contrast to the apathy of everyday Christian living, that means in contrast to all those Christians who were worshipping or attending mass every Sunday ignorant of what had happened, Metz realized that it was time to develop a theology which is unable to distance itself successfully from the suffering of others.

Addressing his intellectual mentor, Karl Rahner, Metz raised the questions: 'Why haven't you told us about these catastrophes in theology? Why do we experience the abyssal misery of the people we face just like an echo from the past or the aftermath of a thunderstorm when we realize everything is over? Why is our theology so far away from the history of peoples' suffering?'[16]

In order to overcome this 'resistant astonishment' (*Verblüffungsfestigkeit*), Political Theology emphasises the 'productive untimeliness' (*produktive Ungleichzeitigkeit*)[17] of the Christian religion. Political Theology defines this 'productive untimeliness' simply as interruption. Christ is not the Conservator but the *Salvator mundi*, he is the dangerous Christ. The Christian concept of God becomes immensely practical. 'It is axiomatic for all Christology that Christ must always be thought so that he is not just thought.'[18]

Therefore the meaning of Political Theology is not just to reflect the connection 'in which religion and theology if they are not yet, become political, i.e. will get a politico-ideological and politico-practical impact'.[19] Political Theology is also a counter-force to the neopoliticization of belief as well as to a neo-clericalization of secular politics. Consequently New Political Theology does not mean to reject the modern distinction between state and society. This anti-totalitarian distinction has

---

13. P. Sloterdijk (1989), *Eurotaoismus. Zur Kritik der politischen Kinetik* (Frankfurt: Suhrkamp), p. 246.
14. J. Metz (1999), 'Der Kampf um die verlorene Zeit.'
15. W. Benjamin (1977), 'Zentralpark', in W. Benjamin, *Illuminationen. Ausgewählte Schriften* (Frankfurt: Suhrkamp), p. 246.
16. J. Metz in F. Schuster and R. Boschert-Kimig (1993), *Trotzdem hoffen. Mit Johann Baptist Metz und Elie Wiesel im Gespräch* (Mainz: Grünewald), pp. 12–55.
17. J. Metz (1981), *Unterbrechungen. Theologisch-politische Perspektiven und Profile* (Gütersloh: Gütersloh Verlagshaus).
18. J. Metz (2002), *Glaube in Geschichte und Gesellschaft*, p. 48.
19. R. Maurer (1983), 'Chiliasmus und Gesellschaftsreligion. Thesen zur politischen Theologie', in J. Taubes (ed.), *Religionstheorie und Politische Theologie. Bd. 1: Der Fürst dieser Welt. Carl Schmitt und die Folgen* (Paderborn: Schöningh), p. 117.

to be implied whenever the term 'Political Theology' is used in this context. At the same time, one has to be aware that due to this difference the meaning of 'the political' has changed. The word 'political' therefore aims towards the history of human freedom.

New Political Theology is a 'theologico-political theology'. Its task is 'to say God in midst of the terrible difficult circumstances of our times' and to 'reserve the whole totality' for him.[20] 'The name "God" promises that the utopia of liberation for all human subjects is not a mere projection, as it would be if it was only a utopia and not God.'[21] To believe in this God demands universal solidarity: forward with future generations and backward with the drowned, the dead.

Political Theology and its understanding of the political is not just orientated towards the 'coming of . . .' or the eschatological, but also rooted in remembrance (*anamnesis*). The principle of the past is not substituted by the principle of hope. Talking about the future, freedom, and hope Political Theology refers to the resources of narratives and memories of failed and unfulfilled hopes. The moment of the 'ought' is empirically to be found in so-called dangerous memories.

Political Theology, and this should be obvious now, does not understand itself as theology in the genitive. It is not a theology of politics. Political theology wants to be nothing else than *theo-logia*, 'speaking of God in our time' (J. B. Metz). As such, theology acknowledges that theological questions have lost their historical, social and cultural innocence. To sum it up, the constituting questions of theology are: 'Who speaks – when and where – on behalf of whom and with which intention – of God?'[22]

IV The Persistence of the Theologico-Political: Redefining the Relationship between Religion and Politics in an Area of Polemical Constellations

In view of Political Theology, the challenge today is not just the question of 'politicization or depoliticization of religion', but the struggle of the political. As we have seen, the process of desecularization takes place within the context of the return of the political in the sense of the old political theology (C. Schmitt). This Political Theology defines the political as the distinction between friend and enemy/foe. Once again I want to emphasize that the danger of defining the political as the distinction between friend and enemy is a seduction for both dictatorial 'societies of fear' and democratic 'societies of freedom'.

Politics based on the notion of enmity in democratic societies are the result of a gnosticly profiled Christianity. Its attractiveness results from the clear solutions of splitting the world into good and evil hemispheres. But, Gnosticism is anti-monotheistic. Dichotomous politics are not an expression of monotheism's violence; exactly the opposite is true! Monotheism is substantially anti-dualistic. Its fundamental cultural function consists in the confession of the one God which

20. T. Peters (1998), *Johann Baptist Metz*, pp. 17–18.
21. J. Metz (2002), *Glaube in Geschichte und Gesellschaft*, p. 65.
22. J. Metz (2006), 'Cultural amnesia', in J. Downey, J. Manemann and St Ostovich (eds), *Missing God?* (Münster: Lit Verlag).

makes it possible 'to conceive reality as a unity and to assume a universal history for mankind. The genuine meaning of monotheism is not to say that there is just one God rather than many. The genuine meaning of monotheism is to provide a world-view; that is that the world is not divided between different divine powers warring against each other nor divided into different dominions. The world is not torn apart by the inevitable dualism of light and darkness, of good and evil; the world is not pluralized by the antagonistic claims of different peoples.'[23]

The speeches by the President of the United States are saturated by a consciousness of mission which must be scrutinized in terms of whether they are an expression of universalism for the sake of the other or an expression of a universal desire to usurp which disagrees with the biblical tradition. Although we can find a so-called 'covering-law' universalism in the Bible, which substantially interprets the belief in one God as one law and one justice, one salvation, one idea of the good life etc., we can also find another form of universalism in the biblical tradition: a '(re)iterative universalism' which is paradigmatically articulated by the prophet Amos: 'Are not you Israelites like Cushites to me? says the Lord. Did I not bring Israel up from Egypt, the Philistines from Caphtor, the Aramaeans from Kir?' (9.7) This seems to indicate that there is not only one exodus, one divine salvation, one time for liberation of mankind. 'Liberation is a particular experience which is made by coerced peoples repeatedly. At the same time, it is a good experience for the individual because God is the universal liberator. Every people experiences its own individual liberation from the one and in all cases identical God. A God who presumably hates every form of coercion.'[24]

There is a tension between this '(re)iterative universalism' and the 'covering-law' universalism. The difference is that the '(re)iterative universalism' is characterized by its particularity and pluralizing tendencies. Key to the biblical understanding of universalism is the covenant God made with all people and animals prior to the covenant with Israel and the covenant with Abraham: the covenant with Noah (Genesis 9.8–17). The remembrance of this covenant destroys all intentions to reclaim God as a property of one particular religion. From this it is evident why this God can be worshipped universally and conceived as being universal. 'Either God is an issue for all of mankind or He is irrelevant.'[25] Consequently, in the light of this universalism, the category of election, which was always religiously abused as a means of gaining political power, has to be reconsidered profoundly anti-elitist. Election is not a privilege, it is rather a burden because whoever is chosen will be judged by stricter criteria than anyone else. 'For you alone have I cared among all the nations of the world; therefore I will punish you for all your iniquities' (Amos 3.2). The biblical belief in the one God does not necessarily imply the idea that there is only one exclusive salvation for all peoples, because the God of Israel is conceived

---

23. H. Zirker (1995), 'Monotheismus und Intoleranz', in K. Hilpert and J. Werbick (eds), *Mit den anderen Leben. Wege zur Toleranz* (Düsseldorf: Patmos) pp. 95–6.
24. M. Walzer (1990), 'Zwei Arten des Universalismus', in *Babylon. Beiträge zur jüdischen Gegenwart*, 7, pp. 7–25, and P. Rottländer (1993), 'Ethik in der Politischen Theologie', in *Orientierung*, 57 p. 157.
25. J. Metz (1999), 'Karl Rahners Ringen um die theologische Ehre des Menschen', in A. Raffelt (ed.), *Karl Rahner in Erinnerung* (Düsseldorf: Patmos), p. 76.

as a God for all human beings. But His injunctions are just addressed to the people of Israel. The one and universal God does not demand homogeneity among people. He is rather the guarantor for the dignity of differences: 'A unity in heaven creates a diversity on earth.'[26] Therefore the absolute injunctions and commandments for the Jewish people are not identical with the universal commandments of the covenant with Noah. Israel knows that it is bound to be obedient, but this obedience is not rooted in a universal law. The particular nature of this covenant is an expression of love. Love never articulates itself in general affections for persons; love is a particular relation to one single person in his/her uniqueness. Such a universalism is the ground for a difference which is the opposite of relativism since it is a difference related to the other as non-indifference. That non-indifference is a challenge (*Heraus-Forderung*), in which the 'I' is related to the other insofar as the other is one's neighbour.

But the difference at stake here is experienced as a threat. For this reason people employ an exclusivist and indifferent concept of difference which is understood in the sense of a binary constellation of identities (black–white or friend–enemy). This concept of difference gives birth to polemical constellations. These polemical constellations begin to flourish also in democratic societies whenever they enter a crisis in which institutions of decision-making are weakened and consequently boundaries of definitions are likely to be blurred. This is also true for the current phenomenon of desecularization which is driven by a deep fear: 'the fear of a chaos, of ungraspable complexity of the world, of pluralism and even of the devil and forces of evil.'[27] The function of a politics of enmity becomes obvious in this context: they are not just used to save their own society from possible external annihilation but also to generate an inner solidarity by creating an external enemy. In short, the external enemy constitutes identity in a very existential sense. Samuel Huntington's scenario of a 'clash of civilization' is grounded in such a *translatio hostilitatis*, which – according to Huntington – no politician and intellectual can ignore because 'for people who are seeking their identity and who redefine their ethnicity enemies are inevitable, and the most dangerous enmities can be found at the boundaries between the great cultures of the world.'[28] Huntington even seeks to ground his thesis anthropologically: 'Hatred is human. People need enemies for defining themselves . . .'[29] Whoever wants to know who he is must know who he is not and whom he is against.

Politics of enmity intend to cement an anti-democratic homogeneity, because they presuppose the people to be a unity and imagined as one. However the empirical people are constituted by the many. They are a people 'composed of the flesh and blood of individuals'.[30] Every imagined substantial unity is deconstructed by democracy. Although democracy also produces unity, the common will can never be grasped as the immediate will of the people: 'What is represented by an election

26. J. Sacks (2003), *The Dignitiy of Difference* (London: Continuum), p. 54.
27. D. Junker, 'Auf dem Weg zur imperialen Hypermacht?', p. 214.
28. S. P. Huntington (1998), *Kampf der Kulturen* (München: Goldman), p. 18.
29. Ibid., p. 201.
30. P. Flores d'Arcais (2005), 'Ist Amerika noch eine Demokratie?', in *Die Zeit* 20.01.05.

is in fact the fragmentation, the divisions and the potential for conflict in a society.'[31] The nature of democracy is not consensus but dissent. Dissent guarantees the liberty of all citizens, i.e., the freedom of the dissident against the sovereign and the freedom of the majority against itself. Democracy is a project for the future insofar as it implies the promise to take the real people seriously as 'the ensemble of struggling individuals.'[32] That is the democratic challenge.

Democracy, as well as monotheism, is the foundation for humans to become a subject rather than a people. If democracy is defined as 'the institutionalized form of dealing with uncertainty in the public'[33] then monotheism cannot be used as an appropriate tool to get rid of this uncertainty. Exactly the opposite is true! Monotheism radicalizes uncertainty. Uncertainty can pave the way for the possibility for new actions. Biblical monotheism is in its very nature a call against deadlocks, a call for a productive exile. Abraham is called by God to leave his home and he is told never to return to his origin. Uncertainty is the site for the formation of the subject. This site in democracy is civil society. It is the site where moral forces are mobilized. Civil society is the genuine motor of democracy. It is 'the source of dissent, innovation, and perpetual public revision'.[34] In other words, civil society is the site of sub-politics. Sub-politics means politics which change the framework of politics. Religions can be a source for a politics which transform the rules. On the basis of its reflexivity, which is a result of the realization of the suffering of the other, biblical monotheism has the potential for transformations. This potential forces democratic societies not to remain where they are but always to raise the question of how a free world can contribute to the transformation of societies of fear into societies of freedom. The biblical God demands an extreme humanism in which there exists no suffering that does not count. Such a humanism conforms with the ethos of democracy. This is illustrated by human rights because human rights are the generative principle of democracy and not simply a code. They are to a certain extent 'a declaration of war against coercion, insanity and slavery'.[35] By this challenge (*Heraus-Forderung*) democratic societies are delimited. Yet there is not only an outer delimitation, but an inner one also. This inner delimitation makes it difficult for democratic societies to be indifferent towards the claims of the stranger. Even justice for the enemy is demanded. At this point we are confronted with what is perhaps the most radical counter-idea to politics of enmity, namely with the commandment 'love thy enemy'! This commandment expresses the rejection of the idea of an absolute enemy. It defines the enemy as someone who hates temporally. This means that whenever we talk about the enemy we have to talk about the other 'for whom we have an inescapable responsibility even in the most excessive situations of collective enmity'.[36] The

31. Ibid.
32. Ibid.
33. H. Dubiel (1994), *Ungewißheit und Politik* (Frankfurt: Suhrkamp), p. 9.
34. Ibid., p. 76.
35. P. Bruckner (1991), *Die demokratische Melancholie* (Hamburg: Aufban Verlag), p. 171.
36. B. Liebsch (2005), *Gastlichkeit und Freiheit. Polemische Konturen europäischer Kultur* (Velbrück: Weilerswist), p. 319.

advocates of a radical secularization thesis should rethink whether they are not dependent upon such a reflexivity when they fight against a neopoliticization of religion. The first step would be, as the philosopher Burkhard Liebsch has argued, to realize that there is no one who is condemned to be an enemy, neither a natural nor an objective one. Enmity is rather the result of a previous process in which enemies are produced.[37] The enemy is not essentially an enemy.

A Manichean rhetoric does not indicate an aggravation but a liquidation of the political. To deny someone's right to exist already transcends the political. The advocates of Manichean politics are on the road to the anti-political. Whenever we talk about the human in terms of a political subject then we should not misunderstand this interpretation of the *zoon politikon* essentially, because it is not true that 'there is something in a human that is the political as such and belongs to it ontologically. Exactly the opposite is true. The human is apolitical. Politics emerge between humans; this is external of what it is to be human. A genuine political substance does not exist. Politics emerge in the in-between and are relational'.[38] The political is based on the plurality of people. It is concerned 'with the being-together of people'. Whenever we see in the fact that people in a society are living together more than just participation, i.e., active participation in the plurality, then 'we imitate God by pretending to be able to transcend naturally the principle of diversity.'[39] This imitation of God becomes manifest whenever humans try to create humans in their own image. The political is not directed towards strongholds and resemblances. Such an ambition leads to a fundamental perversion of the political because it nullifies the basic quality of plurality. It even destroys the quality of plurality by introducing the concept of a homogeneous unity. The political is the space in which humans can be different without fear. Thus politics and polity must be grounded in the political, if they should not lead to old mistakes.

Nevertheless, in this world we cannot just omit self-defence and intervention as options to act especially for those confronted with unjust violence. But Christians must always be aware of the ambivalence in such legitimate application of violence. Bishop Kamphaus rightly states: 'Pacifism in the sense of the gospel is not a principle, it is rather an advice. We cannot demand pacifism from those whose lives are threatened. But violence and bloodshed must be seen as an abomination by those who use force in the case of an emergency.'[40] Unconditional pacifism always risks reducing justice to an empty shape. Facing the extreme, it is very likely that counter-violence becomes mimetic. How can a society resist this temptation and, at the same time, protect itself from terrorism with which one cannot negotiate and which does not make claims (as with 9/11, only ultimate declarations were disseminated in which our own livelihoods were nullified)? 'You love life – we love death!' This unconditional situation challenges and seduces into producing a

37. Ibid., p. 207.
38. H. Arendt (1993), *Was ist Politik? Fragmente aus dem Nachlaß* (Munich: Piper), pp. 9–12.
39. Ibid.
40. F. Kamphaus (2002), 'Pflugscharen zu Schwertern? Gerechter Friede für eine Welt des Terrors', in H. Lutterbach and J. Manemann (eds), *Religion und Terror. Stimmen zum 11. September aus Christentum, Islam und Judentums* (Münster: LIT), p. 198.

radical counter-force which for its own part transcends every rational political measure. Political action must not be orientated towards irrationality like terrorism. On the contrary, it must be orientated towards rationality and justice. The West will have to learn to live with a radical and exceptional threat of annihilation. At this point I just want to bring attention to the illusion of a final victory over the enemy. The promise of an ultimate peace is an eschatological one and not something within the power of human beings to achieve.

Whoever wants to fight a violence that goes hand in hand with the renaissance of public religions should not, like the advocates of secularism, simply trace this violence back to its religious grounds. Whenever we want to resist the new form of terror, it is not sufficient to see Islam as the only cause. The war of terror by the Jihadists is not a continuation of politics by other means. This war of terror nullifies every politics and also every symmetry of force. Moreover, the terrorist as a suicide-bomber contradicts the principle of self-preservation. His embrace of death makes this terrorism destructive and untouchable in a unique way: 'Shock and awe cannot threaten this terrorism. Whoever does not fear death cannot be threatened by death.'[41] Although the violence of the terrorist is not unconscious, he knows exactly what he is doing. The terrorist experiences the use of violence as an absolute sovereignty, as an expression of absolute freedom. 'Absolute freedom here means primarily the freedom to die.'[42] To participate in the power of death generates an incomparable self-consciousness, a negative sovereignty of transgression. Suicide-bombers and killers who run amok seem to be modern people. By their act they gain a surrogate for what seems to be absent from modern society: a coherent meaning which offers the individual a place in the society. It also seems that only those who die and kill for their belief are taken seriously in modern societies. Consequently the act of destruction could provide an ultimate meaning.

The new form of terrorism bears some features which suggest we understand it as a fascist syndrome. Consider, for instance, the maximization of differences by an ontological fixation that turns differences into essential characteristics 'which seem to be innate and unchangeable to people or certain groups'.[43] According to the demand of Bin Laden, 'The Americans' and 'The Jews' are to be killed wherever they can be found. The principle of the 'Führer' is as essential to networks of terrorism as for fascism. Furthermore, fascism needs permanent mobilization that arrests lethargy. This implies a perpetual personalization and emotionalization of anonymous processes. The homogenization of these movements is based on a paranoid and closed world-view. An essential characteristic of the fascist syndrome is that the entire personality is linked to a total politicization. It demands total loyalty and every other loyalty (family, religion, individual conscience, etc.) is suspended. 'Hardness, intolerance, thoughtlessness become virtues of the clearly sado-masochistic "new human" who prefers the extreme "final solution" [*Endlösung*] and wants to achieve it as soon as possible.' Contrary to civilized societies, which temper aggression,

41. W. Sofsky (2002), *Zeiten des Schreckens. Amok – Terror – Krieg* (Frankfurt: Fischer).
42. W. Sofsky (1996), *Traktat über die Gewalt*, (Frankfurt: Fischer).
43. See, for the following quotations, F. Hacker (1992), *Das Faschismus-Syndrom. Analyse eines aktuellen Phänomens* (Frankfurt: Fischer).

fascism permits aggression. In fascism an intimate relation to violence becomes evident. Although there are other forms of government which are extremely violent, fascism prefers to use 'violence thoughtlessly and without hesitation but also as a preferred means'. This violence is libidinous. 'Violence is a surrogate for love or, rather, an object of love, since violence (as it should be in true love) not only will be preferred because of the satisfaction of someone's interests and other advantages, but because it is loved for its own sake.' Those who are made drunk by self-sacrifice gain fulfilment; fearlessly and without any conscience they present their readiness to use violence. It is important to keep in mind that the temptation of fascism is not only a result of economic crises: 'the temptation of fascism is primarily caused by real psychological needs, by "spiritual crises". . .' The fascist syndrome grew up in the soil of modern societies. Therefore, without self-criticism in modern society, this violence cannot be fought by modern society.

Nevertheless, this terrorism cannot exist without a religious element. In this context, the US American sociologist Mark Jürgensmeyer points out that the cosmic war does not accept a compromise: 'War suggests an all-or-nothing strug-gle against an enemy whom one assumes to be determined to destroy. No com-promise is deemed possible.'[44] Cosmic war entails the idea of martyrdom, and martyrdom is always related to self-sacrifice. Religious self-sacrifice intends the inversion of that action which transforms death into victory and life.

V Politics is 'the Art of the Impossible' (S. Žižek)

We should be rattled awake by the process of desecularization. Its advocates are products of global society, and this fact indicates deficiencies that we cannot just counter with the critique of capitalism. Therefore the economic situation cannot be discussed separately from the condition of solidarity in society. And if people are willing to cooperate and to share – this is not just an economic question but a question of meaning. Human beings are not just seeking the meaning of their own lives, for the meaning of their lives arises from the question of the other, i.e., it is a meaning which transcends their own meaning.

The society of late modernity is in danger of splitting the question of the meaning of life so that only the privileged are involved and those who have wealth to own the future. But a society which is engaged only in the future of what is current, which is disconnected from solidarity with the past and disconnected from the right of the dead, is profoundly inhuman. It forgets and denies past misery. 'In the last resort, no happiness enjoyed by the children can make up for the pain suffered by the fathers, and no social progress can atone for the injustice done to the departed. If we persist too long in accepting the meaninglessness of death and in being indifferent to death, all we shall have left to offer even to the living will be banal promises. It is not only the growth of our economic resources which is limited, as we are often reminded today, but also the resources of meaning, and it is as if our reserves here

---

44. M. Juergensmeyer (2001), *Terror in the Mind of God. The Global Rise of Religious Violence* (London: University of California Press), pp. 148–9.

are melting away and we are faced with the real danger that impressive words we use to fuel our own history – words like freedom, liberation, justice, happiness – will in the end have all their meaning drained out of them.'[45]

In a globalized world, as we commonly understand it, it seems that only that and those count which or who have a future. Future becomes a value. There is no room for those who do not have future any more: the marginalized and the dead, those lacking a voice. What kind of society is it in which those who cannot bear the stress of the globalized world, and those who were lost in the process of transformation, are forgotten? What kind of globalized world is this, which avoids death and the dead for the sake of eternal progress, because it cannot accept interruption and finality?

As we can see today, religions have the potential to be a temptation for democratic society, i.e. to close the openness which is constitutional for democracy. But, of course, they also have the potential to guarantee this openness by reminding politics not just to maintain the status quo and to subscribe to an illusion of pure immanence. By the challenge of religions, society experiences a confrontation with something which it cannot produce from its own resources. This confrontation is the *conditio sine qua non* for self-reflexivity which at all times presupposes a certain exteriority. 'That human society has an openness for itself only if it is taken into an openness, which is not self-produced.'[46] But 'advanced societies have already begun to produce the cultural conditions of their own existence.'[47] If culture, however, were reduced to that which is produced by the society, the potential for transformation would disappear, and democracy with it.

In the age of the politicization of religion, a democratic society is well advised to take note of the potential for transformation of the biblical tradition. Since morality is not generated, as the Bible makes clear, by equality, but by being the servant to the poor, the orphans and the widows. By this claim of the recognition of the misery of the other, the theory and praxis of justice, i.e., equality in a liberal society, is examined in terms of the problem of the non-identical. From that arises the injunction to take account of the individual perspective. Taking into account their lamentations is the motor of self-reflexivity. The egalitarian attitude of the member in a democratic society is complemented by that individual justification. 'Individual justification here means to react in solidarity against all that make suffer and lament the other.'[48] The idea of morality expressed in this view is not rooted in the idea of equality but is based on proximity. Such an egalitarian and anti-elitist perspective is based on a feeling for solidarity and is therefore embodied. Such a morality is founded upon a negative universalism entailing the axiom 'that there is no suffering that doesn't count' (P. Rottländer). Contrary to that, the longing for order as part of polemic politics is an ideology which seeks to justify

45. J. Metz (1975), 'Unsere Hoffnung. Ein Beschluß der gemeinsamen Synode der Bistümer in der Bundesrepublik Deutschland' *Synodenbeschlüsse* 18, Bonn; and J. Metz, *Glaube in Geschichte und Gesellschaft*, chs 1, 3.
46. C. Lefort (1999), *Fortdauer des Theologisch-Politischen* (Vienna: Passagen), p. 45.
47. H. Dubiel (1994), *Ungewißheit nund Politik*, p. 149.
48. C. Menke (2000), *Spiegelungen der Gleichheit*, (Frankfurt: Suhrkamp), p. 38.

morally the hatred of human beings. This hatred of other human beings is rather a rejection of responsibility than an expression of the rejection of plurality.

The continuation of the theologico-political, and not its evaporation, could contribute to the breaking up of isolation. It would serve as a motivation for the correlation of the particular and the whole in a twofold manner: first, the suffering can assume that nobody else wants to experience such pain and misery and refuses it; second, the implied change is orientated towards the whole because it redefines the whole. Only then can we talk about 'genuine politics' (S. Žižek). Nevertheless, at the moment, a kind of politics which Slavoj Žižek calls a 'post-politics' is fashionable. It is a politics which mobilizes the entire apparatus of experts, social workers, etc., in order to reduce the full demand of a particular group to a particularity.

In the contemporary situation of crisis, monotheistic religions could serve as a hinge, and become the motor for human and political processes of transformation. This function will consist in the repoliticization of the private sphere and the renormativization of the public sphere, in confronting personal morale with public problems and the public with questions of private morale.[49] Its contribution would be to overcome post-politics which hinder the impact of concrete political demands on the system. Genuine politics would seek to change the parameters which are characterized as 'possible' and 'real'. In short, it would be 'the art of the impossible' (S. Žižek) and therefore a messianic, i.e. interrupting politics. Such a politics would not be satisfied with the meaning of reality but would provoke the meaning for possibility. Only this politics would be the beginning of the end of enmity.

49. J. Casanova (1995), *Public Religions in the Modern World* (Chicago, IL: Chicago University Press), p. 5f.

Primary Sources

Augustine, Saint (1945), *The City of God*, ed. E. Rhys (New York: J. M. Dent & Sons Ltd.

Aquinas, Thomas (2002), 'The treatise "De regimine principum" or "De regno"', in *Aquinas: Political Writings*, trans. and ed. R. Dyson (Cambridge: Cambridge University Press).

Dante, Alighieri (1879), *The 'De monarchia' of Dante*, trans. F. Church (London: Macmillan).

Luther, Martin (1910), 'Address to the Christian Nobility of the German Nation', in *Martin Luther*, ed. C. Elliot (New York: P.F. Collier).

Luther, Martin (1910), 'On the Limits of Secular Authority', in *Martin Luther*, ed. C. Elliot (New York: P.F. Collier).

Machiavelli, Niccolò (1883), *Discourses on the first decade of Titus Livius*, trans. N. Thomson (London: Kegan Paul, Trench & Co).

King James VI/I (1930), 'The True Law of Free Monarchies' in J. Tanner *Constitutional Documents of the Reign of James I: A.D. 1603–1625* (Cambridge: Cambridge University Press).

Hobbes, Thomas (1909), *Leviathan* [1651] (Oxford: Clarendon Press).

Rousseau, Jean-Jacques (1913), *The Social Contract and Discourses*, trans. G. Cole (London: J.M. Dent and Sons).

Paine, Thomas (1792), *Common Sense: addressed to the inhabitants of America, on the following interesting subjects: . . . A new edition, with several additions . . . To which is added, an appendix; together with an address to the people called Quakers* (London: H.D. Symonds).

Tocqueville, Alexis de (1946), *Democracy in America.* trans. H. Reeve, ed. R. Steele (London: Oxford University Press).

Maistre, Joseph de (1974), *Considerations on France*, trans. R. Lebrun (Montreal: McGill-Queen's University Press).

Marx, K. (1844), 'Introduction to the Critique of Hegel's "Philosophy of Right"' in *DeutschFranzösische Jahrbücher*, February (Marxists.org).

Schmitt, Carl (1985), *Political Theology: Four Chapters on the Concept of Sovereignty*, trans. G. Schwab (Cambridge, MA: MIT Press).

Lenin, Ilych 'Socialism and Religion', in *Lenin Collected Works*, vol. 10 (Moscow: Progress Publishers), pp. 83–7 (Marxists.org).

Weil, Simone (1952), *The Need for Roots*, trans. A. Wills (London: Routledge).

Index of Names

283

Index of Subjects

Index of Scriptural References